HAL HOLDER
RENO
2002

Neon Metropolis

Neon Metropolis

HOW LAS VEGAS STARTED THE TWENTY-FIRST CENTURY

HAL ROTHMAN

WITH PHOTOGRAPHS BY VIRGIL HANCOCK III

Routledge
New York • London

Published in 2002 by
Routledge
29 West 35th Street
New York, NY 10001

Published in Great Britain by
Routledge
11 New Fetter Lane
London EC4P 4EE

Routledge is an imprint of the Taylor and Francis Group.

Printed in the United States of America on acid-free paper.

10 9 8 7 6 5 4 3 2 1

Library of Congress Cataloging-in-Publication Data
Rothman, Hal, 1958-
    Neon metropolis: how Las Vegas started the twenty-first century / by Hal K.
Rothman.
    p. cm.
    Includes index.
    ISBN 0-415-92612-2
    1. Las Vegas (Nev.)—Description and travel. 2. Las Vegas (Nev.)—Social con-
ditions. 3. Las Vegas (Nev.)—Economic conditions. I. Title.

F849.L35 R68 2002
979.3'135—dc21   2001041829

For Lauralee, Talia, and Brent
Who've made Las Vegas home for me

Contents

Acknowledgments

It is hard to write a book about the town you live in with detachment and passion. Numerous people have not only encouraged me, but tempered my intensity and sharpened my focus in the process. No one deserves more credit than Nancy Scott Jackson, who took time out from her other work to read the entire manuscript twice and parts of it even more. Her critique was invaluable and provided help when I needed it most. Dave McBride came into the process later, but made great contributions; he shepherded the book to the finish with a keen eye and a willingness to challenge my assumptions. Peggy Shaffer offered her always outstanding commentary. My colleague Gene Moehring contributed his vast knowledge of Las Vegas in countless ways; even when he didn't like what I had to say, he was willing to hear me out. Gingy Scharff was always willing to offer her thoughts. Dave Gutierrez, Carl Abbott, Elliott West, Char Miller, Cathleen Dooley, Virgil Hancock, Keith Eggener, Irv Solomon, Bob Kuhlken, Phil Gruen, Matt Wray, Clark Whitehorn, and many others read parts of the manuscript and added their suggestions. To them and to all the people whose names I've inadvertently left out, I'm grateful.

In Las Vegas, I was fortunate to be surrounded not only by exceptional colleagues at the university, but also by an active community that found my writing worthy of attention. The list is endless, limited only by my ability to recall everyone who helped over the past five years. Peter Michel, Raquel Casas, and Kate Hausbeck at the university all contributed their time, energy, and expertise. Bill Thompson and Keith Schwer gave me their very different perspectives on the local economy. John L. Smith, Geoff Schumacher, and Jon Ralston helped me pick my way through the minefield of local politics and culture. Mike Green offered his own unique perspective. Barry and Amy Fieldman, Henry Chanin, Scott Page, Mike Weissenstein, Amie Williams and Glen Arnodo, Steve and Marla Polott, Leo Behnke, Mark Goldstein, Elise Axe, Tim Anderson, Doreen Leindecker, Steve Sonnier, the late Susan Berman, Don Hall, Ruben Maldonado, Jose Rodriguez, Manolo Saenz, Russ Roberts, Mike Squires, Hugh Jackson, and many more read parts of the book or talked with me about it and all added something unique to the evolving picture in my head.

I've also been fortunate to receive the complete support of the University of Nevada, Las Vegas. A sabbatical leave supported this project, and I was fortunate to have colleagues who engaged in this work as well as a helpful department chair, Andy Fry, who had much to tell me about my adopted city. My colleagues read and commented on this work, and Greg Brown, Andy Kirk, David Wrobel, Chris Rasmussen, and others all added to it immensely. My assistants, Dave Hollo, Dave Sprouls, and Eric Nystrom, not only read this over and over, they ably handled other projects to free my time. Peter Michel and his staff at Special Collections at the Lied Library provided me with friendships, resources, and the space to write. The imprint of my spine will forever be on one of the reading room chairs.

In the end, one of my primary sources for this project was my family's life in Las Vegas. We moved here in the early 1990s, when about half the people who live in the Las Vegas Valley today were here, and in many ways we've grown up with the city. Our children, Talia and Brent, have never really known any other city as home, and Lauralee and I now only dimly remember other places. For better and worse, this has become our home and I can only hope this effort contributes not only to explaining Las Vegas, but to inspiring people to help make it a better place.

Introduction

A LOOK DOWN LAS VEGAS BOULEVARD, MORE WIDELY KNOWN AS THE "World Famous Las Vegas Strip," on New Year's Eve 1999, revealed the triumph of postindustrial capitalism, information and experience, over its industrial predecessor. Billions of dollars from the world financial markets had been fashioned into the long line of multicolored casinos that lit the night sky. This spectacle of postmodernism, a combination of space and form in light and dark that owes nothing to its surroundings and leaves meaning in the eye of the beholder, is one of the largest private investments in public art anywhere. It produces no tangible goods of any significance, yet generates billions of dollars annually in revenue. Here is the first city of the twenty-first century, the place where desire meets capital, where instinct replaces restraint, where the future of a society, for better and worse, takes a form that had been inconceivable even a generation before. In the 1990s, Las Vegas came into its own, became a city on par with other American metropolises in its significance, but one that generates its sustence in a different way than any other city on earth.

In the twelve years since the opening of the Mirage on New Year's Eve, 1988, the Strip has become a world-class center of entertainment encased in a fantasyland portrayal of time and space. The golden Mandalay Bay at the southern tip, the pyramid-shaped Luxor, and the faux medieval castles of the Excalibur melds fake history with an illusion of the exotic. The green glow of the MGM Grand and the raucous architecture of New York, New York, graced by the Statue of Liberty, arm thrust in the air somehow more aggressively than in the original, offers American life recast on a scale and in a style that reminds one of Disney but promises something entirely more fantastic. Paris Las Vegas, complete with Eiffel Tower, and the Bellagio, a little Lake Como with its orchestrated fountains presents Europe and its cultures as Americans wish they were. The Mirage's volcano and Treasure Island's hourly battle between a pirate ship and the British Navy offers imaginative fantasies of adventure in the South Seas and the stories of Robert Louis Stevenson. Caesars Palace, gaming's most recognizable brand, with its tacit promise to make every man and woman a Caesar, gives the public gladiators and Cleopatras, and the Venetian's gondolas mark the newest claimant to the throne of preeminence in the war for the heart of the visiting public. These little city-states, interrelated little kingdoms, entirely self-contained and at war for customers, run by their own logic. They share a purpose, making money by providing pleasure, but they pursue this objective in varying ways. Against a backdrop reminiscent of commercial competition during the first great age of exploration, the Strip offers the past, the present, high, low, and Nobrow culture, all in the space of one long city street. It offers a world fantastic and unreal, yet simultaneously tangible and available for purchase. Here is the unbelievable made temporal, held in your hands. Here is America in the new millennium.

As it does every night, Las Vegas offers much more than a visual spectacle during the New Year celebrations in 1999. For pleasure that millennial weekend, the city presented Barbra Streisand, a Tina Turner and Elton John co-bill, Bette Midler, the Eagles, Celine Dion, Carlos Santana, Rod Stewart, Gladys Knight, Hall and Oates, and a host of other headliners; for experience, the sheer thought of hundreds of thousands of people in the same place celebrating was enough to make anyone who craved that sort of thing giddy. The national television networks covered Las Vegas; NBC, Fox, and CNN could be found at Caesars Palace. Connie Chung and ABC 2000 broadcast live from a floating platform in the Bellagio's artificial lake. Some wondered if she'd need an umbrella when the fountains did their dance, sending water as high as 240 feet in the air.

The media and the 300,000 people who flocked to Las Vegas that night had come to participate in an orgy of the unruly combination of experience, self, and commodity that is what culture has become in the United States. We crave experience as affirmation of ourselves; the packages of experience we buy in all its forms set us apart from one another and grant us our claim that we're unique. In an age when goods alone no longer offer true distinction, we use experience to prove that we're special, to set ourselves apart from others, to win the ultimate battle of the cocktail party by having the most interesting story to tell. Through its own bizarre alchemy, its chameleonlike ability to imitate so well that the copy it creates is more enticing than the original, Las Vegas accomplishes a neat trick: it lets any visitor believe that they are at the center of the experience the Desert City offers. Las Vegas intuited the needs of the baby boomers, the group who look like the elephant a boa constrictor swallowed if you chart their progress through American society, and the changing national and global culture they created; the city replicated that culture's DNA and made it more palatable, more satisfying, and strangely more meaningful than the places, events, and concepts it mimicked. Like Disneyland, Las Vegas encapsulates what we are. Every year millions come to bask in its reflection. No one thinks Las Vegas is real; it is illusion, but visitors willingly suspend disbelief and pretend. Only snobs look down on Las Vegas these days, for its magic is green and gold, the colors of power and status in the postindustrial world.

Las Vegas blends entertainment, experience, and opportunity for a broad swath of the American and world public. It fulfills the desires of the baby boomers, reflects the abundance that they take for granted and the selfish indulgence, the hedonistic libertarianism, that is the legacy of the American cultural revolution of the 1960s. Las Vegas is the therapeutic ethos of our time run amok, our sociopsychological promise to ourselves to be eternally young writ large on the landscape of aging self-indulgence. In its promise of a luxury experience for a middle-class price, Las Vegas pretends to encourage social mobility; it guarantees escape from the mundane—with you at the center of the story. It is the freedom to experience to which the baby boomers feel entitled, and every dimension of their impact on American society reflects this desire. Postmodern, postindustrial capitalism is about consuming experience, not goods, about creating insatiable desire that must be fulfilled in front of an approving audience. Las Vegas is geared to meet this challenge, to provide the audience, to deliver more than anywhere else and hold out the possibility of still more. The ability to quench desire brings people; the chance to dream of more brings them back again and again.

Two generations ago, modern Las Vegas was born with a sophisticated cachet that quickly degenerated. Only a generation ago, in the late 1970s and early 1980s, Las Vegas retained its stigma as the sleazy home of tawdry sex and mobsters. Its face then was different, more twisted to the mainstream, yet alluring in powerful ways. Cleaned up, Las Vegas was what we wanted to become. It was the epitome of American deviance, and as such, it seemed headed toward a dismal end as visitation totals dropped in the late 1970s and early 1980s. Las Vegas seemed played out, passe, soon to be cast aside as a flimsy relic of a laced-up pseudomorality.

From that nadir, the merging of a constellation of forces, the liberalization of American culture, the growing premium on the self, and the normalization of Las Vegas prominent among them, has made Las Vegas the place to be and be seen as the new century begins. The former capital of deviance has become the linchpin not only of national obsessions—Las Vegas has long been a canvas on which Americans paint their neuroses—but of individual aspirations as well. Las Vegas simultaneously looks backward and forward, attracts and repels. Reflection demands both affection and dismay. Only the baby boomers could demand Las Vegas and the Strip. Only capitalism, with its peculiar genius for catering to desires it creates, could build it.

Topped by an enormous thirty-five-foot-high Coca-Cola bottle but still overshadowed by the billion-dollar behemoths around it, Showcase on the Las Vegas Strip offered something new when it opened in 1997. Next to the MGM Grand and sporting SKG Gameworks with Surge Rock, named for Coca-Cola's latest soft drink, in the middle, and the All-Star Café, this cutting-edge entertainment power center had not a single slot machine. No twenty-one tables, no buffet, none of the customary enticements of Strip properties could be found there. Instead, Showcase presented mainstream entertainment, wholesome and for the kids, packaged for the young of today and their pliant parents. From the All-Star Café, huge pictures of Joe Montana, Tiger Woods, Martina Navratilova, Andre Agassi, and Wayne Gretzky looked down on the new Las Vegas. Their images—all sports stars, all in sports on which you can legally wager in Nevada—gave the new Strip, the haven of leisure and entertainment for a society that has become more visual than textual, the figurative thumbs-up.

The brainchild of two young entrepreneurs, Barry Fieldman and Robert Unger, Showcase anticipated a future that was already here and pointed to changes not only in Las Vegas but in national culture as well. Showcase wasn't a casino and it wasn't a hotel. The development was a symbol, a project that could occur only in the context of the growth around it. Its $160 million price tag made it minuscule compared to the nearby hotels, a number of which topped $1 billion in cost. No one came to the city specifically to see Showcase, but, joined to the visual and psychic transformation of the Strip, the property brought the future another step closer. Showcase articulated important links between what had once been the nation's capital of deviance and the core of the liberal consumerism that now passes for culture and has become American faith.

The enormous Coke bottle affirmed the new Las Vegas in a way that no other brand could. No better representative of transnational capitalism than Coca-Cola existed, and few companies were more conscious of their image and their place in the global economy. Robert Goizueta, Coke's chairman from 1981 until 1997, piloted the company to preeminence in the emerging global economy. From Turner Field in Atlanta to Fenway Park in Boston, Coca-Cola picked its spots. Coke's red-and-white logo was ubiquitous, but only a few chosen places received its symbolic anointment. In 1990 World of Coca-Cola, a prototype for Showcase, opened in Coke's hometown of Atlanta. It stood as a testimony to a future that no one thought would ever grace the Las Vegas Strip.

The sponsorship of the symbol of global capitalism—service, quality, and refreshment melded together—was a major coup for the American desert city. The participation of Forrest City, the Cleveland-based developer and a critical player in downtown redevelopment across the country, further enunciated the new significance. Las Vegas offered a development opportunity like no other, a reprise of other booms in a new and different shape. The home of the lounge singer had become safe and profitable. The new Las Vegas could stimulate, titillate, and be clean and fun at the very same instant.

Showcase was a small piece of a much larger transformation. One year later, in October 1998, Steve Wynn opened the Bellagio. The $2.1 billion hotel included Wynn's $350 million collection of masterpiece art, Rubens, Picasso, Degas, Monet, Gaugin, Van Gogh, and Warhol among them. Within eighteen months, Sheldon Adelson at the Venetian had entered into an agreement with the Guggenheim and Hermitage museums and hired renowned architect Rem Koolhaas to design a 35,000-square-foot satellite gallery. When Wynn sold his empire to meta-financier and impresario Kirk Kerkorian and MGM Grand in May 2000, he kept much of his art collection, and the MGM offered the rest for sale. High art seemed to reach a dead end in Las Vegas, but to the surprise of many, the gallery did not disappear. Instead, MGM negotiated with the Phillips Collection of Washington, D.C., for a traveling exhibit that recorded more than 200,000 visitors in its first five months of display. Wynn planned to display his collection in the property he intended to build at the Desert Inn, and Koolhaas's Guggenheim opened in fall 2001. After the purchase of the Mirage group, Las Vegas ended up with more masterpiece art, a counterintuitive result that reflected the city's new status. Mainstream commercial culture arrived, and so had the tattered remains of highbrow culture, the very cultural elitism that had long led its adherents to disdain Las Vegas. In the clearest reflection of the rise of Nobrow culture, high art seemed likely to become permanent in the desert.

The combination accelerated the transition of Las Vegas. The town had once been a risqué aberration in a society persuaded of its own morality. Las Vegas was excluded from the main patterns of post–World War II American prosperity in industrial America. The corridors of growth and development bypassed it, and the city had to forge its own divergent, idiosyncratic way. Until 1970, the centers of power in American society did not invest in the desert oasis. The idea of an initial public offering of stock in a casino was ludicrous. The rare attempt fell flat, victim of a marketplace that disdained casinos and looked down on places that condoned vice. The wealthy and the powerful wanted no connection to gambling and corruption. Gambling had been a pastime for the lazy, those who wanted a shortcut. The neo-Victorian culture scorned it as a vice and more: not only sinful, but demeaning to individuals and their society as well. Even those who were tempted by dollar signs feared disapproving friends at the country clubs or scathing editorials in the newspapers. The financial markets would not touch gambling. With money to be made elsewhere and the gambling industry marred by the stigma of hoodlums, Wall Street saw no percentage in backing deviance. Gambling was illegal everywhere else. American society grappled with the transition from deferred gratification to immediate self-indulgence, and Las Vegas's idea of fun as excess was too much. In a society in which Ward and June Cleaver were the iconography of normal, how could staid bankers, pillars of the community and first pew at church, finance casinos—with half-naked showgirls—run by guys with accents?

As late as 1980, as the baby boomers began to reach positions of power, this stigma remained powerful. Even though American morality had loosened considerably, Las Vegas was not yet truly legitimate. In 1983, CitiCorp located a service center in Las Vegas. This financial giant so worried that its credit-card clients would balk at mailing payments to a Las Vegas address that it invented a fictitious town, "The Lakes, Nevada," to soothe its customers. No one in Las Vegas minded. "We would have let them call it Citibank City then if they'd wanted to," recalled Somer Hollingsworth, then a leading banker and president of the Nevada Development Authority in 2000. The tarnished image of Las Vegas stood, solid and visible, almost twenty-five years after the Del E. Webb Corporation simultaneously owned the New York Yankees and the Sahara on the Strip; seventeen years after Howard Hughes departed from his train car and pulled up to the Desert Inn in his combination ambulance—luxury vehicle; seven years after Atlantic City legalized casino gaming; four years after Chemical Bank determined that the Sahara needed $25 million more than it had asked for to renovate its property on the northern edge of the Strip; and as Circus Circus secured almost $500 million in bank loans near the prime rate to support its growth. CitiCorp recognized the economic advantages of a Las Vegas location. Wall Street already knew. But in the view of corporate executives, the American public—at least those who held credit cards at the onset of the great spasm of loosening credit—was still dubious of even a primary American corporation's ability to be responsible in the face of endlessly encouraged excess.

The opening of the Mirage began a new era, grander than any in the city's past. The Mirage Phase started with impresario Steve Wynn, the hard-edged but smooth former liquor distributor who morphed into the progenitor of a Las Vegas that blended gaming and entertainment, and his Mirage Hotel and Casino. The Mirage cost $630 million, $500 million more than any previous casino, and needed to clear $1 million a day to meet its overhead. The new hotels completed since then—Excalibur (1990), Luxor (1993), Treasure Island (1993), MGM Grand (1993) a few blocks off-Strip, the Hard Rock Hotel (1995), the Stratosphere Tower (1996), Monte Carlo (1996), New York, New York (1996), Bellagio (1998), Mandalay Bay (1999), the Venetian (1999), Paris (1999), and the new Aladdin (2000)—turned the city into a 125,000-room paradise of enormous properties, a metropolitan area of a mere 1.4 million people with twice the number of hotel rooms of New York or Los Angeles. Wynn's Bellagio was the capstone, a $2.1 billion casino, easily the most well appointed casino anywhere and a candidate for the most gracious public-private space as well. Wynn envisioned the Bellagio as a casino-hotel in which women would be comfortable, a different framing in a town known for pandering to male pleasure. The Bellagio enjoyed the "best assortment of shopping on the planet," Wynn proclaimed, and with amenities like the $350 million art collection, remarkable restaurants, and superior drinks—women swear that the Bellagio makes the best Cosmopolitan anyone's ever tasted—the attraction was obvious. Wynn made his reputation on service, and there was simply no place anywhere like the Bellagio. The ante in the Las Vegas poker game had become astronomical. Only the boldest of the bold could afford a seat at the table. In the space of a decade, Las Vegas had gone from gambling to gaming to tourism to entertainment—the culture of the future.

At the same time, American society underwent a remarkable shift. The old rules and standards were tossed out, and new ones, defined through media, evolved in a world without clear cultural distinctions. In this new world, experience has become currency and entertainment has become culture. Experience is what Americans trade, how they define themselves. Entertainment is the storehouse of national values. Authentic and inauthentic have blurred. It's not that people can't tell the difference—they can. But in a culture without a dominant set of premises or common values, topped by a strong twist of relativism, it's hard to communicate why conventional authenticity is better. "Better" becomes preference, and people do as they please, encouraged by talk shows, self-help books, and twelve-step programs. When the value is on the self, when people rationalize their pleasure as socially useful, when it's all "me, me, me, now, now, now," what they seek is Las Vegas.

To generations of Americans, Las Vegas is a code for self-indulgence and sanctioned deviance. It is a town of fun, of excess, where anything and everything is possible and for sale. It is Bugsy Siegel and the Rat Pack, Shecky Greene and Wayne Newton, Tom Jones, the Lido de Paris, the Folies Bergere, and countless bump-and-grind joints. Las Vegas is the place that you promise your mother you'll never go, then break that promise with a wink and a leer. No place in the United States gives permission like the Las Vegas of myth.

But there is another Las Vegas, a real place found now on the business pages of the *Wall Street Journal* instead of the police blotters or the scandal sheets. To date, the money people have best grasped the city's recent change. For almost fifteen years, this Las Vegas has been the fastest-growing place in the nation. In the process, Las Vegas's population doubled and then nearly doubled again as its physical expanse exploded all over the desert. Rapid growth obliterated the old company town and replaced it with the postmodern metropolis, the leading tourist destination in the world and the only city in the world devoted to the consumption of entertainment. In 1999, Las Vegas surpassed Mecca as the most visited place on earth. This Las Vegas is featured in *Worth* magazine and is considered by entrepreneurs the best city in America to start a business, where despite sexual exploitation in the core of the economy, a phenomenal number of women open their own businesses and succeed. People are born by the thousands in this Las Vegas, a lot more in the 1990s than in the 1950s, and they live, go to school, work, start businesses, marry and raise families, and attend church, synagogue, and mosque here.

The new Las Vegas is a fast-moving place, through which billions of dollars travel—for land acquisition, for infrastructure development, be it roads, sewer pipes, water and waste water projects, airports, and a plethora of related structures and systems, for hotels, casinos, homes, and the like. New strip malls and doctors' offices spring up daily, serving the never-ending stream of newcomers. Orange cones dot the roads, always under construction, ever longer and wider. Growth came so quickly in southern Nevada that when Senator Harry Reid ran for reelection in 1998, incumbency was neither advantage nor disadvantage; it was meaningless, a cipher. His constituency had no history with the senator. More than half the state's registered voters—almost all of them in Clark County, home to greater Las Vegas—had not been Nevadans during his 1992 campaign.

Out of this outburst of people, ideas, and money came something remarkable: an index of the economy, social mores, and culture of a changing society. As *Time* magazine announced in 1994, the nation had become more like Las Vegas. At the same time, Las Vegas became a lot more like the rest of America—in where its financial capital came from and who lent it, in the distribution of its demography, in who lived there and what they did, in its residents' levels of education, in the businesses that catered to the community, and in countless other ways. The flimsy aberration became more than a reflection of the salacious desire of the underside of American life. It offered a primary outlet in a self-indulgent and fast-changing society, the ability to reinvent the self to the applause of a paid audience. When roller coasters were good clean fun, Las Vegas was risqué.

Now that casinos are a legitimate recreation and entertainment choice, Sin City is mainstream, nowhere near as shocking as pierced privates, gangsta rap, or the admissions fourteen-year-olds routinely make on the *The Jerry Springer Show*. Las Vegas is still socially sanctioned deviance. Its brand is just more comfortable to more Americans than it used to be.

Las Vegas is different from much of the nation precisely because it is a part of the future that never shared in the prosperity of the past. It is a rare human who has eaten an apple grown in an orchard in the Las Vegas Valley or worn a sweater from the wool of sheep that grazed in the valley. Few machine tools have ever been ground to a fine edge in Las Vegas. Even fewer people have made their living in its automotive plants. Las Vegas's past is on the margins of American society, in the places now abandoned, forgotten, overlooked, or just hanging on. Its history shares more with Carlsbad, New Mexico, whose city officials were ecstatic to receive the nation's first low-level transuranic nuclear waste dump, than it does with New York or Los Angeles or even Omaha. Las Vegas doesn't have traditions unless they're staged for visitors. It recognizes the past for what it is, an ephemeral and malleable story line, and remakes it not for the present but for the future. Among the places that never found their way in the industrial world, Las Vegas is unique: it forged a divergent future at which the good people at the center of American culture turned up their noses, and made it into a remarkable success. While small towns around the nation withered after 1945, Las Vegas became a city—at odds with the rest of the nation to be sure, but a real city nonetheless—and then the rest of the nation caught up, tried it out, and found that it had a lot more in common with Las Vegas than most would care to admit.

Las Vegas has pieces of the puzzle of the future, ways to solve its problems, but not in a form that may translate to other places. The rhythms of Las Vegas are different from those of the rest of the country. They spring from different sources and lead to different results. Wearing lens of industrial America, the constellation of premises and expectations that shaped the first eighty years of the twentieth century, only fogs the Las Vegas landscape. The convergence so central to the future is obscured, cropped from the picture.

"This is America," the narrator in Neal Stephenson's 1992 futuristic classic *Snow Crash* asserts. "People do whatever the fuck they feel like doing . . . because they have a right to." In Stephenson's world, there are four things his "we"—the people who live in North America—do better than anyone else: they make music, movies, and microcode (software), and they deliver pizza. One of those, microcode, belongs to Silicon Valley and its offspring. The rest—service and entertainment—belong to the new Las Vegas.

From its twentieth-century inception, Las Vegas was ripe to become anything that paid. In the desert, away from the systems that sustained American cities, Las Vegas had to forge its own destiny. When middle-class America subscribed to a largely uniform set of values derived from the Victorian era, there were clear lines of conduct outside of which people strayed only at great risk. This created a culture of confinement, of proscribed values and behaviors, and a world in which a minor deviant turn at the wrong time or place could put someone entirely beyond respectable society. If you stepped over the line, you couldn't come back. "They hung a sign up in this town," Tom Waits writes of that world in "Hold On," "if you live it up you won't live it down." Everything went on your "permanent record," as the vision of venal authority, Dean Vernon Wermer, trumpeted in 1978's *Animal House*.

Such a controlled society desperately craved a release, a place to blow off its internalized steam, and to the post-1945 world, that outlet was Las Vegas. In the desert, you could indulge yourself, even sin for a fee without paying the social price. Slot machines and gaming tables were everywhere. Food and drink were abundant and free. Nevada even had legalized brothels and casinos engaged in a furtive sex trade. In Las Vegas, you could exercise your fantasies. Everything, it seemed, was for sale. In the 1930s Las Vegas offered an image of the mythology of the nineteenth-century West, where an individual could thrive and institutions could not impinge upon personal desire. This persisted beyond Bugsy Siegel's Flamingo in 1946 and continued for a generation. Las Vegas was first chic deviance, a place to sin with impunity, where actions that at home would certainly bring disgrace and might even land a person in jail were perfectly acceptable. This scapegoat of a town, a place to cast off sins in a morally and socially constricted society, was an absolute necessity for both its devotees and its detractors. Its patrons needed its freedom, the glitz and glitter it promised, while its opponents needed its image to contrast good and evil. In this, Las Vegas served a clear, necessary, and widely accepted role. Occasionally there were scandals—the Kefauver hearings investigating organized crime in the early 1950s were a prominent example—but Las Vegas survived with a sense of humor and a bawdy irreverence. And why not? Its people had, to an individual, chosen a life at variance with the norms of their society.

Las Vegas changed before the rest of American society did. Its limitations forced Las Vegas to bend to the will of whatever would generate its revenues. This dependence gave Las Vegas a fluidity, a way around the rules of midcentury America, that locals learned to treasure. The city learned that its shape was always transitory, always flexible, not only because it responded to the emotions of a larger culture, but also because the forces that were behind the city were on the borders of legality. Even in moments of great success, Las Vegas had a powerful sense of impermanence, a strong intuition that whatever ruled today might well not tomorrow.

Malleability served Las Vegas well when both American society and the world economy were reinvented as American industrial preeminence came to an end. OPEC and the oil shortages it caused, inflation, and the end of postwar prosperity all hit at once, epitomized by the long lines to pay for even more expensive gasoline in 1974. In an instant, the pillars of postwar prosperity, cheap energy, the rising value of wages, and low inflation came crashing down. Gerald Ford, with his WIN—Whip Inflation Now—button, was the best response politics could muster. In 1974 the United States entered a twenty-three-year period that represented a regression to the American economic mean. The catalyst was the annual drop for each of those years in the real value of hourly wages. Simply put, people worked longer hours to stay where they were on the socioeconomic ladder. One-income families became more scarce. It took more hours to make the grade in each successive year, and middle-class women entered the workforce in greater numbers than ever before in American history. The reasons for this transformation of the so-called pink ghetto of teaching and nursing were as much social as economic, but the change in economic direction of the nation spoke of a harder, more competitive workplace with fewer opportunities to rise.

The global economic realignment that began with the OPEC oil embargo and the post—Vietnam War inflation masked larger considerations. The fundamental basis of the world economy shifted away from natural resources—of which Las Vegas had few—and toward a combination of information and entertainment that took advantage of an array of new technologies, from the VCR to the Internet. This transformation was as comprehensive as the industrial revolution. The global economy moved from its basis in industry to an information and service configuration. Knowledge and the ability to manipulate it became genuine power. When you could get anything you wanted in virtual time and space, a new premium was added to real experience. In an age when anyone with $399 a month to spend could lease a BMW, when you could ski the Alps virtually from your computer terminal, actual experience, the commodity that Las Vegas specialized in, gained rather than lost significance. The microchip spawned a new world with a new set of rules. Against all odds, Las Vegas became one of the winners.

At the same time, changes in the nature of American society made Las Vegas part of a broader American mainstream. The United States had been a place where Baptist preachers threw rock 'n' roll records onto Friday-night bonfires and Elvis Presley could be shown on television only from the waist up. The change to the individual-oriented culture of personal choice of the cusp of the new century created the context for the rise of leisure and the transformation of socially unacceptable "gambling" into the recreational "gaming." Las Vegas had perfected the service economy long before the rest of the nation encountered it. The rise of entertainment as a commodity increased the cachet of the city. With Frank Sinatra and Sammy Davis Jr. in the 1950s and 1960s and the Hard Rock Hotel thirty-five years later, Las Vegas captured high-status, commercial, cutting-edge culture. In the process, the town became more sophisticated at reflecting the desires of the public back onto it, at creating a script for visitors that placed them at the dead center of all that swirled around them.

Las Vegas's ability to change itself into the newest fashion is the root of its success as a purveyor of the low-skill, high-wage service economy. With more than a half-century's head start in offering people what they demand and in a culture that insists that the act of buying turns the purchaser into the focus of a story, Las Vegas has more to export than mere gaming. In the transformation to entertainment as the basis of culture, Las Vegas leads all others. Perfecting the art of putting a smile on every face, creating a city that implodes its past, pursuing theming that has replaced the desert of the Sands and the Dunes with the Italy of the Venetian and the Bellagio as well as the tinytowns of the Orleans, Paris, and New York, New York, Las Vegas has reached an astonishing maturity. At any time of the day or night, any day of the week, month, or year, the corners of Tropicana and the Strip and Flamingo and the Strip are jammed. Hundreds of thousands walk the Strip to see the sights, from the Statue of Liberty at New York, New York, to the fountains at Bellagio, the Eiffel Tower, the volcano at the Mirage, and the pirate battle at Treasure Island. Locals muse that someday a hotel on the Strip will surely accommodate those who stroll the Strip to marvel at its faux wonders; called "Las Vegas, Las Vegas," it will be a cutdown version of the Strip with all its hotels inside a Strip hotel. People will be able to see the Strip—at five-eighths scale—without ever going outside and they won't get sunburned in the process!

Las Vegas remains different, harder, tougher, and a little bit stranger than most places. It is a true desert city, built on a small oasis rather than a flowing source of water. *Las Vegas* means "the meadows," and underground artesian wells created the lush wide spot in the desert that became the genesis of the community. Now that ground is a wild patch in the city, a part of the Las Vegas Valley Water District's holdings. The underground water is diverted before it reaches the surface and the land is managed to be as natural as it can be in the middle of a metropolitan area. Las Vegas is the largest American city that truly began in the twentieth century. Its nineteenth-century incarnation as a Mormon outpost was an isolated moment rather than a piece of continuity with the present one. It is the only city that can claim that its very survival hinged on Americans' willingness to transcend the norms of their society.

As the twentieth century ended, Las Vegas became the court of last resort for displaced humanity from around the globe. If you couldn't make it somewhere else, if your factory closed and you didn't want to wait around the union hall or go through retraining, if your logging job disappeared, if a friend lost a finger at the plant and the risk seemed too real for you to go on working there, if the crops finally gave out, Las Vegas offered the same promise it made to visitors. You could reinvent yourself there. For a generation, most came expecting to beat the odds. These "something-for-nothing suckers" genuinely believed that they would defy probability and strike it rich in the biggest way. This wasn't just thug—turned—local—philanthropist Moe Dalitz's town or later Steve Wynn's—it was everyone's fantasy town. At first these migrants were foolish, desperate people living on the very edge. Many wised up and realized that the real opportunity in Las Vegas was unskilled blue-collar work at union scale plus tips in a town with a low cost of living and no taxes to speak of.

The transformation created a town that was like everywhere else and simultaneously apart. Las Vegas seemed equal parts Washington, D.C., a transient place where everyone was on the make; Los Angeles or Miami, as more and more conversations were in Spanish and signs restaurant and grocery store advertised *pollo* and *carne asada*; Phoenix, as almost 20 percent of the population was retired and medical care became a huge industry;

Detroit of the old days, with its vocal and powerful semiskilled unionized workforce; and New Orleans, the city that, as Etta James still sings, "care forgot, where everybody parties a lot." At the same time, Las Vegas was different, newer, less structured, more vital, with fewer rules and wider degrees of what constituted normal. Its mythic status made it into its own place.

Las Vegas was and is a hard town that will make you pay for your inability to restrain your desires. "It turns women into men," comedian Alan King quipped, "and men into asses." "You have no idea how many families have lost daughters to the strip clubs," a well-dressed middle-aged African American woman told me with real pain in her voice. Atop Binion's Horseshoe, the casino that his legendary father, Benny Binion, built, Jack Binion stood next to mob lawyer Oscar Goodman, who was elected mayor of Las Vegas in 1999, and surveyed the city he knew so well. The lights twinkled, the city shimmered, and Binion observed, "Las Vegas is a wonderful place if you don't have any weaknesses." It was a remark only a survivor could make. If you have a weakness, Las Vegas will punish you.

People come, desperate for a last chance or a new beginning, fall flat on their face, and then find, in Jimi Hendrix's lyrical description, "tire tracks all across [their] backs," run into the ground by a place that is clear about what it values: winning and money. In this, the Desert City is only more frank than the rest of the nation. The thin veneer of civilization is rarely applied and when it is, it cracks in the baking sun. Class and wealth won't protect you. Doctors as well as bartenders succumb to their own excesses. As many as three thousand people a month move from Las Vegas, often leaving no forwarding address and a mailbox stuffed with creditors' notices. Those who think that they're the lucky one who will hit Megabucks, the progressive slot machine game that offers a multimillion-dollar payoff, find an enormous gap between their expectations and their abilities, and usually end up headed out of town, ground to a nub, happy to see the dust rise behind them.

Las Vegas is also a frontier town, maybe the last in the United States. The better part of the twentieth century passed before the American nation came to grips with its margins. New Mexico, with its long-standing Hispano dominance, has submitted to Anglo America only since 1945. Technological transformation and the pipeline turned Alaska from a frozen federal province into an oil fiefdom and now into a dependent of the Princess Line. The desert was equally harsh. Las Vegas's growth was pos-

We Buy Gold

sible only with air-conditioning and the other mechanisms of industrial society. Only then could Americans turn the desert into something tolerable, could build the endless suburbs with their minuscule but neatly cropped lawns, rolled out like a kid's playmat and tended by armies of Spanish-speaking gardeners. Where the technologies of an industrial society are applied, communities like Las Vegas can flourish. Where they aren't, as around the Salton Sink in southern California or in nearby Pahrump, Nevada, Mad Max's world takes hold and anarchy is rampant. But in Las Vegas, the road from an older American society of industry is being paved to one version of a new, postindustrial world of service and information.

Almost by accident, Las Vegas has become the place where the twenty-first century begins, a center of the postindustrial world. It has become the first spectacle of the postmodern world. In this transformation, the old pariah has become a paradigm, the colony of everywhere, the colonizer of its former masters. Old Nevada allowed people to come there to cast off their sins; when prizefighting was illegal in every state in the union but one, Nevada filled the void with title bouts. This once dubious trait has become a virtue in the postindustrial world, where the people who once made things at respectable wages now stock bottles in convenience stores. Las Vegas has a peculiar cachet. It was the first city of the consumption of entertainment, and to be first at anything in a fluid culture guarantees significance. Las Vegas offers an economic model to which cities, states, and regions look to create their own economic panacea—even as they hold their nose. Its consistent reinvention, once scorned as flimsy and fraudulent, shaped its transformation from peripheral to paradigmatic and has become a much-envied trait. Las Vegas has become normal; even more important, it points to the twenty-first century. What people see in Las Vegas today, as in Los Angeles, New York, and Miami, is what they can expect everywhere in the near future.

Las Vegas now symbolizes the new America, the latest in American dream capitals. As New York once defined the commercial economy and Chicago, the city of big shoulders, epitomized the industrial city, Las Vegas illustrates one of the pillars of the postindustrial, postmodern future. Not only in its economy, but in every other aspect of its development, Las Vegas has become an icon. It is the place to be as the new century takes shape, for in its ability to simultaneously attract and repel, it characterizes American hopes and fears. Las Vegas tells us what has happened to American society and what we now aspire to: simple possession of the ethos of status. It articulates what we value: our freedom and legal restraint of others. Las Vegas is rewriting the relationship between law and power as it privatizes public space and splits the definition of the First Amendment along public-private lines. In a world where entertainment is culture, Las Vegas's version is magical. As the bonds of cultural continuity and transmission fray in the proliferation of visual youth culture at the expense of text-bound literacy, Las Vegas's position improves. As travel becomes more important, Las Vegas's position as the mecca of postliterate faith will become even more secure.

Las Vegas leads in other ways. It offers the most fully developed version of a low-skilled, high-wage service economy in the nation and possibly the world. The power of unions in southern Nevada has made Las Vegas the "Last Detroit," the last place in the world after NAFTA where unskilled workers can make a middle-class wage and claw their way toward the American dream. With one-quarter of its population retired, Las Vegas already grapples with the future of the nation, and almost perfectly represents one of the socially complicated features of the coming decades: an older, mostly white, affluent population being served by a younger, increasingly non-white, far less affluent population with fewer options. This typicality is stunning. Only in a world that crossed a divide equal to the industrial revolution could such a rapid transformation of a city so large be possible.

Understanding Las Vegas requires that the observer discard the notions of space, order, economy, and standards derived from the industrial economy and replace them with a new kind of intellectual organization that is still being formed. In recent years, Las Vegas has been dubbed the "new all-American city" by *Time* magazine; Robert Brustein pilloried the town in *The New Republic*; Paul Goldberger chided its architecture in *The New Yorker*; and it even graced the cover of *The Nation*, the famous "Degas in Vegas" quip. Why do Angelenos fear the rise of entertainment in Las Vegas? Because Las Vegas has more concert venues and more sources of revenue from acts and promoters than the City of Angels? How can Los Angeles be the leading city of the future if so many of its residents move to Las Vegas each year? How did Nevada become the state that gave more to both political parties than any other during the 1996 elections?

Clearly, a significant transformation has occurred. A city without any claim to a past, one that purposefully markets the destruction of its history, has taken its place among powerful American metropolises. In the twenty-first century, Las Vegas will lead. Its models, already exported, will be more widely copied as the shifting of the global economy away from traditional economics makes the anomaly of Las Vegas more tempting. Other places already copy casinos. Soon they will mimic the structures of companies such as Mandalay Resort Group and Steve Wynn's Mirage Corporation, the second most widely admired American corporation in *Fortune*'s annual ranking in 1997, and the capital formation strategies of Las Vegas. They already covet the entertainment options and the malleability of identity that defines the town. With 20 percent of the population retired and 20 percent Latino in 2001, Las Vegas foreshadows the coming retirement of the baby boomers and the native non-whites and the immigrants who will likely provide the bulk of their care. In all of these ways and so many more, the future, for better and for worse, has already arrived in Las Vegas.

PART I

Making Money

CHAPTER 1

Inventing Modern Las Vegas

THE NUMBERS ARE THERE, BUT THEY DON'T MEAN MUCH. HOW DO YOU explain a town that began as a railroad land auction in 1905, reached eight thousand in 1940, and topped one million people in 1995? There's no precedent for Las Vegas, no way to put its experience into the framework of other American cities. Distinct from the American whole, away from the arrows of progress and prosperity, Las Vegas was an insignificant part of the great government-industry matrix that defined the twentieth century. No set of circumstances led to Las Vegas. It didn't have fertile land or rich mineral veins; railroads didn't meet, highways didn't cross there. Banks didn't seek out Las Vegas, developers didn't fashion it into the next paradise, corporations didn't come to the desert to establish new headquarters, and people certainly didn't come looking for the little oasis to put down roots. Las Vegas's attractiveness was lost on Americans until after World War II and to the mainstream until well after 1975.

The reasons are obvious. Las Vegas was nowhere, a "miserable dinky little oasis town," the mobster Meyer Lansky supposedly called it, and without transportation that made it easy to reach or air-conditioning to make the stay bearable, Las Vegas's appeal was as seasonal as any ski resort. Before 1945, it had little to recommend it. Las Vegas had no markets, no hinterland to colonize. Even today, nearby St. George and southern Utah, heavily Mormon, look north to Salt Lake City; Kingman, Arizona, is a highway crossroads of its own; Flagstaff is fast becoming a suburb of Phoenix; and Barstow occupies its own dystopic universe. Las Vegas did not even have enough water to make it prey for Los Angeles. At its twentieth-century birth, Las Vegas was podunk, weak, and dependent, an inconsequential speck on the map.

The new town was typical of the small-town West. Modern Las Vegas began atop the remains of a nineteenth-century Mormon settlement that left only a few cantankerous ranchers. It started as a railroad town, a repair shop for the San Pedro, Los Angeles, and Salt Lake Railroad. Like so many other places in the West, its sustenance came from the rails, and when they prospered, as they did with the opening of the silver mines in Bullfrog and Rhyolite before 1910, so did the town. By 1910, Fremont Street, the heart of the old downtown, was paved, guttered, and flagged with sidewalks, and ten miles of local dirt road had been oiled to reduce the dust. The company built sixty-four workers' cottages and offered easy terms to workers who wanted to build their own. When the railroad's fortunes dipped, so did the town's. A track washout in 1910 sent the population spiking downward from twelve hundred to eight hundred. Only an upsurge in regional fortunes redirected the number upward. A pattern that typified the rural West in this period and ever after defined Las Vegas was set: the town was dependent on decisions made in other places.

Las Vegas's circumstances mirrored the history of the state. Nevada has always been a colony, dependent on the whims and needs of other larger, more powerful states, some adjacent like California, others farther away. Shoehorned into the Union to guarantee Abraham Lincoln's reelection in 1864, Nevada enjoyed the privilege of statehood at the cost of its dignity and, some said, its independence. Some nineteenth-century senators from Nevada never lived in the state. Some of those who did never bothered to attend the Senate. Nevada may be the only state in the union that faced the genuine prospect of losing its statehood. By 1900, the state's population had so dwindled that its status was in question. Representative Francis Newlands, a Californian who transcended the carpetbagger label, decided that farmers would save the state. In 1902, he engineered the Reclamation Act, which created the Reclamation Service, later the Bureau of Reclamation, to impound water for yeoman farmers. The bureau became a dam-building monstrosity, a remarkable example of what political scientists call the "iron triangle" that took on a life of its own. Despite Newlands's intentions, the

Reclamation Act created a new colonial master for Nevada, a federal agency that controlled the most basic need of an arid state.

For two decades, Las Vegas was a simple small western town. Its main industry was the Union Pacific, which bought out the San Pedro, Los Angeles, and Salt Lake in 1921, kept the maintenance shop, and became master of the railroad town, responsible for its infrastructure as well as for its open social climate. Las Vegas had all the virtues and vices of such places. It was tough, raw, and sometimes mean. The rules of high-tone America not only did not apply, they simply didn't exist. Like many similar towns, Las Vegas did not explicitly forbid prostitution. As long as it was confined to one square block, block 16 of the original town plat, "quasi-legal" best defined its status. Railroad fiat restricted gambling, legal in Nevada until Progressive reformers barred it in 1910 in a prohibition that lasted until 1931 and alcohol to the same area. Illegal but only in a technical sense, such activities were part of the compact the railroad made when it created towns that functioned like the port cities of yore. The railroad brought life and it tacitly condoned behavior at odds with Victorian norms. Railroad companies well understood the advantages and drawbacks of the rails, and towns that grew up along them made accommodation, even in the most moralistic of times.

Las Vegas's circumstances were typical of the rural West and even more characteristic of railroad towns. The railroad provided a capital regime; it was the only consistent source of funding for the town, and its goals determined those of the city. Much like the cattle trade of the nineteenth century, the rails brought a rowdy element with plenty of cash and a feeling of mobility. Workers lived in Las Vegas, but travelers passed through, and the sense of movement along the rails freed people from place and time. Vice flourished and became an integral part of local commerce. Although still considered not quite proper, it was recognized as necessary. Catering to other people's desires proved so lucrative that even the most upright small-town burghers held their noses and looked away, as they had in the cattle towns. The accommodation made life palatable. Without vice there wasn't enough business to eke out a living.

This condition reflected a larger theme in the state's history. While Nevada liked to bill itself as the Old West, where the rules of modern civilization didn't apply, it was equally true that the state had few choices. Neither of its two nineteenth-century industries, mining and railroads, encouraged stability. Mining exploded on the landscape, peaked in great rushes, then left huge visible scars as testimony to its transience. The railroad epitomized nineteenth-century mobility, defying the rooted ideals of the time. Its reputation in American folklore for encouraging transience and license and freedom inspired generations of songwriters and other artists. The state embraced these industries because it had no other choice. If Nevadans seemed more willing to mind their own business than most, this incipient libertarianism was a product of the limits of its land and infrastructure in a harsh climate.

One-owner towns had their drawbacks for the people who lived in them. Even though they allowed locals considerable autonomy and leeway, outside power maintained tremendous control. Early Las Vegas was wise to heed and placate its masters. When it didn't, disaster resulted. After the Union Pacific purchase in 1921, the new owners laid off sixty workers, earning the ire of the town. The next year, an opportunity arose for railroad workers to pay back their new overlords; workers shut Las Vegas down during the national railroad strike in 1922. The new masters were not amused. In retribution, the Union Pacific signed the town's death warrant: it moved the maintenance shop and three hundred jobs to Caliente, about 125 miles uptrack toward Utah. The railroad regime ended as arbitrarily as it had started, and Las Vegas was consigned to the fate of other small western towns. It had to adapt—or diminish, wither, and finally go under. The period just following the railroad's departure was the bleakest in modern Las Vegas's short history. The whistle-stop easily could have become a ghost town.

Only California and its imperial need for water saved the city. Since the remarkable fiction that created modern Los Angeles, the City of Angels became a vacuum for every drop of water it could collect. Southern California's growth demanded ever more water and threatened its neighbors near and far, paralyzing even distant states like Colorado. Largely to prevent California from taking all the water in the Colorado River, the other river states sued for peace. The result was ratification in 1927 of the Colorado Compact, which adjudicated the waters of the Colorado River on a state-by-state basis, and the decision to construct the Boulder Dam, now Hoover Dam, the largest public works project of its time, in Black Canyon about thirty miles from Las Vegas.

The dam was the signal event in the history of southern Nevada with ramifications far beyond the region. Beginning in 1931, construction lasted nearly four years, which meant four years of paychecks to almost five thousand workers at the height of the Depression. When Franklin D.

Roosevelt dedicated the dam on September 30, 1935, the 760-foot concrete face presided over a technological miracle: a holding tank for all the
water in the river, distributed by legal agreement between haves and have-
nots. The dam created life, an economy, infrastructure, business, and even
tourism. Secretary of the Interior Dr. Ray Lyman Wilbur decided he wanted
no part of the sinful railroad town of Las Vegas for the project. A stern
moralist, Wilbur preferred the dry style of the Coolidge administration that
preceded his tenure. Although Wilbur built a government town called
Boulder City, dry and free of gambling, the road to the dam led through Las
Vegas. Wilbur's puritanism had inadvertently given Las Vegas a new future.

The synergy the dam created was tremendous. Its success paved the way
for the the Bureau of Reclamation to become the preeminent federal
agency of the 1930s and a powerful engine of federal spending until the
1970s. After Boulder Dam, the Bureau of Reclamation engaged in forty-
year orgy of dam building until it controlled the distribution of most of the
water west of the Mississippi River and created legions of dependent local
oligarchies in the small-town and mini-city West. As the dam revived Las
Vegas, it also provided a new master, one that carried other federal beneficiaries in tow.

Las Vegas was entirely typical of other western towns in the 1930s. The
region's economy survived or thrived based on the size of the federal contribution. Compared to places without a Civilian Conservation Corps
camp, which housed young men paid a dollar a day to work on federal projects, or a WPA project, Las Vegas fared well. The dam pumped $19 million
into the region. Another $4 million went for federal dole to the many dis-
appointed people who showed up in southern Nevada for a job only to find
that they were all filled. In the desperate 1930s, Las Vegas was little different from Wichita, Omaha, Billings, or Prescott. It responded to the same
stimuli and felt the same losses, held to same sentiments and emotions and
aspired to the same things. There wasn't a tube of neon to be found, and
when Slats Jacobs, a Las Vegas cowboy who competed in the national rodeo
circuit, won the annual competition held in Sun Valley, Idaho, in 1938, he
was the archetype of the moment. Despite the preeminence of the National
Finals Rodeo in Las Vegas every December since the 1980s, Jacobs might
have been the last real cowboy of any note to come from Las Vegas.

There was one way that Las Vegas could stand apart from the multitude
of similar towns. It possessed a sense of itself as a place out of time, left over
from an older western past. A certain amount of the Old West was consid-

ered ribald by 1930s standards, but Las Vegas wasn't really sinful, its symbolism seemed to say. It just hadn't changed while everyone else had, and so held a convenient place in memory that allowed it—and you, when you visited—to get away with things that you couldn't at home. In a society quick to condemn aberrant behavior yet nostalgic for its lost roots, ribald could be packaged as individual freedom.

This tradition became the crux of the vaunted Nevada individualism, the most appealing and vexing characteristic of the state then and now. Nevada was and is wide open, a dream for anyone who was ever a sophomore in college and entranced by Ayn Rand, even for a moment. In their rugged self-image, Nevadans pride themselves on having real freedom, not the namby-pamby eighteenth-century Paul Revere–style freedom within the constraints of the community, but the right to do what you want, whenever you want, wherever you want, and with whomever you want. Fusing its rugged history with economic necessity, Nevada put as few constraints on the individual as possible. Your property is *your* property more in Nevada than in any other state in the union; you can carry a concealed weapon with less red tape than in most places, and the concept of self-defense—your right to protect yourself—is carried further in Nevada law than elsewhere in the nation. The desert alone was not the sole attraction for James "Bo" Gritz, the survivalist who negotiated the surrender at Ruby Ridge in Idaho. Nor is it accident that within a mile of the state capitol in Carson City, legal houses of prostitution flourish. Nevada is the home of the Sagebrush Rebellion, an attempt to privatize most federal lands in the West under the pretext of furthering private property rights. Nevada still sells this same nostalgia. All of this individualism pulls on the nation's emotions in an age when we're oppressed by institutions and information and told that the self is all there is. But this romanticism embodies a difficult paradox: with ideals like these, it's hard to run a modern society.

The next capital regime, federal dollars, illustrated the perils of colonial existence. Lacking industry or infrastructure, Las Vegas depended first and foremost on outside money. Almost as an afterthought, the state permitted activities that were regarded as scandalous. Southern Nevadans especially recognized the perils of dependence. An arbitrary change in federal policy could threaten not only individual livelihood, but the economic viability of the entire region. Before air-conditioning, attracting newcomers to a town where summer temperatures routinely topped 110 degrees was a difficult task without the lure of easy prosperity.

As a result, Las Vegas shaped itself to the needs of the outside. In the West of the 1930s and 1940s, this was not unusual. Oklahoma City, Richmond, California, and countless communities did the same. Only Las Vegans recognized that their opportunity to capitalize was time-bound, and that long-term sustenance required other strategies. Southern Nevada especially welcomed the federal money and encouraged those dollars to stay. At the same time, its people looked for new ways to diversify their income base.

After the completion of the Hoover Dam, a new strategy became imperative. The dam brought five thousand paychecks each week into the regional economy, and after the work was completed their absence left an enormous hole. Tourism to the dam filled part of the gap. Las Vegas soon advertised the dam as the greatest engineering marvel in the world and even created annual events to attract visitors. Divorce, long a mainstay of the state economy and even more prominent after 1931, when the state's residency requirement shrank to six weeks to trump Idaho's and Arkansas's reduction of their own standard to three months, also helped, but even with Ria Langham, who gave the town a boost as she whiled her six-week wait in Las Vegas's clubs and casinos while her soon-to-be-ex, Clark Gable, did Hollywood with Carole Lombard, the prosperity of the dam years did not return. Only World War II rescued Las Vegas from post-dam doldrums as the federal government again propped up southern Nevada's economy. An air base northeast of town was commandeered by the federal government, which ultimately spent more than $25 million on the construction of facilities there. The Las Vegas Gunnery School, as the installation became known, supplied the Pacific Theater with tail gunners, graduating four thousand every six weeks by 1942. The Basic Magnesium Incorporated factory in what became Henderson, on the road between Las Vegas and Boulder City and the dam, also brought in federal dollars. By the end of the war, Las Vegas had become accustomed to a two-pronged economy. Federal money provided the base, and the old Nevada stand-by, sanctioning behavior that was forbidden at home, added another dimension.

Federal money was the dominant capital regime of the era, driving local decision-making. Access to it came by means of construction contracts, service work, or the opportunity to liberate paychecks from the pockets of federal workers. This capital was so important that the community compromised its Nevadan ideal of individual choice and gave in to decidedly unfamiliar demands: in 1942 Las Vegas closed its red-light district to

accommodate the military brass, and after November 1942 bars and casinos were closed from 2:00 A.M. to 10:00 A.M. But closure was worthwhile
if the alternative was to be completely off-limits to military personnel.
Southern Nevada once again proved that it understood its colonial status.
Just as the region had once catered to mining and the railroad, it agreed to
the demands of the government.

As World War II ended, a little red sports car came up Highway 91 from Los
Angeles, and from it emerged a strong-jawed if ragged-looking man with
hard eyes. Benjamin "Bugsy" Siegel, a mobster and close associate of
underworld leader Meyer Lansky, inaugurated the next capital regime in
Las Vegas. A vicious and probably psychotic thug and hit man, Siegel had
been flirting with Hollywood before he came to Las Vegas. He didn't
understand why he hadn't been cast in movies; he was handsome, he
thought, rugged-looking, and a good actor to boot. He should be in film.
But his real business called, and Siegel headed down the road.

His arrival was part of a larger plan. Lansky and his associates eyed Las
Vegas as early as 1941, but in most accounts Siegel receives credit for envi-
sioning the complicated relationship between gambling and status that
turned the Flamingo Hotel into Las Vegas's first national destination.
Siegel transformed Las Vegas from a western, institution-free center of vice
into a world-renowned spectacle of gambling, entertainment, and fun by
blending the themes of Monte Carlo, Miami Beach, and Havana with the
resortlike character of the hotels that preceded the Flamingo on Highway
91. Siegel had a bizarre idea of class, but in the process of painting it onto
the dinky little oasis, he inaugurated an era in which the capital to fund
gaming resorts, the newest dominant industry in Las Vegas, came first from
the pockets of organized crime and later from legitimate money the underworld could control.

Siegel did not conceive of the Flamingo. Instead he followed Billy
Wilkerson's initiative. Founder of the *Hollywood Reporter* and a Los Angeles
restaurant impresario, Wilkerson envisioned Las Vegas as Beverly Hills in
the desert. He planned a swank and elegant resort that appealed to a fashionable crowd in ways that the sawdust-covered floors of the western-
themed casinos could not. Wilkerson's project faced a typical problem: his
plans outstripped his resources, and with little capital in the state and less
chance to borrow it from conventional sources, Wilkerson needed
investors. Siegel and his friends purportedly bought two-thirds of the

THE FLAMINGO

project for $650,000, presumably to be paid with a $600,000 loan from Walter Bimson's Valley National Bank of Phoenix that was arranged in complicated circumstances. It's doubtful that Wilkerson received any of that money from Siegel and his hard friends.

Locals did not object to this seemingly nefarious involvement in what was becoming the primary local industry. There was only one other significant source of capital in postwar Las Vegas, the Nevada Test Site. Cold War spending in support of aboveground testing between 1951 and 1963 and underground testing afterwards provided as many as nine-thousand jobs. Although certainly significant, such spending only went so far: it provided jobs for the most specialized workforce in the area, offered a considerable number of well-paying but dangerous jobs, and became the baseline for the regional economy. But federal spending after 1945 was only the starting point. In southern Nevada, the need for capital was so great that almost everyone looked the other way when it came to mob dollars. Even the strait-laced Mormon culture welcomed the newcomers. The mobster's arrival opened a new pipeline to the capital for which Las Vegans thirsted. Siegel's well-known association with Murder Incorporated, the sensationalized mob killers from 1930s New York, did not scare away locals. Anyone with money to invest was welcome, even Benny Siegel.

Lansky was perhaps the shrewdest of the mobsters, carefully covering his tracks. When Siegel purchased the El Cortez in 1945, his investors included locals as well as gangsters Lansky, Gus Greenbaum, an Arizona bookmaker, Davie Berman, the mob boss of Minneapolis, and his ne'er-do-well brother Chickie, and Israel "Icepick Willie" Alderman, who ran typical 1930s gaming roadhouses called "carpet joints" in Minneapolis, and Moe Sedway, a Siegel associate from Los Angeles. The purchase of the El Cortez initiated a pattern that marked two decades of Las Vegas development. In every subsequent purchase or development of a resort on the Strip, "connected" illegal gamblers, who became legal in Nevada, participated. In nearly every new casino in the 1940s and 1950s, a visible relationship between locals and newcomers effectively linked outside capital with respectability. Locals who could easily be licensed or individuals with ties to organized crime but no significant criminal record held visible and often sizable percentages of new casinos. Most of these "owners" appeared to have recently come into money. Who truly owned their percentage was not a good question to ask.

The story of the funding of the Flamingo Hotel and the death of Bugsy Siegel has become legend, but its meaning is easily overlooked. Construction of the Flamingo went well over budget. Siegel had never run a construction project before, and his contractors robbed him blind. Siegel got stuck with the bills. The initial estimate of $1.5 million ballooned to almost $6 million, aggravated by Siegel's insistence on providing a private sewer line to each room, which added $1 million to the cost. In 1946, when Siegel tried to extort $2 million from the Chicago mob to complete construction, he had $1 million of his own money in the project and $3 million of shoebox money, the piles of cash that mobsters, almost always immigrants or the children of immigrants, pulled from under their beds and invested in $50,000-sized shares. Not a dime of legitimate money financed the Flamingo after Siegel took it over from Wilkerson.

This pattern of financing was typical of Las Vegas casinos and hotels until the late 1950s. Even resorts with legitimate origins, such as Wilbur Clark's Desert Inn, became part of a vast and only lightly concealed organized crime network. Clark, his brother, and two investors began the Desert Inn in 1947 with $250,000. They soon ran out of money, and for nearly two years the framed structure sat in the hot desert sun, looking more like an ancient relic than a nascent casino. Clark even tried the nearly defunct Reconstruction Finance Corporation (RFC), a New Deal–era agency, as a source. In 1949 Clark met Morris B. "Moe" Dalitz, and within a few months Dalitz and his partners in the notorious Cleveland Mayfield Road gang contributed $1.3 million and purchased 75 percent of the project. When Wilbur Clark's Desert Inn opened in April 1950, local newspapers called it "the most brilliant social event in the history of the Strip." Clark became a glorified front man at the resort that bore his name. The Desert Inn proved that the Flamingo was not a once-in-lifetime opportunity. Mob money easily found its way to Las Vegas, and hotels such as the Sands, completed in 1952, the Tropicana in 1957, and the Stardust in 1958, shared similar stories.

The mob and its strange habits with money created the Las Vegas of myth, the town where, as Debbie Reynolds observed, "nobody got killed who didn't deserve it." Las Vegas became a world of shadowy individual investment, usually hidden and always untaxed, with deliveries of the skim, paper bags, and briefcases full of money to distant cities. These individuals held "points" in Las Vegas, percentage investments that were not on the record but that returned monthly profits skimmed off the top of the casino's profits and never recorded in their ledgers, taxed, or made known to aboveground stockholders. Insidious and nefarious to be sure, most of these investments were also small-time, amounting to as little as a few thousand dollars a month in profit. On paper, Jack Entratter, the head of the Sands in the early 1960s, ostensibly owned 12 percent of the operation. A former headwaiter at the Copacabana in Miami Beach who had become a player and philanthropist in Las Vegas—the social hall in the oldest synagogue in town, Temple Beth Sholom, was constructed with his donation and named for him—Entratter owned 2 percent himself. The other 10 points he held for various people, including the real power at the Sands, an old associate of Lansky's named Vincent "Jimmy Blue Eyes" Alo. The mythic Las Vegas was a personal world where everyone knew everyone else and all knew who buttered their figurative bread.

This world provided much to celebrate for those who came to Las Vegas to legitimize their lifestyle. After the construction of the Flamingo, the town became a magnet for every gambler, hood, and small-time entrepreneur in the country. In every other state in the union, activities that went on every day in Las Vegas could land you a jail term. It was a relief to be in a place where their business was legal. Such people came by the thousands, swelling the population and creating a new kind of company town. Even local political culture was transformed, as politicians found gamblers the only major source of campaign contributions. Las Vegas became one big carpet joint, a place where the mores of illegal gaming culture became the norm and where the only casinos that lost money, after Siegel's famous initial fiasco at the Flamingo, were run by people who did not understand the rules of the new game.

In the open political and cultural climate of southern Nevada, Las Vegas became the center of gaming in the Western Hemisphere. With the rise of Fidel Castro in Cuba and the closure of the Havana casinos, only one location in North America provided legal big-time gambling. Combined with improvements such as the expansion of McCarran Airport in 1963, Las Vegas took advantage of the growing affluence and changing cultural mores of American society. In Nevada, gaming masked its social cost. Despite the reality that many casino employees gambled their paychecks, most of casinos' winnings came from visitors. The industry consistently produced positive numbers for the state economy.

This new importance led to a much greater demand for capital than had existed during the 1950s. Until 1963, when the Fremont Casino skimming scandal was derailed by illegal Federal Bureau of Investigation wiretaps, Las Vegas was a small-time operator's paradise. Accustomed to seeing their occupation as risky, the individuals who ran casinos operated as fly-by-nights. Skimming was endemic. A piece of the profit went in the celebrated "three for the hotel, one for the government, and one for the boys" formula, and the real powers, mob bosses in other cities, received it in paper bags. They looked at the short-term profit that could be put in their pockets as the best profit, almost instinctively feeling that the idyllic moment could not last. They believed that their run of luck would soon end. The laws would change, the moralists would come out of the woodwork, the police would crack down, and they'd be on the run again, without their increasingly expensive tangible assets, the larger and larger casino hotels along the Strip.

When the hammer fell, as it did repeatedly, its impact was usually negligible. Americans were increasingly willing to experiment with self-indulgence. In a world where leisure and recreation were becoming more important, gambling ceased to be a moral violation and began its road toward acceptance as a legitimate recreational pastime, a journey completed sometime in the 1990s. The new emphasis on gambling as a form of entertainment rather than a tawdry pastime put pressure on operators to cater to a broader audience. To get Mom and Pop America to Sin City demanded that operators see the openness of Las Vegas as more than a moment that would soon end. It also required a lot more money.

The limitations of the shoebox phase of mob financing became evident. After a spate of hotel construction during the 1950s that ended with the Stardust in 1958, no new hotels were completed on the Strip until 1966. A number of hotels were renovated, and a nongaming resort, the Tally-Ho, was built by New York stockbroker Edwin Lowe; but without a casino, Lowe's endeavor soon ended in bankruptcy. The limits of small-time mob rule and its capital were exposed for all to see. Siegel, Dalitz, and the other early mob entrepreneurs dug into their own pockets, but as costs and consumer expectations increased exponentially, the pockets that had previously funded the growth of the industry proved insufficiently deep.

The financial markets still eschewed gaming resorts. The only legitimate source of such capital in southern Nevada was a local bank, the Bank of Las Vegas, founded in 1954 and reorganized as the Valley Bank in 1964. An arm of the empire of Walter Cosgriff of the Continental Bank of Utah, the only non-Mormon financial institution of significance in the Beehive State, the Bank of Las Vegas mirrored Cosgriff's willingness to loan money outside of the conventional channels of midcentury America. In the 1950s, the Bank of Las Vegas became a primary local source of capital, but despite its significance and that of banker E. Parry Thomas, growth still outstripped available funding. Casinos lined up for money from Thomas's bank, but the capital needed to transform Las Vegas into a first-class resort would have to come from somewhere else.

Again, the mob was at the center of the story. The Teamsters' Central States, Southeast, and Southwest Areas Pension Fund, run by Allen Dorfman, the stepson of mobster Paul "Red" Dorfman and an associate of the Chicago mob, provided the source. In the early 1950s, the Teamsters boss Jimmy Hoffa hand-picked the younger Dorfman, then a college physical education instructor, to handle the Teamsters' insurance to repay a favor to his stepfather. In 1967, as Hoffa prepared to go to jail, he gave Dorfman complete control of pension fund loans.

Moe Dalitz, who knew Hoffa in Detroit when both were starting out, and St. Louis attorney Morris Shenker, a Hoffa confidant and an attorney for the American National Insurance Corporation of Texas, shepherded the introduction of the pension fund to gambling. Dalitz borrowed liberally from the pension fund. The insurance company had its own nefarious roots in the empire of Texas crime boss Sam Maceo and business mogul W. L. Moody Jr., both of whom were friends of Nevada senator Pat McCarran. The Hoover-era FBI described Shenker as the most highly paid mob attorney in the country. American National became a conduit through which capital for casino funding reached the Bank of Las Vegas, and Shenker soon held a stake in a number of casinos. In 1963, the Teamsters Pension Fund had more than $167 million in assets, and 60 percent of its resources were in real estate, compared to the 2.3 percent typical of similar investing consortiums in that era.

Early Teamsters pension fund forays into Las Vegas had little to do with gaming. In 1958 *Las Vegas Sun* publisher Herman "Hank" Greenspun, one of the few American newspaper publishers to challenge Senator Joseph McCarthy's reign of terror and loudly critical of the influence of organized crime on his adopted state, received $250,000 from the pension fund for a golf course. Teamsters money funded other developments. On April 14, 1959, the one-hundred-bed Sunrise Hospital opened, built by the Paradise Development Company, whose officers included Moe Dalitz, casino executive Allard Roen, who had been indicted in the United Dye and Chemical stock fraud case, and two young Las Vegas businessmen, Irwin Molasky and Mervin Adelson. Hoffa ensured its profitability by delivering the Teamsters union health care contracts to the new hospital.

Subsequent construction by the Paradise Development Company, especially the 1967 Boulevard Mall, drew accolades from the community. With access to capital for developing noncasino projects, the company effectively planned the future of nonresort Las Vegas by turning Maryland Parkway, a two-lane road that paralleled the Strip about two miles to the east, into the main commercial thoroughfare for the growing city. Nearly everyone in the city with any kind of aspiration, workers and executives alike, came to live in the area east of the new commercial center. The enclosed Boulevard Mall, the first modern shopping center in Las Vegas, capped this process. With its completion, Las Vegans needed only a little self-deception to believe that their city had amenities for its residents to match those of the resorts that catered to visitors.

This was the most complicated dimension of mob rule in southern Nevada. In a colony lacking internal capital, in the middle of substantial growth, and dominated by an industry that the mainstream would not fund, Las Vegas hungered for fresh capital, no matter what its origins. Largely invisible to the public, unconventional financing helped shape the direction of the city. Teamsters pension fund money invested in social projects, albeit profitable ones like the hospital and the mall, made that capital even more palatable. To most of greater Las Vegas, which had grown from roughly 8,000 in 1940 to 269,000 in 1967 and was comprised of casino workers who regarded legalized gaming as the solution to legal woes they experienced elsewhere, the hospital and mall were community assets. Similar developments continued to normalize Las Vegas, offering people a sense of typicality that had been hard to sustain in the 1950s. For that, Las Vegans were grateful, and they were usually willing to overlook the unusual origins of the money that financed their normalcy.

In the mid-1960s, pension fund capital, along with a flamboyant, visionary style that could be traced back to Bugsy Siegel and the Flamingo, made its way from local development to the Strip. Even after Hoffa went to jail, his model sunk its claws ever deeper into Las Vegas. The new money was a clear shift from the first generation, when mobsters reached under their beds for shoeboxes of cash. Teamsters pension fund money begat a distinctive brand of new hotels, the most important of which was Caesars Palace, funded by a loan from the Central States Pension Fund and run by Jay Sarno, an eccentric but brilliant entrepreneur.

By the mid-1950s, Sarno was an experienced hotelier who borrowed Teamsters pension fund money in the late 1950s to finance hotel projects in Atlanta and Dallas for his Cabana chain. He'd developed a friendship with Hoffa, and Allen Dorfman supported Sarno's endeavors. In one instance, Sarno was offered money from the fund at a lower interest rate than he'd requested, a gesture that led law enforcement to treat the hotelier as a mob front. Sarno was not deterred. By the time he conceived of Caesars Palace, he possessed the combination of vision and access to funding that allowed him to realize dreams of grandiose projects. Sarno injected new glamour into casinos. Three decades later, his vision had become gaming's primary brand name.

Caesars Palace's $19 million price was the most money ever spent to develop a Las Vegas resort, and the hotel reflected Sarno's idiosyncracies. The casino was elliptical, following the hotelier's belief that egg-shaped structures relaxed people. A frieze showing the battle of the Etruscan Hills graced the wall next to the Noshorium Coffee Shop, itself a tongue-in-cheek combination of the Yiddish word *nosh* for "snack" and a Roman-sounding suffix. Classical fountains and statues graced the property, with eighteen huge fountains bordering the 135-foot driveway. The eight-hundred-seat Circus Maximus Theatre, patterned after the Coliseum in Rome, hosted only the top acts of the day; Frank Sinatra and Barbra Streisand headed the first bills.

By 1966, the pension fund had become the dominant source of development capital in southern Nevada. The rising cost of resort development, particularly after Caesars Palace, demanded more than $100 million in development capital. The traditional means of capital formation, stock offerings and bonds, were still blocked. Wall Street was not ready, leaving gambling's lucrative rewards to the pension fund and the organized crime bosses who ran it. That made Las Vegas beholden not to conventional financial powers in America, but to the parasitic forces that preyed upon it. People in gaming were not bothered by the prospect of silent and powerful control. In the 1960s, Las Vegas's veneer of typicality was thin. Although Las Vegans insisted that behind the glitz, they lived in a "normal" town, their definition of normal was quite at odds with the one held by the rest of the nation.

Even with the mall, the hospital, and other trappings, Las Vegas lacked the hierarchies of the rest of the nation, an old, entrenched elite, physical infrastructure like factories that made goods, vast railroad yards, and even shipping and trucking depots. In Las Vegas as late as 1969, there was really only one economy: gambling. There was the Nevada Test Site, but everything else revolved around the casinos. Locals worked in the casinos, hung out on the Strip, cruised it with their kids in the back seat, and dreamed of hitting it big. Their children aspired to show business, not to medical school. They were service workers and proud of it, beneficiaries of a unique American internal colonialism. Long before anyone else in the United States understood this principle, Las Vegans recognized that putting smiles on the faces of visitors paid very well.

Nevada's gaming laws contributed to its well-paid colonial status. To counter what state authorities perceived as the menace of organized crime, gambling was regulated at the state level during the mid-1940s. Before the

Flamingo, gambling had been small-time. Counties and their sheriffs administered it in their own idiosyncratic ways. Siegel's well-publicized murder in 1947 sparked new statutes, giving the Nevada Tax Commission the power to investigate, license, and monitor gaming, but this remedy accomplished little. The grandstanding Tennessee senator Estes Kefauver arrived in 1950 to root out corruption and further his presidential aspirations. Not surprisingly, he found the mob everywhere. Las Vegas's dirty secret was exposed and not in the charmingly roguish way that the city would have preferred. Locals, already feeling the pressure of new powers in town, echoed Kefaurer's refrain. Clark County commissioner Harley Harmon, from a powerful family in the region, complained during 1952 licensing hearings for Sands entertainment director Jack Entratter that the tax commission "has let every syndicate in the country into Las Vegas." Subsequently, the Nevada Gaming Control Board and the state gaming control commission were charged with the tax commission's responsibilities. Even the establishment of a legal mechanism to bar undesirables like "known hoodlums," as the board's first announcement attested, from casinos in 1960, the "Black Book," formally known as the List of Excluded Persons after 1976, amounted to little more than a public relations ploy to clean up the state's image.

The efforts to keep mob money out backfired. After 1955, one cardinal state regulation determined the pattern of investment in gaming: every stockholder of a gaming establishment must be licensed by the state. The regulation was part of a public relations blitz. To counter stories of shady games and illicit activity, blackmail and rigged cards, Las Vegas needed a shot of respectability to survive in a puritanical moment. The 1955 regulation effectively barred large publicly held corporations from owning stock in the gaming industry, but it had a dramatic unintended consequence. Instead of freeing gaming from the influence of organized crime, the state inadvertently strengthened its power. The law made the Teamsters pension fund the only source of capital upon which Las Vegas could depend, and as long as the only money in town came from organized crime, the county commission and other civic leaders needed the mob as much as the mob needed them. Hostility between locals and the mob existed, but as part of a much more complex relationship. In the 1960s and early 1970s, Las Vegas was a partnership between local interests that needed capital and mobsters who were the only source that locals could reach. With the sole exception of the Del E. Webb Corporation, which simultaneously owned the Sahara Hotel and Casino and the New York Yankees, corporations were barred from the casino business. The combination of stigma of gaming and Nevada statute denied legitimate capital to the gaming industry when it needed it most, leaving the town and its hoods in a twisted but entirely necessary embrace.

The transformation of Las Vegas from a mob-dominated gambling town to corporate-owned modern resort began with two related events. The first was the arrival of reclusive billionaire Howard R. Hughes at a suite atop the Desert Inn in Las Vegas in his typically bizarre fashion on the eve of Thanksgiving, 1966. Hughes had been a frequent visitor to Las Vegas in the 1950s, living there for a year, often talking of bringing his entire business empire to Nevada. In 1966, the billionaire was ferried from his private railroad car and hustled upstairs to the floor of penthouse suites reserved for the high rollers on whom the casino depended. After a few weeks, the management of the Desert Inn sought to persuade Hughes to leave; they'd expected an increase in gambling as a result of the presence of the world's richest man and were sorely disappointed. Hughes had so far cost them money. They couldn't put the high rollers they needed in the hotel because Hughes insisted on having the entire floor. Gamble or leave, they told Hughes's representatives.

Instead of doing either, Hughes bought the place for about $13 million and remained cloistered in the penthouse for four years. The purchase was the first in a buying spree that included the Frontier, for which Hughes paid $14 million, the Sands, $14.6 million, Castaways, $3 million, the $17 million Landmark and its nearly $9 million Teamsters pension fund loan, and the Silver Slipper. All of Hughes's purchases had been Lansky-dominated casinos. Hughes added a television station, airlines, small airport facilities, one hundred residential lots at the Desert Inn Country Club, and thousands of acres of undeveloped land, including more than twenty thousand acres called "Husite," where Hughes promised the federal government a guided missile base in return for the nearly free land. Hughes made overtures to purchase Caesars Palace, the Riviera, and the Dunes in Las Vegas as well as Harrah's in Reno and Lake Tahoe, but an antitrust suit halted negotiations. Before the Nixon administration received a bribe and overruled Justice Department objections to Hughes's purchase of Harold's Club in Reno and the Landmark Hotel, the tycoon controlled about one-seventh of the state's gaming revenue, one-quarter of that in Las Vegas, and more than one-third of the revenue generated on the Strip.

A public relations dream for Nevada, Howard Hughes's entrance into gaming was a pivotal moment for Las Vegas. In 1966 another in the seemingly endless series of scandals in Las Vegas had broken wide open, and the FBI simultaneously impugned the integrity of state oversight of gaming and offended the state's libertarian tendencies. Hughes's reputation as a brilliant entrepreneur who would only invest in a genuine money-maker removed some of tarnish from Nevada gaming.

Hughes served as a harbinger of a new era, the first set of truly deep pockets to seek to make Las Vegas his own. He arrived at the ideal moment for a newcomer, exactly as the fortunes of his predecessors began to give way. The first generation of mob impresarios, men such as Meyer Lansky and Jimmy Alo, were aging, and some grew tired of the constant federal surveillance and other hassles that accompanied a move to the legitimate American economy. Selling out to Hughes, whom they regarded as the quintessential sucker, seemed a good idea. They took their profit and departed.

In some ways, Hughes was more like the gangsters he replaced than the corporate America that revered him. Gaming was a natural for Hughes. He was a confirmed risk-taker who flaunted rules all his life, he was beholden to no one, and even more important, owed no one. Hughes was the sole stockholder of Hughes Tool Company, meaning that only he had to pass gaming commission investigations. A man of his stature and wealth had little problem manipulating regulatory bodies in a state with weak government. As was the case with the development of the Flamingo and its peers, Hughes's capital was private and personal. The reclusive and idiosyncratic billionaire's vast empire had no public association with organized crime. A forerunner of the new Las Vegas whose patterns resembled the old, Hughes's interest helped legitimize investment in the gaming industry.

The second change made the mobsters who sold out wince. In 1967, at the behest of William F. Harrah and Baron and Conrad Hilton, with the support of Nevada governor Paul Laxalt, the state passed the Corporate Gaming Act, which eliminated the requirement that each stockholder had to pass a Gaming Control Board background check. Governor Grant Sawyer had fought this law while in office, believing it would only institutionalize organized crime, but Laxalt had no such qualms. Passage of the law opened the door for an infusion of corporate capital and raised the stakes in gaming. Corporations could now invest, inaugurating a new capital regime that brought Las Vegas closer to the primary avenues of capital formation.

The first purchases by major multinational hotel chains quickly followed. In 1970, the Hilton Corporation purchased the Flamingo and the International from Kirk Kerkorian, another self-made multimillionaire seeking to make Las Vegas his own. A highroller in his own right, Kerkorian made his money in crop-dusting and airlines, moving into gambling with the purchase of a small piece of the Dunes Hotel in 1955. He bought raw land across from the Flamingo and sold it to Caesars Palace before acquiring the Flamingo and the International. The two hotels were preludes to his dream of a new, world-class resort, the MGM Grand Hotel, which was to be the biggest hotel in the world. Selling the Flamingo and the International moved Kerkorian closer to his goal. With the arrival of Hilton and its enormous success in Las Vegas—by 1976, 43 percent of the gross revenues of the 163-hotel chain came from its Las Vegas operations—legitimate capital became widely available. Holiday Inn and Ramada followed close behind Hilton, and a new financing supported the development of Las Vegas.

In this climate, organized crime suddenly became financially obsolete. Hotel chains pioneered the way, and financial markets slowly changed their view of gaming. In a few seconds, Wall Street could muster a great deal more money than organized crime ever could. The $269 million of Teamsters pension fund money in late-1960s Las Vegas might have remained the largest investment in southern Nevada, but it ceased to represent the growth sector of gaming capital. In an instant, the passage of the revised Corporate Gaming Act redistributed power in Las Vegas away from mob-controlled dollars and toward Wall Street.

Quickly and harshly, the old ways of doing things in Las Vegas came to an end. In 1974 Allen R. Glick, a largely unknown San Diego businessman, received a $62.7 million loan from the Teamsters pension fund to purchase Recrion Corporation, a mob-owned company that controlled the Stardust, the Fremont, and the Marina hotels. What followed was predictable. At the Stardust, under the watchful eye of Frank "Lefty" Rosenthal, the chairman of Glick's Argent Corporation executive committee, a 1950s-style mob skimming operation was installed. The skills of slot cheat—turned—counting room boss Jay Vandermark made cash disappear, and the enforcement power of Tony "the Ant" Spilotro, a small-time Chicago hood who took advantage of chaos in the mob hierarchy to claim the streets of Las Vegas as his own, guaranteed that no one challenged the operation.

It was a typical Las Vegas story, but the outcome was different. In the mid-1970s, other sources of capital meant that Nevada authorities neither needed to nor chose to look the other way. The Stardust was beset by problems almost from the moment Glick signed the papers. The arrangement reeked of hidden power. In January 1976 the Gaming Control Board informed Glick that Rosenthal could not be licensed to run casinos. Droll, sanctimonious, and arrogant, Rosenthal tried to be a man about town while he cleared his name. He hosted a local television show so bad that people watched it just to see how bad it would get. Long-time Nevadans recall getting stoned before tuning in. A May 1976 Gaming Control Board raid on the Stardust counting room uncovered a skim that totaled more than $7 million from slot machines alone in a single year. In a pivotal 1979 Gaming Control Board hearing, Rosenthal's license was permanently denied. Perhaps naive, certainly megalomaniacal, Rosenthal expected to have his license restored when he challenged the state's right to regulate his ability to work in the gaming industry and in the process, the state's right to regulate the industry at all.

The permanent denial of Rosenthal's license showed that a corporate vision had crystalized in Las Vegas. Before 1970, Rosenthal would have easily cleared the gaming board, but as Atlantic City legalized gaming in 1976 and state lotteries began in many states, Nevada no longer felt the need to license people with shady pasts. Rosenthal's case held the gaming profession to a new corporate standard that no one from the first generation of Las Vegas gaming executives could have met without political intervention.

Clearing the mob out was easier said than done. In 1979, after a nearly three-year battle to rid the Aladdin of James Tamer, an affiliate of the Lebanese underworld, and Sorkis Webbe, its legal counsel, the Gaming Commission suspended the Aladdin's state gaming license. Later the Gaming Commission gave the Aladdin a sell-or-close order. On August 6, 1979, gaming control agents entered the Aladdin casino and sealed the slot machines and the tables. It was a sad fate for the hotel where Elvis and Priscilla married. Even though Judge Harry Claiborne, who was later impeached by the Senate, issued an injunction a few hours later and the casino reopened, never before had a mob casino been shut down simply for being a mob casino. The closure was revolutionary. A little more than a decade after the Corporate Gaming Act, Nevada state government was making unprecedented efforts to rid its primary industry of organized crime.

The 1980s completed the process of excising the mob. The arrival of FBI agent Joe Yablonsky as special agent in charge in Las Vegas led to a half-decade of vigorous prosecution. The city became tense, and city leaders screamed that Yablonsky pursued a vendetta against them. Senator Paul

Laxalt, a close confidant of President Ronald Reagan, squawked so loudly about Yablonsky that it attracted attention to corruption in Las Vegas. A scandal at the Tropicana led to further prosecutions, and the mob's hold, always tenuous, convulsed and released. Losing Las Vegas, mobsters muscled in on Laughlin, tossing a young lawyer who worked for Louie Weiner, Bugsy Siegel's attorney, into a trunk to persuade Weiner to abandon his interests in the river town. But even these eruptions did little to slow change. Yablonsky's task force put the mob on the run. Even though dozens, even hundreds, of high-level executives in various casinos still had ties to or had experience with the mob, by 1985, Las Vegas was largely free of mob ownership of casinos. Legitimate capital had replaced the underworld, and all the tough guys in the world couldn't change that.

Throughout the 1970s, national banks generally shied away from Las Vegas, but large profits in Atlantic City persuaded a few East Coast and California banks that Las Vegas might be a legitimate investment. Through the Del Webb Company, the Sahara received $135 million in 1979 from New York banks for improvements to the resort, $25 million more than the hotel requested. At about the same time, Aetna Insurance Company loaned Caesars World, the parent corporation of Caesars Palace, $60 million. Soon after, First Interstate Bank developed a sizeable casino and gaming loan portfolio. By 1980 the state's five dominant gaming entities, Harrah's, the MGM, Del Webb, the Hilton, and Caesars World, were all publicly traded corporations.

Las Vegas was yet again transformed by the nearly unlimited capital that public financing could generate. Impresario Steve Wynn, a protégé of Parry Thomas, raised the ante of casino financing, laying the foundation of a new and presumably competition-proof Las Vegas. Large-scale funding meant that Las Vegas could become more than the mecca of glitz and excess. Once its capital came from the mainstream, its attractions could be shaped to the tastes of the mainstream audience. Las Vegas promised a luxury experience at a middle-class price; now it could offer that price to the entire middle class. The gradual easing of the stigma of gaming and the willingness to merge gaming with conventional postwar attractions on the scale of Disneyland increased Las Vegas's reach. Not only did gamblers come to the transformed desert town, so did people who wanted to see the spectacle and have a vacation in a classic but updated sense of the word. Sin City became more palatable and maybe even marginally less sinful.

As the apocryphal story goes, Wynn parlayed a small share of the

Frontier and a liquor distributorship into the purchase of the only piece of land that Howard Hughes ever sold. The tract was a parking lot next to Caesars Palace. Hughes's policy was to never sell land, but once the young Wynn showed him that it cost him money to keep it, the tycoon and his representatives relented. Wynn then sold the property, netting a $766,000 profit, large enough to let him buy a controlling interest in the downtown Golden Nugget. By June 1973 he was vice-president and ran the casino. In 1978 Wynn bought into Atlantic City, securing the backing of his cousin's college roommate, financier and later convicted felon Michael Milken, and the Wall Street firm of Drexel Burnham Lambert. Wynn's casino became the most profitable in Atlantic City, securing his ties with a major source of capital.

Milken supported Wynn's plan to transform gaming. Throughout the 1980s, Wynn marshaled his resources and planned a monumental project. In 1989, Wynn opened the $630 million Mirage resort. Through Milken and Drexel Burnham Lambert, Golden Nugget Inc., the parent company of Wynn's enterprises, borrowed $535.1 million to finance the Mirage in what observers of the financial markets called "a work of art," engineered through junk bonds Milken sold. DBL funded other new industries such as cable television; its financing of casinos did not seem unusual. Wynn's equity came from the sale of the Nugget in Atlantic City. With "fantasy become reality" as a theme and a fiery volcano that erupted hourly cooled by water in the desert locale, the Mirage embodied the essence of what Las Vegas could offer a tourist: an invented reality that only occasionally demanded the suspension of disbelief. Siegfried and Roy and their famed white tigers were part of this ambience, as were a tank of live dolphins, and later, the nouvelle circus, Cirque du Soleil. In the process, Drexel Burnham Lambert became the dominant financial force in Nevada gaming. By 1989 the $2.57 billion that DBL invested in the Silver State created 100,000 new Nevada jobs during the decade. In 1989 Parry Thomas, whose little bank had become a $270 million conglomerate by the mid-1970s, told a reporter that "Milken has been the primary mover [in Nevada] for the last several years." In a nod to the difficulties of the old days, Wynn called Milken's influence equal to Thomas's during the 1960s and 1970s.

The "Mirage Phase," the rush to build that followed Wynn's announcement of the Mirage, altered not only the skyline of the Strip but the culture of Las Vegas as well. Wynn led; corporate planners followed. In the decade after the opening of the Mirage, the number of hotel rooms in the city doubled. The skyline of the Strip in 2000 was dominated by eleven major resorts that had not been there ten years before. These resorts redefined what Las Vegas meant to visitors. By 1998, 300,000 people per day walked along the Strip near its intersection with Tropicana Boulevard. In the old Las Vegas, nobody walked anywhere.

Even more important, the combination of widespread credit, the new availability of cash, and the great stock run-up of the 1990s extended the market for gaming and leisure. In the late 1970s, consumer interest rates were deregulated and companies located in states that permitted high interest rates could export them to customers in states with lower ceilings. The credit card revolution began. Within a few years, anyone with halfway decent credit and the prospect of paying back at least part of what they borrowed received offers of credit cards with limits that sometimes exceeded their annual income. With credit, people could truly attain the be-all and end-all of post-1960s culture: they could have whatever they wanted now and pay for it later, if at all. Cash flow was no longer a barrier to a weekend in Las Vegas.

The Mirage opening coincided with another important technological change, the easy accessibility of cash from automatic teller machines. Before 1992, the only way to get cash in a casino was to bring it in yourself or obtain it from the cashier's cage. Casinos rated players for a reason—and it wasn't to provide players with free meals and rooms. Pit bosses and casino managers had to believe that a loser could pay back an advance from the house, called a marker. With the installation of ATMs, anybody could charge up their credit cards without so much as a raised eyebrow from a cashier. Not only did cash machines infuse casinos with a never-ending stream of dollars, they did so at no risk to the casino. It wasn't the house's problem if a visitor couldn't pay the credit card bill. Once you got to Las Vegas, the party could go on forever, or at least until you reached your credit card limit. And during the mid- to late 1990s, reaching that limit seemed impossible. Recreational spending matched other consumption, and combined with the changes that made Las Vegas's brand of leisure more palatable and more au courant, the magic of the moment was right.

The presence of gifted entrepreneurs who intuited the core of American desires in a moment of prosperity also turned the American scapegoat into a national center of leisure and pleasure. The metamorphosis occurred in stages. In the early 1990s Wynn, Kerkorian, William Bennett of Circus Circus, and others in Las Vegas recast the town as a family entertainment resort. The exotic, decadent Rat Pack—era themes of earlier resorts, the Dunes with its Sahara sultan motif, Caesars Palace and its

Greco-Roman theme, and others, were pushed aside by an iconography derived from contemporary popular culture. The opening of the Grand Slam Canyon, a theme park at Circus Circus, the Luxor, Wynn's Treasure Island resort, and the MGM Grand in 1993 signaled a new Las Vegas tied to mainstream visions of fantasy and leisure. The Hard Rock Hotel extended the successful café into a resort for the young. "This is part of a major metamorphosis in Las Vegas," then-mayor Jan Laverty Jones said as the MGM plan debuted. "Las Vegas is changing from just adult entertainment to a resort destination." Timeless, chameleonlike, and supple, Las Vegas once again obliterated its past.

In a 1994 cover story, *Time* magazine declared that Las Vegas had become an All-American city, the new American hometown. The rest of the nation had become more like its former capital of sin, Kurt Andersen of the magazine averred, granting Las Vegas a leading role in the service economy that has become, for better and worse, the future of the nation. What this glitzy and superficial analysis failed to note was that at the same time, Las Vegas had become a lot more like the rest of the nation.

Las Vegas had solved one of the major problems of the transition from industrial to postindustrial economy. In this mecca of gaming, unskilled individuals with barely a high school education could still earn a middle-class income. The Culinary Union helped keep wages high, and some hotels provided wages and benefits that exceeded union contract in order to discourage unionization. Las Vegas had become the "Last Detroit" in the way it provided solid pay for unspecialized work; for anyone with a modicum of skill and grace, it was an easy place to do well in service positions.

The transformation was completed by the way in which the Las Vegas experience became a part of the business of professional leisure. By the 1990s ITT-Sheraton, Hilton, and other major hotel chains owned major casino-hotels. Graduates of Wharton Business School made decisions, and the gaming industry developed a hierarchy that resembled the army's. Special training was required before anyone received the opportunity to lead. There was even a glass ceiling in gaming, but its defining trait wasn't gender: dealers could no longer work their way off the floor to management positions. In the large resorts, the upward mobility that being "connected" once ensured disappeared. Pit boss was now as high as a dealer or floor worker could expect to go. The management positions were filled by MBAs, professional businesspeople who did not truly understand the gaming industry. The personal side of gaming, where a floor manager recognized and took care of regular patrons, disappeared as gaming became an industry like any other.

Corporate entertainment culture had its advantages. The scope and scale of corporate wealth meant that Las Vegas could offer a new level of extravagance and fantasy. Between 1993 and 1997 Las Vegans were treated to the demolition of much of their recent history. Four hotels, the Dunes, the Sands, the Landmark, and the Aladdin, were all imploded to make room for new construction. The Bellagio and the Venetian replaced the Dunes and the Sands, substituting Italy for the desert, and with the construction of a faux Venice at the Venetian, a Paris at Paris Las Vegas, and Sinatra's New York at New York, New York on the Las Vegas Strip. Plans for San Francisco— and London-themed resorts were on the drawing board early in 2001, delayed first by the slowdown in the economy and again by the atrocities of September 11. Las Vegas had replaced itself, becoming every city on the planet. It offered the tangible to accompany fantasy. Gambling had become gaming, then tourism, and ultimately entertainment.

After a decade of predictions that each new hotel would create an overbuilt city, the Mirage Phase came to an end. Steve Wynn forced the rest to keep up with his ideas, but he got caught with his stock at a low point early in 2000, and Kirk Kerkorian pounced. Publicly traded companies respond to their quarterly earnings report, called the EBITDA, and, hurt by the downturn in the Asian economy, Wynn was trapped. The MGM's offer looked sweet to Mirage Corporation shareholders, and Wynn couldn't block the takeover. For $6.4 billion, the entire Wynn empire changed hands in an instant.

Wynn had been the creative spark, the one everyone tried to top, and his departure changed the scene. "When Steve Wynn ran the Mirage it was his corporation, it looked like him, acted like him, and dressed like him," Las Vegas's most astute chronicler, John L. Smith, observed. "The corporate veil doesn't permit a lot of individuality." Innovative entrepreneurs had fashioned the conceptual future and then watched as corporate money scarfed up their ideas. Las Vegas became a city of publicly traded companies that cared mostly about the bottom line. The first thing to go was Wynn's art collection, the centerpiece of his idea of the Bellagio as high culture. The flourishes of the individual entrepreneur, the guy who wanted to do his place his way, vanished in a heartbeat.

Without Wynn, the Bellagio wasn't the same. "It's ordinary now, all bottom-line," observed Mississippian Gordon Parker, a young and keen observer of the workings of Las Vegas. "It doesn't have the same attention to detail." Parker pointed to the introduction of bars on the windows of the cashier's cage. Wynn had eschewed this common dimension of casino architecture as part of his effort to make the Bellagio unique. Under MGM, the bars came up as in an old bank or railroad station, ruining the illusion that Bellagio, with its fabulous layout and wide open spaces, was anything more than just a well-appointed casino. Even more, observers thought that the very first thing MGM did was replace Wynn's custom coin trays, which muted the clink of the coins, with the more conventional, louder ones.

As the Mirage Phase ended, it was clear that Las Vegas would not continue to build behemoths as it had through the 1990s. Its dinosaur baby, the new Aladdin, struggled, discovering that last-born is a dangerous position. The Aladdin muffed the Las Vegas formula: instead of offering a luxury experience at a middle-class price, it offered a middle-class experience for a luxury price. The results were predictable. The Aladdin went into receivership in September 2001. The Aladdin imitated the imitation that the new Las Vegas did so well, becoming merely a slightly different choice on the same menu. It was hardly the key to success in a crowded town. Even with Sheldon Adelson of the Venetian loudly rattling on about a new tower for his hotel and Wynn planning what to do next, Las Vegas was unlikely to add another fifty thousand hotel rooms. Reticence on Wall Street contributed to the slowing. The financial markets were glad to take profits from Las Vegas, but they were not quite willing to let Las Vegas be Las Vegas. They didn't quite trust the rivers of cash, and on some level, they watched the navigators who guide the boats along the stream of greenbacks with suspicion. They wanted to see the bottom line. The flow of money that characterized the 1990s slowed as 2000 began.

Despite their wealth, corporations haven't given Las Vegas its best moments. The city's lowest point came in the 1980s, before Wynn conceived of the Mirage. The corporations had plenty of cash, but they lacked verve and flair. They weren't entertainers and they felt uncomfortable with the excesses and eccentricities built into the fabric of gaming. They made decisions by committee, sanitizing the look and feel of the city and keeping both eyes firmly fixed on the quarterly earnings report. Corporate thinking built the towers that put Bugsy Siegel's pool, the pinnacle of his vision of leisure, in the shade all day long. As the twenty-first century began, they consumed Wynn's ethos, creating a pale image of it that was designed to lull rather than excite.

This exclusively bottom-line thinking offered one great advantage for Las Vegas's creativity: it created opportunities for entrepreneurs in the mid-sized hotels that remained. Answering to shareholders and Wall Street analysts, the biggest groups tread cautiously. The ferocious competition among them—MGM/Mirage, Mandalay Bay, and Park Place, each with more than ten thousand rooms on the Strip alone—and the constant demand for profit led them to shed attractive properties that didn't fit their formula. They carefully scrutinize their assets, cutting properties loose at the first sign of decline. Age is a telling condition; casino hotels get a lot of use and they wear quickly. Smart corporate managers dump properties in advance of the need for expensive renovation, creating an opening for anyone with a couple hundred million dollars who wants to own a casino. A combination of seemingly easy profit and need for status pulled an entire range of well-heeled entrepreneurs into Las Vegas.

Wynn and other such entrepreneurs, not subject to all the constraints of publicly traded companies, could run these properties according to their own vision, not for the raw numbers of the bottom line. After the sale of the Mirage Group, Steve Wynn purchased the Desert Inn from Starwoods for $270 million, a little more than one-quarter of what he and his wife, Elaine, netted from the Mirage Group sale and about $70 million more than ITT spent to renovate the Desert Inn just three years before. Wynn promised a new era of innovation that would redefine the city once again. He created room somewhere in the middle of the market, where enormous corporate casinos can't quite fill the desires of specialized niches.

The rise of entrepreneurial owners mirrors the moments of Las Vegas's greatest success, when visionary individuals created the context into which corporate money poured and growth followed. This pattern revived the ethos that began with Bugsy Siegel and continued through Jay Sarno and Steve Wynn. It promised individual flair, hotels designed by people who saw their properties as a reflection of themselves and cared in personal way about what their guests thought. Some of these would certainly be wacky; some could be brilliant, redefining once again the meaning of entertainment and leisure in a rapidly moving society.

The individual entrepreneur may not be a blueprint for the future. Siegel was a crooked and enterprising megalomaniac who used the Flamingo to feed his ego, allowing him to proclaim his importance to the Hollywood that rejected him. There's a quality of intoxicating hubris in this model, a certain amount of equating access to money with genius. Las Vegas's scale and scope is so far beyond the ante in most places that the game has a surreal quality about it. "People who come here for a score get eaten alive," John L. Smith recounted. "You either get an understanding of the community or you're dead." Even $100 million to invest doesn't grant de facto credibility. Yet these newcomers persist, seeking to redefine the town. If the wave that appears to be building fails to capture the essence of the nation as Wynn did in the 1990s, such people could end up erecting nothing more than expensive monuments to themselves, certain candidates for short-term implosion.

In the end, it comes down to access to capital. The last remaining feature of Las Vegas's colonial heritage is the fundamental lack of indigenous capital. The money that builds Las Vegas rarely comes from in town. It's always somebody from somewhere else, looking for financial success or merely status. When the capital became more expensive and even scarce, as it did early in 2001, tight financial markets made it harder to find the financing for new casino-hotels. A nearly $1 billion dollar San Francisco–themed resort plan was on hold; another one with an identical theme was on the drawing boards. Two attempts to make London on the Strip stalled. Another group with seventy-seven acres at the south end of the Strip searched for the right partner, and even Steve Wynn, the progenitor of it all, sought financial support from Aruza Corp., the Japanese pachinko maker, for the Desert Inn.

As the twenty-first century gathers momentum, Las Vegas is finally sharing greater commonality with the rest of the nation. It depends on the same sources of capital that other communities do and has accepted many of the same rules and regulations. It's not only that the rest of the nation normalized the behaviors that used to make Las Vegas exceptional; in its hierarchy, distribution of wealth and status, demography, and stratification of its labor force, Las Vegas has become more like the rest of the nation as well. Once a pariah, Las Vegas has become a paradigm of the postindustrial economy. As gaming spreads throughout the nation—usually run by Las Vegas companies—the colony is being transformed. Las Vegas has become a colonizer, exporting its version of the new economy to New Orleans, Missouri, Detroit, and elsewhere. Las Vegas has always reflected America onto itself. It has always been the mirror people held up to their faces to see what they hoped for and, equally, what they feared. As it became normative, the entire historical equation of the city was thrown on its head. Las Vegas is the first city of the new century, the one that owes its allegiance to the shape of the new universe, to the signs and symbols of a culture of entertainment.

CHAPTER 2

It's Hard to Be Elvis in Las Vegas
Entertainment in the Malleable Metropolis

A New Yorker who left the city during the social and civic turmoil of the late 1970s once told to me: "New York has magic moments. You stand in Yankee Stadium and look out at Joe DiMaggio's centerfield and Babe Ruth's short rightfield porch, you're by the Rockefeller Center and the light hits you just right, you catch Central Park at just the right moment, when the ducks are swimming and the glaze of the frost is beginning to melt, and it'll take your breath away. In New York, you can get that magic. You just have to put up with a lot of shit in between. You're living in shit, hour after hour, day after day, and you live for the magic moment. Poof! It's there. Then back to the shit." He cocked his head. "Las Vegas gives you the moment without the shit, over and over. It's magic, alchemy. It's better than real." This hard-bitten cynic, twenty years from the New York of his youth, hit the nail on the head. What Las Vegas does better than any place else on the planet is plane off the rough edges of a visitor's experience and make the traveler, however ordinary, the center of the story. A well-known Hollywood actor passing through town found the same phenomenon exciting: "I've never been anywhere except here where they give you the stage, the setting, and the cast of supporting characters and let you write the script with yourself as the star!" Here's the secret to Las Vegas in a nutshell: it can always be whatever you want it to be as long as you're willing to pay for it.

Entertainment has become king in American society, and no place, not New York, not Hollywood, offers more of it in more forms than Las Vegas. It is entertainment and not gaming that has redefined Las Vegas. The dollars from gaming grease the wheels, but since 1996, they have comprised less than 50 percent of the city's income. In 2000 the net win from tribal gaming finally surpassed Nevada's total, but more visitors gave Las Vegas more profit than ever before. The new lifeblood is the spectacle of Las Vegas and its unmatched ability to make you who you want to be—to entertain, amuse, and make you, the visitor, feel special. Las Vegas gives the middle-class visitor a luxury experience at a middle-class price. That is its genius. So what if the features aren't real? Everyone knows they aren't. But they are Las Vegas, the emblem of the postmodern city. For the same reasons that Americans of wealth and taste once toured Europe, the middle class of the age of media come to Las Vegas. It contains the spectacle for their world, the first wonder of postmodernity.

In an age when faux beaches and resorts captivate tourists, Las Vegas appears no more inauthentic than any place else. In Las Vegas, the state flag is a ten-dollar bill and people know where their bread is buttered. New York, New York, the casino-hotel that mimics the Big Apple, creates a New York experience that makes the wide cut of America comfortable. In the Gotham-themed casino, the change cages look like subway token booths. They're cute instead of imposing. The people manning the mobile change carts painted like Yellow cabs speak English, and the faux streets are safe. Hey, this way, New York can be for the suburban middle class. The fear is gone.

It took me a while to get New York, New York. New York had fallen so far from its apex as the center of the universe by the late 1970s that it became trite to abuse it. "Bite the Big Apple; don't mind the maggots," Mick Jagger sang, epitomizing New York's push-and-pull with middle America. New York's image had suffered so much that a hotel that offered you the experience of a city where the public believed people are rude, the streets are noisy and dirty, everything is expensive, and everyone tawks funny seemed risky. Local cynics figured the hotel would flop. People would flee New York, New York; enough of them had fled the real thing to populate the desert three times over.

When I saw the place, it finally made sense. New York, New York was

New York for the American middle class, mom and pop from Des Moines, who were put off by the real thing. The hotel wasn't the New York of *NYPD Blue*, the one filled with crime and grime and every ethnicity under the sun. It captured Frank Sinatra's "New York, New York," simulating that great postwar burst of energy when no other city in the world could compete. It evokes a mythic moment when all was right with the world, when Americans finished making the world safe for democracy and were going back to the business of their lives. The streets of this mythic space were filled with well-dressed young white people on the make, back when everything had promise, before Americans had to take a hard look at their institutions. No wonder it inspires nostalgia.

If you're younger, New York, New York offers a romantic stage full of mythic characters, a place you never knew but surely heard about or have seen on TV. Here is a cross-generational experience. You could feel the charm of Coney Island before the gangs took it over, get a shave in the Euphoria Barber Shop, and eat in a faux Little Italy and pretend that the

NEW YORK, NEW YORK

Sopranos were close at hand. Never mind the tinytown of Bleecker Street and Greenwich Village abutting Columbus Circle and the Upper West Side; the Statue of Liberty was holding her skirt down à la Marilyn Monroe! Even the Motown Café—"Didn't Motown used to be Detroit?" a baggy-pantsed, shaved-head queried a pal. "Yeah," his friend answered, "but so what?"—didn't ruin the image. When it opened in 1997, the Moments, faux Temptations and faux Supremes, broke into the DJ's act and sang live once an hour, dragging diners to dance with them. The customers, especially women in their thirties and forties, were thrilled. I watched one get so into her dancing that when she realized everyone at the 70 tables was watching her, she blushed a full crimson. Here she was, Dolores from Ottumwa, or more likely Ashley from the San Fernando Valley, living her dream—on stage for just a second with the Temps and Supremes. She was the star, the center of the script, and for a minute it all seemed possible. And no wonder. One faux Supreme and one faux Temp were white!

In the worst of moments, New York, New York, acquired a strangely deeper meaning. After the atrocities of September 11, 2001, people treated New York, New York as if it were the real place. It became a shrine; people brought flowers, pictures, remonstrations of patriotism and of personal sentiment, and innumerable other expressions of feeling and placed at the base of the faux Statue of Liberty. Part of this was real kinship. So many New Yorkers live in Las Vegas that the town sometimes seems like the sixth borough. But another part was clear sentiment, a place to express emotion, a stand-in for the real. Strange as it seems, the faux pleasure of New York, New York became a powerful expression of the real pain of Americans.

Although the New York press was touched by the shrine at New York, New York, New Yorkers hated it from the moment it opened. Residents of other copied cities found Las Vegas doppelgangers less objectionable. Before the Paris Las Vegas hotel-casino opened in 1999, the resort ran a series of commercials: as a catchy French tune played in the background, a truck pulled up, workers hopped out and snatched tables from French cafés, art and statuary from French parks, and finally even French apparel from a store, crated it up, stamped "Las Vegas" on the side, and sent the material essence of France to its destination in the desert. The commercial ended with a toppled Eiffel Tower astride a flatcar with a desert sunset behind. The effect was cute—we're fake, we know it, but we know what we're doing. It isn't France, but you'll like it anyway. The few French hanging around Paris Las Vegas when it opened just before Labor Day 1999 found themselves charmed by the illusion. "We feel like we're in France," Claude Ayache told a reporter. "We're afraid people won't come to France," Celine Molière agreed, "because there's a little part of France here." Then again, the French adore Jerry Lewis. Under a kitschy sign advertising "Le Jacque Pot," with three legs of the Eiffel Tower anchored in the casino, the illusion was complete, if you could buy in. So what if you spoke your high school French to one of the attendants and after "Bonjour," the response was; "Uh, my name is Eric and I'm from Orange County"? Fake accents and faux architecture notwithstanding, Paris offered audiences France as the American middle class would like it, without the rudeness and condescension Americans so expect. At Paris Las Vegas on the Strip, the beret-wearing faux French act like Americans and offer Las Vegas–style service. What more could the real Paris have to offer Americans of the new century?

Las Vegas is the most malleable tourist destination on the planet. It holds up a figurative mirror to visitors and asks, "What do you want to be, and what will you pay to be it?" When you ask for your dreams and fantasies, the only object is the cost. Las Vegas is in the tourism business, selling the experience you want, not trying to teach, indoctrinate, or offer insight. In Las Vegas, the past is truly prologue. Who you were or what you were yesterday makes little difference. The Strip is a skin, to be shed at will, when culture, custom, or capital demand.

In the past decade, the Las Vegas Strip has undergone a visual transformation that has given the city a new skyline. As major global corporations pumped bewildering sums of money into palaces of play, they built a new facade, an edifice that perfectly mirrored American and global consumer culture as the twenty-first century began. Every city is defined by its downtown skyline; *Dallas* showed the Sun Belt boom against the hard Texas sun, *L.A. Law* gave us Bunker Hill, both visions of steel-drenched commerce and competition. Seattle used the Space Needle as the symbol of its futuristic identity even before Microsoft came to town. Las Vegas offers the lights of the Strip and Venice, New York, and Paris. It is everywhere and nowhere, not here and not there. The desert is gone, replaced by Italy. The Bellagio is the Italian Rivera, more upscale than reality. The Venetian gives you the canals and gondolas of Venice without the stench or the pigeon poo. What's next? After Oscar Goodman, the criminal defense attorney who defended a generation of mobsters and, with pornographer Larry Flynt, one of the few remaining defenders of the First Amendment in the

United States, was elected mayor of Las Vegas, the next hotel could be a mob knock-off, enshrining Las Vegas's roguish past: Chicago, Chicago, Al Capone's town. The bellmen will wear pinstripes and speak in gravelly voices. They'll carry faux tommy guns. "Your room is over there, sir," the concierge will say. "Mr. Luciano," he waves for the next bellman in line, using the name of Mafia *capo di tutti capo* Charles "Lucky" Luciano, "will take you for a ride."

The malleability of the city makes it possible. After sixty years of never-ending growth, Las Vegas has yet to develop a fixed identity. No core population enforces tradition. Las Vegas is about options, nearly infinite, a choice of packages. This isn't Santa Fe, which claims one exotic moment out of the past as its authenticity, or even San Antonio, with the Alamo and all its baggage. It isn't Key West, with its paean to Hemingway, or New Orleans and the Vieux Carre, or even Fisherman's Wharf in San Francisco Bay. In Las Vegas, nothing is real and you know that. By admitting it is fake and compensating with amenities, Las Vegas becomes how the world should be, how it would be if you told the story and it really was about you. Las Vegas is the script. You write it, you pay to produce it, and it's yours to do with as you please.

Las Vegas will entertain you. It is truly devoted to your pleasure. Critics have railed about this kind of fake world since the 1960s, when subdivisions sprang up, and the cultural snottiness that Tom Wolfe demolishes in "The Land of the Rococo Marxists" made them instantly devoid of culture. Growth almost everywhere inspired the same critique. In the 1960s and 1970s, with its back-to-the-roots ethos and ongoing search for authentic, such an argument resonated. In a later age, when people clearly understood the difference between authenticity and inauthenticity, but no longer accepted the cultural framing that made conventional authenticity better, Las Vegas made perfect sense.

A cynic might say that the emphasis on entertainment is an outgrowth of the spread of gaming, a way to hedge bets. When I arrived in the early 1990s, a friend derisively wrote to me "now that everywhere has gaming, Las Vegas will soon ride off into the sunset, a victim of its own success," but that hasn't been the case. Despite Bob Stupak, the last of the old-time gamblers who came to Las Vegas with a small bankroll and built a hotel, the Stratosphere, who inexplicably told a national television audience that Las Vegas didn't need visitors who didn't gamble, Las Vegas has developed a second stream of revenue: pure tourism, people who come to see the spectacle and maybe play a little. "You can gamble anywhere," the Coulter VIP Tour guide told his audience of pasty-skinned midwesterners aboard the monorail from the D gates at McCarran Airport as spring began in 2001. "Las Vegas, you have to see!"

You can spot the real tourists. They're everywhere, day and night, in shorts and hats, with cameras and fanny packs, walking, riding, calling to friends or relatives. They stroll the Strip by the thousands. Tourists walk with camcorders, filming the town, but they don't look through the camera eye. Instead they walk and watch, their camera recording a version of it at shoulder-height for eternal replay on the home VCR. They buy T-shirts and bottled water, eat meals, see the sights, and shop and shop. They crowd the walkway in front of Treasure Island, where they await the battle between the pirates and the British man-of-war and the cannonfire over their heads that accompanies it. They stand near the Mirage's volcano to watch the hourly eruption, wait for the fountains in front of the Bellagio to shoot water skyward, lunch at the Eiffel Tower in the Paris, but more likely stop by a buffet or McDonald's. They crowd the corners at the stoplights, walking, walking, always walking. Las Vegans take cabs or drive. The ribald comic Shecky Greene claims to have taken cabs across the street in the old days. No one from Las Vegas would dream of *walking* from the corner of Tropicana and the Strip to Flamingo.

While the old-timers like Stupak disdain the tourists, the bean-counters know their value. By 1997 nongaming expenditures made up 52 percent of the total revenue in Las Vegas, and the percentage is rising. Gaming is still crucial. "In other boom towns in western history, when the gold plays out the boom comes to an end," John L. Smith keenly notes. "We import the gold. The veins don't play out." Gaming remains first among the menu choices in Smith's view. "Gambling is the fuel for investments," he continues, the reason corporations build in Las Vegas. The profits from gaming come easy, but they aren't the entire picture. The tourists who don't gamble or don't gamble much outspend the ones who do. The growth came in entertainment, and the evidence of the change was everywhere: in the gradual upward creep in the price of buffet meals and rooms, the proliferation of brand-name souvenir shops and the new shopping conglomerations like Desert Passage at the Aladdin, the ever-expanding number of stunning one-of-a-kind restaurants and the upscale restaurant chains that follow in their wake, the new arenas hosting never-ending music and shows, and the escalating prices of tickets to shows and concerts. Las Vegas still offers what it always has, a luxury experience at a middle-class price. It is still an exceptional vacation value—a $300 room in Vail or Aspen is still $99 on a Las Vegas weeknight—but the gap is narrowing.

Still sporting the golden-boy good looks that made him a 1970s teen heartthrob, an older and only slightly subdued David Cassidy strode to the podium to introduce Smokey Robinson at the 1999 EAT'M, Emerging Artists and Talent in Music, convention at the Mirage Resort. A lunchtime audience of one thousand music-industry representatives, musicians, and journalists heard Cassidy declaim that Las Vegas "is now the entertainment capital of the world." From him, this hyperbole was no surprise. After all, Las Vegas had turned Keith Partridge back into a working performer. But the pronouncement carried more weight among attendees when Rod Essig of the Creative Artists Agency, the man who brought the world acts as varied as Jim Croce and the Red Hot Chili Peppers, echoed it.

Las Vegas's claim as the city of entertainment is formidable. Entertainment was always essential to the Las Vegas package. Rose Marie at the Flamingo in 1947, Jerry Lewis and Dean Martin in 1949 at the height of their nightclub fame, Frank Sinatra, Sammy Davis Jr., and the Rat Pack, Elvis Presley, who sold out the Las Vegas Hilton a record 837 consecutive times between 1969 and 1976, and Wayne Newton, Mr. Las Vegas to so many, Tom Jones, and Liberace made Las Vegas simultaneously epitomize the hip and the trite, the edge and kitsch. "Viva Las Vegas," so many sang, caustically, tongue in cheek, and straight from the heart as well.

A moment of illusory sophistication accompanied Las Vegas's modern birth. Las Vegas entertainment began as center stage, with Jimmy Durante opening the Flamingo in 1946, Frank Sinatra's arrival at the Sands in 1952, the interracial Moulin Rouge's brief moment at the pinnacle of after-hours cool in 1955, and it peaked in the early 1960s with the Rat Pack and Louis Prima. Then Las Vegas stumbled; instead of cutting-edge it became middle-brow before the concept really existed. Las Vegas became Wayne Newton's town, where entertainment placated and did not challenge, a place so unhip that it was bound to become a caricature of whatever it intended. This was the era of Sonny and Cher, and the town created the lounge singer, an icon now parodied beyond cliché. After they got booted from television, Tony Orlando and Dawn headlined 1970s Las Vegas in their slide toward oblivion.

In that initial era, when Las Vegas was hot, American chic was nightclub culture and Las Vegas mirrored it with a sharp edge. Throughout the 1950s, Liberace, Rosemary Clooney, Lena Horne, Jimmy Durante, Milton Berle, Danny Thomas, and others headlined the various clubs. Liberace received $50,000 a week to open the Riviera in 1955. The casinos consistently tried to outdo one another, investing more in their entertainment with little thought of profit. Performers were a throw-in, a perquisite attached to the central activity of the time, gambling. In the late 1940s when she performed at the Flamingo, Rose Marie was encouraged to gamble and hang out with the patrons between shows. Bugsy Siegel handed her chips to play. She once won $10,000 and tried to return it, but the dapper hood insisted it was hers to keep.

Dancers and the intimation of sex were an integral part of that early Las Vegas. By the early 1950s every hotel had its own line of dancers. The El Rancho offered the June Taylor dancers, the Desert Inn, the Arden-Fletcher Dancers, and the Thunderbird, the Katherine Duffy Dansations. "I was running a girl factory," recalled impresario Donn Arden, who became the progenitor of the Las Vegas extravaganza shows. The showgirl, the Las Vegas icon, emerged in conjunction with the dancing lines. In 1952 the Sahara opened its doors featuring a George Moro production of eight dancing girls and four showgirls. At the Sands, Jack Entratter became famous for the money he spent on entertainment. The hotels competed furiously for innovative acts, seeking an edge in the competition with their neighbors. Bing Crosby, Perry Como, Ella Fitzgerald, the Mills Brothers, Nat King Cole, Harry Belafonte, Andy Williams, and even Ronald Reagan headlined 1950s Las Vegas, Reagan bombing as a stage-show host at the Last Frontier in 1954. As casino owners exceeded one another with wilder costumes and more suggestive dance routines, they engaged in a kind of push-the-envelope competition that paralleled 1990s television: they tested the limits of accepted taste in an effort to remain cutting-edge but simultaneously balanced on the precarious edge of entertainment respectability.

By the mid-1950s competition drove Las Vegas entertainment toward the overtly sexual. Harold Minsky, from a family that worked vaudeville and burlesque, became the catalyst. Minsky's Follies first played Las Vegas in the late 1940s and drew raves for mimicking the extravaganza revues of Paris. Lou Walters, a London-born impresario who owned the Latin Quarter nightclubs in New York and Boston, created the Latin Quarter Revue. The effect was stunning, titillation within the guise of art. Sexuality sold, but it was still veiled. Finally, on January 10, 1957, Minsky crossed the line. The girls in Minsky's Follies at the Dunes appeared topless.

Nudity on the stage reflected both the competition that dominated early Las Vegas and the dangers of selling entertainment in a gambling-based economy. It went hand in hand with the convention trade, a growing part of Las Vegas's visitation. Minsky was comfortable in the burlesque tradition, but the city around him was not. The push for preeminence—Entratter, who opposed nudity and never permitted it at the Sands, was reputed to have spent more than $1.5 million on entertainers in 1954 alone—demanded a response. Hotels that couldn't or wouldn't spend at the Sands' level could only compete by attracting patrons with shock value. No matter how good the entertainment was in the 1950s, it still served one objective: getting gamblers into the casino to improve the $200 million annual profit. Bare breasts seemed a good bet to produce the same results as million-dollar contracts.

Donn Arden's Lido de Paris became the epitome of the topless revue and of the Las Vegas show. When Moe Dalitz and the Desert Inn crew took over the Stardust in 1957, they sought a headliner. Dalitz's entertainment director, Frank Sennes, persuaded Arden, then producing the Lido's review in Paris, to open a Las Vegas version of the show. Arden mounted the first full-scale French show in the desert, complete with the original costumes and dancers. The dancers, it turned out, were actually English, but they were the real thing. Nudity en masse swept the Strip.

The Lido de Paris became the archetype, lasting at the Stardust until 1991, and Arden became the most renowned producer of Las Vegas shows. Within a few years, his shows and the showgirls they spawned became a symbol that defined Las Vegas experience. After the Lido closed, Arden produced Hallelujah Hollywood at the MGM Grand and then produced Jubilee, the last of the old-time Las Vegas shows, at Bally's, until his death in 1994. Jubilee continued into the new century, but more as a curiosity, a gaudy relic, than as front-line entertainment.

Arden was instrumental in bringing more than vaudeville to Las Vegas stages. Spending considerable time in Paris, he recognized the value of a range of specialty acts, including the animal performers and illusionists Siegfried and Roy. Circus trainer Jon Berosini's animal acts stood out in the 1960s, and Siegfried and Roy became one of the longest-running shows ever. They arrived in Las Vegas in 1971 and worked in Arden's shows until 1981, when circus impresarios Irwin and Kenneth Feld mounted an entire show around them. Siegfried and Roy transformed from a specialty act to a headliner, using magic to reach the pinnacle of Las Vegas success with Beyond Belief, the hottest ticket in town for the next seven years. When they signed on with the Mirage, they became intrinsically identified with the Las Vegas of entertainment. Siegfried and Roy anchored the new Strip.

Magic, an element that Siegfried and Roy developed as they transformed from specialty act to headliner, played a transitional role in Las
Vegas. Magic was a vaudeville staple, a breather between acts on the variety
circuit, and it came into its own as illusions made it more fantastic, more
in tune with the tenor of the 1960s and 1970s. By the early 1970s, magicians proliferated in Las Vegas, so popular that a number made their living
as stand-in acts. If a performer was too ill or inebriated to take the stage, a
magician could walk on without rehearsal, lights, or a band and do a routine that covered the evening.

Magicians became headliners as magic reflected the transformed image of
the city. Las Vegas always sold magic, but the deception enjoyed more currency as Las Vegas entered the American mainstream. It seemed natural, a
synergy between the city and the art of illusion. In 1992 one survey showed
thirty professional magicians regularly playing Las Vegas. David Copperfield
earned a nationwide contract with Caesars Palace, performing eight weeks a
year in Las Vegas. Lance Burton became the epitome of close-up magic, playing at the Hacienda until he was rewarded with a long run at the Monte Carlo.
The sarcastic antimagicians Penn and Teller made Las Vegas their home,
finding the city of illusion the perfect foil for their exposés of the field. In
2000 Leo Behnke, a lifetime professional magician, asserted that Las Vegas
had fittingly become the center of magic in the United States.

Las Vegas excelled at translating the nation's tastes onto its own stages.
In the age of the television variety show, Las Vegas offered on-stage variety
that routinely went further than anything broadcast over the airwaves. It
had an edge, but not a threatening one. It allowed performers to capitalize
on their popularity and to extend an act to its limits, sometimes risque,
sometimes designed to offend. Johnny Carson had a record-breaking stint
at the Sahara; David Frost, Mike Douglas, and Merv Griffin also hosted
their own shows, with less success. It is little wonder that George Carlin, the
comic who made his reputation in the 1970s with the "seven words you can't
say on television," remained a Las Vegas staple a generation later.

By the 1990s the old entertainment in Las Vegas was going or gone,
consigned to Madame Tussaud's Wax Museum at the Venetian, where one
of the displays presented wax models of Wayne Newton, Liberace, Tom
Jones, and Lance Burton. Even the showgirl was becoming extinct,
replaced by a more athletic, less remote archetype. Although magic
remained an important draw, a combination of entertainment and illusion
that mirrored Las Vegas's role in American society, the rest had become

memories or anachronisms, reflections of the city's past and its never-ending battle between kitsch and cutting-edge entertainment. The cycles of
entertainment roughly mirror the evolution of the city. Las Vegas may
never have been truly hip to the cognoscenti, but it was cool twice: first
when it symbolized the nation's aberration in the 1950s, when to America
the city meant deviance, but simultaneously gave permission to sin, second
as Las Vegas became mainstream. Only then did it compete in the truest
form for the widest American market, the truly broad expanse of the
American middle class.

The passing of the great extravaganzas came as Las Vegas in the early 1990s
once again reinvented itself, this time as the first city devoted to the consumption of entertainment. Once a town of roadhouses—carpet joints—
that still retained the taint of their illicit origins—Las Vegas became a casino
town, a place where Americans could engage in socially sanctioned recreational activity that let them believe that they were original and apart from
the mainstream. As casino gambling took hold elsewhere, Las Vegas needed ways to broaden its reach and further distinguish itself from places that
offered a comparable experience. The influx of corporate dollars granted
the flexibility to experiment.

Circus Circus pursued this market long before the 1990s. After its initial quirky phase under Jay Sarno, when Hunter Thompson famously
described Circus Circus as "what the whole hep world would be doing on
Saturday night if the Nazis won the war," Circus Circus took aim at volume
and succeeded magnificently. The rooms were cheap and the parking lots
filled with recreational vehicles. At Circus Circus rooms were $19 a night
for almost twenty years and as low as $39 a night in the late 1990s, but there
were stipulations: the reservation was prepaid and guaranteed until 8:00
P.M.; after this witching hour, the room reverted to the hotel. Circus
Circus was always full, 365 days a year, and routinely sold 103 percent of its
rooms. The hotel turned room reservations into a bet. If you showed up on
time, you won. If you didn't, they resold the room.

For a decade and a half, Circus Circus had the only activities for kids
on the Las Vegas Strip. The move from camp to good clean fun was subtle
and cost-effective. Without a hotel when it opened, the property lost
money its first few years. Baby elephants pulling slot levers or human can-
nonballs arcing above the casino floor drew people's attention away from the
games. Sarno even tried charging admission, but no one wanted to pay to go

into a casino when there were plenty of free ones around. Only when William Bennett, who had worked his way up at Del Webb Corporation, and William Pennington bought Circus Circus did the property prosper. The owners built a tower for guest rooms and moved the circus attractions to a mezzanine midway. They separated kids' and adults' attractions, allowing parents to delude themselves into believing that their destination was kid-friendly and assuaging the baby boomer's dilemma: do for the self or do for the kids. If you didn't look too closely, Circus Circus offered a superficial solution. You could simultaneously do for both. Circus Circus became the first Las Vegas property to truly benefit from the liberalization of American culture. Baby boomers reached parenthood but refused to give up the prerogatives of their youth, and Circus Circus catered to their desires. On an average day in 1999, the place felt as crowded as a major airport at Thanksgiving.

Circus Circus was unique until the Mirage Phase began. Even during Las Vegas's nadir in the early 1980s, it continued to thrive. The rest of the town was entertainment for adults, and until Wet 'n' Wild, a water park on the Strip, opened in 1985 as a place parents could leave the kids while they gambled, only Circus Circus made room for the whole family. It claimed this niche and held it tight. The attractions were always entertaining if not sophisticated, and the "whales," the gamblers who wager enormous sums, were not part of the formula. Circus Circus was middle America, ordinary people, farmers from North Dakota, clerks from Cleveland, increasingly Spanish-speaking families from southern California, and even the occasional academic on a tight budget. It catered to their tastes. The buffet at Circus Circus served more meals than any restaurant in the world.

Calling Steve Wynn a genius and a visionary is a cliché, but his conception and the boldness of his execution still inspire awe. Everyone thought that the $1 million a day that the Mirage cost was simply too much to generate, but the Mirage wasn't put together on a hunch. Wynn clearly saw something that neither the old-time gamblers, the Benny Binions and the Bob Stupaks, nor the new corporate owners grasped. The gamblers who invented the town were simply gamblers. All they cared about was the roll of the dice, the turn of the card, or the whir of the slot machine reel. Everything else was a frill. The corporations that owned hotels were endowed with cash, but lacked imagination. The mopes who built the towers at the Flamingo in 1972 and 1977 typified the breed. Architecture critic Alan Hess says that architects Rissman and Rissman's 1972 addition "could have been taken for an office building anywhere in the country." As businessmen, the gamblers were garish and idiosyncratic. The corporations weren't very exciting. Keeping an increasingly corporate town interesting took real imagination. Wynn fused together three things that none of his predecessors possessed: easy access to capital, creativity, and an intuitive understanding of the direction of American culture. Even though critics thought Wynn was in too deep before each hotel opened, it turned out that he'd gauged the nation and the world just right.

Wynn's hotels were like no others. The $30 million volcano in front of the Mirage erupted every thirty minutes. David Hersey of *Cats* and *Les Miserables* designed the lighting. Wynn made Siegfried and Roy into household names and introduced the nouveau circus, Cirque du Soleil, to the nation. The elegance and mystery of the Mirage proved irresistible. The art and shopping of the Bellagio, with its collection of masterpieces, a $10 million Dale Chihuly glass canopy in the lobby, and a formal conservatory, created the right atmosphere. Wynn understood the public's desires: experience they could taste that gave them the illusion of culture. The gamblers understood only their wallets, and the corporate hotels their business needs.

Wynn's inventiveness spurred imitation by powerful corporations. During the Mirage Phase, an unparalleled spate of construction changed not only the character of the resorts and the look of the city, but its very purpose. All of a sudden Las Vegas became upscale and even chic. It was the place to eat out and to shop, to take the kids to a roller coaster or theme park. Las Vegas imported many of the best chefs in the world. Wolfgang Puck came first, followed by a parade of world-class chefs. Billboards showed James Beard Award–winning chefs beckoning patrons, a far cry from the days when Caesars Bacchanal Room, where waitpeople dressed in Roman attire and serving girls seductively placed grapes in the mouths of male customers.

All of a sudden, high-end consumer experience dominated the city. Sephora occupied the space that the All-Star Café vacated when the chain folded, F. A. O. Schwarz opened in the Forum Shops, and Prada beckoned the Bellagio. Trendy shopping malls graced the last Mirage Phase gargantuans, the Aladdin and the Venetian. Las Vegas had two grand canyons, the Grand Slam Canyon theme park at Circus Circus and the Grand Canyon shops in a faux canyon at Showcase. For the adventurous, roller coasters sprang up atop the Sahara, New York, New York, and the Stratosphere, which also sported an attraction where the truly foolhardy strapped on a jet pack to be rocketed to the very tip of the tower, 1,100 feet above the street.

The roller coasters and theme parks were themselves only preludes to another in the ongoing series of reinventions. As it was during the heyday of the Rat Pack in the late 1950s and early 1960s, Las Vegas has again become a place where, as in Doug Liman's 1999 hit film *Go*, the young come to play. There's no limit to what properties will do to bring in young spenders, and an entire ancillary industry has sprung up to serve them. Peter Morton's Hard Rock Hotel gets much of the credit. "If the house is rockin', don't bother knockin', c'mon in," the inscription above the entry reads, and like Stevie Ray Vaughn, from whom the quote is taken, the place rocks. A shrine to rock 'n' roll, the Hard Rock is more like Mecca than anyplace else in Las Vegas. Rock 'n' rollers make pilgrimages to it. Where better to dive from a second-story hotel room balcony into the pool than the Hard Rock? What more powerful iconography could there be for the rock 'n' roll generation?

By 2000 Las Vegas had developed an even more envied nightlife than ever before, touted as one of the hottest club scenes in the country, with nightclubs such as the Ra at the Luxor or the reprise of Studio 54 at the MGM. Impresarios like twenty-seven-year-old John D. Guzman, progenitor of Naked Hollywood, a high-end takeoff of the sinfully exquisite mansion parties of Los Angeles packaged for nightclubs that seek to offer the titillation of the old Las Vegas, thrive. Club Rio atop the Rio Hotel became the setting for THUMP, a nationally syndicated television show. Musicals like *Chicago* presented another dimension. Then there were the staples: Lance Burton at the Monte Carlo; Penn and Teller everywhere; Siegfried and Roy and their white tigers at the Mirage; Mystere, and O, two versions of Cirque du Soleil, at Treasure Island and Bellagio; the $45 million EFX music and special effects extravaganza at MGM Grand that featured Michael Crawford of *Phantom of the Opera*, David Cassidy, Broadway's Tommy Tune, and 1980s down-on-his-luck pop star Rick Springfield in succession; *Splash* at the Riviera. The Blue Man Group at the Luxor offered a gentle cutting edge for performance art. Intel featured them in a TV ad campaign as the show opened. Dance clubs like Utopia and Beach thrived, raves happened weekly at the Candy Factory, and to cap it all off, there were more venues for live music than anywhere else in the country. The proliferation of venues for national acts as well as the club scene gave Las Vegas an exciting and viable music scene.

By the late 1990s music had become a crucial piece of Las Vegas's offerings. In Las Vegas, you don't have to wait very long to see every act you ever saw in the 1970s, 1980s, and 1990s, and all the ones competing for your heart in the new century. "Four to six years ago," Rod Essig observed in

1999, "there were Vegas shows in the showrooms." With fifteen arenas, outdoor stages, and showrooms of fifteen hundred or more seats, Las Vegas attained an unequaled capacity to present music. On any night, a major headliner or three is playing somewhere in Las Vegas. A typical two-month period bookended by Tom Petty's August 21, 1999, show at The Joint at the Hard Rock and his October 15 return to the MGM Grand Garden included Little Feat and the Neville Brothers, the Righteous Brothers, the Bolshoi Ballet, Donna Summer, Leann Rimes, Cooper, Dwight Yoakum, N'Sync, Linda Ronstadt, Alanis Morrissette and Tori Amos, Alan Jackson, the Beach Boys, Jeff Beck, George Carlin, Ray Charles, Lenny Kravitz, Sting, and dozens of others. The city's essential malleability ensured a continued response to the demands of popular taste. In 2001 Mandalay Resort Group chief Glen Schaeffer decided to pursue a Latin-themed show modeled on Ricky Martin's successful stint at the hotel. "There's only one universal language now," he told a reporter, "and it's called MTV."

For pure grandiosity, nothing on the Las Vegas entertainment scene matches the MGM Grand. Since it opened, the resort has billed itself as the "City of Entertainment," featuring such behemoth events like the Rolling Stone's "No Security" tour. The MGM's venues have hosted title fights and rock extravaganzas among other giant acts. Mike Tyson and Evander Holyfield fought there, and Barbra Streisand came out of hiding to kick off her six-city 1994 tour there. None of this is accident. The MGM offers the consumer a complete experience, one-stop shopping for entertainment. Top-rated restaurants, gaming, and other options for a night on the town are there on the way to and from any show. The 650-seat Hollywood Theatre; Catch a Rising Star, the city's premier comedy club; Studio 54, modeled on New York's hot dance club of the 1970s; and EFX fill out the entertainment options.

Tall and powerfully built, Mark Prows exudes the confidence of a man who knows his business. The vice president in charge of the MGM Grand Arena, he is one of the loudest voices proclaiming Las Vegas the entertainment capital of the world, now and in the future. "It's a five-sense experience we provide," he said over lunch at one of the many fine restaurants at the MGM. "You see, feel, smell, taste, and hear."

Until the MGM Grand Arena opened, the primary theater in Las Vegas had long been the Aladdin Theater for the Performing Arts at the Aladdin Hotel. The $10 million, seven-thousand-seat venue opened in 1976 and booked everything; "one week, it was *Joseph and the Amazing Technicolor Dreamcoat*, the next it was *Motley Crüe*," Prows observed. "It was all over the place." Without a clearly defined mission and a few thousand seats short of making the biggest acts pay, the Aladdin couldn't really dominate the market. The theater was a cultural center for a town that had not yet defined itself, a B-level stop on most tours.

The Grand Garden's only competition was the Thomas and Mack arena at the University of Nevada, Las Vegas, home to the UNLV Runnin' Rebels, the sole venue with more than ten thousand seats. A "stand-alone" venue, where the only sources of revenue are the Big Four of the entertainment industry—tickets, parking, concessions, and merchandise—the T&M had more than enough seats, but faced other limitations. It could not offer gaming or rooms, and so its patrons arrived for the show and immediately departed. Bands and their managers sought a cut of the revenue, but without any other way to make money, the T&M could never give those up. Without the enticements Las Vegas visitors and residents demand, the T&M could never be a destination in the Las Vegas market.

Rock 'n' Roll offered a way to fill smaller halls, something The Joint had proved could succeed. Between 1995 and 1999, new arenas opened at nearly every hotel in the town; the most prominent was Mandalay Bay's House of Blues. Booked by well-known agent Kevin Morrow, the House of Blues immediately succeeded. By 2000, every major hotel offered concerts. Mandalay Bay's special-events center hosted frontline entertainment; if nostalgia was your bag, rock 'n' roll retreads could be found most summer weekends on the faux beach at the hotel. An REO Speedwagon concert that opened there in 1999 brought my youth back for an instant.

All the bother just for music? In a town many think is still devoted to gaming? Music is one of the many catalysts of the transition to entertainment. The expansion of venues has helped to create a menu of choices for visitors. Music entices people who would not otherwise be in Las Vegas, and their choice of one activity encourages them to engage in others: gaming, dining, another show, or something else. It's one of the many reasons why Las Vegas remains special, better than the gaming palaces that have sprung up across the country.

But music has limits. Nothing quite competes with boxing for drawing in gamblers. Mike Tyson has an immense following that contains celebrities and professional athletes who spend freely. This crowd often brings violence and leaves trashed rooms, bruised bouncers, and enormous bills behind. The rapper Tupac Shakur was murdered after a Tyson–Bruce Selden fight in 1996. But Tyson can't fight every night and no other boxer delivers the gaming crowd as well as he does, which is one of the factors that turned casinos toward music. Rock 'n' roll acts aren't quite like heavyweight boxing, but they can be close. A Rolling Stones concert generates as much revenue as an Oscar de la Hoya–Felix "Tito" Trinidad fight does. Major concerts bring the Hard Rock's audience to the big hotels. Profitable on their own, rock 'n' roll concerts also bring people through the casino doors who might not ordinarily come to one.

Las Vegas is an "excuse market," Prows suggests. "People are looking for an excuse to come here and music can provide it." If you live in Los Angeles and want a weekend away, your favorite band at a big Las Vegas hotel provides an opportunity to wrap different kinds of recreation together. Not only do you see a band you crave, you can stay in luxury, eat at a fine restaurant, and maybe play a little too. As I waited for a flight the morning of the Rolling Stones MGM Grand show in April 1999, the airport in Tucson was clogged with concert-goers, dressed in their Stones wear and ready for twenty-four hours of partying. The anticipation was palpable. The next morning, on an 8 A.M. flight back to Tucson, they were satiated. The ones who were awake talked about the show.

On a Tuesday afternoon just before the Stones concert, the inside of the MGM Grand felt like a city. As the crew set up the stage for another show, the prospect of Las Vegas being the city of entertainment didn't seem far-fetched. Las Vegas has always excelled at giving better than value. Music was one more variation on the oldest theme in modern Las Vegas's history.

"Well, the joint was rocking, going around and around," Tom Petty belted from the stage at The Joint, the twelve-hundred-person-capacity hall at the Hard Rock Hotel in August 1999, and the fifteen hundred people who paid $100 a head for a general-admission ticket rocked along. The crowd was a mix of vacationers and excuse travelers—I met a fan who came from L.A., liked the Hard Rock, and felt like he needed a weekend off—locals and rock 'n' rollers, button-downs, and aging Harley enthusiasts. Such is the audience for a band with twenty years of hits and an antisocial edge. Petty put on a two-and-a-half-hour show that had the entire place moving. In songs like "Free Falling," the crowd chanted the chorus. In the late 1970s Petty was known for fighting his record company to keep prices down, and even in his late forties, he is still edgy, prone to bite the hand that heaps caviar onto his plate. The Hard Rock displays guitars, clothing, and other rock 'n' roll memorabilia as if they were religious icons. "If you see any of my shit up there," Petty tersely told the cheering crowd. "You have my personal permission to rip it down and take it with you!"

Still, $100 for general admission seemed like a lot, especially for a band that made its rep in part by fighting the commercialism of rock 'n' roll. A few months before, the Rolling Stones "No Security" tour played the eight-thousand-seat MGM Grand Garden. The Rolling Stones' attitude had changed since the 1970s, when guitarist Ron Wood announced that he'd rather be dead than play in Las Vegas. Like every other band, the Stones chased gargantuan paydays with a vengeance. The attraction was obvious when top ticket prices reached $300, but at least the seats were reserved. The Stones came out and rocked as they hadn't in years. In the end, it was one of the best rock 'n' roll shows I've ever seen—and I've seen hundreds. But $300? Even for a small venue? When the 1998 "Bridges to Babylon" tour peaked at $75?

The price of live music has gone through the roof in the 1990s. *Rolling Stone* called 1999 the year of the three-digit ticket, an uncomfortable reality Las Vegas had been experiencing since the mid-1990s. The battle to bring clientele in the doors has driven the cost of entertainment way up. "In the old days, shows used to be a loss leader," Las Vegas native Pat Miller, the grandson of an entertainer, observed. "Now the owners [of venues] are laughing all the way to the bank." The variety costs. As rock 'n' roll audiences have gone gray and affluent, they've been more selective about what they see and more willing to pay to see it on their own terms. For anyone in their right mind over the age of twenty-five, the idea of waiting in line for days to get premier seats is ridiculous. Call a broker and pay to sit where you want. No one over thirty wants to fight the crowds, the noise, the parking, and the endemic violence for a glimpse of their youth. They'd rather pay more to be transported as spectators, be able to drink good champagne or Absolut and tonic and sit in comfort as the memories roll over them.

Las Vegas offered a way into higher-priced shows. With only the Sam Boyd Silver Bowl, the thirty-thousand-seat football stadium, as an outdoor venue and in a climate where summer outdoor shows were nigh on impossible, Las Vegas could not host the big stadium shows that played Busch Stadium, the Coliseum in Los Angeles, or the Meadowlands. The exception was the Grateful Dead, who began an annual three- or four-day run at the Silver Bowl in 1989 that lasted until Jerry Garcia died in 1995. But the

Dead reached Las Vegas only after they'd become the highest-grossing band in rock 'n' roll. Culturally, the legions of Deadheads and their pseudovillages outside the arenas made a four-day stint possible and palatable. For ordinary concert-goers, the village served as a counterpoint, a memory of where you might once have been but were damn glad not to be twenty years later. The Joint brought the smaller venue, more intimate, comfortable, more like you were there instead of squinting at faraway figures on a stage.

The more intimate venues were an aging rocker's dream. If you weren't going to two shows a week—and you weren't—and you were there to hear the music rather than make new friends, what could be better than a two-thousand-seat hall, an eight-thousand-seat theater, or even the faux beach at Mandalay Bay? These were rock 'n' roll clubs, so they expected you to dance—no cries of "down in front" with general-admission or theater seating—and you could always stay in your seat and see pretty well if you didn't want to boogie. The drinks were expensive, but you had your choice. No need to drink swill. The concerts in the smaller venues felt more like parties than concerts, more like the Stones were playing your fiftieth birthday party instead of a concert hall.

The economics work in Las Vegas. There are two obvious markets, affluent locals and the myriad visitors in town any given night. Las Vegas residents are more likely to splurge on a show than their peers elsewhere. Excuse tourists and people in town who see that there's someone playing they want to see—the Microsoft millionaire and his wife staying at the Hard Rock who see that the Neville Brothers are at the House of Blues—make up the rest. On an average Labor Day weekend, more than 250,000 people crowd the 125,000 hotel rooms in Las Vegas. They'll fill a lot of seats at almost any price.

"Now it's an agent's dream and an agent's nightmare," observes Rod Essig. The goal is to make an artist consistently profitable while increasing both exposure and fees. Every booking runs the risk of outstripping the market, of becoming the moment when the ticket prices are finally too high and the revenues don't equal the band's guarantee. With so many choices, the market can become saturated in a heartbeat. It's easy to "oversell your acts," says Essig. "There are so many places to play that you can't repeat too often. I tell acts there's something unique about Vegas—change your show, make it different, make it better." Three-digit tickets cut out a large section of any audience. The situation is a real dilemma for artists, managers, and agents in an age when the number of venues played and the price of tickets combine to accrue status. To have both in Las Vegas is a very hard thing.

So the $50 Tom Petty charged for his return to the MGM Grand in October 1999 made sense. It let Petty continue to claim that he, like Garth Brooks and a few other artists, cares enough about the fans to keep prices down. The reduced price guaranteed a largely different audience than the one he drew in August in The Joint, and with Sting across town at $200 the same night, Petty was a bargain. Las Vegas's newfound status as a leader in the consumption of music demands more from the acts that play there: bands put on a better show in Las Vegas than elsewhere because they have to, because they need to, because they want to come back to the neon lights and the big payday.

The television cameras covered Oscar Goodman as he stood on a New York street with David Stern, commissioner of the National Basketball Association, and Gary Bettmann, his peer at the National Hockey League, on September 28, 1999. A few months into his term as mayor, Goodman and billionaire John Moores, owner of the San Diego Padres, came to New York to plead Las Vegas's case for a "Big Four"—National Football League, Major League Baseball, National Basketball Association, or National Hockey League—franchise. Goodman was Las Vegas's Jesse Ventura, a mildly roguish and candid straight-shooting populist who spoke with élan for those whom the rapid growth of the region helped least. He sought his first symbolic conquest: Las Vegas's inclusion in the figurative limousine. A major-league sports franchise was a status symbol for the city, proof positive that the new Las Vegas was entirely mainstream. "Las Vegas is a major metropolitan area," Goodman told the press. "In order to be number one, you have to have every good quality that every other major city has."

Despite its reputation as the sports bettors' mecca, Las Vegas has never come to grips with professional sports. The number of such teams is endless and their histories sadly similar; a few fans, a few seasons if they're lucky, and one day the makeshift office is locked. Football, basketball, soccer, or hockey, Las Vegas has always been a losing proposition for teams. The evidence is everywhere. A few billboards left, a former player or two who goes on to play elsewhere or maybe announce on a local radio station, and the memories of a few diehards. The Las Vegas Posse—a minor-league football team whose local nickname became more anatomical—had been gone five years by 1999, but their headquarters, a beat-up old storefront in a transitional neighborhood, was still adorned with their name and a larger-than-life drawing of their helmet. In no other way does Las Vegas show how completely it is a winner's town than its basic, fundamental, and complete lack of attention to teams that don't capture the local imagination. There's only one way to do that: win with flair and win a lot.

Before 1990, Las Vegas was simply too small to even entertain the prospect of an NBA, MLB, NFL, or NHL team. Without the hometown ownership and populated hinterland of deeply loyal, rabid fans that keep a town like Green Bay in the NFL, Las Vegas could not overcome being smaller than 1 million people. Even Phoenix, more than three times the size and with Tucson, one hundred miles to the south, only became major-league in the 1990s. Before that the Phoenix Suns were the only game in town. When the St. Louis Cardinals moved to the desert after the 1987 season, they added to the one-sport town, but their arrival smacked of theft, of Robert Irsay fleeing Baltimore in the of the middle night with that city's beloved Colts. The opening game of the Arizona Diamondbacks' inaugural season in the Bank One Ballpark in 1998 gave Phoenix major-league status. By 2000, the Diamondbacks were hemorrhaging money and the voters had approved a new stadium to keep the hapless Cardinals in town. Professional sports were expensive. Denver attained this status only when the Rockies debuted in 1993; even though the Broncos appeared in two Super Bowls before 1990, they and the Nuggets were relics of the AFL and the ABA, upstart leagues that folded into existing leagues in the 1970s. Before Coors Field opened in 1995, the only reason to go that neighborhood was to buy drugs.

When Las Vegas's population topped 1 million in population in 1995, only a few cities of similar size in the United States other than Green Bay had a top league team: Buffalo's NFL franchise started in the AFL, Milwaukee's synergy mirrored that of the Packers and was helped by Bud Selig's local ownership and his other job as commissioner of baseball, San Antonio's Spurs were another ABA holdover, and Paul Allen's money kept the Portland Trailblazers afloat as it did nearly every other pro sports team in the Northwest. Basketball's global reach and small squads—one great player, a Tim Duncan, can change a team's fortune in basketball in a manner impossible in any other sport—kept the Spurs in San Antonio, where they won the 1999 NBA championship. Few remembered how close they'd been to leaving the Alamo City just a few years before.

In the pro sports franchise derby of the 1990s, the winners were Sun Belt cities that experienced rapid growth. Charlotte, North Carolina, with its Hornets and Carolina Panthers; Tampa Bay, which added the Devil Rays and the Lightning; and Jacksonville, Florida, with the Jaguars, took the most prestigious prize, an NFL franchise. Each capitalized on a booming economy and publicly funded arenas. No wonder Oscar Goodman seemed entranced. With Steve Wynn endorsing the idea, a major-league franchise conferred a legitimacy in postmodern America that made Goodman salivate.

Beyond the questions of small population and no hinterland, sports betting loomed. In Nevada, wagering on sports events has been legal since 1931. Nothing scares professional sports more than wagering. Gambling, even legally, appears to diminish not only the integrity of the game, but the significance of competition. Despite the money that people pay to see and bet on professional sports, the vast television contracts that drown leagues in money and make stadium fans mere props, and the huge sums that accrue from licensing, professional sports insist that they offer pure competition, a primal contest beyond the pale of money. Gambling is the greatest threat, the overarching concern, the ultimate corruptor. Betting scandals have dogged professional and college sports throughout the twentieth century. Scandals at Northwestern and Arizona State in the 1990s recalled an earlier, more tainted time. From the CUNY and Long Island University basketball scandals of the early 1950s, Paul Hornung and Alex Karras in the NFL in the early 1960s, and Denny McLain and especially Pete Rose in baseball in the 1960s and 1980s, the stigma of fixed games and threat of pay for less-than-utmost performance sends chills through not only owners and fans, but television executives who've paid billions for broadcast rights. Las Vegas is too close for comfort for any league in a solid position.

A team in Las Vegas would create considerable tension. When the line between real and unreal blurs, when people embrace the identity that is intrinsically wrapped up in their local sports team, the threat of losing, catastrophic in itself, but blamed on someone tanking a game or worse, shaving points by not trying, is too great a risk to bear. The idea that people paint their bellies for a game that isn't played by real gladiators, but instead by participants who might tweak their performance to ensure an outcome smacks of jai alai or dog racing, neither of which have fan bases outside of bettors or say much about American culture. Baseball, basketball, football, and even hockey push American buttons. People live and die with their teams, and their teams must live and die with them.

The threat didn't stop people from trying. In the early 1990s talk surfaced about locating a major-league franchise in Las Vegas. Professional

sports had become dysfunctional. Owners held up towns for bigger and better stadiums with luxury boxes, promising prosperity but draining regional economies and perverting tax bases. Teams sold personal seat licenses,
the right to buy and then keep a seat for an annual fee. Instead of civic
pride, pro sports extended crass capitalism, precisely the metier in which
Las Vegas excelled, from labor relations to civic arrangements. The down-
side was huge. Sports betting, small population, no hinterland, and the
stigma of the town's shady past stood in the way. The surprise was that
leagues even considered the idea.

In major-league sports of the postindustrial world, NFL football is the
only genuine prize, the real marker of legitimacy for cities as the twenty-first
century begins. Football long ago supplanted baseball as the national pastime. A fundamentally corporate game, football fit post-Vietnam America.
The spectacle of the game matched the image of Las Vegas: its gladiator
nature, a gridiron of players in sculpted uniforms surrounded by thousands
of screaming fans, seemed a page out of Caesars Palace. No sport inspires
more passion nor fills the sports books more than pro football. The largest
sums wagered are always on the NFL. The logistics and economics of the
game seemed to work too. An NFL season contained only eight home games,
even at 75,000 fans per, it would be far easier to fill the stands than 10,000
seats at forty-one NBA games or 25,000 at eighty-one baseball games. An
NFL franchise seemed natural for Las Vegas. A combination of avid local
fans and a multitude of tourists could easily make football work. In the most
optimistic scenario, the big hotels would buy thousands of season tickets for
comps. Local businesses would buy many more. Las Vegans would become
fans instead of bettors. The numbers made sense.

No professional sports league needed Las Vegas less than the NFL. Its
position in American society was secure and the league floated on money.
The Super Bowl is bigger national holiday than President's Day. That
makes a pro football franchise the hardest to acquire, unless you hook up
with a renegade owner like Al Davis, Irsay, Bill Bidwell, or Art Modell, and
wait a decade for the stigma of your conquest to disappear. After Howard
Milstein and Daniel Snyder bought the Washington Redskins for about
$800 million in 1999, slightly more than the cost of Paris Las Vegas, the
NFL perched even higher atop the world of professional sports and it
looked down its nose at Las Vegas.

This didn't stop people from trying. An instant whirlwind, Paul
Tanner, a Texan with a knack for getting attention, purchased one of the

best tracts in town, sixty-one acres of the old Union Pacific rail yard just off the Fremont Street Experience in downtown Las Vegas, and late in 1996 announced his plans for a 110,000-seat stadium. Tanner was the talk of town for a couple of weeks. He told the press that "four NFL teams have already talked to us about moving" to Las Vegas. Recognizing the limits of the local market, he added, "If it's going to be tourists filling the majority of seats, so be it." Tanner promised college football events like the Kickoff Classic and hinted at the Super Bowl, and soon even local sportswriters, who should have known better, believed. Anyone who read the press clippings would have thought the stadium alone would reverse the fortunes of the sagging downtown economy, pounded by the growth of the Strip.

Tanner initiated one of the great fictions of Las Vegas sports, that out-of-towners could fill a stadium when locals wouldn't. The argument reprised the "excuse market" thinking of the music industry—visitors would use an event as an excuse to come to town and do other things—or vice versa—but it ignored a larger issue. A sporting event, even an NFL game, isn't a prize like a great concert ticket. It can be replicated every weekend throughout the season. A ticket for any game wasn't in itself special, unless you had genuine affinity for one of the teams. Fans would come to town, but if they were season-ticket holders at home, any single event had less appeal. A Las Vegas team in the NFL would likely share a problem with the UNLV football team. Schools such as the University of Wisconsin fill Sam Boyd Stadium with visitors when they come to town, but NFL cities were not Madison. Maybe if the Las Vegas team could regularly play the Packers.

The NFL was a lot less interested than Tanner anticipated, and when the attempt to acquire a team stalled, Lehman Brothers Holding Company foreclosed on him. Tanner's public relations man blamed it on the tight-knit local business community and its suspicion of outsiders, but Tanner needed to look in the mirror too. The adventure left a taste, a sniff of big-league-city status, and Las Vegans were ready to jump at the next opportunity. By 2001, the city had acquired the tract and planned another version of downtown redevelopment.

In 1999 major-league sports reared its head once again, this time in conjunction with Oscar Goodman's election as mayor. Pro-sports were a symbol of the city's growth and newfound prominence and a manifestation of the constellation of construction, dollars, and identity shift that made the new Las Vegas. As summer arrived, Wynn announced that if the city built him an arena, he'd buy an existing NBA team or bid for an expansion franchise. It was only a concept, he insisted, but when Wynn talked, ears in Las Vegas and the financial markets perked up. Wynn had manipulated government before, but he consistently had his market research right. He translated his cachet into self-interest, telling the audience that a team would help fill the city's burgeoning supply of hotel rooms. Business leaders got interested in a hurry, and it spiraled from there. "Mark June 30, 1999, down in your Las Vegas sports history books," wrote the usually cynical columnist Joe Hawk. "That was the day this city let it be known it was going major league." Stern and Bettman gave Wynn the impression that putting a team in Las Vegas would not "cause World War III." A Wynn-commissioned survey showed that Las Vegans overwhelmingly favored the deal, but support skidded down a slippery slope when taxes and especially property tax increases were added to the mix. The libertarian, anti-tax, and anti-institutional nature of the state never became more clear: stick it to the tourists with regressive tariffs like sales tax or with a $1 surcharge on hotel rooms or car rentals.

Wynn, the most influential individual in the state in 1999, followed a strategy pioneered by other sports franchise owners across the country. From Baltimore to Oakland, team owners portrayed their needs as the public good, and in some cases blackmailed cities and regions into supporting new and expensive arenas that benefitted only the team's owners. Some communities spent hundreds of millions of dollars to keep their storied local franchise. In a few cases, Coors Field, Cleveland's Jacob's Field, and Baltimore's Camden Yards, all new baseball parks made to look old and filled with people on eighty warm summer nights, the stadiums actually contributed to area revitalization. By the mid-1990s, some cities actually rejected new stadiums, saying to teams: pay your way or go somewhere else.

This public-private battle was not new to Wynn. The year before, he sought a tax deduction for his $350 million art collection at the Bellagio— the one with the signs that said "Now Appearing: Monet" on billboards near the Strip—arguing that it was public culture and enlightening for school tours. The legislature balked, one of the few times the savvy and well-connected Wynn, accomplished at lubricating local, state, and national politics, didn't instantly get his way. Wynn was told he would have to forego the $10 entrance fee for schoolchildren to get the tax break, an offer he declined.

For Goodman, Wynn's proposition was at once exciting and vexing. Goodman won election as a populist, an incorruptible man with enough personal wealth to be immune to temptation. He supported a team in a new arena, but assured everyone that the city would not finance a new stadium. Goodman and Wynn had a long-standing relationship. They were two of the winners—in very different ways—left from the mob era, and in their new roles as civic leaders they needed one another. The prospect of finally making Las Vegas major league appealed to Goodman. The cost of it to the city, the one governmental entity that needed a new pony in the ongoing effort to stem the decline of downtown, had to be carried elsewhere. The operators of down-town hotels, accustomed to watching Wynn slide through resistance, waited not a second to jump on the bandwagon. The project "would be advantageous for downtown," Bill Noonan, general manager of Fitzgerald's, a prominent downtown hotel-casino, observed. "The Fremont Street Experience was the first component but you can't stop with one thing."

Despite Wynn's claim that a team would generate pride and identity for the new Las Vegas, everyone else who looked at it saw once again the rescue of the battered and sinking ship called Glitter Gulch. The megaresorts on the Strip pummeled downtown throughout the first decade of the Mirage Phase, and even the infusion of nearly $70 million for the Fremont Street Experience did not reverse the trend. Two very different goals, first-class-city status and prosperity for downtown and the City of Las Vegas, quickly melded. The two goals weren't mutually exclusive, but they didn't have a lot in common either.

Reaction in the town was mixed. John L. Smith called the new push for a pro sports team "narcissism at work" in 1999. Dean Juipe, a sportswriter for the *Las Vegas Sun*, observed that Wynn could afford a team, an arena, and even the outrageous salary demands of players—or at least he could get financial backing for it—but "he doesn't want to take that serious plunge and he prob-ably never will." Others took a less jaundiced view. A downtown sports arena "will happen as definite as a Shaquille O'Neal thunder-dunk. As certain as a Jaromir Jagr slapshot," Hawk insisted. "It will happen because Steve and Elaine Wynn want it to." Hawk represented a minority, the few who believed Las Vegas would finally get its due in the world of sports.

When Oscar Goodman came back from New York, he sounded chas-tened and a little chagrined. No one said no, but they didn't say yes, either. Stern was especially harsh. His league has had countless troubles with drugs and gambling, probably including a few the public doesn't know about. The new generation of NBA stars, epitomized by Dennis Rodman, aren't the kind of people who would restrain themselves in a town of excess. Stern took the high road, telling Goodman that the NBA would be interested only if the sports books gave up wagering on the league. In 1999 the NBA was flush and didn't need Las Vegas. Bettman, whose NHL was the most rickety of the four, was more amenable. He didn't offer firm stipulations, but he didn't say that betting on hockey had to be outlawed. Who bets on hockey anyway?

Goodman's trip exposed the flaws in the idea of a Las Vegas sports team as well as the soft underbelly of the local sports fan base. Even though a lot of Las Vegans would pay as much as $40 a ticket to see an NBA team as many as three times a year, the NBA and the NHL were not quite right for Las Vegas. Basketball was hot, but really it was the UNLV Runnin' Rebels with roguish Jerry Tarkanian at the helm who captured the local imagination. Pay for play didn't have quite the pull. The NHL? Who's kidding who? There are plenty of fans and snow-country expatriates, but they would support a hockey team—only if it won—a lot. What about tourists? They're going to make the trip to Las Vegas to see *hockey*? The only sport that could really fill a stadium in Las Vegas is football, NFL football. "The game is so good it sells itself," says Kevin Byrne, the Baltimore Ravens vice president of public relations and marketing. "Football makes for great television and great in-stadium entertainment and that isn't going to change." Eight games works; football is king in the American heart these days. But as long as the NFL rides Byrne's crest, it won't need Las Vegas.

When Elvis Presley first came to play Las Vegas in 1956, he was still young, ripped, and taut, not the blimplike caricature he later became. The booking came about at the last minute, and Elvis found himself in the Venus Room at the New Frontier, a thousand-seat venue. He and his band were backed by Freddy Martin and his orchestra. Elvis's new manager, the wily Colonel Tom Parker, took the credit. Parker had previously booked Eddy Arnold, the first mid-South country singer to reach Las Vegas, and he knew that his new phenom had real crossover power. Even by March, 1956 had been a good year for Elvis and the neon city of excess promised more. In pure Las Vegas style, a twenty-four-foot-high cutout of the twenty-one-year-old appeared in front of the hotel. Las Vegas could always recognize a star.

Elvis bombed. For two weeks, he, guitarist Scotty Moore, bass player Bill Black, and drummer D. J. Fontana played. At the opening, they were, according to Elvis biographer Peter Guralnick, "a very nervous, very out-of-place hillbilly quartet." Elvis even introduced one of his hits as

"Heartburn Hotel." They were just the wrong fit, too eccentric for the older, pseudosophisticated Las Vegas audience. One prominent guest leaped up from his seat at a ringside table, shouted that the music was too loud, and headed back to the casino. Elvis was the fringe, and Las Vegas only did well with the center. When he returned in 1969, he was a star. He began a record seven-year stay and performed 837 sold-out shows in a row beginning at Kirk Kerkorian's International Hotel and remaining after Hilton bought the property. After the army, after the rock 'n' roll revolution, during the Vietnam War, Elvis was a Las Vegas act. The years, the weight, and the changes in society conspired to make him an anachronism, perfect for Las Vegas in 1969.

Las Vegas doesn't create entertainment. It packages music, art, and like it or not, culture to a wider audience than those concepts could otherwise reach. A good portion of the 200,000 people who passed through the Phillips Collection during the first five months of its exhibition at the Bellagio never would have gone to see masterpieces in a conventional museum setting. Certainly more people saw Elvis in the showroom of the Las Vegas Hilton than anywhere else in the world. But what they saw in the fading star was a memory, a package, a wrapper for desires that they once held or to which they aspired. In this sense, Las Vegas's claim as the City of Entertainment rings truer at the box office than in the coffeehouses. The city takes mutable forms and fixes them, makes them palatable. As for Elvis in 1956, the stamp of Las Vegas, positive or otherwise, signaled his emergence from the ghetto of hillbilly and his arrival in the larger market. But it cost him something too, both immediately and in the long term. After two and a half years of girls screaming, he'd finally reached a little Waterloo, a place where his act didn't fly, where the audience turned him back. Although Scotty Moore thought "people that were there, if you'd lifted them out and taken them to San Antonio, the big coliseum, they'd have been going crazy," he was wrong. A Las Vegas audience in 1956 wasn't made up of teenagers, didn't hail from the Bible Belt, and wasn't entertainment-starved.

Elvis loved Las Vegas. There was plenty to do, and a guy who didn't sleep much didn't have to worry about the town closing. He also recognized a future in Las Vegas, a way to reach an audience that was ambivalent toward him in 1956 a decade or more down the road. This failure with a future became the paradox and promise of the City of Entertainment. Las Vegas doesn't nurture entertainment; it only buys it. An artist can hold the town, can become it, and be it, but Las Vegas will push you as an artist and compromise you at the same time. Las Vegas does to entertainment exactly what it does to experience: it planes off its rough edges, the unique traits that give it critical acclaim, and repackages it as fashionable. No wonder the city's contribution to the world of rock 'n' roll is a band called Slaughter.

CHAPTER 3

The Last Detroit

The New Service Economy

"STRIKE'S OVER—EVERYONE WELCOME," DECLARED THE FRONTIER HOTEL sign on the Strip early in 1998. After the longest labor action in American history, the Culinary Union, Las Vegas's largest and most powerful, won an enormous victory not only over the Frontier Hotel and its owners, Margaret Elardi and her sons Tom and John, but in the ongoing contest between labor and management in what has become the most unionized city in the United States. When the grueling strike finally ended after six years and four months, the Elardis left the Strip and the Culinary Union reasserted its leadership in defending Las Vegas's unique economic climate. In the space of a decade, the union had been transformed from chaos and disarray and become one of the most powerful entities in Nevada. In the process, they ensured Las Vegas's place as "the Last Detroit," the last place in American society where unskilled and semiskilled workers can make a middle-class wage and have those dollars create the prosperity that once was the hallmark of the unionized American working class.

Only in Las Vegas can ordinary workers achieve a semblance of yesteryear's American dream. Unionized gaming recycles workers from the scrapheap of economic history, from being excised from a well-paying, benefit-laden, blue-collar workplace. It saves such workers from the morass of minimum-wage work in the new economy. In Las Vegas, relatively high wages and the "toke," the tipping that is the elixir of local working life, combine with the low cost of living to offer hope in ways that the retraining clinics of the Rust Belt can't match. Las Vegas's unique economic circumstance is playing a crucial role in creating the middle class of the future.

As it once was in the industrial core of the nation, Las Vegas enjoys a relationship between the cost of living and the local wage scale that lets people of ordinary skills, achievements, and means live a comfortable, middle-class life. In no small part as a result of unionization and the high-pay, low-skill work made possible by the profitability of casinos and the generosity of tippers, local workers are extremely well off by postindustrial blue-collar standards. They can own nice homes in good school districts and buy new cars and even lake cabins and boats. They receive health care benefits and put money away for retirement. They send their kids to college in the fashion of Americans who endured the 1930s. The parents see themselves as fortunate and want, even demand, better for their kids. They look at their children and say, "I don't want you doing what I do. I've sacrificed to give you an opportunity to get out and by God, you're gonna take it. If you come back to the casinos, you're coming back in the management suite instead of on the floor or in the back of the house." It's a powerful message that resonates. Here's a way up in life; do better. Don't pay the price that I did to get ahead.

The union gets considerable credit for creating this cross-generational transformation. In its consistent effort to ensure quality working conditions and living wages and its ongoing organizing efforts to bring new hotels and their workers into the fold, the union has accomplished what seems unattainable in postindustrial America: it has made ordinary workers valuable parts of the company's endeavor, not replaceable cogs that can be outsourced or shipped overseas for assembly. Almost fifty thousand culinary union workers project a new future for American labor, one that speaks Spanish and includes African Americans, Asians, Eastern European immigrants, and plenty of others. No wonder the AFL-CIO kicked off its revival campaign in Las Vegas in 1997. No wonder Las Vegas mayor Oscar Goodman, a longtime friend of the union, refused to cross a picket line to be honored at the nonunion Venetian Hotel in 1999. No wonder AFL-CIO president John Sweeney called Las Vegas "the fastest growing union city in America" and observed that "just as surely as New York set the standards for the past 100 years, Las Vegas will be setting them for the next 100 years." Unions had a place in the desert. They'd become a cornerstone of local prosperity. They benefitted not only workers but the community at large.

The success of the unionized workforce in Las Vegas is an anomaly. Like most western states, Nevada is a right-to-work state where there is no such thing as an exclusively union shop. In 1952, a referendum was placed on the ballot ensuring an open shop provision. Even at the height of the Cold War and McCarthyism, the measure passed by only one thousand votes out of 76,000 cast. As a result, workers do not have to belong to a union to work in any hotel, and without membership, they still receive the same wages and benefits as union workers. Some nonunion houses pay well above union scale in a costly effort to keep the union out. To any individual, there's no clear-cut economic benefit from belonging to the union. To want to belong, a worker has to look at a larger picture, has to understand that the presence of the union sets the pay scales even in the nonunion houses, that the $108.12 a day that a union fry cook made in 2000 translates into very similar wages in nonunion megaresorts and the other major hotels. A nongaming cocktail waitress in 2000 made $9 an hour plus tips under Culinary Union contract; a gaming cocktail waitress started at $14 per hour. Without the union the daily rates would be much closer to minimum wage, surely incapable of sustaining a middle-class family even in a low-cost town like Las Vegas.

The inability to rely on the traditional union emphasis on higher wages forced the Culinary to devise more sophisticated rationales. Members stress not only wages, but better working conditions in the labor-intensive and physically difficult service industry. The hotels insist on strict rules, and in a pro-business state, without union protection, workers are always vulnerable to the caprice of managers. Many back-of-the-house jobs characteristic of the Culinary are physically hard, housekeeper prominent among them. Others require people skills, intense interactions with customers in a full range of moods, some of whom think it is funny to abuse and demean service workers. The union offers something tangible: a promise to fight for better workplace conditions.

The union's emphasis on working conditions resonates in Las Vegas. The nonunion shops might pay as much, observes Geoconda Arguello-Kline, a native of Nicaragua who came to the United States in 1979 and works as an organizer for the Culinary, but there aren't any guarantees. Nonunion shops offer no seniority, no consistency in hours per week, and less protection from arbitrary workplace rules. Peggy Pierce, a lounge singer–turned–banquet server, agrees: "Nothing protects you [from capricious management] in a nonunion hotel. We're the guys that keep the bottom from sinking." Seniority and protection in the workplace became watchwords of the union's message.

Persuading the hotels to accommodate the union required a different strategy: the union had to show its partners that contented workers were essential to the expansion of leisure and entertainment in American society. The real strength of the Culinary stems from its ability to convince managers and casino owners that the work union employees provide is better, more dependable, more professional, and will do more to keep their customers happy and coming back. More than fifty thousand new hotel rooms opened in the 1990s, placing a premium on quality labor. A new hotel opening generates as many as forty thousand applications for between five thousand and eight thousand jobs. The town is flooded with workers, newcomers mostly, but there's more than meets the eye to service work. Sorting through applicants from everywhere, with every kind of background and variety of limitations, is an enormous task for management. It is easier to find large numbers of union workers than to recruit from the population at large. Union workers consistently demonstrate higher skill levels and more commitment to both the work and the employer. They stay with the company longer, show up on time more consistently, and provide better service than random people recruited off the street. Most of the major hotel groups recognize their value. "The unions have brought professionalism and stability to the workforce," observed Alan Feldman while spokesman for Mirage Resorts. "The modern Culinary Union has established a standard of service that has served everyone well."

The value of labor is preserved in Las Vegas because what the city offers can only be had there. Unlike a factory, management can't send the work overseas for cheaper rates and get the same product; unlike trendy retail, you can't get the feeling of Las Vegas from the Internet. "Service" means personal attention, and it is at its smoothest when contented people deliver it. People protected by the union are happier than other workers and they work better as a result.

Local 226 in Las Vegas is the Culinary Union's single biggest affiliate and the most important local in the country. Beginning in the 1970s, unionism in the United States declined, and the membership of the Hotel Employees and Restaurant Employees International Union, the Culinary

Union's international umbrella organization, followed the trend, declining from 421,000 in 1975 to 258,000 in 1995. HEREIU was beset by organized-crime scandals during that time and was considered the most mobbed-up union in the country. Its troubles made it irrelevant in most communities. As HEREIU slid, Culinary Union Local 226 grew from the mid-20,000s to almost 50,000 in 2000. The transformation of Las Vegas, its growth from about 25,000 hotel rooms in the mid-1970s to more than 125,000 in 2000, created endless opportunity for more workers. The megaresorts that characterized the Mirage Phase hired thousands upon thousands of housekeepers, new restaurants and buffets needed cooks and food servers, and the millions of visitors needed bellmen and porters. Even as membership in the international union declined, Las Vegas's growth served as counterpoint to a changing workplace climate. In a culture that elevated the meaning of experience to self-definition, service that made experience special, something Las Vegas excelled at, was essential.

In Las Vegas, the cost of labor added to the bottom line. The megaresorts offer two successful models, union and nonunion. In the union hotels, labor and management have a partnership because both have a stake in success. Union contracts ensure that there are enough workers to do the job well. Service differentiates desirable properties from less popular counterparts. Because the heart of visitor experience is labor-intensive service, labor is a drag on a property's bottom line. It has to prove its value with quality. Nonunion hotels try to save costs by using three people to accomplish the work of four at a union property. It can work, but it is a long-term risk. After more than a year of heavy losses, the lightly staffed and nonunion Venetian started to show a profit in June 2000. About the same time, observers complained that the service was terrible. There weren't enough waitresses, bellmen, and desk clerks, and each was asked to do too much to be able to do it well. As a result, the staff seemed surly. In a competitive market, complaints from guests don't bode well and bad service defeats the purpose of paying $300 a night to feel special at an upscale resort. The hotel's first-quarter earnings in 2001 fell dramatically, which management attributed to an unlucky quarter at the tables. People in the know looked at the hotel's labor situation as one source of the decline.

Local 226 remains different than most hotel and restaurant workers unions. Las Vegas's unique conditions altered the typical culinary union profile. Front-of-the-house workers, bellmen and -women, bartenders, cocktail servers, and change people, not behind-the-scenes staff like cooks and maids, built the Las Vegas local. As a result, they play a much greater role in union activities in Las Vegas than anywhere else, and contracts in Las Vegas are weighted to their concerns. In Las Vegas, contract language has as much to do with tips and other front-of-the-house issues as it does with the workplace conditions so important to the back-of-the-house. This difference reflects the union's evolution and history. Until the Mirage Phase, most of the hotels were small, and the largest component of the workforce was floor staff. The rise of the massive megaresorts has created a new workforce, comprised of larger numbers of maids, cooks, and porters, people excluded from the IRS-mandated tip pools, but unlike elsewhere, tipped employees receive the same hourly raises as employees who don't receive gratuities.

Union demographics have changed dramatically over the years. Women make up a majority of the union, and better workplace conditions are particularly important to them. In 1997 36 percent of culinary workers were Anglo, 36 percent were Latino, 15 percent African American, and 12 percent were Asian. The influx of Latinos is the most pronounced trend. Asians, especially Thai, Vietnamese, Chinese, and Filipinos, make up the other most rapidly growing segment of the workforce. The presence of both results from changing immigration policies after 1965, the changing demography of the nation as a whole, and the increasing emphasis on education, especially a college degree, as a way up the socioeconomic ladder for Americans. For people who don't follow that route or who can't afford it for their children, unionized service work in the Culinary Union is among the best opportunities in a postindustrial economy. The Culinary in Las Vegas provided some of them with a chance to pull themselves out of the morass of minimum-wage work in a maximum-consumption society.

There are other prominent unions in Las Vegas as well. Two public-sector unions, the Nevada Service Employees Union/SEIU Local 1107, with 5,000 members, and Service Employees International Union Local 1864, with 3,032 members, represent state, county, and city employees. The United Food and Commercial Workers Union, grocery-store workers and meat cutters, have 3,049 members, the Teamsters have 4,500 members, the International Brotherhood of Electrical Workers Union Local 357 counts 1,814 members, and others, including the Musicians Union of Las Vegas, with 1,200 members, top the 1,000-member mark. As much as 30 percent of the workforce is unionized, providing a remarkable base for economic and workplace security.

Workers recognize the benefits of a semi-unionized economy. Dan Topps, a bulky man with graying close-cropped hair and the loud nasal voice of the South Side of Chicago, worked as an electrician in Chicago. The weather was hard on an electrician there. "You get all weather-beaten quick," he recalled, and he'd read about the boom in the desert. The move to a union job in Las Vegas improved the Topps' standard of living and helped them to a new life. "I made $68,000 last year," he beamed. "My best year ever there was $55,000." He added, "And the cost of living here is cheaper. $68,000, that's real money in Las Vegas. You can live good on that."

The Culinary Union's roots date back to the 1930s, part of the rise of labor in the West during the New Deal. The union was small then and became influential only after World War II, when the dapper Elmer "Al" Bramlet arrived in 1946. He was only twenty-nine when the war ended, but he had already enjoyed a full life. Born on a farm near Jonesboro, Arkansas, the small, slight man came from the poverty-stricken milieu of the southern plains, a historically impoverished region that only got worse with the Depression.

A lot of important people in Nevada and throughout the West shared Bramlet's background. Oran K. Gragson, who served as mayor of Las Vegas from 1959 to 1975 and was as close to a good government executive as the city ever experienced, caught a freight train out of Oklahoma in 1932 and six days later landed in Las Vegas. He never went back. Neither did Robert Maxson, the president of UNLV from 1984 to 1994 and the man who forced out legendary basketball coach Jerry Tarkanian as a result of the coach's troubles with the NCAA. Kenny Guinn showed that same intense desire to break free and better his lot. Born in Garland, Arkansas, in 1936, he was raised in Exeter, California, a small agricultural town in the Sierra Nevada, and after attending Fresno State, arrived in Las Vegas in 1964 and began the civic career that culminated in his election as governor of Nevada in 1998. Many more hailed from the region of John Steinbeck's fictional Joad family. The enterprising and desperate left the southern plains as soon as they could and never went back except to visit. They could not afford to fail. Giving up meant that they returned beaten, without riches or success, without the baubles to prove they'd triumphed, to endure the mockery of the ones who lacked the gumption even to try. The people who left not only Arkansas but the entire Southern Plains were flinty pragmatists who understood that there was no net below them if they fell.

By the time he was fourteen, Bramlet was out of Arkansas for good. In

1931 he began work as a dishwasher in Joliet, Illinois. A hitch in the navy during World War II followed, and when he was discharged in Los Angeles, he found work as a bartender, joined the bartenders' union, and became its business agent. In 1946 the union sent him to Las Vegas to help the fledgling Culinary Union. It was a match made in heaven. Bramlet had the traits the young city prized: toughness, competence, energy, and flamboyance. He walked the walk, talked the talk, even if he willingly bent the rules, and some said, was a little crooked. Bramlet built from the ground up, organizing workers and finding new ones for the rapidly growing city. He was gone for months, off on long recruiting trips, and he returned with the labor that Las Vegas so desperately needed. In small towns in the South, he'd pull up to a gas station or talk to waitresses in a diner, ask if anyone wanted to make real money. He'd collect a carload of excited young workers, ferry them to Las Vegas, and put them to work. Bramlet had a leg up in recruiting people from the Southern Plains. He'd come from their world, knew who they were—the ones who hopped in his car were younger versions of him—and understood the enticement of a faraway place where money

INDUSTRIAL, INDUSTRIAL, INDUSTRIAL

could be made. The train whistle, so loud in the American consciousness, couldn't free them, but Bramlet could. A delivery system began, carload by carload, catapulting Bramlet to real power. By 1954 he'd become the general secretary of the Culinary Union.

Bramlet had stumbled upon Las Vegas's greatest need: consistent, dependable labor. He converted that need into power because hotel bosses were prepared to make an exchange to secure reliable workers. They accepted the union in return for the constant supply of labor in a town that was not big enough to generate its own workers and had no hinterland from which to draw. Labor was in such demand that Bramlet established a hiring hall in Las Vegas, an anomaly in a right-to-work state. With legal restrictions against union-only or closed workplaces, a hiring hall seemed extraneous, but demand so far outstripped supply that Bramlet could line newcomers up and send them out in the morning for a good job. In return, the union screened workers and vetted their credentials, weeding out undesirables at little direct cost to the industry. It wasn't in Bramlet's best interests to send out drunk or addicted workers, nor was it in the hotel's best interests to hire such people. The synergy was stunning and the relationship smooth. The hotels needed the union as much as the union needed the hotels.

Funding for the city's growth, which during the 1960s came from the Teamsters Central States Pension Fund, helped cement hotel-union relationships. Las Vegas operated as a company town in those days and every part of the company cooperated. The hotels paid the salaries and the health care contribution and workers took those dollars to Sunrise Hospital, which used them to pay the loan from the Teamsters pension fund. The proceeds ended up in the same pockets.

Bramlet was rough and maybe even unethical. He played favorites, helping those he liked and ignoring the needs of others, and enjoyed living large. He always had a beautiful girl on his arm, and he favored Cadillacs. In the early 1970s he sported a fine set of fashionable muttonchop sideburns. They lent him a simultaneously hip and slightly menacing air, like an uncle you loved but knew enough about to fear. Bramlet maintained iron discipline through a combination of charisma and bullying. He did favors for people because he wanted to and because they built loyalty. In one instance, Bramlet personally arranged for a union widow to receive benefits even though her deceased husband hadn't qualified for them. He cultivated a dedicated cadre around him and took care of them, ensuring their allegiance with money, power, and in some cases a piece of his action in other businesses. Autocratic and blustering, fiercely competent, fixed on results, and politically astute, Bramlet was not someone to be trifled with.

There was no one like Al Bramlet when it came time to negotiate contracts. The union didn't even have a negotiating team—just Al. He met with the hotel owners himself. The owners were "working-class guys in those days," one old-timer remembered. "They were guys you could talk to." Bramlet understood that his workers were vulnerable. They could easily be replaced or made to do each other's jobs, so firm work rules, specific duties for different jobs, limits on what employers could ask of their workers, and because many of the occupations depended on tips, a guaranteed minimum tip per customer became the hallmarks of a Bramlet contract. In the lucrative banquet trade, he demanded a cut of the profits for workers. "The owners knew they were being taken," Robbins Cahill, who headed the Nevada Resort Association during the early 1970s, said. "But money came easily." Bramlet simply ensured that the workers got a piece of the pie. "Al Bramlet negotiated very good contracts," D. Taylor, a 1990s Culinary Union leader, reflected. "He had employers over a barrel." Since the cost wasn't terribly important to the bosses, the negotiations were often easy. They didn't sign contracts in those days. Bramlet shook your hand and you had a deal. No one, neither management nor workers, welshed.

Nor was Bramlet above getting tough to solve labor problems. In an open-shop state, he had only solidarity to guarantee the union's success. Bramlet made his people toe the line and leaned hard on business owners who didn't want to go along. A showroom captain once defied Bramlet's walkout order. He found himself without a job and unable to find a new one. And pity the poor restaurant or hotel who sought to get rid of the union. Bramlet threatened reluctant property owners, cajoled them, negotiated, and if none of that worked, pickets appeared. Herschel Leverton, who opened the Alpine Village Restaurant in the 1950s, claimed that one day in 1958, Bramlet told him he had fifteen minutes to sign up his workers or Bramlet would put him out of business. "Take your best shot," the owner told the organizer. Fifteen minutes later, twenty pickets started marching outside the restaurant—and they remained there until Bramlet's death twenty years later. The recalcitrant operators were fewer and fewer, and Bramlet found himself one of the power brokers in the most unusual city in the nation.

Bramlet was also prescient about the basis of his power, going to the weak and politically disenfranchised and carving out a place for them as well. Blacks loved him because they thought he was fair and honest. His right hand was Sarah Hughes, an African American woman who worked with him to solve grievances. Lucille Bryant, a maid and linen-room attendant, remembered Bramlet as "a fighter. Some of the people were saying, 'he's got a boat, four or five houses, a Cadillac, a Mercedes,'" she remembered. "I don't care what he gets as long as he takes care of us, as long as he takes care of the people. He fought the hotels for us. When he called for a strike, every door of every hotel was closed!" To the people looking up from the bottom, Bramlet was all they could hope for in an authority figure in mob-run Las Vegas. He might not have been perfect, but he was theirs. Bryant recalled Bramlet as "the Great White Father."

Bramlet earned his power the hard way. He built the union into a sizeable and powerful organization and turned it into a political force. When Bramlet became general secretary in 1954, membership stood at about two thousand. In 1967, at the time of the first major walkout, the Downtown Strike, membership topped sixteen thousand. Even though the hotels could hire nonunion workers, they generally didn't. It wasn't worthwhile. Then as now, they couldn't control either the quality or the flow of workers. It was easier to let Bramlet recruit workers and then use his union hall to screen and hire, saving the hotels a lot of money. A partnership evolved between labor and management that worked to everyone's advantage. Las Vegas still felt like a game to its players and they didn't want to mess up a good thing by getting into a public scrape that invited wider interest in their profits.

The system worked very well as long as Las Vegas retained its old flavor. Workers and owners shared a lot, even during the six days of the 1967 strike. That year, the union nearly struck the Strip, but in the end the strike was only downtown, where most of the casinos were family-owned and -operated. The strike was quintessential old Las Vegas, impenetrable to the outside world. The walkout was actually pleasant. Benny Binion, the hard-nosed Texas raconteur and gambler who opened the Horseshoe in 1951 and became a real power in the city, brought food to workers who struck his hotel. Italo Ghelfi, the owner of the Golden Gate, snuck cold drinks and smokes out to the strikers, hiding from his own security force. The familial relationships at the core of 1960s Las Vegas prevailed even over economic tension.

The onset of the corporate era, brought on by Howard Hughes and his transformation of the rules of casino ownership, altered the tacit arrangement. Unionization worked because gaming made the hotels so consistently profitable, and the union's ability to produce labor contributed to their success. After the Corporate Gaming Act, corporations brought an entirely different set of assumptions about labor-management relationships. Hilton, Holiday Inn, Ramada, and their successors took a much harder attitude toward labor and focused on making each sector of the hotel profitable. They willingly battled the union. Hughes's Summa Corporation was the leading antagonist, refusing to negotiate with labor lawyer Sydney Korshak, a powerful and slippery figure whom the Justice Department called "one of the five most powerful members of the underworld and the most prominent link between organized crime and legitimate business." The shadowy Korshak and Summa Corporation had wrangled before, and Korshak had become anathema to the corporation. But Korshak was useful. He could step in at the last minute and avert a strike for a fee, and his ouster changed local labor relations. The corporate show of force highlighted the new power in town as it simultaneously closed the door to the easiest solution to most labor disputes. After Korshak's ouster, there was no one to put the pieces together, and the familiarity between management and labor diminished. In 1968, the Culinary joined the Teamsters and the bartenders union in a strike pact. In any strike, the unions promised not to cross each other's picket lines. The handshake contracts soon disappeared. Now all the documents bore signatures. The two sides watched each other warily.

The new climate led to ongoing testing of the boundaries of the labor-management relationship. During the early 1970s posturing on both sides dominated the local scene. When a wage dispute could not be settled, a strike against three hotels in 1970 inaugurated greater strife. The Nevada Resort Association, the trade organization for about half of the unionized casinos, retaliated by closing the three hotels and declaring a lockout. Everyone faced the consequences. The Strip lost more than $2 million during the four-day lockout, the city lost $125,000, and the county $64,000 in tax revenue. The cost dampened the taste for friction, leading to a three-year contract in 1973 without incident. When that contract expired without resolution in 1976, the Culinary Union struck over a wage increase and the terms of a "no-strike, no-lockout" clause. In this first major city-wide strike, the union stayed out for sixteen days, and Nevada governor Mike O'Callaghan, the one-legged Korean War veteran, school teacher, and former Boys Club boxing coach who was the only real populist ever elected in the Silver State, mediated. State and local government experienced severe losses of tax revenue and hundreds of workers were laid off as the Strip lost money. Summa Corporation executives declared the strike "a power play between Bramlet and us." Bramlet considered the strike a victory; management conceded the wage increases and gave in on most of the other provisions.

The demise of the mob had a profound impact on the union. After 1970 power shifted away from the mob and its Teamsters pension fund money, moving toward legitimate corporate capital. More money made the old arrangements increasingly anachronistic, as the availability of enormous sums created a new scale for local development. As casino companies tapped into conventional funding, Las Vegas no longer needed mob money and the trouble its presence caused. Its people and its institutions sidled away from their old benefactors and toward their new corporate masters. As its power dwindled, the weakened mob resorted to intimidation of a kind it had previously outlawed in Las Vegas, in the end revealing how little power the mob had left.

Crucial in the old Las Vegas, Bramlet got caught in the transition to the new. By the early 1970s he owned a number of businesses that traded with the union, and some of the rank and file eyed him suspiciously. The leader appeared to forget the interests of ordinary people. At the same time, Bramlet also collided with Tony Spilotro, who capitalized on the inattention of Chicago and Kansas City mob bosses to solidify his hold on local street action. Spilotro leaned on Bramlet to enroll the local in a mob-run dental plan. Bramlet resisted; one of Spilotro's minions beat up Bramlet in a bar, breaking his ribs. Stories about funds missing from the local's pension account appeared in the local newspapers, and five local restaurants sought to decertify the union. Two of them, including the Alpine Village, were firebombed. The situation had all the makings of a mob putsch, with Spilotro pushing Bramlet out and installing his own people. The firebombings were puzzling. Bramlet was tough, but no one had ever seen him use bombs as a way to make his point, and for five lousy restaurants, when the Culinary Union membership topped 27,000?

The body count became the stamp of Spilotro's power play, and Bramlet became its most well known victim. Landing from Reno on February 24, 1977, Bramlet called his daughter to tell her he would soon arrive home. He never made it. Three weeks later, hikers found his naked body in the desert west of Mount Potosi, about thirty miles southwest of Las Vegas, his hand protruding from a shallow grave. Three men who claimed they killed Bramlet because he hired them to bomb the five restaurants and refused to pay were convicted and sentenced to prison, but their explanations made little sense. Many saw the bloody hand of Tony Spilotro behind the killing, but who killed Bramlet was insignificant in the end. The charismatic figure who built the union was gone. The strong leader left a weak organization.

The Culinary had been a proud force, dedicated to the community and to its workers. On a certain level, its accomplishments had a smoke-and-mirrors component. Al Bramlet and his combination of charisma, skill, and drive were the union. His successors were flunkies, people who exercised little imagination in carrying out Bramlet's directives before his death and who found themselves in positions they barely understood and could not master after he was gone. Catapulted to the limelight by Bramlet's murder and the complicated times they inaugurated, the new leaders contributed to the union's rapid decline.

The nadir began as soon as Bramlet was buried. Lacking Bramlet's ability and charisma, Ben Schmoutey, the newly elected secretary-treasurer, had little negotiating skill. Finally in the limelight after two decades as Bramlet's underling, Schmoutey fancied himself the foremost labor leader in the state. Few agreed, and when he lost an election for the state AFL-CIO chairmanship, Schmoutey pulled the Culinary out of the umbrella organization. Legal and image troubles mounted. News accounts linked Schmoutey to Spilotro, and when Schmoutey hired Spilotro henchman Steve Bluestein as a labor organizer, a job for which Bluestein had no qualifications, many believed that Spilotro had taken over the union. Schmoutey was indicted for attempting to bribe a Las Vegas district attorney in 1979 and was tied to the restaurant bombings. The former fry cook negotiated a contract in 1980 that hurt the union with the inclusion of a no-strike provision and enraged the other unions that had counted on the Culinary since the strike pact of 1968. When the first nonunion hotel opened on the Strip in 1979, the Imperial Palace, the membership was incensed. Leadership seemed to have given away their hard-earned gains. Jeff McColl trounced Schmoutey in a 1981 election that featured mob goons intimidating McColl supporters as they went to vote, but McColl was hardly a panacea. He lost internal support, seemingly wasting Bramlet's two decades of organizing. Membership dwindled to below twenty thousand, down almost 30 percent from the peak of Bramlet's reign just a few years before. The struggling union became a shell of its former proud self.

In the union's version of what followed, the corporate casinos picked this moment of weakness to challenge the Culinary's power. Nationwide, unions were on the run during the Reagan administration. Detroit's autoworkers were no longer a force, reduced to building the obnoxious K cars while Americans bought Toyotas and Datsuns. American steel had become an oxymoron. Rabid anti-unionism permeated the country. The Reagan administration smashed PATCO, the air-traffic controllers union. American labor was on the ropes, in its worst situation since the early 1930s. In the new climate in Las Vegas, corporate casinos no longer regarded food and beverage as loss leaders. Every aspect of the hotel's operation had to show a profit, and labor-intensive service work provided an opportunity to cut costs, translating into reduced wages and benefits. The Nevada Resort Association looked at the struggling union with glee. After years of being at the mercy of the union, management could turn the relationship to its own benefit. In 1984, the hotels offered a contract that rescinded many of the work rules that Bramlet had won, gave the NRA control of the union health care insurance fund, eliminated the forty-hour work week, and reduced tip guarantees. The sop was a minimal increase in wages.

Without support from the rank and file, McColl was in a difficult position. He could fight, but he had little support and possessed none of Bramlet's political pull. Still, no union leader could accept such terms. McColl had to fight; he publicly called the contract offer "garbage," tension mounted, and on April 2, 1984, the union struck. Management appeared united. Only Circus Circus, long a bellwether union house, flush with cash, and in the midst of enormous expansion, stayed out of the fray. Everyone settled in for a long strike. Both sides believed a loss in the battle threatened their very existence.

While the NRA appeared to be comprised of like-minded companies, serious rifts emerged that highlighted the differences between newer corporate casinos and the older family-owned businesses. With smaller operations and narrower profit margins, the family enterprises went their own way. Eighteen non-NRA casinos, most of them privately owned, settled. The corporations' influence soon dominated NRA policy, and the families that ran casinos felt uncomfortable in a fight that wasn't their own. The downtown Nevada Hotel and Casino even produced advertisements in support of the strikers. As the Hilton and MGM Grand led thirteen other houses into the strike, independent casinos positioned the Culinary Union as an ally in the battle against growing corporate dominance of Las Vegas.

The split between different types of casinos seemed likely to benefit the strike, but the results were so brutal and so murky that in the end, no one could be called a winner. The strike lasted sixty-seven days. At thirty-three days, the Hilton settled. At fifty-three days the Culinary Union agreed to a contract, but the strike continued for two more weeks as Culinary members honored the bartenders' and stagehands' picket lines. A few hotels held out. The result was chaos. Although the contract was not bad, individual workers bore the brunt of the losses. They received a wage increase, but it was not enough to compensate them for lost income. Some found their finances wrecked by the strike. Some lost homes, had vehicles repossessed, and struggled for years afterwards. Others never got out of debt.

The union was rocked too, its already diminished stature compromised. The Culinary lost six hotels, Sam's Town and the California of the Boyd Group, Elsinore Corporation's Four Queens, the Marina, the Holiday Inn South (currently the Boardwalk) and the Holiday Inn International, which became Main Street Station. The strike had been designated an economic strike, about wages, rather than an unfair labor practices action, about work practices or conditions. Under existing rules that governed economic actions, after a year, the properties could hold decertification elections in which striking workers could not vote. Management at the six refused to join the new contract, and in elections at the six hotels in 1985 the union was decertified. Striking workers watched as the hotels permanently replaced them. Nonunion workers parked in their old parking spaces, ate their meals, served their customers, took their wages, and visited their doctors. The loss was devastating. The union's weakness, the vacuum after strong leadership, had been exposed, and powerful new adversaries seemed ready to crush it. In 1985, a lot of people did not expect the Culinary Union to survive.

The Culinary's worst moments came as Las Vegas catapulted from the periphery of American society to the very center of the future. Las Vegas's nadir came in the late 1970s and lasted into the mid-1980s. Corporations increasingly controlled the town, few new hotels were built, countless renovations were stale from the onset, service became standardized in a bland way, and two disastrous fires, one at the MGM and the other at the Las Vegas Hilton, put a damper on the city's image. Between 1979 and 1981, visitation actually declined. In 1984, when I first visited the town, just after the end of the strike, Las Vegas seemed tawdry, down at its heels, and past its prime. Nothing could have been further from the truth.

What I couldn't see in 1984 was the constellation of forces that became the Mirage Phase. By 1984, the mercurial workaholic Bill Bennett had built

Circus Circus into a prime operation on the Strip, his then-protégé Glen Schaeffer had persuaded banks to provide conventional funding for casino growth and development, and Steve Wynn had begun the first casino Disneyland, the Mirage. The three thousand rooms Wynn proposed at the Mirage were almost immediately topped by Bennett's announcement of four thousand at the Excalibur, and a few years later by Kirk Kerkorian's construction of the newest MGM Grand, the world's largest hotel, at five thousand and nine rooms. Every one of those rooms needed service. Every one of those guests ate, slept, and hopefully played the tables or the slot machines. The new hotels required an army of workers, as many as five per room, to meet the needs of thousands of visitors each day.

In a bizarre reprise of Al Bramlet's original circumstances, the demand for labor far outstripped supply and the highly leveraged megaresorts needed a dependable source. In 1989, the population of Clark County, which stretched from the Colorado River at Laughlin to Mesquite at the Utah border, barely topped 700,000. Even in the worst economic years, the labor market remained tight. The opening of just the seven thousand or so rooms at the Excalibur and the Mirage meant a need for more than thirty thousand workers, and they simply couldn't be found in Clark County. For the beleaguered union, the lack of labor was a gift. Instantly, the union again became a human resources department, recruiting workers and delivering them to cooperative owners like Bennett and Wynn. The recent enemy had become a friend. No other entity could supply the labor necessary to staff the new hotels, much less maintain any semblance of quality control. Once again, the Culinary Union attained importance, this time as a partner in the new corporate Las Vegas.

Bennett and Wynn both welcomed the union, initiating a new relationship between the Strip and its workers. As late as 1986, the union was still reeling. Both Bennett and Wynn came out of the older Las Vegas where unions were prominent and valued. Circus Circus had been a union shop since it opened in 1968. Wynn's Las Vegas ties stretched to E. Parry Thomas, the financier who brokered the first infusions of bank money into Las Vegas, and were tightly woven into the Las Vegas that Al Bramlet helped create. Another motivation propelled Wynn. Like all the other casinos except the flush Circus Circus, Wynn carried enormous debt and required an uninterrupted flow of cash to meet his $1 million daily overhead. The only way Wynn could guarantee that he could staff the hotel was with the union. The new Culinary sought a partnership with management, and in a

groundbreaking five-year deal, Golden Nugget Inc., Wynn's parent corporation, agreed not to oppose union organization at its current and future
properties in exchange for the union ceding its right to economic action
against the company. Along with some changes in work rules, increases in
wages, and benefits that ensured no-cost health insurance for workers, a
partnership developed. As a result of loyalty, necessity, and desire for quality, the two most important players in late-1980s Las Vegas signed on with
the union. In the process, they revived the union's fortunes.

The decision changed the future of the union and the community.
Instead of dwindling into irrelevance, the Culinary gained strength and
status, and it more than doubled, to top fifty thousand members in the next
decade. The election of an experienced labor leader, Jim Arnold, as secretary-treasurer in 1987 helped replace recent trouble with a new vision.
When Hattie Canty, an African American housekeeper, was elected president of the union in 1990, a new leadership team apart from Bramlet's
successors took the reigns. A team of organizers arrived in 1987 to help
rebuild the union. They focused on creating a genuinely grassroots democratic process within the union, recruiting committee leaders from every
department in the union houses. When a federal judge ordered the downtown hotels that decertified the union in 1985 to pay millions of dollars in
back wages and benefits to the displaced strikers, and the union organized
a campaign that almost stymied an effort by hostile management at the
Showboat to enact a poison pill that would have protected the hotel from
the grasp of a pro-union buyer at terrific expense to shareholders, the
union again became a force on the local scene.

The first test of that new status came early in 1990, when the union
struck Binion's Horseshoe. In the 1980s, the casino industry had come
apart into two groups: the family-held and the corporate casinos. Only one
organization, the Boyd Group, which acquired larger, Strip-style properties while retaining its family-sized operations, straddled the line, but in
the late 1980s it functioned as a smaller operation. Headed by Bill Boyd,
the family casinos felt that their interests differed from the big Strip hotels
and that they deserved a less stringent contract than the one that covered
the big properties. Backs against the wall and unwilling to recognize that the
Mirage, Excalibur, and all the drawings of planned hotels raised the standard not only for service but for entertainment as well, the independent
casinos sought to turn the clock back. Rather than renovate, they tried to
cut their labor costs. After Binion's Horseshoe illegally fired the union's

rank-and-file negotiating committee, on January 19, 1990, Super Bowl Sunday, the union struck.

Benny Binion had been one of the titans of the old Las Vegas. A gambler's gambler, he founded the Horseshoe in 1951, and until he died on Christmas Day, 1989, he remained one of the venerated old men of the city despite a shady history that included a stint in Leavenworth for tax evasion. Binion's Horseshoe was an icon of the old Las Vegas. Binion displayed $1 million in a horseshoe in the door and promised to take any wager of any size, an extraordinary short-term risk that paid off in the long run. "Your first bet's your limit, sir," the Horseshoe refrain went, and a gambler, William Lee Bergstrom, once actually bet $1 million on a single roll of the dice. He lost. Binion hosted the World Series of Poker, the primary gamblers' event in the world, as well. The sheer pluck of his approach won him adherents among serious gamblers and made his operation wildly profitable. By 1990 the operation enjoyed almost $100 million in retained earnings, made between $20 million and $40 million each year, and was mostly debt-free. Binion became a political power, providing campaign contributions to candidates from the sheriff's race to the statehouse. His heirs were well positioned to fight the union if they chose.

The strike turned into a long, drawn-out affair that demonstrated the tenacity of the resuscitated union. The Horseshoe's clientele was intensely loyal, a testimony to the old man's verve, and his recent death had made them even more so. Downtown Las Vegas remained viable after the Mirage opened, but increasingly it served locals. That market had begun to change, and the Horseshoe was losing ground to the new neighborhood casinos like the Boyd Group's Sam's Town and Frank Fertitta's Palace Station. Slowly the customer base dwindled, cutting into profits. The union remained determined. Culinary members voted to double their monthly dues to pay $200 a week in benefits to strikers. In 1990 individual strikers would not bear the brunt as they had in 1984. Union strategists fended off the threat of decertification, presenting the National Labor Relations Board with complaints of the Horseshoe's labor practices. The NLRB declared the strike an "unfair labor practice strike," protecting the Horseshoe strikers. The strike could not become the pretext for decertifying the union. With pickets in front of the casino, business slumped, and by November 1990, when the Horseshoe settled, the casino's business had fallen by as much as $16 million. At its end, leaders of the union could look around and say with confidence, "We're back."

Comfortable with the new megaresorts, the union turned its attention to the family-owned casinos. The end of the Horseshoe strike sent the union out to regain hotels it had lost in the 1984 strike. The Boyd Group, which had decertified the union at the California and Sam's Town—Sam Boyd, the founder of the group, joined the strikers against the hotel as his son Bill, the new CEO, watched from a window above—had become one of the premier groups. After 1985, it acquired the Stardust on the Strip and the Fremont downtown, both mandated sales after scandals, and as gaming became national and the company went public, Boyd Gaming developed riverboats and other properties in Illinois, Indiana, Missouri, and Louisiana. It acquired enormous financial liabilities in the process, and when negotiations began, it lacked the financial capacity to weather a strike. Faced with the prospect of a picket line as it opened a new tower at the Stardust, the Boyd Group settled, and most of the downtown casinos followed. For the Boyd Group, the decision to abandon anti-union tactics was pivotal. As it mirrored the actions of the megaresorts and formed its own partnership with the union, the Boyd Group catapulted from the periphery to a central position in the multiproperty market. For the union, the contract was one more triumph, along with the addition of five thousand new members from the opening of the Mirage, Excalibur, and others, demonstrating that the Culinary was back to stay.

If the old union faced its Armageddon in the 1984 strike, the Frontier strike became its equivalent for the new union. As the corporate Strip grew more glorious, the older properties along it became a golden trap for a city looking to redefine itself. They were a drag on the transformation into tourism and entertainment. Small and generally owned by individuals or family corporations, they could not compete with the megaresorts. They offered cheap and even nearly free food and drinks, but their real appeal remained gaming, slots and table games. Margaret Elardi and her two sons, Tom and John, entered this situation when they bought the Frontier and the Silver Slipper from the Summa Corporation in 1988.

Margaret Elardi was a Las Vegas story, someone who through sheer determination built a small empire that she ruled with rigidity. She called her family business Unbelievable Inc.; *Gambling Magazine* once called her a "grande dame with brass knuckles." Parlaying her retirement from her husband's contracting business, she arrived in Nevada as part-owner of the Pioneer Club in downtown Las Vegas. She sold that property and bought the Pioneer Hotel and Gambling Hall in Laughlin, Nevada, a miserable little resort town nestled between the Colorado River, I-40, and the coal-fired Mohave Generating Station, one of the leading sources of air pollution in the Southwest. The union never took hold in Laughlin, and wages and working conditions were awful. In Laughlin, some workers lived in their cars in the extraordinary heat. Laughlin was so bad that the union often pointed to it as prima facie evidence of the reasons for organized labor in Las Vegas. Laughlin catered to the low-budget crowd. That market received little in the way of amenities, but Margaret Elardi fashioned her club into the most important property in the little town. She sold out in 1988, before the area was overbuilt and before Indian gaming took off. Elardi took her $112 million stake and brought her low-budget, scrimping mentality to the Strip.

It wasn't a good moment to try to turn the clock back. Las Vegas's visitation soared after the Mirage opened, reaching 19 million in 1991, and the new visitors wanted more than just gambling. When the Elardis came in, they tore down the Silver Slipper and turned the Frontier into a grind joint, a casino with little in the way of amenities. Siegfried and Roy, on whom Steve Wynn staked the entertainment revolution in Las Vegas, had been the mainstays of the Frontier's showroom. Under the Elardis, the room was dark. It was a telling distinction. The Frontier was filled with slot machines. There was no entertainment and nothing resembling the amenities elsewhere on the Strip. It was a cheaply run casino for the desperate, even if it was on the Strip.

Margaret Elardi's cost-cutting extended to every facet of the operation. Like the older family-owned casinos, the Elardis shaved their costs, and labor became their target. Their actions precipitated the strike. On September 21, 1991, after the Elardis illegally implemented new work rules, cut pension contributions, slashed wages by $4 an hour, and switched health care to an inferior plan that made more than a hundred workers ineligible, the Culinary Union and three other unions struck the property. The Strip had been firmly union throughout the 1980s, and the union had just regained respectability. The Frontier strike was a showdown of mythic proportions.

The union's position in 1991 was much better than it had been in 1984. The corporate revolution was a fait accompli. Up and down the Strip, huge properties were under construction. Union membership had grown by more than fifteen thousand workers since its early-1980s nadir. With Circus Circus and the Mirage in the fold, times were good. Even the political machinery, usually anti-union in Nevada and decidedly so in both the 1984 and the Horseshoe strikes, opposed the Elardis. The notoriously anti-labor Las Vegas *Review-Journal*, a newspaper so far to the right that it made the *Washington Times* look liberal, counseled a quick end to the strike. Under these circumstances, the union could muster the strength and continuity to fight with one little hotel, and the battle could help it reclaim its power. The Frontier strike was a proving ground for the revived Culinary. The flinty Elardis unwittingly cemented the links between the union and the new corporate Las Vegas.

The Elardis proved as determined as the union they faced. For more than five years, they refused to give an inch and even alienated other Strip hotels by paying for advertisements in the Los Angeles papers that made it sound as if the union was striking every Strip hotel. The Elardis rejected calls for mediation, and when Nevada governor Bob Miller appointed an experienced mediator to seek a compromise, the Frontier participated only under duress. Miller shook his head and publicly denounced the Frontier's intransigence. The Elardis became such renegades and reflected so badly on Las Vegas and gaming that the other hotels assisted the Culinary. Bill Bennett of Circus Circus sent his company's food truck to feed the strikers three times a day. The gesture showed how well the partnership between labor and management worked and how disgusted the big players had become with the Elardis, but it did little to resolve the strike. Even a 1995 ruling by the Ninth Circuit Court of Appeals that the Frontier's changes were illegal and strikers were entitled $60 million in compensation for their losses did not deter the Elardis. For almost two more years, they resisted the state, the federal judiciary, and the union. "One day longer" became the union's rallying cry. The strike lasted six years, four months, and ten days. Late in 1997 Phil Ruffin, a Wichita, Kansas, investor who owned a dozen Marriott Hotels, worked with Culinary Union general president John Wilhelm to buy the hotel and settle the strike, and early in 1998 they ended the rancor at the Frontier. "I believe we're going to make a big success out of this project," Ruffin told reporters after the state gaming board granted his license. Labor was certainly behind him.

The first ever Local 226 Culinary Shop Stewards Convention opened with a flourish in June 2000. The theater at Cashman Field, the Triple-A ballpark—cum—community center was packed with raucous delegates and it sizzled with energy. The meeting had the intensity of a political convention and a lot more flair. It was loud and Latin-flavored; Gloria Estefan blared over the speakers. Seventies-style soul followed. People danced in the aisles as the day began, hugged, and clapped each other on the back. The room looked a lot more like the future than the past. More than half the people in the room were African American, Latino, or Asian; almost two-thirds were women. Headsets provided translation in Spanish, although for some of the speeches they didn't need it. A lot of power and more than a little pride filled the room.

The gathering was organized like a national political convention. Each union hotel had its standard and each group presented a standard-bearer to tally their numbers at the extended roll call. Hilton, MGM, Mirage, even Aramark, the commercial food service provider at UNLV and many other institutional settings, and EG&G, one of the primary contractors at Yucca Mountain and the Nevada Test Site, were represented. The roll call went on, with cheers for each hotel. The union's position had become so strong that most of the stewards asked for the day off and got it from their properties. The MGM, once the scene of a huge battle to unionize, presented a delegation of 118. The cheering reached a crescendo.

Then, union organizer D. Taylor stopped the action and called the workers from the Rio Hotel, across I-15 from the Strip, to the stage. When the Brazilian-themed Rio opened in 1990, it was the hottest place in town, the one that gave the Strip back to the locals—though just a little to its west. Locals loved the Rio. Built by Tony Marnell, of Marnell-Corrao Associates, the company that built most of the new Strip with union labor, it became a staple, a real value for anyone who wanted the amenities of the Strip but fewer tourists. With suites instead of rooms, with the Carnival World Buffet, quickly the favorite buffet in the *Review-Journal*'s annual poll, and cocktail waitresses in skimpy costumes, the Rio epitomized the new Las Vegas: fun, chic, and a genuine value. Consistently rated a best value by Zagat, the Rio found a niche in the market. After a $200 million addition that made the little Brazil into Mardi Gras, with Fat Tuesday every two hours in an airborne parade called the Masquerade Show in the Sky, *Travel & Leisure* declared the Rio the best hotel value in the world. Its $79 a night suites compared favorably with the cost of the second-highest-rated MalaMala Game Reserve in Africa at $1,148 a night.

The new status made the Rio a takeover target, and in 1999 one of the largest casino companies, Harrah's, engineered a $767 million buyout that made Marnell and another Rio executive, James Barrett, the largest individual shareholders in Harrah's. Harrah's was excited about the buy. The company was among the largest gaming concerns, but it had only a few more than five thousand rooms in Las Vegas. The Rio operated without a union, and even though Harrah's was a union shop, the Culinary had reason to worry. Harrah's owned twenty gaming properties, but only three were unionized. Difficult negotiations indicated that the Culinary had an opportunity at the Rio, but they were likely to have to fight for it.

By late June 2000, when the shop stewards' convention took place, the Culinary's fears had become reality. Harrah's revenue at the Rio didn't even reach half of their projection. At first, the shortfall was attributed to an unusually low hold, casino parlance for an unlucky quarter when gamblers took home a disproportionate share of wagered money. Typically investors don't punish gaming companies for an occasional quarter of low hold. Gaming is a risky business, made more so by the introduction of Baccarat, James Bond's favorite game, with its dizzying ebb and flow. Sometimes players walk away with lots of money, and earnings waver. It's just life in gaming, fluctuation in the market. But the slowness in retained earnings persisted. Analysts attributed the shortfall to the migration of high rollers to competing properties. The MGM had just opened its fabulous Mansion, and other properties featured better restaurants and shows. The Rio had perfected a niche. It offered the best luxury experience for the middle-class dollar, but despite all its accolades, it wasn't truly a luxury hotel. Off-Strip, it was more of an Oldsmobile than a Mercedes. The cash-flow problems changed the hotel, and Harrah's reassessed the desirability of a relationship with the Culinary. When the union tried to organize the Rio, management leaned heavily on workers, singling out immigrants for pressure. Immigrant women especially felt the company's pressure.

Seventy members of the Rio Organizing Committee came forward to tell of their desire to unionize. I watched as they crowded the stage and saw row after row of people, more women than men, mostly Latinos, Asian, and African Americans. These were the parents of the middle class of the future, people who wanted to send their kids to college, who'd sacrificed more than the rest to be here—they alone among all the stewards had not been given a day off to come to the convention. No cheers in the course of the day were louder than the ones that the crowd gave up for the Rio organizers.

The stories they told could have been out of an earlier anti-union time, the days of Taft-Hartley or the 1980s, when immigrants were roundly despised and unions were on the run. These tales of people struggling for decent life pushed every emotional button I had. Mercedes Castillo won the lottery to get out of Cuba, came to the United States, and got a job as a porter at the Rio. When the union organizing drive began, she volunteered. Three months pregnant, she told the crowd in Spanish—this time the translators spoke English—she helped sign up workers and was threatened by a manager. A campaign to harass and intimidate her and other organizers began. She was roughed up, suspended, then threatened with termination. "It is impossible to intimidate me," the translator repeated her words. "I know my rights."

Castillo was the union's dream spokesperson, an attractive young woman who came to the United States from a place that wasn't free, only to find the kind of intimidation Americans associate with Russia at work in their own backyard. That she'd become so American so fast—"I know my rights," she'd said—was testimony to both the power of American ideas and the triumph of the individual even in the guise of collective action of a union organizing drive. She and other Rio workers, Poasent "Andy" Duangrudeeswat, a cook who'd struggled all the way up from poverty in Thailand and spent a couple of years sleeping in the bathroom of a Los Angeles gas station, among them, stood, hearts bare, as standard-bearers in a revolution of work in the United States. These were the newest Americans, to whom America unselfconsciously meant opportunity. They thought nothing of twelve- or even sixteen-hour work days and saw work as the opportunity to climb in socioeconomic standing and increase their choices. They valued work, they sought fair wages. It seemed only fair.

Early in 2001 the Rio quietly went union, but the Culinary's plate held other battles. Although the union's alliance with the corporate Strip remained close, fissures existed. Some corporate hotels avoided the union, and the Culinary battled for its position. The rapid growth of the 1990s was a double-edged sword. There were far more members of the Culinary in 2000 than there had been a decade before, but there were many more nonunion workers on the Strip as well. Even though the history of the union clearly indicated that hotel casinos that brought in the union made money and that those that didn't had a much harder time, some owners still did not believe that the union provided value as well as consistency in labor. After its many successes, the union still faced the recalcitrant Venetian, Sheldon Adelson's understaffed anti-union shop. The new Aladdin opened without a union contract on August 17, 2000, the project so far in debt that it seemed that its desire to exclude the union stemmed not from animosity but from a simple lack of cash. The MGM's contract expired in November 2000 and after an attempt to decertify the union failed, an agreement came easily. The victories were substantive and meaningful, but the battle would never be over. The aftermath of September 11, 2001, led to almost fifteen thousand layoffs in the hotel industry, and the Culinary scramble to provide social welfare and to encourage hotels to rehire as soon as possible. No matter how much ground the union gained, there was always another battle, another struggle, another fight. Watching the triumph of the Rio workers foretold a new reality taking shape in unskilled American labor. At more than fifty thousand strong, the Culinary Union really was the last hope for blue-collar workers in America.

In this respect, Las Vegas answers a question that vexes much of the rest of the nation: what to do with the large number of people whose skills have little relevance in the postindustrial age. Long the core of American society, stable home-owning voters, these people have been the losers in the move from industrial to postindustrial economy. Las Vegas's unionized economy and its high wages for service positions rescue such people and give them a chance to make their children's lives better. As a result, Las Vegas retains a stable middle class, where ordinary people with ordinary skills can make enough money to live a decent life. This model served American society well; its resuscitation in Las Vegas's form or any other will help stabilize the economic rifts in American society and lay the basis for a prosperous and more tenable future.

CHAPTER 4

Freedom and Limits in a City of Pleasure

THE MEDIA CALLS A LOT THESE DAYS, MOSTLY ON VERY SHORT NOTICE. One afternoon, a crew showed up from the Travel News Network, an outfit that produces those ninety-second travel shorts broadcast at the end of local news programs. They were excited, interested, and really into it. We did a filmed interview in a hotel room and then they wanted me to show them the Strip. Off we went.

We drove up and down the Strip, the camera following me as I narrated and pointed out the window of the car. We talked back and forth, cameras rolling, about the hotels, their history, their prospects, what visitors might find there, about how the Strip had become an incredible economic engine. Finally we parked and walked around, cameras still rolling, in front of Bellagio, across the street at Paris Las Vegas, and by Caesars. The questions were sharp and focused and the day was exquisite. I couldn't imagine a better opportunity to explain the new Las Vegas.

Outside Treasure Island, we stood on the wooden walkway, and the energetic on-air reporter fired a few questions at me with the camera rolling. I looked around to make sure we were in the clear—the hotels are private property and they require permission from the PR office to shoot on their property. Because the Strip tour was not planned, I hadn't called.

This could have posed a problem, but we were on the wooden sidewalk, what I assumed was public property open to anyone, on the street side of the manmade lagoon where the Jolly Roger pirate ship and the British man-of-war battle hourly. In the middle of the interview, I felt a tap on my shoulder. I turned around and looked up—way up. Glowering down at me was a very large security guard who wanted to see our permit. I grinned sheepishly and tried to charm him. I have a good relationship with all the hotels. They sort of know me, some follow what I write about the city, and a few try to do me favors, which I always decline. I don't take comps, free rooms, meals, or tickets, and they seem to respect that.

Under Steve Wynn, the Mirage group had always been easy to work with. They promoted much more than just gaming and were always happy to have anyone who understood that they were in the entertainment business talk about them. I was sympathetic; the volcano and the pirate ship, Siegfried and Roy's tigers, and O, the newest Cirque de Soleil show were all part of my repertoire. Our lack of permit here would be no problem, I thought. We could work this out. I tried to tell the guard about my contacts in the PR office, but he wasn't buying. No permit? You have to leave. As a last resort, I said, "I thought we were on the public sidewalk here." He smiled a wry smile and took me by the arm to the street side of the upraised wood platform eight feet above the traffic below, pointed over the edge to a thin ribbon of concrete at street level inches from moving traffic. "That," he said emphatically, "is the public sidewalk."

Since the individual rights revolution of the 1960s, Americans have again contested the meaning of freedom. The 1960s gave us freedom as the right to do, in postmodern America, whatever we want, wherever we want, however we want, whenever we want, and with whomever we want. This "freedom to" greatly contributed to the cultural revolution that made Las Vegas seem normal. When what had once been a vice became a choice, the overarching pressure of generations of neo-Victorian morality lifted its weight from even the middle and upper-middle classes. Individuals, not their pastors or the PTA, set their own moral compasses. They defined their own standards instead of taking their cues from a larger, amorphous, but clearly articulated culture. In the process, they redefined the boundaries of freedom.

As a city built on personal prerogative, Las Vegas is a funny place to discover the next stage of this revolution: the transformation of the idea of "freedom to" into "freedom from," the ability to use the idea of individual freedom to regulate and otherwise limit the prerogatives of others when

they are offensive or threatening. In this sense, "freedom from" is not freedom in the conventional American sense. It is its selfish descendant, when
freedom means the right to have the world the way you want and everyone
else's choices be damned. "Freedom to" bred "freedom from." One could
only lead to the other as individual rights superseded community sanction
and personal obligation. When anyone could see anything as a right, there
had to be some way to exclude, even control. In a confessional culture, where
readmittance to what passes for polite society hinges on the approval of a talk
show audience after the transgressor confesses on air, the only way was to
change the definition of space. After the end of legal segregation, the law no
longer functioned as a tool to exclude. Only commerce and the American
obsession with private property could draw such exclusive distinctions.

This construction, "freedom from," which a crime- and now terrorist-
fearing nation has often contemplated as a solution to the woes of a society
that demands experience and encourages personal expression, crystallized in
corporate Las Vegas. In a town where there is little public space for meetings
or play, where government is weak on its best days, private entities fill the
gaps left by authority to serve a useful function while appearing to have long-
standing commitment to community. In Las Vegas more than anywhere else
in the United States, the line between public and private space blurs and the
boundaries become indistinct. You can stumble across them with the best of
intentions. That's how I got thrown off of Treasure Island's private sidewalk.

Las Vegas has always faced a dilemma. When you cater to other people's sins,
you have to control not them, but yourself. Can't have the help acting like the
patrons, even though for the longest time they did. The casinos used to be
filled with off-work employees. Old-timers claims that in the old days, dealers were often players on their own time. People would finish their shift, take
off their tuxedo and bow tie, walk out from behind the table, slap down a fifty,
and sit in a chair on the other side. That's why they were in Las Vegas. They
got paid so they could play. But, he insisted with a knowing look, they could-
n't make it through a day off without their tips so they came into work every
day, scheduled or not. With the help of the unions, the hotels eventually
secured contract provisions that forbade employees from playing where they
worked. Ways to maintain that distance, to caution and discourage locals from
hanging out, became part of local culture.

But these rules weren't legislated by government. They came instead
from agreements between labor and management. Nevada's traditions as a

state were anti-government. Libertarian heaven, a place where people left each other alone, was the Nevada of lore. The state had long been poor, and its leaders believed that the government that governed least—and especially least expensively—governed best. Nevada's government couldn't be too picky, couldn't afford to stand in the way, as some thought state government in California, Massachusetts, New York, Minnesota, Wisconsin, and even Washington State did. Without the mills and plants of industrial America, how could Nevada attract new industries? The same way the rest of the Southwest did: by letting business do entirely as it pleased.

In such a climate, developing institutions that put any conception of the larger public good ahead of the rights of private commerce was a quixotic endeavor. Anything the private sector wanted to do that governments usually did—pay for streets and traffic lights, for example—was fine with the county commission or the Las Vegas city council. Since holding the line on taxes was civic religion in the Silver State, when business paid, government had one less thing to fund. It seemed a sweet deal for all involved, a sop to the remarkable business climate in Nevada, both evidence of the state's accommodationist tendencies and an explanation for the businesses' enthusiasm setting up operations in the desert.

Even in the best of times, government in Nevada is ineffectual and parsimonious, a handmaiden to power. The state's odd tax structure, simultaneously invisible and powerfully regressive, is one of the primary culprits. Nevada has a constitutional amendment against a state income tax, barring the most reliable revenue source available to most states. In most of Nevada, you can't find your property tax with a microscope, but in a sparsely populated state, even paltry property taxes were a mainstay of state revenue. In 1981 Governor Robert List abruptly changed the structure of state taxation. Property taxes were higher in northern Nevada, where he lived, and his friends owned large parcels of land, taxed by the acre. Beholden to the casino industry, like most Nevada politicos, List feared a Proposition 13–like anti-tax revolt in Nevada; just two years after Howard Jarvis and Paul Gann engineered the revolution that ultimately destroyed California's ability to serve its citizens, List could feel a cold wind blowing. He believed that cutting the property tax rate would ensure his reelection, and he fancied himself a supply-sider, following the skewed logic that said that lower tax rates would increase investment. At his behest, the state legislature lowered the property tax and then raised the state sales tax.

List badly miscalculated. He catered to the north and let the cash cow in the south suffer, as had politicians throughout the century. In the first salvo of what one southern politico called in 1999 a "fifteen round fight now in round three," the strategy blew up on List. What played well in the north bombed in Las Vegas, where homes had lower valuations and smaller parcels. The increase in the sales tax seemed like a personal income tax to southerners with their higher incomes and more lavish spending patterns. The gaff cost List reelection, and left the gaming tax, the lowest in the nation at 6.25 percent, and sales tax as the bases of state taxation. Seventy-five percent of the states revenue comes from two sources, making state revenue eternally unstable and leaving the state perennially on the brink of financial chaos. It hit home first during the 2001 legislative session, when the already meager state budget was adjusted downward by $121 million as the public squalled.

Regressive taxation meant that the state sloughed off responsibility and handed it over to the counties, and while no one ever suggested that the Clark County Commission was rational, it responded as rationally as it could to the stricture to build for itself. When developers offered to build something the county was supposed to, the commission simply let them. It saved a lot of money, and throughout Nevada's history, such distinctions made little difference. But during the Mirage Phase, the ante went up, and with it the need for greater control of image. Managing image meant control of access, which in turn guaranteed struggles about what was public and what was private space.

The second MGM Grand was as close to a privately funded megahotel as Las Vegas had ever seen. Billionaire Kirk Kerkorian built the property. He'd been a leading player on the Las Vegas scene since 1969, when he parlayed a share of Caesars Palace and his sale of Trans-World Airlines into the construction of the $80 million, 1,512-room International Hotel, at the time the largest in the world. Kerkorian sold the International to the Hilton chain, which turned it into the Las Vegas Hilton, the place where Elvis Presley played endlessly and spent his nights in the penthouse shooting out the lights on the Hilton sign. After the International, Kerkorian built the first MGM Grand Hotel in 1973, again the largest hotel in the world at the time, with 2,200 rooms and at a cost of $106 million. Intensely private, Kerkorian has offered little insight into his motivations, but when the $1 billion, 5009-room new MGM Grand opened in December 1993, it was once again the biggest in the world. Kerkorian and his immediate family owned 73 percent of the stock, and given his penchant for hands-on management, it was certainly privately managed.

The president of the newest MGM Grand was an old union-hater, Robert Maxey, an engineer with a long career in both financial management and casinos. He'd been senior vice president at First Western Financial in Las Vegas and then attached himself to Steve Wynn's rise. He and Wynn had a falling out. Maxey left, ending up as CEO at the Elsinore Corporation, the owner of the downtown Four Queens Hotel, where he extended the 1984 city-wide strike for fifteen months until he decertified the union in July 1985. At the same time, Elsinore reported nearly $3 million in losses at the Four Queens and more than $30 million in losses at its Atlantic City property, the Atlantis. Within a month of Maxey's resignation in October, Elsinore filed for Chapter 11 bankruptcy and remained insolvent for a decade. His operation to get rid of the union was a success, but it killed the patient. But that didn't derail Maxey, who earned a reputation for successfully opening new hotels, a difficult task that kept him in executive positions. A couple of stops later, Maxey opened the nonunion Rio and went on to open the MGM.

At the MGM, Maxey wanted nothing to do with unions, refusing to negotiate with the Culinary. In 1992, a full year before the hotel opened, Maxey broke ranks with the other leading gaming companies and promised higher wages and better benefits to entice employees to eschew unionization. He planned to offer the roughly four thousand MGM employees whose jobs were unionized at the other Strip hotels a better benefits package than the union contract specified. The MGM would have an in-house medical clinic, Maxey announced, a flextime vacation package, and a company pension plan. The reinvigorated Culinary Union, less than a decade from the devastating 1984 strike, had to fight. On December 17, 1993, pickets lined up outside the MGM as the property opened to the public. Union organizers stuck to the sidewalks, assuming they were public property. They were as wrong as I had been at Treasure Island.

Maxey had outfoxed the union. In 1991 he hired a leading land attorney to write an ordinance that permitted the hotel to build its own sidewalks on its own property. Two years before the opening, on December 17, 1991, the Clark County Commission approved a traffic participation agreement that contained a requirement for a private sidewalk. There didn't seem to be anything nefarious about it. The decision was typical of the county commission, a way to save a few taxpayer dollars. The right-of-way remained public property, and presumably the county could build its own sidewalks. But why should it? The hotel had already built wide, attractive ones that teemed with pedestrians even before opening night. In Nevada, when a municipality could lay off costs and services on private business, it did. The request was standard operating procedure, sanctioned by the history of government in Nevada. If the MGM wanted to pay for a sidewalk on the Strip, why on God's green earth should the county commission stop them?

None of this was a problem until union organizers stood on the sidewalks to protest Maxey's nonunion paradise. The MGM announced that since its sidewalk was private property, it would not allow union demonstrations on it. When almost five thousand people, including Governor Bob Miller and other politicians, showed up on opening night, the police refused to let them assemble on what everyone assumed was public sidewalk. Booted off private property, the union filed suit, and Nevada's deputy attorney general, Chuck Gardner, wrote a scathing report that determined that the state had allowed the MGM to own the sidewalk with safeguards that permitted passage for all. Gardner excoriated not only the MGM and the county, but the most prominent law firm in the state, Lionel, Sawyer, Collins, architects of the statute. Despite Gardener's opinion, the court ruled that since the county required MGM to create a private sidewalk to save taxpayer money, government could not require that the MGM offer a public forum.

Americans have long assumed that sidewalks belong to everyone. Almost everyone has heard stories about people discovering that the ground between the sidewalk and the street belonged to the municipality and not the homeowner. Public space is an American virtue that dates back even before Frederick Law Olmsted and Central Park, an idea embodied in national parks and that was central to the Civil Rights movement. In public space, there are no favorites. It belongs to everyone all the time. The sidewalk serves as the archetype for public space, and no clearer image of 1960s-style "freedom to" could be found. The battle over the MGM sidewalks went well beyond the union's rights. It also addressed the obligations of government to the people of the state.

Private sidewalks offer what Americans now desire: the ability to make private space free of anything they find offensive. Even more, the property owner retains the right to determine who uses the space. Private sidewalks provide "freedom from"; they give control over the outside world at the expense of civic rights, a sure sign of living in a society dominated by fear. They also exclude on the basis of private property, an old refrain in American law. Private property rulings let segregation flourish. In 1883 the U.S. Supreme Court ruled that while states could not discriminate, private property owners were under no similar compunction. This distinction became the basis of legalized segregation in the United States. The motivation of the MGM, to exclude the union, was far less onerous, but the battle over sidewalks became a reprise of a century-old debate in American law. As in the nineteenth century, private property had been allowed to supersede civil rights because of weak public culture. Racial discrimination didn't result, but some narrow version of class warfare seemed likely.

On Memorial Day weekend in 1994, the union staged a massive sit-in at the MGM. Thousands of Culinary Union workers, their families, friends, and activists from across the country carried tiny American flags and clogged the sidewalks. MGM security men in blue blazers stood behind signs that declared the sidewalk private property as union loudspeakers blasted Bruce Springsteen's "Born in the U.S.A." to a crowd that included a large number of immigrants. "We got real sensitive about music right after that," laughed Glen Arnodo, the Culinary Union's political director. After a brief rally, the marchers submitted to arrest. In groups of forty, the police hauled them away as tourists watched from behind the barricade. After five hundred arrests, the police stopped. Hundreds of union protesters complained that they too wanted to go jail, but the police refused. No more seats on the bus to jail, no more arrests.

The moment was a combination of public relations and symbolic warfare, designed to let the MGM Grand know that the union wouldn't roll over. It energized the union and provided the MGM workers with a different vision than the one the company was offering. Wages were no longer the only workplace issue. Workers told of arbitrary cuts in hours—one woman went from eighty hours in one two-week pay period to twenty-seven the next—and they valued the security, the privileges of seniority, and the camaraderie of the union. After the arrests, the union filed a lawsuit that charged that the county, the MGM, and county manager Pat Shalmy conspired to deprive union members of the right to free speech. The battle continued to a standstill, but market economics provided the union with a victory. As a nonunion hotel, the MGM didn't make much money. Maxey again sacrificed financial health on the altar of his anti-unionism. After its first year, revenues were flat, operating income fell, and Maxey was booted. J. Terence Lanni, former CEO of Caesars World, who was more favorable to unions, replaced him, and the hotel became a union house. A year later, the MGM produced a 525 percent increase in net income, and the MGM's stock price doubled. The sidewalk remained private; the hotel became a union shop. Go figure.

. . .

Noxious is in the eye of the beholder, and to Steve Wynn in 1999, the smut peddlers who hawked graphically vivid images of outcall escort specialists in front of resort properties were truly obnoxious. At Wynn's newly opened Bellagio, his genuine attempt to take Las Vegas beyond gaming, on the beautiful promenade he'd built, Wynn didn't see why his visitors should have to endure tawdry pornography agressively handed to them by sleazy people. In a city with more than a little sexual exploitation in its fabric, Wynn built the Bellagio to be the casino where women would be comfortable, where the spaces and the amenities would make them want to stay another day. But in front of the hotel, on the sidewalks he built under the same ordinance as the MGM, smut peddlers disseminated lurid pamphlets, making a mockery of Wynn's vision.

Wynn was outraged. Over a lavish breakfast at his exclusive $48,000,000 Shadow Creek Golf Course, he vented his anger at smut peddlers. They were tacky and indiscreet, an affront to the dignity of women. They held the city back, limited what the Bellagio and indeed Las Vegas could and should be. By 1999 he'd tried everything to stop them. His lawyers worked constantly for a solution, but none was forthcoming. The very freedom that made Las Vegas also made it possible for smut peddlers to disrupt Wynn's vision and cut into the future he planned. Las Vegas could overcome the stigma of gambling, but it couldn't forbid the exercise of even noxious First Amendment rights. The issue drove him to distraction.

It is impossible to think of the old Las Vegas without thinking of sex. The image of the city was purposefully risqué, an effort to enhance its status as the first city of sin at a time when Las Vegas served as an outlet for the nation's excesses and a scapegoat for its moral shortcomings. The combination of mob roots, gambling, and distance from the norm made the city the place to be for people looking to get laid. Even though Las Vegas's legalized prostitution ended during World War II and a number of postwar prostitution scandals brought down local law enforcement officials, exploitative sex was part of what brought people to Sin City—and what they bought into by coming.

As with every other commodity, sex is displayed more openly and less modestly in Las Vegas. It commodified the risqué and gave it a quirky place in culture. If you believed that Las Vegas was a zone where sin was impossible, its public displays of sexuality were respectable. After Minsky's Follies, the city's entertainment took on an adult cast. The big extravaganzas came to be known as "Las Vegas shows," and everybody knew what that meant: topless. The last of them, Jubilee at Bally's, struggled to survive in 2000 before reviving in 2001.

Titillation was the norm in 1950s and early 1960s Las Vegas, and sex was even more widely available. The mob world from which so many gamblers came was filled with available women—gun molls or dames in the popular literature—and sex became part of the appeal of Las Vegas, personal prerogative in a space outside of morality. Showgirls dated high rollers, and an active and seemingly independent world of prostitution flourished. Individual women made fortunes as prostitutes, asserted Ralph Pearl, the city's premier gossip columnist during the era. Ian Fleming, the creator of James Bond, so admired Las Vegas that he included it in *Thrilling Cities*, his paean to the exotic. Fleming reveled in Las Vegas's openness, comparing it to other cities without the normative rules of disintegrating Victorian culture: Singapore before Lee Kuan Yew, Macao, Havana before Castro. Fleming understood Las Vegas in that frame. He glorified it, stretched and changed it, but he recognized in it a social scapegoat, a place where Americans could distance themselves from the society they created. *The Green Felt Jungle*, the classic 1960s Las Vegas exposé, called Las Vegas "one huge whorehouse" and announced that 10 percent of the city's 65,000 people were involved in the sex trade. Although authors Ed Reid and Ovid Demaris sounded indignant, they did little more than whet the public's appetite for more salacious exposés. Even boosters like Ralph Pearl couldn't help but use sex to sell their stories. Before it was fashionable to explicitly market sex, Las Vegas excelled at its commodification.

The American cultural revolution, the constellation of behaviors and practices that hit conventional America with full force in the 1960s, transformed commercial sex in the United States. Once the "new morality" hit, selling the image of sex became easier. As Hugh Hefner's *Playboy* magazine and subsequent empire provided men with a model for sex without commitment and Helen Gurley Brown's *Sex and the Single Girl* and her revamped *Cosmopolitan* magazine gave women a similar message, Victorian mores finally collapsed. The birth control pill freed women from the constraints of historical morality. Without the threat of pregnancy, personal behavior really became a private choice. Properly managed, it did not have to have consequences, and after *Roe v. Wade* in 1972, it theoretically didn't even have to be managed. With the stigma removed, the American middle class exercised its desires. Young women no longer guarded their chastity with the supposed vigor of old, and as they became more amenable to the entreaties of young men, sexual transaction became social rather than commercial. Even more, communities soon set their own standards. Court cases established local standards for obscenity, which translated as grudging permission for public sexuality. After the *Miller v. California* decision in 1973 that established a three-part standard for pornography, a community's level of tolerance became the governing standard.

With liberalized law and technological innovation, the modern sex industry was born. The VCR was catalytic. Pornography on videotape became widely available. People could watch porn in the comfort of their homes and often could rent it nearby. Home camcorders meant that anybody with a little money could put their own kinkiness on tape and keep it for themselves or sell it as widely as the traffic would bear. The porn industry became massive. Wide exposure to pornography again softened community standards and further enhanced demand. The proliferation of "gentlemen's clubs," a euphemism for the high-dollar, upscale strip clubs that cater to businessmen, couples, and even women, followed and became places to be seen as well as to see. In 1990 a national stripper's convention at the Sahara became an HBO special. By the late 1990s Internet pornography services accumulated unbelievable numbers of hits from consumers. The sex industry had gone upscale and acquired pretensions of respectability.

By any American measure, Las Vegas was tolerant. Its public displays of sexuality and the way it accepted casual and commercial sex made it a natural for the sex industry. Porn stars soon called Las Vegas home and some even found semipornographic work in town. Linda Lovelace, the star of the 1972 pornography classic *Deep Throat*, starred in an ill-fated dinner theater production, *My Daughter's Rated X*, in 1976. Porn star Veronica Hart was eventually revealed to be UNLV theater student Jane Hamilton, a Las Vegas native. Jenna Jameson, who struck porn gold with a nude appearance in Howard Stern's *Private Parts*, hailed from nearby Boulder City. With adult superstores all over the valley, the Yellow Pages listing 105 pages of adult entertainers, the emergence of gentleman's clubs, and the array of topless, nude, and other sex clubs throughout the valley, and in 1999, 46 of every 100 businesses housed on the world wide web, a trend observers believed reflected the predominance of cyberporn, Las Vegas offered a mature sex industry as public sex became more widely accepted.

When the sex industry discovered the Consumer Electronics Show

(CES), it became even more visible. Since the 1970s CES had been the most important trade show for electronics, drawing cutting-edge industry types as well as the usual hangers-on. Plenty of them were easy marks for adult entertainment, and adult entertainers flocked to town during the show. The porn industry added its own trade show and faux academy awards to coincide with the CES each January. In 1993 the organizers staged a free speech fundraiser that was simultaneously a live sex show at an off-Strip adult bookstore. The place was packed and the audience ate it up, but the police didn't find it funny. They moved in and arrested the performers. The existence of the zone without sin did have limits. You could look, but you couldn't touch. If you did, the performers and the proprietor were arrested, not you in the audience.

By 1997 the porn industry found even more lucrative timing for its meeting. Comdex, the giant computer show, brought in 250,000 of the most puzzling conventioneers around. Unlike the cowboys who came for the National Finals Rodeo or the rappers and NBA stars who followed the heavyweight boxing circuit, the computer geeks had none of the obvious Las Vegas vices. They didn't drink much and they sure didn't gamble. The hotels adjusted to their profile. During Comdex, hotel rates in Las Vegas paralleled the rest of the nation. A room that could regularly be had for $89 was $250 or more. The hotels had to make their money some way.

But Las Vegas will find your weakness, and the largely male entourage of computer geeks had a clearly evident one: sex. Saddled with the image of being pimply faced nerds with pocket protectors and desperately wanting to be suave, the male prototypes of the dot-com revolution wanted girls, girls, girls. AdultDex, what reporter Joe Schoenmann called "the illegitimate child of Comdex," emerged as a profitable outlet during the most unusual week in the city's year. In 1997 excitable computer types pressed into the third floor of the Imperial Palace for AdultDex '97. Among them were a number of undercover vice police, who issued nine citations during one of the shows. Seven were for "lewd and dissolute conduct," a misdemeanor that occurred when some of the vendors bared their breasts. The final two, for performing a live sex act, was handed out to two women who touched each other on stage. The arrests came, Vice Sergeant Robert Duvall told the press, because AdultDex did not require entrants to prove they were of age.

This conventional free speech issue pushed the buttons of libertarian Las Vegas. AdultDex really was an exercise of constitutionally protected speech, loosely defined. It was also offensive to many. But Las Vegas's history and tradition of tolerance dictated that such behavior had to be tolerated. After all, the porn industry's trade association was called the Free Speech Coalition, a concept that defined the old Nevada. The *Review-Journal*, the local daily, well to the right of the mainstream press, but libertarian in its political outlook, defended AdultDex as free speech. It ran photos from the porn confab on page one, a decision that brought some criticism from the larger community already on the demographic road to normality. The new Nevada was prepared to look the other way in the best state tradition, but it didn't want to confront the adult industry on the front page of the paper. When local columnist John L. Smith defended the decision to run the photos, a barrage of letters to the editor hammered him. With all the in-migration, Nevada's tolerance had become something new; "freedom to" had become "freedom from," at least for some vocal members of the public.

There were other defenders of public morality out there in southern Nevada, not the least of which was the Clark County Commission, the governmental entity that benefitted most from the growth of the valley. Late in 1996 a draft ordinance circulated that would have banned "off-premises canvassing," the practice of standing on a public sidewalk to hand out leaflets or fliers advertising a business transaction. Despite Nevada's hardcore tradition of personal freedom, most politicians and the Las Vegas Convention and Visitors Authority (LVCVA) board enthusiastically supported the ordinance. Although the measure didn't specify adult entertainment, it did relieve the city of one major embarrassment during the transition to mainstream entertainment. Being handed material from outcall services or legalized prostitution in nearby counties clashed with the veneer of respectable entertainment like theme parks and roller coasters as the city shed its past and reinvented itself once again.

There was also a class dimension to the handbill issue. A lot of the people passing them out looked poor and many appeared to be immigrants. A significant number were Latinas or Asian women, often with young children in tow. They reflected the lack of choices of people at the economic bottom. In New York in 1910 they might have sewed shirts in sweatshops. In Las Vegas in the 1990s they handed porn to upper-middle-class tourists, reprising the old class hierarchies of early-twentieth-century America. The women Steve Wynn wished to protect came from far more comfortable circumstances.

Despite Nevada's libertarian traditions, a move against the handbills was no surprise. The state remains an oligarchy, and in a place where money dictates and conventional power meekly falls in behind it, the big money lined up against porn on the street. Despite the state's pretensions, freedom in Nevada first and foremost meant freedom for big business to do as it pleased. The illusion of freedom extended to smaller business concerns and even individuals, but Heaven help them if they got in the way of the big boys. The purveyors of gaming and their own classier but still risqué entertainment sought to stop the advertising of smaller, sleazier operators, and no mere law could make them back down. On January 22, 1997, the county commission voted unanimously to ban the distribution of handbills on the Las Vegas Strip.

The battle lines were clear, if perplexing. On one side stood most of the power in Clark County; Glen Schaeffer of Circus Circus told the county commissioners that his customers "have a right to feel safe" and "not be harassed" near hotel property. Public officials echoed Schaeffer's sentiment: "We need to make Las Vegas Boulevard a showplace, not a garbage dump," said county commissioner Lorraine Hunt, who went on to become lieutenant governor in 1998. "We want to make it an enjoyable experience, free of harassment and intimidation of people." In opposition stood a few handbill companies, an anonymous man who was referred to by his own attorney, JoNell Thomas, as a "major smut peddler," and the ACLU. The scenario had all the makings of a David and Goliath–style showdown. Opponents asked for a temporary injunction, but when U.S. District Court Judge Lloyd George ruled, he followed local power as much as law. He denied the motion for an injunction in early March and the ban took effect. Stunned, opponents appealed George's decision to the Ninth Circuit Court of Appeals in San Francisco, which remanded the case back to George and ordered him to issue an injunction banning enforcement of the law pending a trial. Even though the case remained in litigation, the law did not achieve its social purpose. Even temporarily, it failed to stop the handouts.

The county ordinance was questionable from its inception, proof that power brought inchoate arrogance that couldn't see beyond the county line. Clark County got creamed in every subsequent court hearing. In August 1998 the Ninth Circuit Court of Appeals overturned the ordinance. Early in 1999 the county wrote a new ordinance to circumvent the ruling. "We ought to give this [approach] one last try," Commissioner Erin Kenney remarked as she moved to approve the new ordinance. "If this doesn't work, we're going to have re-evaluate what we're doing here." It didn't work. Chastened by the appeals court's reversal of his earlier decisions, Judge Lloyd George promptly declared the new ordinance "over-broad" and ordered the county to remove its anti-handbill notices from the Las Vegas Convention Center. "I don't consider it an obscenity case," the judge said. "I consider it a First Amendment case." After George's decision, there wasn't really anything the county could do. The most powerful industry in Clark County had been defeated by a bunch of smut peddlers.

The handbill controversy really was about much more than distributing sleazy pamphlets. Because the entire debate focused on public spaces, off-premises canvassing became closely linked to the larger but more amorphous discussion about the sanctity of private space and the growing preference for it over conventional public spaces. In public spaces, even political heavyweights couldn't exclude activity, and they well knew it. But casino owners couldn't get their patrons into their carefully designed private spaces without crossing public space, a First Amendment gauntlet where any guest could be hassled and their experience disrupted. At its core, Las Vegas was a script for the visitor: every major operator worked to fashion their script so that visitors left their concerns behind and found themselves center stage. The process had to be controlled from beginning to end, and people offering handbills at the entrance to imagined paradise intruded in a way that threatened every other dimension of the experience.

This measure of control was particularly important for Wynn, who was the master of this process, as well as such a perfectionist that some thought of him as a bully. During the 1990s Wynn's needs ran the state; nearly every politician kowtowed to him and in most cases his vast power carried the day. Wynn was classic Las Vegas, a curious mix of benevolent captain of industry and sometime tyrant who bent the state to his will. No one invested more in the quality of visitor experience, in making private feel not only public, but friendly. State law influenced the pattern. In Nevada until 2001, all gaming space has to be open to the of-age public. Million-dollar baccarat hands were theoretically as public as nickel slot machines. Wynn's approach was born of a desire to transform experience, the key feature of the latest transformation of Las Vegas.

It was commonly assumed throughout the 1990s that what was good for Steve Wynn was good for Las Vegas, but even he couldn't get handbilling stopped. In a one-industry state, its primary industry's most important purveyor spent enormous political capital and millions on lawyers. Though Wynn told people he would do anything to solve this problem, even he could not get around the First Amendment. Despite efforts to curtail the

First Amendment across the nation, exclusion remained an all-or-nothing proposition. Either you could exclude everyone or no one. Public space is "still the place where some guy can stand on a soapbox, shout what he wants to, hand out what he wants to and if the tourists don't like it, that's the price we pay for freedom," observed Allen Lichtenstein, an ACLU attorney. "It doesn't mean that harassment can't be stopped or littering can't be stopped." The alternative was insidious to conventional definitions of freedom. "If in order to prevent First Amendment activity, all government had to do was quitclaim the sidewalks to private enterprise," Lichtenstein insisted, "there'd be no place in the town, in the world, where people have the right to express themselves. That's a scary thought."

Well before the 1990s, downtown Las Vegas had a serious problem. The old Glitter Gulch, the place where people spilled from the train depot into the streets of Mammon under the waving hand of Vegas Vic, the neon cowboy in the sky, had been overshadowed by the Strip for a long time. After the construction of Caesars, the Aladdin, and Circus Circus in the mid-1960s, visitation tipped toward the Strip. By the 1980s corporate money dominated the Strip, and local money, much less of it, resided downtown. The Mirage Phase made the differences even more stark. Downtown couldn't compete. Most of the downtown hotels were small. None even resembled a megaresort. They lacked space, glitz, and amenities. By 1990 downtown served a niche market of one kind or another. While the Strip built theme parks and attracted families, serious low-dollar gamblers, locals, and people who liked the old days, the looser slots, and the cheaper buffets and meals, came downtown. Fremont Street, the heart of Glitter Gulch, was funky. It felt like a real city instead of a movie set, a relic of the past, with casinos that opened into the street. The million-dollar horseshoe in the entry to Binion's Horseshoe and the ever present ninety-nine-cent shrimp cocktail at the Golden Gate were its trademarks. For a while, downtown housed Las Vegas's only reggae and blues club. Street people hung out, panhandlers sat with palms up, and streetwalkers in high boots and ridiculous get-ups paraded up and down. Simultaneously Glitter Gulch had the feel of the 1960s, when homelessness and vagrancy seemed almost cool, anti-materialist statements against the prevailing values in American society, and the 1980s, when they were frowned upon as a failure of the individual. Fremont Street felt like a carnival, a boardwalk, a place of nighttime recreation in the American memory—except with slot machines and a little more sleaze than you'd want your kids to see.

As the city spread out, the area around Fremont Street deteriorated. Once the center of town, it had been given over to the official functions of the county and city. Las Vegas is the county seat, but that's meaningless in southern Nevada. The county clerk's office was there, with its always packed marriage license bureau. Even today, people come to Las Vegas to marry. The day before Valentine's Day, the line for marriage licenses stretches around the block, sometimes three times. Las Vegas's high rate of marriage skews the demography for the entire West. To the south of Fremont Street, along Bridger Avenue and a few blocks to the south, the town's original California bungalows stood, turned into law offices, and sprinkled with urban blight. It didn't have quite the same kind of problem most American downtowns have, that you could shoot a cannon off after 5 P.M. and never hit a soul, but most people in downtown Las Vegas in the evening—excepting hookers and the homeless—weren't locals. Downtown was populated by tourists and by the people who preyed on them, and that was not the image 1990s Las Vegas wanted to project.

Downtown suffered from some of the problems of similar public spaces around the country. The old middle class, the people who lived nearby in the 1940s and 1950s, had long since fled. In their place came commercial use and lower-income people, and the street scene of the early 1990s followed. Latinos became more prominent. To the east of Las Vegas Boulevard on Fremont Street stood a block that I call the Bodega. It looks like the business district of any South American city, or of almost any port in the world outside the United States. Small businesses selling all kinds of goods abounded, large hand-lettered advertisements in their windows. People walked along the street, customers and owners haggled over prices, and traffic stopped in the middle of the road for no apparent reason. The block had a vibrant hustle and bustle that reminded me of Caracas, Haifa, Manila, even Athens. The signs were in English—mostly—but the nature of the area's commerce felt international. I expected to see old men with worry beads, the rosarylike strands favored in the cafés of Greece, and felt sure to hear Arabic or Turkish along with the Spanish so common in the American Southwest.

East of the Bodega, Fremont Street slopes downhill, and it was hard not to construe the physical descent as a metaphor for social decline. The Metropolitan Police Department headquarters stood prominently, and both the Bodega and Glitter Gulch sported officers on mountain bikes. The El Cortez was across the street. Bugsy Siegel got his Las Vegas start by buying the El Cortez, and the mob accelerated into Nevada because he turned a 27 percent profit on their investment in six months. Now the El Cortez is the bottom, the place where newly trained dealers start and leave as soon as they can.

From there it was down the hill, to rent-by-the-week motels that sold package liquor, liquor stores and check-cashing storefronts, bawdy street-walkers even in daylight, low-level drug trafficking—the pathos of humanity on the street. Only the Las Vegas backpacking hostel broke the detritus of decline. The freshly scrubbed kids, even those with dreadlocks who looked like they belonged in the area, who walked toward Glitter Gulch sporting their backpacks were clearly different from the people they strode past. While not the poorest area in Las Vegas, east Fremont Street filled with people who had either just arrived, eager to grapple their way up the ladder, or those who couldn't escape the grip of poverty and their own demons.

The grittiness of the area intrigued some, but it was also threatening, hard to sell in a town that had been promising better than real for three decades. As greater Las Vegas upscaled throughout the 1990s, the seediness of Fremont Street lost its appeal to the new constituency. Panhandlers and streetwalkers increased, and downtown didn't seem like the new Las Vegas, sanitized to keep your fears away while pushing you to your desires. The casinos downtown were really just grind joints with specialty entertainment. Even the downtown restaurants, once among the most renowned in the city, were overshadowed by the nationally known chefs on the Strip. Hugo's, in a cellar of the Four Queens, once the city's premier gourmet dining experience, could not compete with Aureole at Mandalay Bay or Picasso at the Bellagio. Only the Golden Nugget, the first property in Steve Wynn's empire, could match the Strip for elegance, but it seemed like something out of a Graham Greene novel, a declining Saigon, a stultified Carribean. The rest were filling small niches; the most surprising of these was the California Hotel, a Boyd Group property, which catered to Hawaiians. Sam Boyd had worked in the islands as a young man in the 1930s and retained an affinity for Hawaii and its people. Walking into the California was like disembarking in Hawaii. The smells and sounds were of the islands, the people the same marvelous polyglot, and the restaurants even served poi, the taro staple of the island diet. A statue of the Buddha graced the lobby, its belly shiny from people rubbing it for luck. Hard to sell to the American mainstream, the California held a solid and impene-trable niche, the real key to success in downtown Las Vegas.

FREMONT STREET

Redevelopment of Las Vegas's core had been an ongoing theme since the 1960s. In the 1960s downtown Las Vegas did not face urban renewal, but it was already in transition. After the opening of the Boulevard Mall in 1967, locals drifted away and did their business elsewhere. The parallel migration to new homes west of the interstate and behind the mall in the early 1970s accelerated the trend. Downtown became a place for visitors, and stores that stocked souvenirs and kitsch did better than those that sold groceries and sundries. The solution proposed was a typical 1960s response: a mall, in this case no more than one block in length, that permitted north-south traffic flow. Little happened.

The idea of the mall didn't go away, resuscitated in 1975 and again in 1986. In 1975 the Downtown Hotel Association retained consultants who trumpeted a new vision of downtown. They too favored a mall, but as more than simply a boon to business. The ambitious plan featured a sports arena, a public park with amphitheater and museum at the location of today's Cashman Field, a greenbelt, development of the Union Pacific's railyard, and revitalization of the downtown core with the mall and a series of construction projects. A 1986 plan echoed the same values, albeit in a climate that emphasized the shift from locals to tourists. The 1975 plan sought to accentuate the existing street. The overarching theme of the 1986 plan was revival. If either had been implemented, downtown would have been different. Without any action, by 1990 downtown's fall was obvious to anyone who looked.

The growth on the Strip and the changing demography of visitation were the catalysts of downtown's decline, and the early 1990s provided a unique window on the chaos that an enormous shift can create in a changing business climate. After Benny Binion's death in 1989, most downtown properties had shifted from their founders, men like Binion and Sam Boyd, to the next generation. In 2000 only Jackie Gaughan held on, still firmly ensconced at the Union Plaza, while his son Michael ran the Gold Coast, the Orleans, the Barbary Coast, and the rest of their empire. The younger men had been raised to be local aristocracy, privileged since early in life and accustomed to accommodation by government, the law, and even people on the street. They took their crowns with zest, only to find new kings just up the road, building enormous palaces that, from the point of view of the old-timers, blurred the town's perception of downtown's importance.

The downtown hotel owners had one entity that they could count on, the City of Las Vegas. Far less significant than the Clark County Commission, Las Vegas city government still had admirable access to resources. Unlike the Strip, located in the unincorporated county, downtown fell within the boundaries of the city. Saddled with debt, watching their share of the local market dwindle, and unable to secure the financing that Strip moguls found with ease, downtown casino owners followed the path of so many American oligarchs in decline in so many towns across the nation: they looked to an entity with taxing power that they could control. It was their last stab at retaining the power their parents once wielded.

Discussions began in the mid-1980s, but no coherent redevelopment plan resulted until October 1993, when eight downtown casinos founded the Fremont Street Experience Company. With help from the Las Vegas Convention and Visitors Authority (LVCVA), the company created a public-private partnership with the City of Las Vegas to redesign downtown and return it to its historic vibrance. As with the sidewalks at the MGM, they had to make law accommodate their desires. In 1993 the state legislature increased the room tax at the downtown hotels that stood to benefit from the development and followed with a bill permitting a pedestrian mall on Fremont Street. A total of $70 million in capital improvement money was raised, $27.6 million from the City of Las Vegas and $8 million more from LVCVA, which designated the Fremont Street Experience a public recreational facility in order to make the allocation. The funds allowed the partnership to hire noted architect Jon Jerde, catalyst of Minneapolis's Mall of America, San Diego's Horton Plaza, Los Angeles's Universal Studios CityWalk, and Rotterdam's Beursplein, to transform five blocks of Fremont Street, from Main Street to Las Vegas Boulevard, into something—anything—with allure for visitors.

Famous for his ability to create liveable urban environments, and using "the communal experience is a designable event" as his motto, Jerde grappled with urban space that was more small town than big city. Downtown had once been the city center, but that time had passed. Local observers such as the prescient Geoff Schumacher, then editor of *City Life*, had long argued that *downtown* was a misnomer, a description of location alone. The city's real downtown was the Strip itself, the skyline that defined the city and the hub from which its economic activity emanated. An equally strong argument could be made that Las Vegas didn't have a downtown at all. The valley had become a series of interconnected and competitive commercial zones that grappled for dominance of geographical sectors of the valley, demarcated by the presence of the local chain, Station Casinos. You knew you were in another sector when you saw the next Station property. In this view, Las Vegas was many cities masquerading under one name.

By the 1990s downtown certainly wasn't where locals went to take care of their daily business. Fremont Street catered almost exclusively to tourists. Gift shops and convenience stores dominated the spaces casinos and hotels didn't fill. Government was the only other industry downtown. Bail bond offices were close at hand. The housing that surrounded the area was mostly lower-income. Located near the junction of the two main arteries through town, I-15 and U.S. 95, downtown seemed trapped by its environs.

Jerde touted his ability to create attractive and livable space, and in downtown Las Vegas he designed and built another of the projects his detractors revile. The plan malled off five blocks of Fremont Street, destroyed the street-level architecture, and converted a bona fide urban streetscape into a sidewalk with pushcarts. But this wasn't CityWalk in Los Angeles, with Universal Studios behind locked gates next door. This was Las Vegas, where every attraction had to compete with every other one.

Jerde tried to rescue the endeavor with glitz. Ninety feet above the street, a five-foot-deep, forty-four-foot-wide canopied frame sported a light and sound show that covered four blocks: 7.8 megawatts of power lit 2.1 million light bulbs in a computer-generated light show of animated images controlled by computer; 540,000 watts of sound completed the show, filled with strobe lights and images. It sounded impressive. In daylight, the canopy looked like a great big circular chain-link fence in the sky.

When I went to see the show, I came away underwhelmed. As soon as the lights went down, everyone stopped and looked up. Music blared. Images shot across the frame. All I remember now is a series of animated buffalo—I think—stampeding across the sky. When it ended, I looked at my friends and said, "That's all? For $70 million?" Nor was I alone in my confusion. Peter Michel, director of special collections at UNLV, observed that the Fremont Street Experience "looks like a shopping mall in Dayton, Ohio, trying to do Las Vegas." The project brought in almost twenty thousand onlookers each day, but it didn't staunch the decline of casino revenues downtown. The show simply wasn't all it was cracked up to be. Jerde's planning made the Experience a B-grade attraction in a town where an A-minus routinely fails.

The project had other important dimensions. When the Fremont Street Experience opened in December 1995, it already had in place one of the preeminent goals of its planners, a series of city ordinances that included prohibitions on solicitation and complete exclusion of panhandling within the four blocks under the screen. The company could also charge admission to the area. With the complicity of government, a sort of welfare project for downtown hotel owners had remarkable social ramifications. It privatized public space with public money, permitting the exclusion of behaviors that were endemic in the area but were noxious to property owners. Allen Lichtenstein, of the ACLU, shouted that the Fremont Street Experience claimed to be a private building by virtue of putting the four-block chain-link fence in the sky, but no one seemed to hear him. The city gave the keys to the property to the hotel owners, admitting that it was abdicating responsibility for the streets. It also created an "order-out corridor" in downtown, in which anyone arrested for prostitution or minor drug crimes could opt for a suspended sentence on the condition that they stayed out of the area for a fixed time. Although this was purported to cut crime around the Fremont Street Experience, in reality order-out functioned liked a broom, sweeping street crime to nearby areas. The combination created a space out of place. While physically downtown, the Fremont Street Experience was no longer there. It was, like so many of Jerde's projects, a faux downtown that happened to be surrounded by the real downtown.

At the time, no one really noticed. The public-private blurring was so typical in Las Vegas, the idea of common good so remote, and the antipathy for government action so great that the failures of the Fremont Street Experience went relatively unremarked. On local television, Mayor Jan Laverty Jones called the area "Las Vegas's town square"; on a national television documentary about Las Vegas, she said that the Fremont Street Experience created the "world's largest casino." Her two different positions were irreconcilable, but since nobody's freedom was affected (at least no one's who counted), few cared. "Freedom from" triumphed, and with the typical Nevada flourish, eyewash for the mind, the deal was done.

There were a few who protested, but their actions were symbolic. In 1995 the city council voted to let the Experience hire its own security force and restrict access for special events such as New Year's Eve. The city retained the right-of-way to Fremont Street, further confusing jurisdiction. No one really knew whether the Experience was public or private. In 1997 Joseph Cartino, vice president of the Laservida Arts Cooperative, organized an activity, a "picnic in the park," designed to test the status of the property. The LVCVA designated the Experience a park, so the broadsides read, "Come frolic in Las Vegas' newest park." Cartino was skeptical. "Everybody knows that it's really a big tourist trap," he told reporters. "They're passing it off as a park, so we're testing the whole idea." Sensing a trap, Fremont Street Experience officials did not rise to the bait.

The cheers turned to boos on New Year's Eve, when the Experience charged admission to the area. The law permitted the charge, and it was just like paying to go to one of the hotels or a swank private party, spokesmen protested. Look at the benefits, they blared. You can walk on the streets and not be hassled. We'll have our security force protect you. All you have to do is pay the twenty bucks to get in. We'll even give you a glass of champagne. But the public disagreed, steaming about being charged to use public streets that they'd paid for—that the law had made private, or at least nonpublic—in a public process that most ignored. The same vaunted Nevada individualism, the quasilibertarianism endemic in the Silver State that let people think that privatizing space wasn't a bad idea, had the opposite effect when people found out that "private" could mean they had to pay to get in.

This battle brought the ACLU in a hurry. The ACLU had fought such battles since the 1960s, and in 1997 it sued the City of Las Vegas over the ordinance that prohibited solicitation on the public-private space. "We think the whole damn law is unconstitutional," thundered Gary Peck, the ACLU's executive director in Nevada. "We will fight it all the way to the Supreme Court if we have to." Peck and the ACLU contended that the agreement between the city and the Fremont Street Experience Company restricted all First Amendment activity except company-sponsored events. This, the suit alleged, "attempted to redefine the Fremont Street Experience's essential character as a public forum." It made public space truly private, in Peck's view, illegally overriding the protections of the U.S. Constitution.

The ACLU's appearance spoke volumes about the changing vision of rights in American society. Closely associated with the Left, the ACLU became the champion of the second generation of the rights revolution, the libertarians, property-rights advocates, and others who embraced the doctrine of "freedom to." In the way that long hair on men migrated from 1960s elites to the blue-collar, take-this-job-and-shove-it types in the 1980s, the political Right became heir to the left-leaning tradition of individual expression inherited from the 1960s. The American cultural revolution, far less bloody than its Chinese counterpart but equally transformative, offered the now hackneyed cliché "do your own thing." But doing your own thing in the terms of the 1960s young was really an interior exploration, an internal activity that took on outside traits. Especially in the West, the inheritors of that idea, many of whom were dismayed by the extension of rights to people they didn't much care for, took the soft edges of 1960s rights and made them absolute. Never mind that Paul Revere and the Founding Fathers would have recognized the right of the individual to be free only within the constraints of the community. In the late 1990s freedom truly meant individual rights *über alles*. Those who embraced that interpretation of the First Amendment differed from the advocates of free speech during the heyday of the rights revolution. Instead of wanting to fix government, as had most of the activists of the 1960s, these new rights activists feared government, blamed it for the chaos that they felt ruined their lives and their society, and wanted to dismantle it and live in a state of armed, near anarchy. To them, the rights of the individual were the only ones of consequence.

The ACLU had another equally powerful rebuttal. Although it escaped notice in Las Vegas, the bastion of free-market capitalism, the city had given away $30 million to create not public, but private space. Recouping that sum from the tax revenues might happen, but it would take a long time. Questioning whether the city could give away taxpayer dollars and property rights together prompted more inquiry. The LVCVA money, the $8 million earmarked for a public park, complicated the city and the company's position even more. The LVCVA had to designate the Fremont Street Experience "public recreational space" before it could give the project money. "It's parochial to think of a park as a field or a baseball diamond," observed Mark Paris, president of the Fremont Street Experience, in a self-serving assessment. But a public park meant that the space was open to the public and that the traditional rules of free speech in public places applied. "They want to call it a public park in order to pay for it," Peck observed, "but then they give authority to a private security force to regulate it." Attorney Chuck Gardner offered an even more direct challenge: "I don't know how the city attorneys can oppose the complaint without violating their oath to uphold the Constitution," he told reporters.

The U.S. District Court did not see the issue in clear terms. In an April 1998 decision, Justice David Hagen decided that the Fremont Street Experience was not a traditional public forum, but it wasn't entirely private either. He deemed provisions banning leafleting and message-bearing merchandise unconstitutional. "The purpose and use of the mall today is revitalization of downtown business," Hagen wrote, "by promoting commercial activity in a safe convenient relaxing pedestrian environment." The decision allowed the city to make the distinction between what it regarded as good and bad public speech. The law allowed unions to leaflet, but no one else could, changing the terms of the battle that had occurred on the Strip. Las Vegas mayor Jan Jones gladly permitted unions, but she didn't want pornography. She had already tried to drive casino executive Herb Pastor's strip joint, the Girls of Glitter Gulch, out of downtown. "If the union's right to leaflet opens up the door for pornographic literature," Jones noted, "that's something we'll have to look at." Both sides claimed victory: The provisions had been declared unconstitutional, pleasing the ACLU. The city and the Fremont Street Experience were ecstatic because the development was not considered a traditional public forum.

The nexus of American law has always been the intersection between property rights and personal freedom. The Bill of Rights lays out individual freedom, but ever since the Constitutional Convention closed its eyes and held its nose about slavery in 1787, American law has been about property. When private property was pitted against individual rights, the right of property owner proved paramount. This made the designation of the Fremont Street Experience as public or private crucial. If it was private, the owners enjoyed certain rights to restrict behavior. If it became public, the plethora of freedoms protected in American law prevailed.

Hagen's decision was based in economics. Since the Fremont Street Experience promoted a more vital downtown, the state could permit it to restrict activities even if they impinged on its public status. Hagen did not address the ways in which the transfer of public space to private hands with public money might constitute dereliction of duty, nor did he engage the dangers that resulted when a free society allowed "freedom from" to exceed "freedom to" in law and practice. The case followed from the Slaughterhouse cases of 1873, which ruled that while states could not discriminate on the basis of race, creed, or color, the court could not forbid individual property owners from doing so. The ACLU appealed.

A practical test of the ruling followed when a religious activist, Amy Donaldson of Progressive Campaigns, and four colleagues were detained by three Metropolitan police officers in front of the El Cortez. The "Fremont Street Five," as they were called, were told that they were being detained under a 1968 case, *Terry v. Ohio*, which permitted holding people to search for weapons if police suspect criminal activity. Donaldson and four others had been soliciting signatures on petitions. When the officers released Donaldson and her friends after an hour, they were told not to return under threat of arrest. They came back with an ACLU escort a few days later. The police observed but arrested no one.

Hagen granted an injunction against the city that permitted leafleting at the Fremont Street Experience, but in October 1999 a group of teenagers passing out leaflets as part of a national protest against police brutality were accosted by police and FSE security guards. The officers threatened to arrest the students and showed one a laminated card with an ordinance that defined leafletting as illegal. Gary Peck of the ACLU was outraged. "There is a real breakdown in the system at Metro," he told the press. "These officers are in violation of a federal court order and it needs to stop now."

Public and private space had blurred, tangling the First Amendment between them. Nevada and Las Vegas's libertarianism proved only skin deep. It protected business, but at the Fremont Street Experience it protected individuals only when coerced by the courts or public opinion. The privatization of formerly public space proceeded, not only in Las Vegas, but around the country. People chose to abdicate their rights in favor of the perception of safety. Law leaned away from communal and community goals toward the enshrinement of local oligarchy. Economics trumped civil rights.

In this regard, Las Vegas pointed the country to a place that the nation might not want to go. In a state that never really grappled with the rights revolution—staunch Nevadans said they didn't need to because in Nevada you were freer than anywhere else in the nation—the new vision of American rights, as protection for liberal consumerism, creating safe, clean environments devoid of noxious behavior, led to a cumulative trouncing of individual rights. In a series of incidents, the police exonerated officers who threatened, harassed, or otherwise impinged upon people passing out leaflets in downtown Las Vegas. It was Kafkaesque, and some feared tht the actions were harbingers of a more tightly regulated state, a fear made worse after September 11, 2001. The protection of liberal consumerist freedom over constitutionally enshrined rights of free expression in Las Vegas meant substantially less freedom, which ran directly counter to the city's image of itself.

But if people didn't care, who was going to stop the curtailment of First Amendment rights? Most Las Vegans and indeed most Americans had become willing to sacrifice rights for safety and comfort, "freedom to" to attain "freedom from." Nearly everyone in Las Vegas found the pornographic solicitation pamphlets disgusting, but the courts ruled in favor of dissemination. People wanted to be free of nuisance in the short term. Most just didn't think about the long run.

The weak institutions of Nevada and its libertarianism have given way to another problem of potentially great proportions, I thought as I sat in a police substation in the suburbs, attending an organization's meeting. There wasn't much in the way of public space anywhere for any purpose, forcing community organizations and nonprofits to meet in unusual places. Most logical places for the sewing circle or book club didn't exist or were booked all the time, and it took a certain amount of creativity and cooperation from local businesses to make the wheels of civic-mindedness turn. One organization in which I participated held its meetings in an eye doctor's office; later, we moved to the patio of a coffee shop that belonged to friendly business owner. Some car dealerships built community centers into their showrooms. They added playrooms for kids, diners, and short-order restaurants that were designed to be fun—one suburban Ford dealership opened a Mustang Sally's diner on its premises—and some even advertised for nonprofit and other civic groups to use their meetings rooms. Startup churches routinely met on the university campus or in public schools. I once gave a talk to a VFW post gathering in a hospital. On another occasion I spoke to midcareer professionals in an assisted living center for seniors. Only on rare occasions were conventional public spaces, public libraries, churches, or community or senior centers, available for such gatherings.

This in itself may seem benign, but it is indicative of a larger trend in American society of which Las Vegas is the most pronounced example. As government loses its luster, the services it once provided, essential to the concept of community, are being parceled out. In a liberal consumerist society, they're handed to people who can make money from them, commercial entities that seek to bring people through the doors. The creation of public-private space attributed an ostensibly civic purpose to a commercial activity; before long the commercial motivations show through and take precedence. Without civic options, these services fall de facto to people with economic goals that at least equal any civic objectives they possess. The result is a democracy of dollars, a place where commerce serves all of our needs in myriad ways.

There's nothing inherently wrong with this scenario—except for its implications about who we've become. There isn't a common American culture anymore, no dominant set of values that dictates norms. The ones we had we threw out in the 1960s after they collapsed under the weight of their own inconsistencies, but their replacement, a rampant and often malignant individualism, doesn't do much for knitting ties between individuals or communities. The decline of civic culture is everywhere, observers like Robert D. Putnam, author of *Bowling Alone* proclaim, and to a certain degree, they're correct. We're not really bowling alone, though. It's more like the parallel play of small children performing nonintersecting dances and glancing out the corner of their eye to see who's watching.

There's no shared space left in American society. In postmodern America, we insult each other in traffic and think of it as communication. Public spaces are open to all, but in a society where we lack faith in government and the ability to talk across fences, that openness is inherently threatening. Polls show that Americans think the tolerance inherent in the First Amendment needs to be tempered. Too much sex and violence in the media, asserted Paul McMasters in *Media Studies Journal* in 2000, have prompted Americans to wonder whether the community's need to maintain order and set limits might supercede the individual's right to express themselves. People have already announced that fear by voting with their feet. Scared of the world they created, they've abandoned the public for the semipublic and the private. They've found what they feel is a better scenario: private space designated for public purposes, which seems a mild compromise if "freedom from" is your goal. This is the type of reasoning that enshrined segregation, that led to the privatization of sidewalks, and that created private space with public money.

But the situation is very comfortable. Sunset Station, one of the ubiquitous Station Casino chain, contains a multiplex movie theater, an ice cream store, a supervised area for children to play, half a dozen restaurants ranging from a coffee shop to high-end dining, bars and a nightclub, and an outdoor stage. It's fun and not at all threatening. There's no sense of being compelled to gamble, although a lot of people do. Instead it feels like a shopping mall. Devoid of civic space, Las Vegans use such private commercial space as public space, a style of use that casino executives and others who point to the value of gaming as an industry tout as an advantage. It costs the state nothing, they say, and in fact generates that paragon of Nevada revenue, sales tax. Station casinos are friendly to everyone, and all kinds of people like them. They were the first chain to include an interracial couple in their television advertising. This subtle portrayal—Las Vegas's sense of freedom extends to personal relationships in ways that don't occur so easily in other places—deftly nodded toward a local reality that most advertisers avoid. So what's wrong?

The use of private space as public space masks something insidious, a combination of the many flaws of government and the hidden pressures that are ripping American society apart. In public space, the postmodern definition of freedom—the right to do as you want, whenever you want, however you want, and with whomever you want—holds. All kinds of obnoxious behavior, from people handing you pamphlets for prostitutes and outcall services to pounding boomboxes with amplified bass, are legal and grudgingly tolerated. In private or controlled public space, whether it's a casino, an airport, or a mall, that isn't the case. The property owner retains the right to exclude as long as that exclusion occurs in an impartial manner. If they forbid by activity instead of by appearance or skin color, the law will uphold their decision. In a public park, you do have to worry about who is out there, who might impose upon you in all kinds of ways. You have to share space in a fashion that requires that you and others regulate the space for yourselves. You have to trust the people around you to live by the same rules as you do. There's no arbitrator, no handy authority to march out and rule against someone who refuses to leave you alone. You have to sort it out yourself.

But in private space, especially in a casino through which millions of dollars float on a daily basis, there are rules and there are arbitrators. Make so much as a hard and fast motion toward someone else, and the eye in the sky will alert a number of the large, suit-coated men whose job it is to make sure everyone gets to play unmolested, and they'll pounce. The offender will be removed from the area and probably from the premises so quickly that whatever happened will be a brief interruption in the eternal quest for excitement. Private space permits security, a comfort we associate with a rose-colored past of shared values and avid citizenship. It was also a shared past because many were excluded on racial, ethnic, religious, and other esoteric grounds, and because the people who determined the values of common culture could enforce that through media, with the law at their back, and if necessary with the force that only wealth could buy. After thirty years of the triumph of individual rights over community, in an era that has scrapped notions of common values, the public spaces have become maddening. It's the private spaces that now articulate privilege and prerogative, that offer privacy and security, that let people be free enough "from" to do as they please.

In this sense, the new public-private and truly private spaces that Las Vegas has engendered are the equivalent of commercial gated communities. In Nevada casinos are open to anyone of legal age. You can enter, but you can stay only as long as you conform. There's a Big Brother atmosphere. The cameras, the eye in the sky, and the security officers are watching, creating an illusion of safety along with that of the perceived danger that seems to insist upon their presence. You're safe from whatever lurks in or out here. Enjoy yourself, secure in the knowledge that you're protected by private security, which keeps you safer than the state can promise to do.

This division is a step on the road to a very different society. Turmoil in the American economy broke the middle class into two distinct groups, the large downwardly mobile cohort of the old middle class and the professionals and entrepreneurs who pushed upward. The 1990s restored prosperity, placing a premium on the trappings of privilege, on the ways people can make themselves distinctive. Even with the uniform crime index on the decline, Americans fear people unlike them. With immigration at an all-time high and the fallout from September 11, 2001, the association is clear.

Everyone knows their rights; few understand that they come with obligations. Once people widely perceive that the protections of the private sector are better than those of the public, "freedom from" will triumph over "freedom to" and democracy will never be the same.

PART II

Filling Las Vegas

CHAPTER 5

The New Emigrant Trail

DOREEN LEINDECKER, A RELAXED STRAWBERRY BLONDE WITH A WINNING smile, laughed out loud as she recounted the story of how a sheltered Catholic girl from the Cleveland suburbs ended up in Las Vegas. "I came here for a job," she reminisced. "I was running a hotel back home—did the front desk, accounting, assistant manager, night manager, all for $7.50 an hour. And I thought: this is ridiculous!" Two of her friends, a young couple from home, called to tell of the opportunities in Las Vegas, and at twenty-three, she came out to visit. "There's *so* much money to be made out here, Doreen," her friend, a sous-chef, insisted. "Look what you do there. You answer the phone, check 'em in, check 'em out, balance the books, run the hotel all night, all for peanuts! You could do half the work and make twice the money here, they said, and they were right. So I went home, quit my job, and came out here." Instead of working eighty hours a week and having no life, doing all kinds of jobs for which she wasn't being paid, in Las Vegas Doreen worked forty hours a week, made more money, and had a life.

More than 150 years ago, white Americans set out along the Oregon and California trails, headed west to make their fortune, becoming an integral part of American mythology. At first they sought land, the rich farms of the West Coast, the wet fertile soils of Oregon's Willamette Valley;

later the Gold Rush destroyed any cohesiveness and made westering a free-for-all. But from this chaos came one of the nation's master narratives, the idea that by going to where new opportunities existed, Americans could reinvent themselves. Everyone came for a better life in its many forms, and they became a transformative force that shaped the nineteenth century and, as a result, the twentieth. Their appearance changed the Far West. Their needs, for property, schools, and churches, fashioned a society, and the institutions they created dominated the region for most of a century. This process of ruling by numbers, called "to populate is to govern," at least since the American takeover of Texas in the 1830s, was a critical factor in bringing about the Mexican War and allowing the United States to claim and keep the American Southwest. It provided a rationale for taking land and clearing its inhabitants away. If you had enough people on the ground, you could in time expect your institutions to dominate.

At the time, Las Vegas was far from the minds of westering Americans. Without air-conditioning, Las Vegas was a dinky little wet spot in the heart of a relentless desert. Even the misguided migrants who found themselves in Death Valley in the winter of 1849 and gave that desolate place its name passed Las Vegas by. Only a stopover, the valley was of interest largely to Brigham Young and his Church of Latter-Day Saints, in search of an outpost at the southern boundary of the Mormon nation-state of Deseret.

But with opportunity created first by the mob-run gaming town after World War II and later by the corporate regime, twentieth-century Las Vegas became a magnet for all kinds of people. Doreen Leindecker is typical of those drawn to the city. The growth after 1945 was remarkable, distinguished by its scope and scale. The 8,000 residents of 1940 became 270,000 by 1970, and more than 740,000 by 1990. In the 1990s alone, the population grew by more than 650,000, almost doubling in just one decade. Even as residents asked questions about the costs of growth, people continued to come down the hill from Barstow, their belongings packed in their station wagons or vans, from Montana and Idaho, in pick-up trucks, from New York in such large numbers that sometimes Las Vegas seems to have a New York accent, from Mexico, El Salvador, and the Philippines, from China, and from nearly everywhere else. Against all odds, this magnet's pull showed no signs of weakening.

The first of the post—World War II emigrants to the desert shared traits with the men who built Las Vegas's casinos. In 1940s America, still a self-consciously moral place, gambling was a sin and the people who enjoyed it were sinners. The bad-boy posture, the swagger made popular by Marlon Brando, James Dean, and Elvis Presley, was still out of bounds, and the people who claimed it were déclassé, losers in a society that embraced middle-class normalcy. In this world, gamblers were still "hoods," as the daughter of one described her father, a bad element, a blight on society and especially on the towns that tolerated them. They looked out only for themselves.

These outcasts could thrive because Americans harbored a passion for vice. A mythology and a generation of legends were built on that passion. The Cotton Club in New York was only the best known of places that catered to risqué desire. Newport, Kentucky; Phenix City, Alabama; Cicero, Illinois; and other small towns, usually near larger cities and often just across county or state lines from the major jurisdiction, became regional purveyors of vice. Every major city tolerated vice in spurts, susceptible only to changes in the moral tenor of leadership or political response to outraged public opinion.

Before the Flamingo, gambling operators had no place to go when it got hot at home. Angelenos were the only exception. They already recognized the advantages of a scapegoat state next door. A late-1930s effort to clean up corruption by Los Angeles's new mayor, Fletcher Bowron, sent Guy McAfee, a Raymond Chandler–like Hollywood vice commander who simultaneously ran illegal gambling joints, Sam Boyd, who operated bingo parlors in Los Angeles and Honolulu, and others scurrying to Las Vegas for the cover of legalized gambling. At the time, they were exceptions, local operators looking for a new locality.

McAfee, Boyd, Tony Cornero, who ran offshore gambling boats off California, and the rest were the prototypes for the generation of migrants who followed them. From 1946 to the 1970s, the people who came to Las Vegas were largely of a piece. The postwar newcomers hailed from the seamy side of American life, the hustlers, the grifters, the sharks who ran gambling from pool halls and saloons, and who were always one step away from at least a scrape with the law. Such a life took a toll on people who chose it, for they were always on the run, looking over their shoulder, always paying someone off. Despite their criminal status, they were keen observers of local politics. They had to be. Their livelihood depended on reading public opinion. When authorities looked away, life was easy. When, for whatever reason—public pressure or a crusading district attorney, say—the heat was turned up on the small world of semilegal vice, "we couldn't even have dinner in peace," one old-timer recalled. "My nerves were always shot."

How they chose the little spot in the desert where they could be legal is the stuff of legend. The stories are endless, sounding the same, but each is somehow different. The phone rang, a friend saw a newspaper story, some-one further up the ladder made a suggestion, or a bust or the threat of one sent someone else packing. Las Vegas was the place to go. Every illegal gam-bling act in Kentucky, Ohio, Minnesota, or Texas could be done with a license in Nevada. For the boulevardiers who operated dice games and car-pet joints, here was not only legitimacy, but freedom from the threat of corrupt and untrustworthy authority. In Las Vegas, with the law on your side, you could have dinner without worry or interruption. Only there could you, a gambler, be an upstanding citizen and a taxpayer. Maybe there was something to this Las Vegas place.

For almost thirty years, people came from all over the country, from the East Coast, New York, from Chicago, Cleveland, Newport and Covington, Kentucky, Kansas City, and the South. They were urban and rural, from ethnic neighborhoods in big cities and from small hayseed towns and rural roads. What they shared was an affinity, even a passion, for games of chance and an entrepreneurial spirit, a willingness to risk more than you would wager in a back alley. Some were among the brightest of their time, denied a real shot at conventional opportunity because of who they were, where they were from, or because their relatives lacked resources. They'd made their choices, sometimes foolishly, and some may have even regretted them. Las Vegas gave them a way out and a fresh start that turned out not only to be legal but surprisingly lucrative as well. They were strivers all, even the something-for-nothing crowd who thought a town like Las Vegas was sure to be their oyster, people willing to seize an opportunity even if what it offered was a little weird by midcentury American standards.

No one epitomized this generation better than Davie Berman, one of the progenitors of modern Las Vegas and among those who stepped in at the Flamingo after Bugsy Siegel was killed. Born in Ashley, North Dakota, to a poverty-stricken Jewish immigrant family, Berman came up the hard way. After the family farm failed on the North Dakota plains, the Bermans moved to Sioux City, Iowa, where young Davie found himself on the fringes of the law. He learned early and quickly: "You've got to use what you have to get by," he often said. In the Midwest early in the twentieth century, Jews had three ways that Berman could see to get ahead: they could bob their noses, change their names, and pass for gentile, his daughter, the late Susan Berman wrote, they could go into men's wear, or they could become gamblers. For a poor kid proud of his heritage and not averse to conflict, there was only one choice. Berman went to the wrong side of the law. The risks were high, but the potential reward and independence was very appealing.

Berman became a perverse success story. Hard-nosed, capable, and dependable by the criminal standards, he rose quickly, and by the mid-1920s he ran his own bootlegging and gambling operation and engaged in other kinds of crime. His heists led him to New York, where in a 1927 shootout an accomplice was killed and Berman captured. "Hell, the worst I can get is life," he said in a phrase that captured newspaper headlines around the country. Berman was instantly known as "the toughest Jew in America." At twenty-three, he became the wrong kind of celebrity, and was sentenced to Ossining State Prison, the notorious "Sing-Sing." He spent seven and a half years there without ratting out his mob confederates.

After his release, Berman settled in Minnesota, where gambling, bootlegging, and other vices were informally regulated by a system of pay-offs. For a decade in Minnesota, Berman managed to stay on good terms with the law. He was, in the strange thinking of the Depression era, a good racketeer, an asset to the community as underworld figures went, but Mayor Hubert H. Humphrey cracked down on vice as the first step toward the vice presidency, and good racketeer or not, life became harder for Berman. After a jaunt in Cuba, Berman was picked to run the new operation in Las Vegas. In 1944 he moved to Las Vegas and played an instrumental role in the purchase of the El Cortez.

With a wife and a new baby, Berman recognized the advantages of Las Vegas earlier than most of his peers. After a career in crime, he could settle down to a weird respectability. As a hotel owner, a man with property and a license that allowed him to run games of chance, Berman could use the skills he'd learned outside the law. Like no place else in the United States, Las Vegas could reward not only what he knew, but also the vast entrepreneurial energy he brought. In fact, the city craved people like Berman. Established, forthright, and as true to his word as a man who spent a decade in Sing-Sing could be, Berman represented the best of illegal culture.

This perverse Horatio Alger story reflected the experience of others, the drug-addicted Gus Greenbaum, the career criminal Joseph "Doc" Stacher, Benny Binion, Wilbur Clark, Moe Dalitz, Jake and Belden Katleman, and more who sat atop the pyramid of legal gambling. Their kind built the first generation of Las Vegas resorts. Many of these founders had long criminal records, involvement in vice and often far worse, and frankly were lousy candidates for rehabilitation. But the city needed them. The very expertise that earned them a criminal label was exactly what Las Vegas determined to sell. It was a bargain, a complicated, tacit one, but an arrangement nonetheless. The city got professionals who could make this new industry thrive and grow. The hoods, or former hoods in the eyes of local law, all recognized safety in Las Vegas that money could not buy elsewhere. No matter how many cops, politicians, and lawyers they paid off, being legal was a far greater prize.

Berman, Greenbaum, and the rest created an empire that needed hotel maids and bartenders, valets and cocktail waitresses, singers, musicians, and people to sweep the streets and collect the garbage. From the late 1940s to the early 1960s, opportunities that stemmed from the new gambling economy drew new residents in stunning numbers. In 1940, 8,422 people called Las Vegas home. In 1950 the valley's population approached 50,000, reaching 125,000 by 1960. They came from all over, from New York and Havana, from working-class neighborhoods and slums in cities large and small. When former Cleveland Browns player George Ratterman was elected sheriff of Newport, Kentucky, in 1960, his reform policies initiated an exodus of gambling operators to Las Vegas. "All you had to say when you landed in Las Vegas was that you were from Kentucky," one old-timer reported, "and you had a new job that day." Most came because they worked in gambling or vice in some fashion. Others opened hardware stores, grocery stores, clothing stores, shoe stores, and every other kind of shop that a town needed. A few probably came because they recognized an opportunity to do better and have more fun than they could at home.

One segment of the wave of immigration came because its members were in the business of catering to customers, and the gamblers who disembarked from trains, cars, and later airplanes tended to be better, more generous customers than those who didn't play. There was a vitality to this Las Vegas, a feeling that made anything possible. Winners gave tips, sometimes large ones, to the people around them, to the bellman, to the bartender, and especially to the cocktail waitress, and the individuals got to keep their "toke," as the tip is locally called, until the IRS forced dealers to pool their tips in the early 1980s. The dollar signs seemed to blind many, newcomer and longtime resident alike. Perhaps that was all many of them sought. They looked the other way at obvious machinations and relied on stale arguments to justify the direction the town took. The money drew some. Others came for adventure. Nat Hart was running a successful San Francisco restaurant when the phone rang: an 11:30 P.M. train brought visitors to Las Vegas each night, and Davie Berman wanted to offer them some kind of meal. Hart whipped up what anyone from an American city would have recognized as a Jewish feast: lox, whitefish, herring, and a few other things, and laid it out on a long buffet-style table. When the people got off the train, they stormed the table, and a Las Vegas tradition, the buffet, was born.

The demand for service meant that Las Vegas provided a niche for almost anyone. After World War II, African Americans heard of the prosperity of Las Vegas and came from the South in search of economic opportunity. They found it, along with many vestiges of the American disease of segregation. Las Vegas had been integrated before 1941 in a frontier, small-town way. In 1930, 150 African Americans lived in Las Vegas, and Clarence Ray, an African American gambler who settled in Las Vegas in 1925, described a community of about fifteen families, all of whom owned property. The war brought workers, the men to Basic Magnesium Inc. in Henderson to work in the war industry, the women to work back-of-the-house jobs as maids, cooks, and laundresses in the thriving hotels and downtown clubs. A strike at BMI gave Nevada the appellation "the Mississippi of the West." While the designation was not quite fair in that it stemmed from the importing of black strikebreakers to undermine the CIO, there was more than a ring of truth to the racism of Nevada.

As the African American population grew in number during the war, conventional American segregation took shape. After the war, blacks were consigned to "Westside," across the railroad tracks and technically north of downtown. The openness of the prewar era disappeared. Like many western states, Nevada had a southern, anti-government flavor and a real lack of tolerance of anyone who was different, especially those of another color. By 1945 the fluidity of the world of mining hardened into rural and southern America's characteristic and formidable Jim Crow restrictions.

The need for labor as Siegel and the others built their hotels in the postwar era helped change Las Vegas. The 178 African Americans of 1940 became 15,000 by 1955. "Come on out here, they're giving away money," Lucille Bryant told her friends and relatives in Tallulah, Louisiana, which along with Fordyce, Arkansas, provided more than half of the African American migrants to Las Vegas in the 1940s and 1950s. "Eight dollars a day and working in the shade," a big step up in pay and working conditions compared to cotton-picking in the South. Despite better jobs and pay, discrimination persisted in Las Vegas. African Americans lived mostly in Westside, where roads were not even paved until the mid-1950s. They worked in service and behind-the-scenes jobs on the Strip, but through the 1950s they were not, figuratively or literally, permitted to enter Strip hotels by the front door.

In a city devoted to meeting customers' desires, licentious and otherwise, such rigidity could not hold for long. Even though in the mid-1950s Sammy Davis Jr. called Las Vegas "Tobacco Road," in 1955 a multiracial casino-hotel, the Moulin Rouge, opened in Westside, cracking another barrier as the rest of the nation grappled with the *Brown v. Board of Education* decision. Not only did whites and blacks share the stage at the Moulin Rouge, but they mingled socially until all hours. For the Mississippi of the West, even the illusion of social integration, a mixing place where the elites of entertainment could fraternize, was a remarkably rapid stride that reflected the city's dependence on its cultural cachet. If African Americans entertained from the stage but couldn't step off it, even their customers had less fun. After a half-decade of tension, a 1960 consent decree integrated the Strip, as liberal cities like San Francisco struggled with similar issues and four years before Berkeley students, inhaling the heady fumes of the Civil Rights movement, forced the Sheraton to hire its first African American behind-the-scenes employees. Las Vegas's deviance prevented it from taking the lead in desegregation—Las Vegas was no one's role model in those days—but the suppleness of a city devoted to pleasure foretold a more malleable future than other places might reasonably anticipate.

It was one helluva way to build a town, from scratch, entirely on one industry that a generation before would have seemed sinful and even bizarre. But people came, salivating after the opportunity to make play their work. It didn't hurt that the living was good, money flowed, pleasure was easy to find, and all were relieved that finally the law was on their side. Money could be made in Las Vegas, and Nevada's opportunities had been slim for so long that the people who preceded this invasion cheered the prospects. In the process, the community abdicated any sense of standards and embraced organized crime and the money it used to make the city grow.

From top to bottom, from the 1950s to the 1970s, Las Vegas owed its allegiance to organized crime. The mob was ubiquitous; Dean Martin joked from the stage that he was the "only entertainer who had ten percent of four gangsters." Most hotels, and consequently most of the jobs created in the town, were mobbed up. Illegal culture had a visible hold on the city, but it also paid the bills. In this Las Vegas, everyone knew where their bread was buttered, and they generally liked that butter thickly applied.

The federal economy that preceded the mob remained, now owing its sustenance to the Cold War and American atomic weapons testing. The Nevada Test Site, located just beyond the Spring Mountains northwest of the city, became the primary location within the then-forty-eight states for the nation to test its atomic and later thermonuclear arsenal. Between 1951 and 1963, the Nevada desert hosted 126 atomic tests, an average of one every three weeks, aboveground, in tunnels, and partially buried. From 1963 until the cessation of underground testing in 1993, the tests continued, producing a periodic low rumble through the desert. Each and every test required the work of specialists, construction workers, miners, and others. Throughout the Cold War, the impact on the economy remained substantial. In 1969 Nellis Air Force Base outside the city employed nine thousand people at a payroll of $60 million, almost 15 percent of the local workforce.

Between 1945 and the late 1980s, those workers and their paychecks played an important if unrecognized and even invisible role in the city's growth. The test site people were different from casino workers. Many arrived after World War II and military service, and most made careers of either government or one of the contractors, EG&G, Wackenhut for security services, Federal Services Inc., or later Raytheon or Bechtel. The few scientists possessed advanced degrees, but southern Nevada was not generally where the science was done. Scientists stood at the top of the rough hierarchy, followed by technical workers in computers, radio, and electronics, miners, construction workers, guards, equipment operators, secretaries and clerks, and manual laborers, cooks, and staff for the living quarters at Mercury, the government town about fifty miles from Las Vegas that served as the headquarters for tests. The workforce were generally high school graduates; those who rose possessed mechanical or engineering aptitude, often honed on farms in their youth. Technological wizards, they fashioned their skills into a living and a way of thinking about the world.

"Test site families," as Dineen Barkhuff, who grew up in one, called them, shared distinct traits. Most of the adult members of Barkhuff's extended family worked at the test site or for one of its contractors. These were "nuclear nuclear families," locals said. Although test site workers were part of the community, except in the most perfunctory ways their world rarely intersected with the gambling world. The test site people mostly socialized among themselves. Nuclear technicians lived next door to casino dealers and their kids played Little League with the children of mob boss-es, but they inhabited different worlds. Test site work provided a secure liv-ing, less lucrative than the casinos perhaps, but solidly middle class and with a different stigma than America associated with Las Vegas. In Las Vegas the test site was the shadow economy, unseen and underappreciated. Tourism and gambling remained the staple.

Test site jobs that required less skill paid well because they were danger-ous, reflecting an aspect of American work that hailed from an earlier age of sacrifice. When a good salary was $10,000 a year, some of the miners who dug the tunnels for the underground tests made three times that when the test site was brimming with activity. The only drawback was radiation exposure. When workers reached their maximum level of exposure for a quarter, they were placed in jobs with less risk of exposure that usually paid less.

In the fashion of midcentury, poor and minority workers were recruit-ed for the most dangerous tasks. High wages compensated them, but work-ers were deceived, told there was no risk. They took the work, recognizing an improvement from pumping gas or other low-skill, low-wage occupations, and remained unaware of the inherent danger. Some jobs were integrated; whites and African Americans worked as miners. Some African Americans recruited in the South served as "rad monitors," forward observers posi-tioned close to the aboveground tests in the 1950s. Others cleaned up after the underground tests in the 1960s, 1970s, and 1980s. Their mortality rate was considerable twenty years later and led to workers' lawsuits in the 1980s and 1990s. Scientists and technical experts received far less exposure.

For African Americans, the sharp edges of the bargain were particularly evident. The income from the test site produced middle-class prosperity, otherwise denied to African Americans, but at a grievous price. In 1968, when Elise Johnson arrived from New York to teach in the still de facto seg-regated schools of Westside, she found that test site and back-of-the-house Strip jobs had created a classic American middle-class community that was black. The tremendous human toll in cancer victims over the following decades placed the brittleness of the exchange in stark relief.

African American and white test site workers alike were exposed to radiation in their daily endeavors by a callous and disingenuous Atomic Energy Commission and its successors. With casual disregard for the risk to workers and hiding behind the cloak of national security, responsible indi-viduals with real power became boys with toys, exploding them with aban-don. The government did what it could to deny the consequences. In the

Baneberry case, when two workers contaminated by a large black cloud that escaped from the 912-foot underground detonation in 1970, sued, U.S. District Judge Roger Foley denied that the men's leukemia was caused by exposure. Widespread testing and silencing of the victims could have happened with so little opposition only in a state like Nevada, where oligarchies of various kinds had governed with impunity since statehood and where the needs of individual workers and the safety of the community could be neatly tucked into a pocket and forgotten in the name of false ideals of money, power, and national security.

Besides the mob and the powerful federal economy, Las Vegas attracted another important group that made its presence in local life felt. Mormons came to Sin City, recognizing not only economic opportunity but a place where their attributes had particular value. Mormons did not drink or gamble, but after the 1940s their doctrine did not prevent them from working in institutions that sold vice. On the rim of Deseret, Las Vegas was a natural location for a Mormon presence, and the Mormon return to the area combined elements of colonization and local economic development. That the Mormon sensibility and etiquette fit well in the new Las Vegas was a fortuitous circumstance. Even before Parry Thomas arrived, Mormons were valued in the gaming industry for their rectitude. Thomas solidified the Mormon presence, and for the rest of the century a healthy Mormon presence influenced community institutions. The county commission and county services, the school district, and the airport authority were among the longtime Mormon bastions.

By the mid-1950s Las Vegas was one of the most unusual towns in the United States. Its population included an overrepresentation of both Mormons and Jews, an anomaly unmatched anywhere. Parry Thomas said it best: "I work for the Mormons until noon, and from noon on for my Jewish friends." The city's unique traits brought together an unusual array of forces. There were others in town as well, those who preceded Bugsy Siegel and who usually owned real estate that gained in value, well-paid federal workers, the group of mob associates who added a colorful presence, business operators often tied to the mob, which provided the raw materials for the hotel-driven economy—towels, uniforms, drinking glasses, and booze. Entertainment drew another constituency, African Americans disproportionate among them. Strays and stragglers who were comfortable in town also found a way to get by in this newly exciting city. A few professionals, an occasional physician, and more lawyers also made their home in the developing community.

During this era Las Vegas thought of itself as normal; no one else in the United States would have agreed. "It's a great town," insisted Dineen Barkhuff, "and we grew up normal," the classic refrain of Las Vegas youth who encountered the outside's curiosity. Las Vegans stamped their feet and said, "We're the same as you!" They pointed to their eighty-one church groups, fine schools, and conventional civic activities as proof. Friends, cousins, and detractors begged to differ. In Louisville, visitors would never ask residents which hotel they lived in, something that happened to me in the mid-1990s. The Kefauver Commission didn't come to other towns, putting the leaders of local industry on the stand for cross-examination and embarrassing them. The FBI did not wiretap the business leaders of other cities and refuse to give their governor information about upcoming raids on the state's leading industry. Las Vegas was scrutinized. Everyone knew that the line between legal and illegal was at best indistinct. Normal towns had shopping centers and hospitals, not shops in hotels and medical care near the concierge desk. In a still self-consciously moral society, Las Vegas's claim to being normal could be easily dismissed.

During the 1950s and 1960s signs of impending normalcy emerged in Las Vegas. In 1957 the University of Nevada opened a branch campus along Maryland Parkway, about two miles east of the Strip between Tropicana and Flamingo. The one small building was in the middle of nowhere, surrounded by desert. Despite financier Robert O. Anderson's dismissive rejoinder—"Who can imagine a great university in Las Vegas?"—the institution grew into an independent full-service urban university, the University of Nevada, Las Vegas, which specialized in educating first-generation college students. Sunrise Hospital brought together local businessmen, transplanted casino operators and workers, and newcomers, and set the terms for a generation of civic growth. Las Vegas soon stretched south toward McCarran Airport, its crowning achievement the construction of the Boulevard Mall.

As if anyone in Las Vegas needed further proof, the hospital and the development of Maryland Parkway and the mall demonstrated where the money came from. Las Vegans knew well that the rest of the country looked askance at them. During the great postwar burst of industrial energy and prosperity, Americans were even more obnoxious than usual. In the 1950s they really believed they had made a genuine effort to make the world safe for democracy and resented the parallel rise of Soviet power and influence. The Red Threat imperiled the nation, many believed, and anything that diminished American will was an equal threat, a drain on much-needed energy and innovation. Cavorting in the desert, having fun for its own sake, as Sputnik circled the globe, was seditious. Las Vegans needed symbols of their normalcy—hospitals, colleges, malls, and the like—and the city embraced whoever gave them that protective cover. They had few choices about who funded the trappings that gave it the cover of normality.

Despite the idiosyncracies, it was possible to lead a normal family life in 1950s and 1960s Las Vegas. The town was truly a company town, in the best American sense, like Detroit, Gary, Indiana, or even Winston-Salem, North Carolina. In each of these towns, a dominant industry ran the community. Autos drove Detroit, steel made Gary, and vice versa, and in an age when everyone smoked, Winston-Salem enjoyed a powerful but peculiar cachet. In each, what was good for the industry was good for the town, and nearly everything that these communities had or became stemmed directly from their industry. They shared a special, insular feel, a dependence on "the plant" in whatever form it took, and a range of amenities that emanated from the company. Whatever inherent weirdness existed, the work made for a good life, more prosperous than could otherwise be expected. The difference in Las Vegas was that the industry was sin.

Las Vegas anticipated the breakdown of the one-income family and the toll it took on children. Even before half of American marriages ended in divorce, a large percentage of children in Las Vegas lived in homes with only one biological parent. In the consummate company town, two incomes were not only desirable, they were essential. Las Vegas had latchkey kids before the term existed. The twenty-four-hour nature of the town meant that some moms "cocktailed" graveyard shift. To their children this was the norm; to kids at sleepovers who woke up in the middle of the night without someone's mom to deal with it, their absence was a source of confusion and curiosity. With few opportunities for after-school care or day care, children had a great deal more leeway than was probably good for them. Before parents truly recognized the risk that independence for children entailed, the danger of too much freedom too young in an anonymous society became one of the hazards of growing up in Las Vegas.

In the end, being a kid in Las Vegas wasn't all that different from growing up anywhere else in the country. Children took piano lessons and dance lessons, played baseball, roller skated, or just kicked stones around. They went to church and were confirmed, became part of the small-town status hierarchy called "popularity" based on their looks, athletic ability, and style, and followed the institutions of midcentury to their logical end.

They cruised the Strip, tried to buy alcohol underage, and otherwise took advantage of the proximity of other people's leisure. No shortage of open spaces, nearly all desert, and construction sites everywhere hid their hijinks as they did everywhere else. They had television, and it gave them moments of great local pride. The Las Vegas Rhythmettes, a local high school dance troupe, performed on the Ed Sullivan Show in 1956, and the city watched on its TVs. Like any other small town, Las Vegas took its identity from local activities.

The signature of local identity came in the persona of a short, round, balding Armenian with a trademark towel stuffed in his mouth. When Jerry Tarkanian took over the UNLV basketball program after the 1972–73 season, he brought a sensibility that Las Vegas easily embraced. Like a lot of small towns, Las Vegas was passionate about local sports and it loved winners more than most. It had been built on the hope of victory. The soft-spoken, even droll, Tarkanian brought savoir faire and an unmatched coaching record at high school, junior college, and at Long Beach State University, and recognized that in Las Vegas he could be the only game in town. With a 20–6 record the first year and an NCAA tournament berth the next, the legend of the Runnin' Rebels was born. With unparalleled speed, the little college in the desert acquired standing and a remarkable mystique. When the UNLV Runnin' Rebels reached the Final Four with their run-and-gun style in 1977, a brand name was also born. UNLV basketball stood for excitement, high scores, and an anti-authoritarian style.

UNLV's rapid move through the ranks of college basketball teams was a major affront to the people who ran college sports. Tarkanian was branded a rogue and an outlaw. Instead of making him an outcast, this label endeared him to Las Vegas as much as winning did. Tarkanian closely mirrored his new hometown. He was disarmingly honest in an increasingly cynical society, and with his trademark towel stuffed in his mouth, seemed a charming eccentric. No one could have fit into a self-consciously different place better than Jerry Tarkanian did; nothing could have reflected more of the winner's persona back onto Las Vegas's fans than did the soft touch of this coach.

The Runnin' Rebels became one of the best-known and most controversial basketball teams in the nation. They were always in the Top 20 even as the NCAA engaged in what the federal courts later decided was a twenty-year vendetta against Tarkanian. The NCAA looked like a bully and Tarkanian like a misunderstood and persecuted hero, and the general decline in respect for authority and the coach's shoot-from-the-hip style made him a genuine figure in a society increasingly made up of fakes. The disaffected and especially young African Americans embraced Tarkanian and his Rebels. They were winners in spite of the system, courageously fighting not only a powerful organization but the worst of entitlement in American culture, an appealing pose in a society that seemed to have lost its bearings. In 1995, three full years after Tarkanian was sent packing, I hopped into a cab in Chicago. When the middle-aged African American driver found out that I taught at UNLV, he took me to my destination for free and refused a tip. He was, he told me, a die-hard Rebel fan and he raved about Tarkanian and his compassion for his players. I didn't have the heart to tell him that I did not much care for the coach. I gave him a business card and told him if he was ever in Las Vegas, my seats for a Rebel game were his. It was the least I could do; the ride from O'Hare to a Loop hotel would have cost $40.

From UNLV's first Final Four appearance in 1977 to the 1990s, there was no stronger marker of local identification than being a Rebel fan. Everyone in town followed the Rebels, lived and died with them, and no single moment in local history, not the opening of the Flamingo in 1946 or the Bellagio in 1998, was as great a moment of local joy as UNLV's NCAA championship in 1990. A generation of Las Vegans had grown up near the Tarkanian family, played at their house, and went to school with the kids. When the Tarkanian children became adults, the number of people who said they knew the family and hung out at their house exceeded the local population. More than Wayne Newton or Steve and Elaine Wynn, the Tarkanians were Las Vegas's first family. They epitomized the local sense of self: they were winners, they were honest, and they took no prisoners.

The success of the Runnin' Rebels basketball program gave Las Vegas its most genuine claim to being normal, its strongest allegiance to a conventional small-town ideal apart from glitz and glamor. Beating Duke in the 1990 national title game was a badge, not only for Las Vegas and its people but for anyone who disliked hierarchy. Duke students, the epitome of American privilege, greeted the Rebels at the title game with a sign that read, "Welcome, fellow student-athletes." Its snotty implication was not lost on the city. Tarkanian's Las Vegas was notable for its lack of pretension, a blue-collar company town where people admired money, not class or breeding, and flash and dazzle, not Brooks Brothers and La Coste shirts. The idea of a well-honed but still rag-tag bunch of Juco transfers beating a premier academic institution tasted good to service workers who routinely catered to people who thought themselves better than those who served them. No wonder African Americans all over the country embraced the Rebels and wore their gear. Their success seemed to spit in the face of a two-tiered society that made its selections at birth.

But by 1990, when the Rebels won their championship, Las Vegas had again become a different place. Corporate capital brought its own generation to Las Vegas, larger in number and better educated than the managers of the old mob hotels. As Hilton paved the way for hotel chains to buy into the desert and investment houses retained gaming analysts, the people who managed Las Vegas hotels were transformed. Unlike Mouse from Detroit, who came up with the Mayfield Road gang, the new class of managers graduated from the hotel school at Cornell or the Wharton Business School. The growth of the city spawned tremendous demand for lawyers, accountants, engineers, and the whole range of skilled professions that accompany any major construction boom. Las Vegas never before had a true professional class; until the 1970s its professionals were either homegrown or idiosyncratic. But as the corporate boom took off, a new generation, on the make and often trained at the very best universities, became part of the town.

They were different, this new generation of Las Vegans. "There aren't as many notorious resumes out there," John L. Smith remarked, and the demography of the new city bore him out. A much larger percentage of newcomers had earned college degrees, and a significant percentage of those had done graduate work. They shared the expectations of people of their class throughout the country. That meant better schools, more parks, new libraries, and more to do. They needed doctors to take care of them, accountants and financial planners to manage the money they made and saved, teachers for their children, churches for their religious observance, and a range of other markers of middle- and upper-middle-class life. While some participated in "the industry," most worked in ancillary professions, only indirectly dependent on casinos and visitors.

Because they were typical of their class, they played an instrumental role in bringing the old company town to an end. The old way in Las Vegas had been taking hits since the 1970s. The corporate-run casinos measured only the bottom line and their stock price. People of that generation, those who were comfortable in the idiosyncratic town, felt alienated and left behind in the new Las Vegas and bemoaned the passing of the old. "It was better in the old days," someone always called in to say when I was on the radio. "You could leave a thousand-dollar bill in the middle of the Strip and nobody would touch it!" Hyperbole for certain, this sentiment revealed with remarkable clarity how Las Vegas had changed. The mob-run city had certain attributes. Everyone knew everyone, and everyone knew where they stood. Street crime was essentially forbidden. "We had two police forces in those days," an old-timer told me. "The regular cops and the boys. The boys were a lot more effective." The old Las Vegas had a mystique that the new corporate-run town nods toward in its incessant desire to cater to all tastes.

The migrants of the past fifteen years, during which Las Vegas has remained the fastest-growing metropolis in the nation, can be divided into loose categories. The community has grafted on an upper middle class, the educated professionals who follow their career from city to city and who see in Las Vegas an opportunity to do better than elsewhere. The job and the job alone draws them; many perceive Las Vegas as another stop on the corporate road, the place where business is happening now and where they can make their mark, make it fast, and move on to a better job in a locale they'd prefer.

This grafted upper middle class includes professionals who came to set up their own practices. Until the 1990s Las Vegas had a dearth of teachers, doctors, architects, and even attorneys. For a long time, membership in the American professional classes demanded a degree of conformity that usually excluded Las Vegas. Why would a gifted young attorney go to the desert when Wall Street and a home in Greenwich, Connecticut, beckoned? But a changing culture, a more maverick approach to life for many professionals, and the marvelous opportunities of an unfettered economy made Las Vegas heaven for professionals in the 1990s.

Before 1985, Las Vegas was low on the list for professionals, a reality reflected in the way locals regarded their physicians. Las Vegans who could went "outside" for medical care. Having a doctor in another town, usually Los Angeles, was a marker of status. When professionals embraced Las Vegas, the community rewarded them with affection and the measure of all status in the town: wealth. This became a habit that continued even after young professionals coveted Las Vegas. "I call it the 'golden handcuffs,'" one young physician said in the splendor of her five-thousand-square foot home with a stunning view of the Strip and the city below. "I can make more money here in a month than in six in California." In the 1990s, no state had fewer dentists per capita than Nevada, and physicians are in prime demand. New doctors' and dentists' offices open daily, and some new strip malls fill up exclusively with medical offices. Despite the overall trend toward the purchase of doctors' practices by HMOs and other medical organizations, independent practitioners thrive in Las Vegas. The numerous independent partnerships and especially the new solo practices suggest an attractive prospect for starting a medical career. Entrepreneurial young practitioners find Las Vegas a haven, a wide-open opportunity that mirrors the experience of doctors everywhere three decades ago, when medicine offered the opportunity for wealth and acclaim.

The number of new physicians in Las Vegas is not as remarkable as their credentials. A generation ago, the town drew only eccentric gambling or desert-loving doctors. A great many now come after earning fellowships at the top medical schools in the country. With the need for medical care growing at an even faster rate than the population as a whole, partnerships add newcomers with monotonous regularity. It's hard to maintain a relationship with a doctor. Between visits, a practice will grow so much that it can be months before you can see the physician you saw on your previous visit. Most people settle for the next available appointment, usually with the newest partner in the practice.

The emergence of a professional community only marginally related to gaming is one of the most overlooked stories in Las Vegas. The city's remarkable growth has brought all kinds of professionals, almost none in sufficient supply even as their numbers increase each year. "Why are you here?" I asked the members of the Clark County planning division. "What attracted you here? How many of you were here in 1980?" No hands rose. "In 1980 nothing here attracted planners, made it worth your while to even think about the place. Only with the growth, and the possibilities and problems that it created, did Las Vegas become worthy of your talents." Las Vegas in the 1990s became the newest frontier, the easiest place to latch on to the American upper middle class.

Among Las Vegas's grafted upper middle class, transience remains the salient trait. They usually don't vote unless the issue is schools or roads and they don't participate in civic discourse. They turn out at school redistricting hearings to prevent having to drive their children farther each day. They complain about roads, but not about sweetheart deals for developers or environmental issues, or even the Yucca Mountain high-level nuclear waste storage debacle being foisted on the state. These folks don't vote unless it directly affects them; they know little and care less about local politics because they think the issues don't impact them. They live in Las Vegas but haven't yet accepted it. I was stumping for a local candidate with Sandy

Watson, a go-to person, the kind who handles the details, who the busier she was the more she got done, perfect for a role in the campaign and to accomplish the daily legwork that makes grassroots politics work. I talked myself blue in the face, extolling the candidate's virtues, reminding her of the work we'd shared and the friendship that developed between us and our families. I'm very persuasive, but to no avail. The pull of local politics hadn't yet reached this two-year veteran of the suburbs. Like her neighbors, she is still fixed on the here and now. Such people don't expect to be around long enough for issues to matter.

More of the grafted upper middle class eventually make Las Vegas their permanent home. Part of it is certainly inertia; after the kids reach a certain age, who wants to move? All your relationships are set, your friendships, your doctors, your mechanic, your restaurants. Plus there's all the junk to shlep. Another dimension is money. Even the upper middle class's money goes further in Las Vegas, and the standard of living in the belt of new suburbs is very high. The homes are nice and spacious, the cars are new, and the amenities are attractive. This phenomenon, the golden handcuffs, has bittersweet dimensions. Some would like to be elsewhere, but for lots of people in Las Vegas, there is nowhere they can go where life is sufficiently better. The money they make offers not only immediate material prosperity but comfort and long-term financial security. Those who once disdained the place and sought ways out come to like it—a lot. They forge bonds, make friends, start churches, and make a life.

Locals, the children of the immigrants of the generation before, sought the same path. Families that inculcated middle class values over those of gaming and leisure measured their aspirations in similar ways, often seeing education as the means to achievement. Dineen Barkhuff typified the pattern; the daughters of test site parents, she and her sister were the first in the family to graduate from college. Growing up on the old east side, she and her family moved to the suburbs. The family couldn't afford out-of-state tuition, so the girls went to UNLV. At first, Dineen worked to supplement the parental stipend. Soon she was working two jobs, forty to fifty hours a week, to pay her own way. Her sister became a librarian; Dineen worked with troubled youth at Child Haven. A stint at Aureole, Charlie Palmer's acclaimed restaurant in Mandalay Bay, followed, and she moved across the cobblestone walkway to Red Square, the hippest grown-up bar in town. Las Vegas provided both a living and an opportunity for an education.

The "Vegas trap" did not beckon to Barkhuff; it was only the means to an end. Jobs like Aureole and Red Square are lucrative, averaging as much as $25 an hour including tips and wages, and they require relatively little accomplishment. Anyone who grew up in Las Vegas knew people who went to work in the hotels after high school, made good money, and remained. For some, this was salvation; they could raise a family on the salary from cocktailing. For others, it became a different version of the golden handcuffs. One Culinary worker told me that she'd planned to work in the hotels for a ten years while pursuing a teaching degree, but when the opportunity to leave for teaching finally arrived, the decrease in pay and benefits from a unionized hotel job was too great a burden for her family. Her aspirations and economics got tangled, forcing her to put aside one set of dreams.

One person's trap is another's opportunity. Striving to attain their status is the wide middle class, primarily comprised of service-sector workers. Hailing from the cities and the middle-class inner and outer suburbs, this group represents the broadest geographic and ethnic origins, and possesses considerably less education and fewer marketable skills than the grafted upper middle class. Las Vegas unionizes these workers, and unionization shields the value of their labor. There is a hustler class, people who see Las Vegas, with its dollar signs, as their kind of place. "I thought about all that money floating loose in this town," Geoff Reese, a car salesman from Florida told me, "and knew I had to be here." Some people work in the hotels and casinos, a lot labor in the construction trades—Oregon, Idaho, and Montana license plates on trucks are ubiquitous—and some think that they will truly be the one who hits Megabucks, the multimillion-dollar progressive slot machine jackpot that captures the regional imagination every time it tops $10,000,000. These "something-for-nothing suckers" think that the hotels along the Strip were built with other people's losses and they cling with fervent faith to the myth of instant victory and redemption. Surely they've suffered enough. Surely they've paid their dues. C'mon, jackpot!

Las Vegas also recycles people, usually from one or another of the mounds that make up the scrapheap of postindustrial economic history. When the widget factory in Nowheresville closes, when industries lay off thousands of workers, when people's personal failings get them in trouble, and when they just plain want to flee, they come to Las Vegas. In a city of illusion, where change is what the city does, it's no wonder. Las Vegas is the court of last resort, the last place to start over, to reinvent yourself in the same way that the city does, time after time. For some it works; for some it doesn't, but they keep coming and trying.

The demography of those looking to start over has changed in recent years. In the early 1990s, during the height of the California recession, almost everyone who showed up in Las Vegas seemed to be an excised blue-collar worker from southern California. When I stood in the interminably long line to exchange my out-of-state driver's license in 1992, I was surrounded by Californians. The fellow next to me, a former aerospace worker who was passing out flyers touting his home repair skills, asked where I was from. When I replied Kansas, he asked, "What part of California is that?" Californians were so prominent in that era that when I surveyed an introductory class at UNLV two-thirds of the students had graduated from a California high school. A subsequent question established their blue-collar roots. More than two-thirds of the white kids from California responded that their grandparents or great grandparents had come from the southern plains in the 1930s, Dust Bowl and Steinbeck territory. They were "reverse Okies," following the road that brought their forebears to the Golden State, but in the opposite direction.

Don Hall, a grizzled fiftyish fellow with a ponytail, tattoos, a big Hog—a Harley Davidson—epitomizes the people Las Vegas recycles. To look at Don, you'd think him a renegade, but listening to him, I heard a survivor. Hall grew up in Iowa and moved to California, where he spent twenty-six years in the aerospace industry in quality assurance for a small company. Both he and his wife worked there, and Don loved the place. "I was as loyal as they come," he said with a laugh, standing up for the company in the best American tradition. Then one day it was over. He was unceremoniously let go. His wife was next, after the company sent her to Mexico to set up the very operation that made her extraneous. The Halls felt betrayed. In his forties at the time and with limits to their skills and education, Hall and his wife faced a crossroads. They needed to catch a break.

The Halls moved to Las Vegas in the early 1990s, as the California recession crippled high-paying, blue-collar work and sent thousands like them streaming over the mountains. Hall's stepfather had been a Teamster, a path he resisted. A Teamster he became, an expedient decision that surely made his stepfather chuckle. In Las Vegas Don joined the union and worked setting up conventions. It was steady work—no shortage of conventions in Las Vegas—and a good living that gave the Halls time to live their lives. They bought a house in an established community and settled in. The job came with good benefits. Don could genuinely plan for retirement. When his wife was ill, health insurance made the burden more manageable.

Las Vegas provided a smooth transition for a semiskilled blue-collar worker jettisoned at the end of the Cold War.

Though his story is representative of blue-collar migrants, Hall himself is different. With his Harley and his tattoos, he is the kind of man who might appear a danger to community, someone who exudes opposition to authority. In his solid, middle-class neighborhood, Don became an upstanding member, a founder of the Neighborhood Watch, the kind of person every neighborhood needs, someone who is around a lot and sees everything. The kids in the area came by his house for a look at the bike and saw in him not an authority figure, but a peer, someone who liked the same things they did. A fifteen-year member of Alcoholics Anonymous, Hall embodies responsibility. "I clean up after myself now," he told me. "It wasn't always that way, but that's what AA teaches. You have to get right with the world to be right with yourself."

This flood of people has done a lot to the city. Most important, it has made the demography of Las Vegas more typical of the nation in its distribution of race, class, and wealth, while also creating a window into the American future. The new Las Vegas looks, talks, sounds, and acts like everywhere else. The twenty thousand new homes sold each year during the 1990s are filled with people who came to capitalize on the economic climate that rapid growth and low-cost living created. They are every color under the sun, from all over the world, and they bring the same expectations of their community as any other group of migrants in the United States. Longtime locals sometimes resent the transformation, but some embrace the breadth such change brings. "I'm one of those old-time Las Vegans who enjoys the fact that you can get more than one good pizza in town," said writer John L. Smith, the most clear-eyed chronicler of his native city. Las Vegas "is becoming more eclectic."

Las Vegas's population long differed from the nation as a whole in essential traits: it was less diverse, less well educated, more prosperous than in other similarly educated areas, more likely to have declared bankruptcy, and more likely to buy high-status goods. The 1990s have made the community look much more like the rest of the America. The rate of college graduates in the population has risen slightly above the national average, and the newcomers have maintained the economic prosperity that has been characteristic. A huge and fast-growing retired population and an equally fast-growing and young Latino and Asian population fill out local demography, a preview of the American future.

Equally significant, the influx has altered the state's perspective, bringing people with an entirely different set of values to state politics, community development, and every other dimension of life. Many of them, especially those from southern California, expect social services in ways that old-time Nevadans did not. They turn to authority to solve problems instead of resolving them by themselves, as Nevadans think they once did. Accustomed to sitting in traffic, they see a thirty-minute commute as a walk in the park. They want parks, infrastructure, and most of all service from local government, state government, and even the federal government, but they remain reluctant to invest their time and energy in the process of creating them. It's not that they won't. Just get them angry and watch the results. But they need to be prompted by a galvanizing situation or event.

This neonative constituency, the newcomers like me who have come to the desert to make it home and who change it with their presence, create a difficult situation in Las Vegas: they pit the state's libertarian traditions, its individualism, against its future, the demands of an ever more crowded city and the community energy needed to make it more liveable. Growth endangers Las Vegas's ability to survive with its older definition of freedom, the right to do what you want, intact. The cumulative impact affects everyone. Neonative expectations demand a powerful state. Nevada traditions present the primacy of the individual. In ample space with few people, most Americans would prefer the old Nevada way. In a crowd, it just doesn't work.

The change is evident in other ways. For a long time Nevada politicians followed a specific model. They were usually Mormon—they'd been equally Catholic through the McCarran era, but after the old senator's death, Catholic power in politics diminished—diffident and soft-spoken, aw-shucks kinds of guys, lanky and understated. U.S. senators Harry Reid and Richard Bryan, the state's pair throughout the 1990s, and Bob Miller, governor from 1988 to 1998, and even Governor Kenny Guinn, who looked like a high school football coach, also fit the mold. They were genuine guys, powerful but careful about public displays of the use of power. In 2000 Bryan retired and Nevada elected Republican John Ensign to his seat. A veterinarian and the son of Mandalay Resort Group executive Mike Ensign, one of the most powerful political influences in the entire state, the younger Ensign had the California blow-dried look of a TV anchor. He didn't have much to say because he didn't have much opposition, but even a commercial to enunciate his deep Nevada roots did little to take the sheen off his vacuous male-model persona. He seemed arrogant and even mean as he tried to be one of those Republicans who sounded like Democrats as the population aged. Ensign was clearly a new species on the Nevada scene, a forerunner of a new urban and even urbane cast to state politics.

This move toward the American mainstream in politics belies the differences of a transient city just settling into an uncomfortable adolescence. For all its recent in-migration, Las Vegas is still a frontier city, there for the taking. "The heart of Las Vegas hasn't changed," observed John L. Smith. "Its sense of itself isn't that different than it was." Las Vegas has fewer rules, its political cadres are less effectual and their reach less comprehensive, and local and regional institutions are nonexistent or still forming. But Las Vegas is on the road to being typical, coalescing at a rapid rate, and the differences are not so telling after all. Las Vegas was wide open and in a lot of ways still is. The great weight of migrants who come not because of Las Vegas's difference, but because of its newly discovered economic opportunities and low cost of living is grinding down the hard-nosed anarchy of an earlier time. Las Vegas was once a rogue's city, a place where you could come to shed the sins of your past. Like other such places, San Francisco during the Gold Rush, third-world cities crammed with expatriates, or any Carribean beachside bar, no one asked who you'd been before. It was exhilarating and it contributed to the exciting, edgy feel about the place. Fluidity and the sense that anything was possible characterized Las Vegas even into the 1990s.

The real change has been recent, most evident in the last half of the 1990s. An average of sixty thousand new residents a year for fifteen years will tamp down a city's fluidity with sheer numbers. These newcomers create a new set of realities that defy the older, hands-off logic. As Las Vegas becomes more typical, as Californians and others take over its institutions, there will more be change. People can't help but re-create what they left behind in their new homes, can't help but transpose their personal and social past onto any new setting even if they're trying to flee that past. One casualty over time may very well be Las Vegas's fundamental flexibility, already diminishing but still a powerful force. It may be crushed by the growing weight of newcomers and their desires.

In 1999 the Clark County School District redrew its school zone boundaries for the umpteenth time. Opening a dozen new schools or more every year means that many children change districts with frightening regularity. There are apocryphal tales of people who stayed in the same house for a decade and sent their children to a different school each year. A lack of continuity was one of the prices of living in Las Vegas and there didn't seem to be much that people could do about it. But the influx of people with higher expectations has started a near revolution. At a public hearing to discuss the latest boundary change, a parade of people trooped to the microphone to make their special pleas. A lot started by saying, "We've only been here a few months, but . . ." or "Back home, we did it this way. . . ." Some had been excluded by one street from the school they wanted; others expected to be included in the newest school but weren't. Some gently asked or even begged for a variance, a bend in the rules to tide them over. Others fumed, shouted, and threatened. It seemed a typical moment in the life of a growing city, when change hits individuals who hadn't been reading the tea leaves, but for the first time in my decade in Nevada, I heard the sound of the treehouse effect, when the newcomers try to pull the ladder up behind them after they've arrived. The schools are too crowded, there's too much growth, they said, and it has to stop. Government should do something about it. There it was, the voice of change, splitting the old Nevada where people did as they pleased from the need for order in a rapidly growing place. The accompanying plea to change the rules of nature to suit their whim marks the cult of self-indulgence that the nation blames on southern California but is truly all of our fault. The new Las Vegas was on the road to normal.

Chapter 6

The Face of the Future

I EASED MY CAR OUT OF THE DRIVEWAY, HURRYING ONCE AGAIN. I WAS late, and for a guy who prides himself on promptness, this ever more frequent feature of my harried daily existence drove me nuts. Out of the subdivision onto the arterial road in record time, I smiled. Just a few hundred yards to the freeway and a fighting chance to gear up, lay some dust, and be there on time. I hate to be kept waiting; I try never to do it to anyone else. It's a courtesy I like to extend, but one that is harder and harder to meet as the pace of life quickens and the demands grow. So I've taken on the look of a frantic commuter, hustling through traffic, biting my lip, afraid that once again someone is going to be standing around waiting on me.

I turned from the winding two-lane street onto the four-lane and accelerated. A spot of clear road opened, and changing lanes, I steered toward it, prepared to zip through it, around the traffic, and on to my meeting. There my nightmare began. Reaching the open patch of road, I nearly ran into another increasingly common phenomenon of daily life in the Las Vegas Valley. Clogging both lanes were slow-moving cars, one a boatlike Cadillac, the other a more characteristic nimble gold Saturn. The heads of the drivers were gray, gnarled hands clutched the steering wheel firmly at 10 and 2 o'clock, plodding along at twenty-five miles per hour in a forty-mile-an-hour zone. They talked in a relaxed way to one another, oblivious to all around them. Old people! I slowed down and began to mutter to myself, "Why can't they stay in the right lane? Who drives the speed limit, anyway?" I angled, tailgated, tried to maneuver around them, all to no avail. If they hadn't driven in tandem, if either of them had just once gotten above thirty miles per hour, I might have made the light and been on the freeway at the pace I'd hoped. But stopped at the red light, the seconds passed and my chances eroded. One of the cars sat in the right-turn lane, obviously going straight ahead; it figured! I continued to stew. It was a conspiracy of old people, a passive-aggressive way of maintaining control in a world that passed them by. Finally, I made the turn, accelerated and was gone, hopelessly trying to make up lost time that was my own fault to begin with. I'm sure passengers in the two cars shook their heads and wondered what could have been so pressing.

The St. Petersburgization of Las Vegas has begun in earnest and its consequences in a harder society are manifest everywhere. In 1998 almost 20 percent of the population in southern Nevada was over sixty-five years of age; another 17 percent was between the ages of fifty-five and sixty-four. Two large retirement communities, Del Webb's Sun City in Summerlin in the northwest and Sun City–McDonald Ranch in the southeast, seeded the territory. Anthem, with its huge upscale retirement community, opened in 1998 and grew rapidly, but retirees were spread throughout the community. A visit to any grocery store would turn up some. Every park and all the libraries were full of them. Three in ten households in the valley, more than 125,000 homes, a remarkable number, enjoyed the presence of a retiree. Statistically, every block had one retiree. Greater Las Vegas was ahead of the curve in the United States, well on the way to becoming a retirement center for a society that sees personal satisfaction as the ultimate end of human endeavor. Soon to be inundated, the rest of the nation watched as Las Vegas became the newest Florida, a refuge for retirees, with all the problems that stemmed from the addition of a population of seniors with few connections to the people who already lived in town.

The almost 20 percent of the population that identified as retired in 1998 were the crest of a remarkable wave. Most were born in the 1920s and 1930s, preceding the baby boom, but these preboomers were a portent of a very different-looking future. The graying of American society is well under way, and the retirement of a baby boomers spells a transformation as great as any in American demographic history. American society has been revolutionized by the needs of baby boomers every step of their way through life. In 1950 the United States needed thousands of kindergarten teachers, in 1957, thousands of junior high teachers, in 1963, thousands of college professors, and in 1969, millions of jobs. As the twentieth century ended, that enormous cohort inched toward retirement. The oldest and most affluent of them, the glimmer of diamond sheen at the top of the iceberg, have already made the transition, but their castles, tennis courts, and pools do not typify the transformation to come. The first to settle down to the eternal routine of travel, golf, and dinners out are of the wealthiest strata, the people for whom cost is not an object. Most of the retirees to come will have to manage on a budget of one kind or another.

For most of this group, the prospects are great. Current retirees are the wealthiest generation in human history, the beneficiaries of the great aberration that stretched from 1945 to 1974. They are the tip of an explosion that will bring an even wealthier generation to the end of their careers, and they too prepare for what will be an extended sunset. They've got money and will also benefit from the greatest cross-generational transfer of wealth in human history. They've got more time and better health than of their predecessors, they'll live considerably longer than their parents and grandparents, and they're disengaged from the wants and needs of the rest of society. As this elephant has done throughout its passage through the boa constrictor of time, retiring baby boomers will again revolutionize American life as they approach life's exit.

Las Vegas's newness highlights this trend. A huge sector of the population, retirees are creating a new kind of service economy. Since the 1940s the Las Vegas Valley has depended on low-skilled service work—cooks, maids, casino dealers, valet parkers, retail, and an entire constellation of similar occupations—to drive the regional economy. Retirement also requires a service economy, but one inherently different from other manifestations in the Las Vegas Valley. Many of the occupations that retirees depend on require higher levels of skill than making beds or cleaning rooms, and such jobs—nursing, physical therapy rehabilitation, and running medical imaging equipment—pay well. The unskilled medical work is not as lucrative as unionized casino work and it certainly doesn't inspire tipping.

The retirement economy is labor-intensive personal service in a way that much work used to be, but only tourism and child care still are in the United States. Retirement communities are often self-sufficient islands that provide their own services specifically for their residents. They inhabit a largely separate universe, which requires labor, some of it specialized, but much of it unskilled—activities such as lifting, carrying, and cleaning. Some retirees need assistance beyond professional service in office visits and clinics. Clerks must handle medical and governmental paperwork. Someone has to push the gurney on which they're transported. From recreation to transportation, these activities require staff, service, and personal attention. Retirees enjoy golf so much that new golf courses have proliferated in the valley. Each requires a staff, not only a golf pro, but a groundskeeper, a maintenance crew and supervisors, bartenders, cooks, and locker room attendants. Retirees also frequent coffeehouses and movies, restaurants, parks, community centers, and especially libraries. With the retired population growing daily, these areas have the potential to be catalysts for changes in the structure of the local economy.

Retirement is a problematic social phenomenon in a city without strong roots. Retirees fit the model of the CAVIE—citizens against virtually everything—and in a city where they've come to retire and don't have deep ties, their desire to take their rewards far exceeds any feelings they have about the future of the community. In this, retirees pose a significant dilemma. Like everyone else in Nevada, retirees take more out of the system than they put in and they don't rush forward to offer more than their share. Their interests seem parochial and self-centered to those who don't share their circumstances. The real numbers are frightening in their enormity: more than 313,029 children under the age of eighteen give Las Vegas an enormous non-working population to accompany its huge service industry. Added to the 188,000 retirees, 500,000 of the 1,246,000 in the county in 1998 put little into the system. Trapped between two different kinds of open mouths, children and seniors, the latter always loudly demanding that their needs be accommodated, the middle class views seniors with the disdain of a society that would readily eat its old. Regressive tax structure and the demands of vocal constituencies who don't pay their way complicate local decision-making. Cross-generational warfare is never far away.

The weight of this burden signals a complicated future. Las Vegas's demography foretells that of the rest of the nation, with larger numbers of retirees for the first thirty years of the twenty-first century, and as a result of the echo boomers and the growth of immigration, especially from Catholic and rural countries, more children. This peak-valley-peak in population already strains institutions across the country, the Social Security system among them. The consequences in low-tax settings are telling, and in no place are they more in evidence today than in Las Vegas. In a state with the eighth highest per capita income and the third lowest taxes in the nation during the 1990s, Las Vegas faced public poverty nudged up against private prosperity. Nevada's social spending was disastrous, low enough to rank the state in the bottom tier and last in the nation in a number of categories. Part of an age-old Nevada sense of people doing for themselves, this lack of social spending created enormous gaps in the infrastructural fabric as well as huge holes in what passed for the state safety net. It also allowed people to lay off responsibility for the cost of social services on others. At the beginning of the new century, an enormous question loomed: Who would pay for the growth? Whose responsibility is it?

Before air-conditioning, few retired to Las Vegas or any other southwestern city. Americans simply didn't choose Las Vegas, and the city had few of the conventional avenues for attracting retirees. No nearby farmers let their children run the operation while they moved to town to sip coffee in front of the feed store. People didn't sell the house and pack up to move to the desert for its beaches, recreation centers, and shuffleboard courts like they did to Florida. Nor did a young city like Las Vegas harbor lots of elderly people who could cease work and stay closely connected to nearby family. With little history, little of the generations of family layered in place that characterized small-town America, the community grew up and later old together, its ties washed over by the ever-present tide of in-migration. The few retirees who lived in Las Vegas before the 1980s likely spent their working lives in town.

Del E. Webb and his corporation altered that pattern. Born in Fresno, California, in 1899, Webb aspired to be a baseball player. At six feet and two hundred pounds, he cut an imposing figure on the mound and spent the 1920s in the old Pacific Coast League, the third major league that existed because the West Coast was too far from the rest of the nation for effective scheduling. The PCL spawned Joe DiMaggio, Ted Williams, and a host of other early- and midcentury major leaguers. Even in such august company, Webb held his own until he contracted typhoid fever. Debilitated by the illness and half his normal body weight, Webb chose Arizona's climate, as did many people early in the twentieth century who thought the dry air would do them good. Before the 1920s ended, he started his own construction company.

Like any good entrepreneur, Webb gravitated to the sources of construction money, and during the 1930s those dollars came from the federal government. By 1933, the first year of the New Deal, Webb's company was grossing $3 million and it grew throughout the decade. He opened a branch office in Los Angeles in 1935, built an addition to the Arizona state capitol in 1938, and by the time World War II began, was firmly ensconced at the top of the second tier of western construction companies, not far behind the "Big Six," Morrison-Knudsen, Bechtel-Kaiser-Warren Brothers, Utah Construction Company, J. F. Shea Company, Pacific Bridge Company, and McDonald and Kahn that incorporated as Six Companies, built Hoover Dam, and laid the basis for an industrial infrastructure throughout the West.

World War II was the greatest boon ever for western construction companies and it confirmed Del Webb's aptitude and secured his new-found wealth. Webb ran an efficient organization and he had experience with the government before Pearl Harbor precipitated an incredible industrial build-up in the West. The war demanded a full industrial complex to support the Pacific Theater. Webb stood in the forefront, building anything the government asked, including the internment camps for Japanese Americans ejected from their homes and isolated as a perceived threat to national security. If Webb had any moral qualms about such projects, he never publicly expressed them. He became a huge success, one of the wartime stories that paralleled Henry Kaiser's, another of the many who made money doing their part to keep democracy safe. By January 1945 wartime construction made Webb wealthy enough to indulge a personal dream. With partner Dan Topping, he purchased the New York Yankees, and the two men owned the team until 1964, throughout the heyday of Yankee dominance. After 1960 Webb simultaneously owned the New York Yankees and the Sahara Hotel, creating an oddity even now unmatched: he owned a casino in mobbed-up Las Vegas and the premier franchise of the national pastime as Roger Maris broke Babe Ruth's home run record. Nobody gave the obvious contradiction a second thought.

An experienced builder before 1960, Webb found a niche in the postwar housing market with Sun City, outside Phoenix, the first master-planned retirement community in the nation. Marketers discerned that older people wanted distance from their families, breaking the age-old pattern of cross-generational kinship in neighborhoods and communities. Webb planned a new city, apart from Phoenix, a revolutionary idea that freed Sun City from paying for school bonds and other services that a typical community required. Sun City transplanted people into an entirely manufactured place, creating a template for an unformed society that expected people to share space and create conventional community from the single fact that they chose to live in an age-segregated place. Sun City recruited people from across the country, ensuring that its relationship with Phoenix remained complicated and even contentious. Retirees looked past the social obstacles, and Sun City succeeded beyond all expectations.

The Sun City model became more important to the nation with each passing year. While Sun City didn't create retirement as a concept, it did institutionalize the retirement community as a separate phenomenon, apart from other stages of life. Webb also displayed prescient command of social desires, picking a segment of society and offering it a "way of life," presaging the increasing penchant for comfort and convenience that marked the aging of the baby boomers. Sun City remained a niche market in the 1960s and 1970s; the people who chose it were the vanguard of a revolution in social behavior, the wave that would be cresting to shore a full generation in the future. Sun City's claim to community stemmed from physical rather than social relationships, but it established a pattern of central authority and management, detachment from surroundings, and vocal self-interest that has come to define American retirement. Even before the Del Webb Company built even one subdivision in Las Vegas, it played a significant role in the shaping the way not only Las Vegas but most of the rest of the desert West eventually looked.

The creation of retirement communities in greater Las Vegas started as a function of unusual patterns of land ownership in the valley. In the 1970s and 1980s developers started such communities, one on a 260-acre parcel near McCarran Airport, but none came easily and quickly to fruition. The market was not sophisticated, large numbers of retirees loomed too far on the horizon, and none of the developers had sufficient acreage to create a self-contained community with more than its own pool, recreation center, and clubhouse. Golf courses, one of the prestige symbols of retirement, were impossible in the available space. Without large plots of land, the communities could offer only age segregation as an advantage. They seemed more like apartment complexes than communities and hardly appealed to people who planned for an active and fulfilling retirement.

The Del Webb Corporation jumpstarted local retirement communities. The company enjoyed close ties with Summa Corporation, the descendant of the Howard Hughes Corporation and one of the primary landholders in the valley. In the mid-1980s Summa planned an area called Summerlin, west of the existing city but within Las Vegas's city limits. The Del Webb Corporation's ties with Summa stretched back to the friendship between Webb, who died in 1974, and Hughes in the 1940s. Hughes still dealt with the outside world in those days and Webb had done the increasingly odd billionaire countless personal and business favors, in particular announcing the ill-fated move of Hughes's operations to Florida in 1956. The Del Webb Corporation was the largest casino owner in the state when Hughes returned to Las Vegas in 1966, and Webb himself advised Hughes on his purchase of the Desert Inn. As the company considered its vast holdings in Las Vegas, Webb and his company enjoyed a nearly exclusive hold on its large-scale development.

The Del Webb Corporation's inside status became evident in a number of ways. Summa Corporation executives worked closely with Webb Corporation leaders as they fashioned a strategy for Summerlin. Even before the announcement of its master plan for the new development in 1988, the Webb Corporation closed on 1,050 acres of the area. The move came at an opportune time, for changes in the casino industry and the difficult real estate market of the 1980s put the company in a tailspin. In 1987 it reported a loss of $96.6 million, and 1988 ended with a similar loss. Webb's signature development, the retirement community, offered a fast way back to financial health. With access to much land in the path of growth well ahead of other developers, Del Webb inaugurated suburban west Las Vegas with a sizable advantage.

Anchored by a golf course designed by legendary professional golfer Billy Casper and architect Greg Nash, the Sun City model was transplanted from Phoenix to Las Vegas. The plan was a "cookie-cutter development," one old-timer recalled, typical of the Del Webb Corporation's retirement communities elsewhere, offering a total of 3,100 homes on 1,050 acres and the ability to expand on an additional 842 acres on which to situate 2,800 more homes. The homes were modest in price, ranging from $70,000 to $150,000, the same market at which the company's earlier Sun City development projects aimed. By the late 1980s Del Webb had perfected the age-segregated community. Bolstered by the low taxes, easy living, and the promise of privacy and protection, Sun City Summerlin, as it was named, heralded another transformation in regional demography. Las Vegas drew retirees from other places in growing numbers, bringing a new component that the city had never before experienced.

The stigma of Las Vegas long slowed the growth of retirement in the valley, but as the nation moved further from its midcentury neo-Victorian pose, retiring in Las Vegas first made sense and then became desirable. As communal social obligation dissipated, moving to a place where you did not have to pay much in taxes, especially ones that provided services for other people's children, had considerable appeal. Golf courses were common, and with cheap food and entertainment in the casinos, Las Vegas became an even more powerful draw. In the 1990s Del Webb dominated the local market, leading the sales per subdivision in most years. In 1996 alone, Sun City Summerlin sold 702 homes, while Sun City McDonald Ranch, Del Webb's southeast site in Green Valley, sold 458. At completion, Sun City Summerlin contained more than 6,000 units. McDonald Ranch topped 2,500 homes when it was completed in 2000.

The Del Webb Corporation also expanded the retirement marketplace, creating an upscale development that included a retirement community clearly meant to seed the future in advance of the massive retirement of baby boomers. As 1997 ended, Del Webb debuted Anthem, atop Eastern Avenue at the south end of the valley, on five thousand acres the company acquired in an exchange with the Bureau of Land Management. The new development, named Sun City Anthem, was the first to tap the upscale retirement market. Instead of a ceiling of about $190,000 in price as at most of the corporation's other developments, Sun City Anthem started at around $240,000 for three-bedroom, one-story single-family dwellings aimed at retirees.

As Las Vegas prepared for more upscale visitors at its new palaces, Del Webb sought to convert some of them into residents at Sun City Anthem. The synergistic strategy had worked before in Las Vegas, and more affluent retirees were attracted to a luxury community located high above the city. Del Webb had again taken the lead in retirement services, offering high-quality living at an expensive local price far beneath the cost of similar properties elsewhere. Again the company sought an out-of-town market; again they pulled newcomers who fit the demographic of their market to the newest Sun City.

Del Webb's success in Las Vegas is not unique. The company led the market and plenty of others followed behind it, but even more telling, the move of the baby boomers through American society made Del Webb's nascent gamble as close to a sure thing as developers could imagine. The combination of excellent amenities, comparatively low cost, and accessible entertainment made the arrangement a winner. With a population growing faster than even Clark County's burgeoning pace, nothing suggests that the number of retirees in greater Las Vegas will diminish any time soon.

. . .

Las Vegas's retirees closely fit the profile of other migrants to southern Nevada. They clearly come for the climate—"it's warm," retirees say when asked about their choice—and for the nearly nonexistent tax structure and the affordable cost of living. "It's cheaper than either California or Florida," one retiree told me, and given the vocal complaints of seniors any time they're asked to pay more, Nevada's notoriously regressive tax system is likely to stay that way. Despite draws like climate and golf courses galore, retirement in a strange town, without a network of family and friends, has to be a daunting prospect. Generations of northeasterners went to Florida and created a community, but they were largely surrounded by their neighbors from back home. Could they do the same in a new city, one that was rising to retirement fame while it simultaneously accomplished a number of other transformative economic tasks?

The Desert Willow Community Center sits atop a golf course, surrounded by Sun City McDonald Ranch. The center functions as a country club for retirees, a place where people go to golf and eat, where come election time the voting booths are set up, where book, sewing, and other clubs meet, and where people come just to pass the time. It offers a lovely view of the mountains to the south, and the golf course wraps around the building and across the street. If you can look past the putting greens and sand traps, it is vaguely pastoral, and you can almost see nature. Citizens Area Transit, the award-winning local bus system, drops passengers right at the center's door, and a bus from a local casino chain comes by to collect those in search of an outside expedition. The center seems idyllic, complete, promising a serene, sedate, pleasant, enjoyable environment with access to the outside—and, equally important, insulation from it.

The retirees in Sun City Summerlin and Sun City McDonald Ranch are as middle class as they come. Working-class and middle-class southern Californians make up a healthy share, as do former federal workers, and union families from the Rust Belt. The voting patterns illustrate the diversity. While middle- and upper-middle-class newcomers of working age in Las Vegas lean to republican affiliation, gradually shifting the political orientation of the state, a large block of retirees retain the voting affinities of their work life. For union and federal retirees, this often means allegiance to the Democratic Party, which in 1999 still maintained a 46 to 34 percent advantage over Republicans in Clark County. This predominance doesn't necessarily translate into democratic sweeps of local or state politics, although it's safe to say that U.S. senator Harry Reid owes his reelection in 1998 to the turnout among retirees, but it does slow the rise of Republican ascension prevalent elsewhere in the interior West.

An increasing number of retirees land in Las Vegas for a clearly personal reason: their kids and grandkids are there. Las Vegas's economic opportunity provided a re-creation of an older cross-generational American society, in which three generations live in proximity and know each other better than they did when the kids and grandkids came for a visit at the holidays. In a booming city with two distinct areas of exclusively retirement homes, families can also avoid the oppressiveness of the grandparents next door—or to turn the equation around, the whiny expectation of grown-up children that their parents will watch their kids so they can go out and play. In many Las Vegas Valley families, the grandparents live west, the children and grandkids east, or vice versa. The distance is short, if sometimes made long by traffic, but the twenty-five miles is a lot less than the 280 to southern California or the 2,000 by air to the East Coast. In post–World War II America, when people followed a sense of destiny far from their roots and forged community in their newly built neighborhoods, kids saw their grandparents three or four times a year at most. In 1990s Las Vegas, smaller holidays and frequent backyard parties encompass not only two, but three and sometimes four generations, only the youngest of which may be native to Nevada. In a fundamentally transient place, nothing provides a stronger sense of being home.

But retirees still have endless days to fill. A few babysit for their kids, more enjoy the freedom of retirement to take up pastimes like golf, and still more tend their yards. The lawns of retirees are well kept, manicured, with hardly a blade of grass or a rock out of place. Retired men, especially those with mechanical or woodworking inclination and who had consigned the house to their wife during their working years, take over the garage and plan endless projects. There's an unmatched market for table saws among Las Vegas retirees. Don Fritz, a retired executive who hails from Ohio and lived his working life in Texas, is in the garage daily by 6 A.M., no matter what the season. He exercises, putters around for a while, then takes on one of the endless tasks he's always in the middle of. Some days he's cutting out dead grass and replacing it with new sod; others, he's working in the garage with a Skil Saw. It's intimidating to younger people on his block, who regularly work seventy hours a week and try to keep up, noticing the weeds in the lawn but not always able to schedule the time to do something about them. We see his labor and remember the houses of our youth. Don's house and yard are the best on the block, and this generous-spirited neighbor not only puts up spectacular Christmas lights, he does the same for his neighbors.

For those who lack Don Fritz's energy or skill or who don't golf, other options abound. Seniors get up and go for a long morning walks in remarkable number. At dawn on summer mornings, the best time for outdoor exercise in the hottest months, the hike-and-bike trails are jammed with retirees. They walk alone or in couples, sometimes in larger groups, arms swinging or casually pumping. Some go for coffee and a paper, some just walk, and others jog, bike, and a few even in-line skate, the sophisticated technology removing much of the pounding of roller skating. Fit seniors can enjoy this often strenuous activity with complete ease. Some seniors work two or three days a week, mostly as a way to meet people or to be involved in something they enjoy. Local churches and synagogues also benefit from retirees, who volunteer their time and share their experience with established and recently founded institutions. Retirees eat out an average of three times a week, see a lot of movies, and spend plenty of time in libraries. They use a lot of public services, getting great benefit from the sales tax and minimal property taxes they pay, and they always turn out a crowd for a public hearing if its topic affects them.

There's a slightly nefarious side to this bucolic retirement heaven. The few studies of retirement have shown a pattern with potentially devastating consequences. Retirees typically enjoy about fifteen years of independent living in the Las Vegas Valley; after that time, either the husband has died and the wife lives with a daughter in the valley or elsewhere, or the couple has become frail and moved on to assisted living. In some cases, retirees can't manage the casinos any better than the most vulnerable of any other group, and they find that within a two- to five-year window, their assets are devoured and they face a less pleasant, less secure future. For most of them this is a signal to move on, but some stay and become part of the underclass of retirees—the 40 percent of retirees who have household incomes below $25,000 annually. The majority of the 18 percent who have household incomes of less than $15,000 a year have always been poor, but some of them are newly vulnerable, made so by their own actions. Las Vegas does capitalize on weaknesses, and will expose anyone, young or old, rich or poor, who can't control their passions or can't reason their way through problems. Senior citizen status does not provide inoculation from personal foible.

• • •

The corner of Wigwam and Pecos in suburban Green Valley tells a lot about the tensions that will come to bear in Las Vegas's future. In a shopping mall stands a twenty-four-hour fitness club, attentive to the all-consuming desire to stay young that obsesses the American upper middle class. If you identify with the professional classes like the people who inhabit the new suburbs, you're likely to belong to a gym like this one. Next to the club is Mira Loma, a recently constructed assisted-living community that also caters to patients with Alzheimer's Disease. This juxtaposition of space is repeated over and over again in greater Las Vegas and it brings a number of awful jokes about overlapping activities to mind, all of which reflect the selfishness of people these days as well as how familial obligations have frayed. The two facilities emphasize the speed with which suburban Las Vegas has become multigenerational. Very different in their purposes, the health club and the assisted-living center illustrate a novel set of relationships that are repeated all over the Las Vegas Valley. Two groups, in entirely different stages of life, unconnected by any kind of relationship or experience, share space in a complicated way. Both entities have their own parking lots, but the juxtaposition and shared space represents the way to an intertwined future.

That neatly intersecting future is everywhere. I picked a local Starbucks located near a large retirement area and a number of other neighborhoods and made camp at about 6:15 one morning. I wanted to see how one space could accommodate a range of different uses and users in the course of a day. A laptop was my only tool; I intended to use it as a recording device. I ordered coffee and sat down to watch who came along and what they did.

The early morning was the province of the young and the middle-aged. The parade of well-dressed, well-coiffed people driving nice cars and hurrying to the counter for a carry-out coffee and maybe a Danish or a biscotti were legion. A few stopped and sat, some eating alone, reading the paper, or just breathing in a moment of solitude. Others were in groups, in casual breakfast meetings. These people knew one another and obviously enjoyed each other's company. One couple, clearly married, were having breakfast by themselves. It looked like a tradition, something they did together regularly, maybe once a week, so that they could have a little time alone to catch up with one another. The café bustled early in the morning, with lots of motion, some of it hectic, some of it controlled. Getting on to other things, willingly or unwillingly, was the overriding theme.

By about 7:30 A.M., a new group became prevalent. Carpooling moms, sometimes with kids in tow, became the dominant presence. They ran in for coffee, grabbed a bagel, biscuit, or even hot chocolate for the kids, and ran out again, on their way to drop the kids off at school or preschool, the best-dressed on their way to work or perhaps another appointment. A few padded in wearing pajamas; a few more sat in their cars in pjs and sent the kids in for the carry-out order. By 8:30 A.M., some of the same moms, the ones dressed in casual clothes, were back, this time meeting friends and sounding more relaxed. They sat this time, in groups of two, three, and four, drinking coffee, laughing, talking, catching a quick breath, a brief interlude before getting on with the day. By 9 A.M., the coffee house emptied, and I thought a long and boring day awaited me.

As if by magic, as the younger people streamed out, retirees appeared. Some walked in, finishing or perhaps in the middle of a morning stroll. One man ambled in, smiled at me as he took off his jaunty cap, strolled to the counter, and began to flirt with the twenty-something counter girl. She clearly knew him, and their talk looked like part of a daily ritual, a game that pleased them both. More retirees came in, some in sweat suits after aerobics or maybe tai chi, an age-old Chinese form of exercise that offers a combination of relaxation, stretching, and mind-over-matter discipline. Tai chi has become very popular with Las Vegas Valley retirees. One class in 1999 was so oversubscribed that the local recreational center offered a second and then a third one. This next group, mostly women, bought coffee and sat in the same places the younger moms favored just an hour before. They too chose the picture windows, the open and in the winter pleasantly sunny spaces in the café. I could not help but think of their choice as a promenade, a conscious selection to be both comfortable and visible. They wanted to see who was passing by and be seen as well.

In one hour, the composition of the Starbucks audience changed dramatically. The first wave, the earliest part of the day, belonged to the people without choices, the ones who had to be somewhere soon. They were harried and clipped, purposeful about their decisions, drawn, and, late in the week, visibly tired. Their presence was part of a routine, but clearly not one they easily controlled. Once they moved into the part of the day where they no longer controlled their time, the tenor of the café changed. Where the professional class strode with purpose, the retirees ambled casually, without pressures and with only the places they chose to be in front of them.

The older people were far more curious about me than were the working moms and dads who hustled through. Not one of the well-dressed men and women on their way to work gave me more than a glance. Who cared? Who had time if they did? Within minutes of their arrival, a couple of the retirees came over to see what I was doing. Partly I was intruding; my hair is not yet gray, and they were unaccustomed to a young one in their midst, observing them and typing away on a keyboard. This was their space, their actions told me, and they were carefully checking me out. The two gentlemen who came to chat me up evinced almost a proprietary sense of the coffeehouse. Once they figured out I was harmless—emphatically I told them I wasn't a newspaper reporter—they concluded our talk and went back to their coffee. Several waves of retirees appeared throughout the morning. Although they came and went, there were always between eight and fifteen in the café. By about 11:30 A.M., newcomers no longer replaced the ones who drifted off. The retirement presence diminished, and I figured that my experiment was coming to an end.

As the retirees cleared out, a wave of younger people appeared and filled the Starbucks. The frantic pace returned, with its air of transience. They came this time in groups of two, three, and four, meeting people dressed like them for what were obviously business discussions. One woman wore a Realtor's jacket; another I recognized worked as a loan officer in a bank. These were hardly power lunches. Although many unholstered their cell phones, and put them on the tables in front of them as if they were gunslingers offering proof of prowess, the phones did not chime and chirp constantly as they did in power settings. They were doing business, but it was friendly, with people they already knew and with whom they felt comfortable. They weren't trying to impress one another with how important they were. The well-dressed continued to stream in, and within half an hour, the café was full of a lunchtime crowd, insistent, with only glimpses of leisure about them.

The afternoon followed the same pattern. By 1:30 P.M. most of the lunch crowd was gone, and different retirees came in, sitting, talking, and sipping coffee as had the groups in the morning. By 3 P.M. moms showed up again with children in tow, and they too met friends, sat, and conversed. Soon after, a parade of people began. By 3:30 or 4:00 P.M, whatever coherent identifiable patterns I'd seen during the day fell apart. Instead of belonging to one or another group, the café truly became common space. Other people sat with laptops, writing. One guy checked his e-mail with his computer through his cell phone. Kids played, people stood in line, and the segregation of time and space came to an end.

The day seemed hopeful somehow, as if different groups could easily share one space in the course of the day without tension or rivalry. The key was respecting the boundaries of time, of observing the unwritten de facto distinctions that kept different groups from treading upon one another. Every group who came to Starbucks shared the same or at least similar purposes. Socializing was high on nearly everyone's list. For most who sat down, the coffee was a backdrop to conversation. People rarely stepped beyond their group, but that didn't seem unusual. Where in American society do people routinely cross boundaries of age and class? They don't really anymore, except possibly when they're teenagers or in college, and maybe they never did. The coexistence of these different groups showed a kind of tolerance that a society that has long dispensed with shared space and civility could use in larger doses. Sometimes the kids were loud, but the retirees did not complain or even look askance at the parents in that way that people who were raised when you could shame someone do. Everyone seemed to respect each other's right to be there. At least in public spaces, the retirees and working-aged people shared interests. When pocketbooks were concerned, the relationship frayed very fast.

While Las Vegas's many generations can easily share space, when it comes to paying for the infrastructure that growth demands, their interests quickly diverge. Nevada's tax system, made up of sales tax and casino tax revenues, makes it a haven for people who seek to avoid paying any share of their communal freight. Twenty-five percent of Clark County's population in 1998 were under the age of eighteen and almost 20 percent were retired, but the burden of paying for all the institutions the community needed fell on less than three-fifths of the population. Retirees and children both make enormous demands on infrastructure and social institutions, and Las Vegas strains to accommodate both.

The maldistribution of fiscal responsibility meant that sooner or later the valley would face difficult choices. The Clark County School District, which grew so quickly that in 2001 it was the sixth largest in the country, with more than 230,000 students spending more than $1 billion annually, became a central flash point. Each year it added as many students as the average American school district contained. By 2000 15,000 new students were entering the system each year, and growth showed no sign of slowing.

Financing new schools and renovating older ones became a crucial test, one that threatened to rip the fabric of what passed for community apart.

Most of Las Vegas's retirees, lured by Del Webb's marketing strategy, the rapid growth of the community, and the ease of living in Las Vegas, had lived their working lives elsewhere. Few of them felt any allegiance to Nevada, and fewer still felt that funding the growth that they were part of should be their responsibility. Like seniors everywhere, they feared a rising cost of living and regarded the prospect of even small increases in their tax burden as a threat to their economic stability. The cost of growth, and especially schools, was not their problem, seniors loudly told the rest of the community in public hearings. They had paid their dues, their school assessments, back home, a long time ago, when their children were young. It was somebody else's turn.

Although it is hard to find Nevada's taxes with a microscope, seniors battled any effort to raise taxes with fervor and dexterity. A higher cost of living was the single overriding threat to their insulated existence. In 1996 a small change in the assessor's rates for Sun City Summerlin nearly fomented a revolt. Seniors lined up outside the city clerk's office in Las Vegas, circulated petitions, attended city council meetings in large numbers, and vociferously spoke against any tax increase. Because seniors had the time and the energy for political organization and a track record of appearing at the polls in disproportionate numbers, the council melted. The rates were turned back, and seniors won an important political victory.

But that victory came at the expense of frightened politicians who needed to curry favor with powerful senior coalitions to win reelection. After establishing themselves as a dominant voter bloc, seniors cultivated their power. Politicians came knocking, in search of support, but the most evident power seniors held was in community-wide races that did not inspire passion. By 2000 candidates for the university system board of regents, the state school board, and the local school board were openly currying favor with seniors. Campaigns that were not too well heeled targeted only seniors. Such strategies affirmed the axiom that seniors voted when others didn't.

But political power had the potential to aggravate as well as yield spoils. In other circumstances, seniors faced the double-edged sword created by the combination of their power and insularity. They too could become careless with power, vain about its sources, and complacent about its persistence. The truth in southern Nevada was that no group paid their own way, seniors no more so than anyone else. Without cross-generational cooperation for the good of the community, the gig was up. If any one group balked at coming up with its meager share, the house of cards would crumble. Funding the schools became the test for weak city- and county-wide institutions as well as for the power of seniors in a transient community.

The Clark County School District became the battleground of cross-generational warfare. No matter what the district did, growth outstripped its ability to keep pace. Since the late 1980s, the stream of new students required the construction of so many schools that it spawned a quaint quirk. Las Vegas may be the only place in United States where schools are routinely named for living people. So many new schools and Nevada's small leadership cadre quickly exhausted the short list of obvious deceased choices, and planners found themselves with a shortage of names for schools. They turned to the builders of the moment. Principals and teachers of distinction often find their names adorning schools even before they retire. Selma Bartlett, long an institution in the city of Henderson, had a school named for her well before she left the workplace. Developer Irwin Molasky gave his namesake school money for equipment and other needs. Current and former governors Kenny Guinn and Bob Miller both have schools named for them. Almost anyone of any longevity and distinction will soon find their name on a gleaming new school building. With at least 140 new schools from just the two most recent bond issues, it's hard to find people to name them for. Washington, Jefferson, and Lincoln were taken a long time ago.

Bond issues in 1994 and 1996 were the largest ever undertaken by the district. The 1994 issue floated $605 million to build 24 new schools, undertake three major expansions, and modernize 113 existing schools. It also earmarked $30 million for the purchase of land. The 1996 issue added an additional $643 million for similar purposes. These huge sums barely kept pace with growth. Some of the new schools, especially elementary schools, found themselves at twice the projected capacity within a year of opening. Year-round schooling has been a feature of the Las Vegas Valley since the late 1980s, and the bond issues were supposed to if not end the practice, at least keep it from spreading. Growth again overwhelmed intention, and the newest of these schools, even when principals adamantly opposed year-round schooling, soon found themselves on a twelve-month schedule.

There was no way to perceive the rapid growth of the district as anything but intense pressure to meet the needs of the young. But in a community with nearly as many seniors, many with a powerful vested interest in maintaining the status quo, any spending program, especially one that held out the prospect of even marginally higher taxes, faced fierce and ongoing opposition. Opponents of spending comprised one of the most powerful emerging political forces in the largely apathetic political climate of the Las Vegas Valley, and negotiating the various interests became complicated at best and tenuous under any circumstances. As hundreds of thousands of new residents made their way to Las Vegas during the 1990s, a showdown between seniors and the rest of the community was brewing.

It began with a second part of the 1994 school bond issue. Between 1985 and 1994, growth changed the valley's demography so completely that the district's piecemeal approach did not meet the challenge. The school district's portion of the property tax was set to decline after 1995, but the district needed even more than the continuation of its mill levy; it also needed new dollars. Early research by the district indicated little opposition to continuing property taxes at the existing level, but considerable antipathy for an outright tax increase, even a minimal one. Rather than run one bond issue, the district got gun-shy. It divided the 1994 bond issue into two parts, one the continuation of the existing mill levy, and the second a new and separate bond issue that would have raised taxes on the average Las Vegas area home by about $39 a year. Seniors revolted, and the situation provided a rare moment of candor in late twentieth-century public discourse. Irate seniors felt no qualms about publicly stating that they didn't feel responsibility for children in the community. "We're on fixed incomes," one said at a public hearing, "and these are not our children anyway." The second part of the bond issue was narrowly defeated, and everyone gave credit—or blame, depending on your point of view—to the seniors. Inadvertently and almost without anyone realizing what had happened, the first salvo in what could have become a war between the generations exploded on the local landscape.

In American history, there has been no more powerful force than public education and none more sacred to the idea of participatory democracy. Made possible by the reservation of a section of land in every township, public education has always been the rock-solid bottom-line basis of American civic culture. In its long history, it served as a means of advancement for generations, an instrument of socialization for immigrants and the native-born poor, and a great equalizing device. Often shorted by cities, counties, and states, public education has long relied on two primary sources of energy and funding: the students' parents who volunteer time and effort and local property taxes. In a nation where different generations of the same family lived close together, finding support for school bonds across the demographic spectrum was not too hard. In Las Vegas, with only a nascent sense of community in place of deep familial ties, selling school bonds to groups interested primarily in self-preservation was a difficult chore.

Seniors were vulnerable. Without realizing the impact of their vocal opposition, they created a firestorm around them. Seniors demanded higher levels of police and fire protection than other constituencies, and they used public programs more frequently than did younger people. Even a casual glance sustained the notion that seniors got more than their fair share from the system. All that younger members of the community wanted in return was support for school bonds. When they didn't get it, the sense of community, always wobbly, took a full frontal blow. If it really was dog-eat-dog, the actions of a whole spectrum of people seemed to say, let's eat!

Within weeks of election, cries of outrage came from all over the valley. The most militant suggested that Sun City and the other retirement communities create their own municipalities and pay for their own services, without help from anybody else. Others decried the lack of community spirit and wondered if the old had declared war on the young. A counter-revolt took shape, and now the seniors were on the defensive. They had called the tune, and whether it was complacency, power-drunk arrogance, or a sense of invincibility, they ran headlong into a buzzsaw of usually quiet but surprisingly powerful competing interests. It did not take a genius to recognize that providing their own services in separate communities was an expensive proposition. Some resolution, compromise, or middle position had to be found before the next time the school district needed more money.

The district was back for more dollars almost immediately. Stymied by the 1994 defeat, officials still had to accommodate twelve thousand new students a year. Each needed a desk, and since Nevada governor Bob Miller mandated classrooms of eighteen from kindergarten through second grade, later adding third grade, the district found itself undertaking an ongoing building program worthy of the Marshall Plan. A 1996 bond issue passed without a hitch; it prolonged the existing mill levy on property but did not raise taxes at all. Sooner rather than later, a new bond issue would offer the prospect of higher taxes. The real question was: Would seniors vote for it?

Growth accelerated, and each year the school district faced larger numbers of students, new state mandates that affected the ability to run classrooms, and a range of constraints and limitations that hampered its ability to educate. The piecemeal approach to funding worked, but it was exhausting. Mounting a bond issue nearly every year drained the district of resources and energy. No one claimed that the school district was perfect, but it could not solve problems without resources. Overcrowding was rife, test scores were generally mediocre, home-schooling, for whatever reason, on the rise, and the district devoted much of its time to annually shepherding medium-sized bond issues. In a bold step, Superintendent Brian Cram sought a long-term solution to growth in one large bite rather than a series of smaller, incremental mouthfuls. Simultaneously daring and dangerous, the strategy stemmed from the need for stability. Growth was really an all-or-nothing proposition. If Clark County wasn't going to fund the incredible growth it experienced, better to know sooner rather than later.

In 1998, with U.S. senator Harry Reid up for reelection, the district added the largest school bond issue in state history to the ballot. The hotly contested race between Reid and U.S. representative John Ensign ensured a reasonable turnout. From the school district's perspective, the higher the turnout, the better the chances of passage; one important group of voters, seniors, were likely to be at best ambivalent—more likely hostile—toward the proposition, and the more people who turned out, the better the chances of negating their impact. The district's share of the property tax rate was scheduled to decline beginning in 2003. Question 2 on the Clark County ballot froze the assessed value at the 55-cent level until 2008. According to its calculations, the school district could raise $2.5 billion of the $3.5 billion it needed to build eighty-eight schools simply by maintaining the existing higher level of property tax. The real estate transfer tax and the hotel room tax would provide the final $1 billion. No one would pay more; they simply wouldn't pay less, $193 a year on a $100,000 house, for a little longer.

Recognizing the risk inherent in any such proposition, the district left little to chance. Private sources provided $300,000 to support promotions. Governor Miller, the Las Vegas Chamber of Commerce, and the Southern Nevada Strategic Planning Authority all endorsed the proposition. Volunteers canvassed neighborhoods, knocking on doors; thousands of homes posted "Yes on Question 2" signs on their lawns and in their windows. Opponents recognized the power they faced. Framing themselves as watchdogs for the public interest, Glenn Nelson, education chairman of Nevada Concerned Citizens, with the Nevada Seniors Coalition, the leading opponents of the measure, claimed to seek to prevent waste and fraud.

Nelson and other opponents presented the vote as a referendum on a more highly taxed future, the result of irresponsible spending.

Opponents truly believed that they served an important public function, but they faced proponents of the measure within the senior community. Two potent coalitions in favor of the bond issue formed in Sun City Summerlin. Headed by former educators and grandparents of valley children, they recognized how fragile their situation was. A combination of fear of backlash and enlightened self-interest led them to favor the measure. School funding was right, they told their friends. At coffee klatches and town hall meetings, pro-bond seniors excoriated their foes and broadened the discussion. With vocal seniors in support, opponents looked like cranks and extremists. Intensely lobbying their neighbors, the kind of time-consuming grassroots activity that only seniors and paid political workers can afford these days, the senior coalitions played an enormous role in crossing the generational divide and building bridges to a future of competing but complementary interests.

It did not hurt that proponents framed the bond issue as a tax freeze rather than an increase. The language was cagy. In 1998 in Las Vegas, no politician in their right mind wanted to be seen as an advocate of higher taxes, but accommodating growth meant greater expenditures, and the money had to come from somewhere. The result was a kind of sophistry, an argument that promised growth without *added* cost, but deemphasized ongoing costs, a transparent but palatable explanation. To the pro-bond seniors, the bill was less a question of money than of larger community relationships. "We all have to live here," one said to me. "We need to learn to better share."

Such sentiments were truly new in the Las Vegas Valley. Since statehood in 1864, and especially since the 1940s, Nevada had been an individualist's paradise. Here was the genesis of a new ethic, brought on by rapid growth, changing conditions, and flat-out need. They all had a pass, dumping the responsibility for paying their own way to the 36 million annual visitors. The Las Vegas Valley became much more crowded, and different constituencies were intertwined, not only financially but socially as well. Common interests served as a hedge against the alienation spawned by the unmatched pace of growth in change.

The school district kept up its promotional campaign throughout the weeks before the election. Even when a poll showed that the bond issue topped 60 percent in a survey of likely voters, Superintendent Brian Cram did not relax. The six-foot-five son of a school custodian, saw the bond issue as the crowning achievement of his decade at the top. Facing a projection of 150,000 additional students by 2008, Cram could not afford to take the result of the vote for granted. The lobbying remained intense all the way to election day. When the results were in, 63 percent of voters backed the measure, a strong majority. The school district achieved the means to a secure future. A restored sense of cross-generational commitment to community endeavors was an added benefit.

Retirees and the rest of the community truly possessed different interests. The question was how parochially each group would behave, and how supple each could be in arranging coalitions that sought something resembling compromise. The future of life in a new city hinged on each group's willingness to find commonality with others. An all-out Hobbesian war would have been disastrous for everyone. The question turned on issue-specific alliances, on the ability of necessarily self-interested groups to throw a figurative bone to competing interests. The shifting balance of power, the obvious growth of the senior population, as well as growing numbers of children in the community narrowed the waist of the demographic hourglass. That middle sector seemed likely to bear an increasing burden in the twenty-first century. The constellation of forces that passed the 1998 bond issue hardly seemed solid and lasting. Maintaining cross-generational alliances would require work, and such an endeavor appeared essential to the continued functioning of the Las Vegas Valley in the coming decades.

Another dimension of the graying of the Las Vegas Valley offered an obvious but hardly pleasant vision of the future. Most of the retirees walking the trails of the neighborhoods in the morning, going to coffee shops, attending movies, gambling in casinos, and babysitting their grandkids were white. A growing percentage of younger workers, especially unskilled workers, were not. More and more, the faces of the workforce were brown, yellow, or black. This situation looked uncomfortable: one color being served, many more serving. It may be that the future of this country will be marked by older, more affluent white people, who experienced opportunity in their working lives, served by younger, less affluent nonwhites with a smaller chance to achieve a higher standard of living. This is not an issue in the Las Vegas Valley; in fact, it is less of an issue only in southern Nevada as long as the high-wage, low-skill service economy creates upward mobility for anyone who can avoid the city's countless temptations long enough to save money for their children's future. Throughout the nation, as the primary beneficiaries of the stock market run-up of the 1990s age, they will increasingly depend on nonwhites to provide their care and services. In situations where the care-providers see no future, perceive a grind of poorly paid and unappreciated service for cranky old people, another tear at the fabric of social civility is certain.

Although it is no longer fashionable to say so, American society has survived because it could integrate people outside of its dominant classes into its socioeconomic and eventually cultural structure. That these folks were white—albeit in 1900, Catholic, Jewish, and eastern and southern European rather than their Protestant and northern and western European predecessors—may have eased this task. The question facing the nation today, already evident in the Las Vegas Valley, is whether in the twenty-first century the United States can create widespread mechanisms of upward mobility for its African American, Spanish-speaking, and southeast Asian and Filipino young. They are the middle class of the future, the voters of 2035, the people who will shape the nation in the middle of the twenty-first century. The retirement economy will play an enormous role in their future and consequently in the future of the nation. If such jobs can create a middle class with a vested interest, as did the factories of industrial America, if they can create reasonable prosperity with the hope of upward mobility for the children of medical service industry workers, if they can provide work that promotes social and personal responsibility, then American democracy should thrive. It will be different: large parts of it will speak Spanish, it will celebrate new holidays, and it will accommodate different traditions in its schools and shopping malls. But it will still reflect the evolving principles of democracy.

The greatest cultural asset of American capitalism has long been its ability use consumerism to plane off cultural difference. As popular culture became the primary means of communication between young Americans, consumerism supplanted abstract ideas as the basis for American life. It came to be cachet itself, a marker of status and belonging, of class and the distinction of the self in a world of uniformity. Essential to that strategy is people's ability to participate in the consumptionfest that is postindustrial American culture. If they can, a crucial socialization process for democracy—at least what passes for representative government today—will continue. If it fails, if work does not provide the young with the chances that the old once received, the future of the nation is far more dismal. In the end, we'll lose the fluidity that has characterized American society and be left with a reasonable-sized elite, a shrinking middle class, and large numbers of nonwhite and multiracial poor. Assisted by racial divisions, class lines will harden and opportunity will mutate into other, harder-to-recognize and harder-to-reach forms. The hopelessness that such stratification would create would bury representative democracy as we know it today.

CHAPTER 7

Aztlán in Neon

Latinos in the New City

AS THE SUN CRACKS THE EASTERN HORIZON ON ANY LAS VEGAS MORNING, a line of cars backs up at the freeway exit on Eastern Avenue, the turn-off to the hottest development in 2000, Del Webb's Anthem. Before 7 A.M., the line reaches back from exit ramp onto the freeway. Nearly every car is filled with Latinos headed for construction work. Young men mostly, they ride four or five in a truck or car. Nevada license plates predominate, but as always California plates run a close second and Mexico is not far behind. The vehicles are old, often beat-up, with the evidence of previous owners remaining in tattered bumper stickers. I saw one filled with five young Latinos sipping coffee, steam rising on a cold morning; the bumper sticker on the back advocated a vote for one of the California anti-immigration propositions of recent years. Sometimes the new owners will personalize their car: "I ♥ Jalisco" is a favorite, with stickers advertising the Jalisco Restaurant or Lindo Michoacan, for many the best Mexican restaurant in town, hailing their Mexican regional points of origin. Once in a while, a new pickup, brightly colored and sometimes cut to a low rider, will display the driver's sense of accomplishment, but most workers travel in groups, in cars left over from the 1970s and 1980s, big Impalas, beat-up K cars, and the ever-present imported pickup trucks.

They come by the hundreds, the thousands it seems, a version of the white separatist's nightmare depicted in Jean Raspaill's 1970s racist futuristic novel *The Camp of the Saints*, the invasion of the third world into an unprepared, head-in-the-sand first. They rattle by, windows down on the hottest and the coldest mornings, half-awake guys getting ready for another day of hard physical labor. Some walk up the hill; from the top you can see a parade of people on foot. They've come by bus, stopping by the convenience store for water and coffee. The coffee's for now as the sun rises; the water for later, when it is hot and dry no matter what time of year. A few ride bicycles, distinct from the groups of cyclists decked out in bright Lycra jerseys who meet on the same road. There's nothing that says recreation or sport about what they do; this is how they get around. A few gather on the corners in a mini–labor market, looking for work for the day, but they're the minority. Most stream onward, upward toward Anthem, toward work, toward a future they hope is better than the lives they left behind.

This is a common picture in the Southwest, where Latinos, Mexicans predominantly, sometimes with the taint of undocumented status wafting around them, have filled the manual and low-skill labor market. Spanish is everywhere, spoken by the people who do the work. They form armies of housekeepers, maids, janitors, and laborers. Most are poorly paid and have little upward mobility. The work they do is supposed to free them, to set them up for life in the middle class, to give them an opportunity to bootstrap themselves upward, to save money, to own a home, to send a kid to college. In most of the nation, this is an illusion, a trick played on hapless immigrants and others, a promise deceitfully made and not kept. Everybody knows these low-level jobs lead nowhere, provide no benefits, offer nothing to people in a postindustrial society. Even the kids of the guys who walk up the hill know better. No wonder they join gangs and flash signs at passersby. They see their parents' efforts as wasted, futile, disrespected. There's no future in such work.

Las Vegas tweaks this picture, and for some it comes out a lot better. Service work is rewarded, the maids are unionized, they make good wages, get benefits, and can forge a life for themselves and their families. With a good union job, a maid can afford her own home, her own car, and can even save enough to have vacations and eventually send her children to college. It's a success story that is easy to overlook in the incredible cacophony of noise, dollars, and growth that is the postmodern metropolis.

No group of people has become more visible in recent years in Las

Vegas than Latinos. They come from everywhere, from East Los Angeles and now from South Central, which is increasingly Latino rather than African American. They leave Mexico in droves, fleeing the poverty of the cities and oppression of the highlands. Middle-class people from Nicaragua, El Salvador, Guatemala, and Panama come, fleeing the anarchic and often lethal dangers of life in societies with private armies and rampant poverty, where riding in limousines surrounded by armed escorts makes you a target instead of keeping you safe. They land all over the United States, but in a new city, with few of the geographic designations of historic neighborhoods segregated by race or ethnicity, these new migrants are everywhere. The Latino population in Clark County jumped from 85,000 in 1990 to more than 300,000 in 2000, an increase that doubled the Latino presence to more than 20 percent of the county's population. Given the propensity of census workers to undercount immigrants and minorities, that figure is surely well below the actual total. Children with Spanish surnames will soon be the majority in Las Vegas public schools. After making up 13 percent of the school population in 1991–92, Latinos increased to 23 percent, almost 45,000 students, in 1997–98. In the lower grades, the Latino percentage jumps even higher, to 35 percent in kindergarten and 33 percent in both first and third grades. Project that growth out over time and the Latino immigration of the last decade is a major force reshaping Las Vegas.

Latinos have not yet begun to put the impact of their demography into play. Their influence on politics is still minimal, even after the 1998 election of Dario Herrera, a twenty-five-year-old whiz kid from Miami, to the county commission and his ascent to chairman in 2000. Although Herrera will likely run for Nevada's third U.S. house seat, added as a result of the 2000 census, much of his support comes from conventional Democratic sources—urban labor, itself more and more Latino, liberals, and working-class whites. The coterie around Herrera in 2000 remained Anglo, illustrating the observation of one political consultant, Mike Sullivan, who called Latinos "the biggest paper tiger in town" in politics. Even though Latinos top 20 percent of the population, only 7 percent of registered voters have Latino surnames. This number exaggerates the percentage of Latino voters, for it includes Filipinos, many of whom have Hispanic surnames. When the Las Vegas City Council expanded from five to seven district-based seats in 1999, the presumption was that at least one would go to someone with a Hispanic surname. One of the new districts was at least 50 percent Latino, but the representatives appointed for the initial term were black and white. Even heavily Spanish-speaking neighborhoods are often represented by native English speakers. A state assembly seat, District 18, was created so that a Latino could sit in the assembly, but since redistricting the seat has been held by Vonne Chowning, a white. Local Latino groups get little of the federal funding that comes to Clark County. Even the ubiquitous CBDG, the Community Block Development Grant, the lifeblood of redevelopment in American cities during the past twenty years, has eluded Las Vegas Latinos. "The reason why," says Tom Rodriquez, the Clark County School District's longtime affirmative action chief, "is Hispanics don't submit grant proposals."

Hailing from a multitude of places, the Latino community looks homogeneous from the outside, but from within is made up of many different and sometimes conflicting interests. It isn't just one community. Rather, Spanish speakers are a loosely connected network of communities that share the Spanish language and sometimes little else. Even their Spanish dialects vary widely, as diverse as the many locales from which they originated. Mexican Americans, many third-, fourth-, or fifth-generation American, new immigrants from anywhere in Mexico and Central America, not to mention South America and the Caribbean, and others combine in an uneasy mix. While each community within the Latino community has its own institutions, few community-wide clubs or groups even venture to represent the whole. Rodriquez identified the root of the problem as "our own unique ability to keep shooting ourselves in the foot. We're always trying to tear each other down." Political representation in local government for Latinos is still limited, and they still inhabit an even more circumscribed place in public culture.

Despite the close-cropped snapshot of today, Latinos are the future. Their population has grown so quickly that the town, like the nation, has not yet recognized the significance of their presence, much less come to grips with it. That oblivious attitude doesn't change reality: Las Vegas will become the third city in the United States to predominately speak Spanish, after Miami and Los Angeles.

The first systematic Latino immigration to Las Vegas was an essential building block in the city's history, an accident of fortuitous circumstances beyond the city's control. The Las Vegas Valley lacked the deep history of New Mexico or California. Mormons, not Spanish or Mexican *vecinos*, settled the valley in the 1850s. Hispanic railroad workers, dam builders, and industrial workers had been a presence before World War II, but transience limited their impact. After the war, American mobsters created a base on the beautiful Caribbean island of Cuba. Meyer Lansky and his friends capitalized on Havana's reputation as the pleasure capital of the Western world, and even before Fulgencio Batista's ascension to power in 1952 mob casinos flourished. Many were crooked, and after a 1952 scandal in which a friend of Vice President Richard Nixon felt cheated in Havana's casinos and complained, a journalistic exposé made Havana's tourism industry disreputable. Into that opening came Lansky, an impressive impresario in any circumstance. Batista looked the other way at the unregulated gambling industry, seeing it as a source of valuable foreign currency. Lansky always gravitated to political power that regarded his activities as benign. Batista gave Lansky an opening, indirectly leading to the first widely visible Latino migration to Las Vegas.

Lansky and Batista grew comfortable with one another, the dictator appointing the mobster his chief of gambling reform in 1953. Both had their own motives, Batista seeing Lansky's ability to operate gambling houses that appeared honest as an advantage for his island. Lansky recognized an opportunity to revive his flagging fortunes; his star seemed on the wane in the 1950s and Havana helped him regain lost wealth. It was a match made, if not in heaven, at least somewhere nearby. The two men grew genuinely fond of each other as their twinned fortunes rose. After the 1952 casino corruption scandal, Lansky cleaned up the mess with the steely force that intimidated far more important but less-controlled men across North America. He even built a number of hotels, including the Havana Riviera, his prize, and offered many of his gambler friends a share of the business. By the mid-1950s Havana was the place to be.

The niche lasted as long as Batista stayed in power, but even the adroit Lansky could not outmaneuver Fidel Castro and his revolutionary government. When Castro ousted Batista in 1959, vice and excess, counter to the revolutionary spirit, went with the dictator. At first, Castro allowed the casinos to run, but he made it so difficult that they lost money. Lansky felt trapped. He could not escape the values that hard-line Marxists like Ernesto "Che" Guevara and Castro's brother Raul brought to the regime. Flummoxed, Lansky turned to the United States government, long his adversary, and tried to persuade the FBI that the rise of communism in Cuba was bad for the United States. The mobster held a losing hand. Lansky and his friends invested $20 million in the Havana Riviera, but that did not prevent the eventual confiscation of the hotel along with 165 other American enterprises. The mob was kicked out of Cuba and so was everyone associated with hotels. Where else could these Cubanos, who had worked with the Americans, go but Las Vegas?

Many of the better-known names among the exiles were Anglo—guys like Jack Entratter, Eddie Levinson, Las Vegas's bagmen deluxe, and Charles "Babe" Baron, the general manager of the Havana Riviera—but the most who fled for sanctuary in the desert were Cubans. Before 1960 the Cuban population in Las Vegas numbered about 250; a decade later, it topped 2,000. Castro encouraged them in the same way he pushed the *Marielitos* out two decades later. He branded his adversaries undesirable and left the beaches open for their departure. Everyone who disagreed with the new regime, especially those tied to Batista and the casinos, found the new Cuba hard going. Castro executed criminals and opponents of the revolution, and the casino workers watched with trepidation as relations between the new government and their employers deteriorated. To them the change was not a game; it was hard, cold reality. The Americans could leave at will, any time they wanted. The Cubanos were in far more danger. Many headed stateside at the first opportunity.

Like other 1950s migrants to Las Vegas, the Cubans brought the skills the Desert City needed. They had been in an Americanized economy in the Havana casinos and they knew the ropes of unfettered capitalism. Experienced casino hands, skilled at service, the Cubanos quickly adjusted. While the Cuban presence in Las Vegas never approached the proportions of Little Havana in Miami, it did add an international flair and create a more evident Spanish-speaking cultural presence in Las Vegas. The Cubanos rarely experienced the direct discrimination leveled at Mexican workers in the Southwest. Most were white and they lived in a niche that valued them for their Latin openness. The Stardust and the Sands imported Cuban baccarat and twenty-one dealers even before Castro, and a number of hotels, especially the Las Vegas Club, coveted their services. Cuban entertainment, style, and verve were all fashionable, and then as now, Las Vegas imitated other places very well. Cubans did well, filling many roles in town. Entertainers like Xavier Cugat and Desi Arnaz were regulars even before Castro. Jack Cortez, a revolution refugee, created *Fabulous Las Vegas*, a prominent entertainment guide, and Manny Cortez rose to the head of the Las Vegas Convention and Visitors Bureau, a post of considerable power and influence. *El Circulo Cubano de Las Vegas* became the primary Spanish-language publication and a community institution. Devoted to preserving the ideals of *Cuba de ayer*, the Cuba of yesterday, the paper became not only the social center of Cuban Las Vegas, but an expression of refugee longing as well.

Most Cubans only peripherally recall incidents of discrimination or antipathy. They were foreigners, exotics in the constrained culture of the time. Few needed real proficiency in English for their work, and most spoke English anyway. That many of the emigres were educated, cultured, or wealthy didn't hurt. The Cubans were an asset in a city finding its way. Their presence and their knowledge marked the transfer of pleasure in the Western world from Havana to Las Vegas, helping to elevate Las Vegas beyond its competition as the place for boulevardier-style leisure. They were essential in making modern Las Vegas, in paving the way for its transformation from idiosyncracy to center of leisure.

The Cubans were unique among Spanish-speaking migrants to Las Vegas. They had skills the community coveted and experience with its overlords of the moment. They fit. Their combination of casino and hotel skills and the passion for living that was the midcentury American stereotype of Latino culture made them a visible asset in a tourist culture. Havana had a certain cachet, and the Cubans brought it to Las Vegas. With its ability to perfectly mirror American desire and a willingness to embrace the exotic, Las Vegas naturally embraced the image of Cuba.

Subsequent Latino immigrants fit into a different category. As occurred throughout the Southwest and as far north as Chicago, Mexican immigration accelerated in the 1970s and 1980s, and invisibly, Spanish-speaking populations coalesced around the country. In many places, Mexican immigrants filled jobs in the bottom socioeconomic stratum, as laborers, dishwashers, maids, and cooks, jobs that few Americans would accept even at good wages. Mexican and Latin American immigrants, many of them *sin papeles*, without papers, kept their heads down. They came from places where the state was venal and vengeful and they avoided it here whenever possible. Unobtrusively, they increased in number, until one day they were so many that American society, which is to say the English-speaking United States, had to notice. By then, Latinos were such an integral part of the workplace that entire industries would have shut down had the United States stringently enforced its immigration and residency laws.

In Las Vegas as in many American cities, Latinos initially attached themselves to economic peripheries. In Chinese restaurants, the cooks were Latino. Invariably so were the busboys. In the 1980s convenience-store clerks were primarily subcontinent Indian or African American. By the early 1990s they too were becoming increasingly Latino. Lawn care were Spanish speaking. Construction workers, especially unskilled labor, were overwhelmingly Latino, and as the 1990s ended a lot of the guys who drove company pickups and front-end loaders were Latino too. So were skilled craftsmen, stone workers, masonry finishers, electricians, plumbers, and practitioners of nearly every other craft. The guy who repaired my air-conditioner was Latino and sounded like an immigrant from his accent. Clean-cut and dressed in a uniform, he had care of a van and equipment worth hundreds of thousands of dollars, demonstrating his employer's trust. Latino immigrants seem to have begun the gradual creep up the socioeconomic ladder. They quickly move from unskilled to skilled labor. Their children now go to college, earn degrees, and join the white-collar middle class. But the transformation can take a long time.

Despite its remarkable level of unionization in service work and the skilled trades, Nevada is a Right-to-Work state. That keeps the largely nonunion building industry a low-wage trap. The incredible construction boom of the last decade has ballooned the construction labor force to more than 75,000, overwhelmingly Spanish-speaking, but wages for the work have stayed at the bottom, as is typical in Right-to-Work states. "I don't think there's anybody who speaks English who builds houses anymore," said one construction industry veteran. Outside of the realm of well-compensated service labor, many Latinos receive poor pay and only the most basic benefits, if any, and they remain transient. Wages are in the single-digit dollars per hour. Even entrepreneurial crews find it hard to make decent money. A crew of four "Mexicans," as Latino laborers of every nationality are colloquially called, will frequently split $500 for two and a half days of grueling work sheetrocking a new house in a trendy suburb. These wages offer little hope of eventual prosperity, stability, or ownership of a home like the ones the workers build, but they powerfully contribute to the affordability of housing for everyone else in the Las Vegas Valley. Construction workers are among the few Las Vegas workers left out of "the Last Detroit," this last bastion of remarkable prosperity for the unskilled.

Yet they come by the thousands and work outside, in the hot sun. "Those Mexican guys work, they really work," the owner of carpet-cleaning business observed, and everyone who works with Mexicans and Central

Americans echoes his sentiments. Workers line up at the day labor market, on D Street in North Las Vegas, in the morning and wait for employers. Many hire a new crew every day, usually for cash. The market is mostly young Latinos, with a smattering of whites and blacks thrown in. "Drive past the white guys; they're all derelicts," the grizzled young Anglo tree-cutter just out of drug rehab looking for help told me. "Drive past the black guys, too. Get the Mexicans. They work." For eight dollars an hour, he hired a guy to work trimming palm trees, hard, nasty work sure to leave you exhausted and scratched-up at day's end. As the sun set, $64 in cash changed hands and the Latino went his way. The tree-cutter was satisfied, and most who rely on such labor are also happy with the arrangement. Latinos are prized. They work hard, they work well, they clean up, and they cause few problems. Not only in Las Vegas but elsewhere, immigrant labor is prized for its durability and quality as well as its comparatively low cost. If you need manual labor in Las Vegas, or in the nation as whole, the odds are strong and growing stronger daily that its purveyors will speak Spanish.

The presumption that such work is reserved for Latinos is as strong as the feeling African Americans once had that the worst jobs were saved for them. A white former student of mine, now in graduate school, returns each summer to cut palm trees for a few weeks. The $1,500 a week he earns supplements his paltry annual academic stipend. When his friend Jaime Aguila heard of the plan, he observed with a smile, "So you're turning Mexican for the summer?" Atop a tree one day with his day help below, this olive-skinned, dark-haired Anglo heard a call from below: "Hey ameeego," a white guy hollered up. "You wanna buy a good work belt?" His position atop the tree and his shock of dark hair had been mistaken for his ethnicity.

Latino laborers are often vulnerable and can be exploited in the workplace. A lot don't speak English. Many find work and places to live through networks of relatives and friends—as did earlier American immigrant groups—and some are indebted to labor contractors, or *coyotes*, who transport them across the border for a fee that they promise to repay from their wages. Latino brokers work the Spanish-speaking world, delivering workers to companies for job sites and receiving a fee from which they dole out wages. The brokers are usually Mexican American; most workers in such situations are immigrants who know little of the obligations of employers under American law. *Sin papeles*, they fear authority and do not feel that they can negotiate. They take what is offered. A lot are paid in cash. In some cases, laborers are paid in beer.

When the wages are good, by law or circumstance, contractors and crew bosses sometimes demand kickbacks from workers. On prevailing wage jobs, public projects for which the state pays workers a rate fixed by the state contracting board, between $29 and $30 an hour in 2000, Latinos have been expected to return a portion of the higher wage to the crew boss. In spring 2000, the Nevada Carpenters Union filed complaints against Jetstream Construction charging that the company paid its Latino workers in cash and demanded kickbacks of between $200 and $280 dollars a week, about 20 percent of the prevailing wage weekly salary. Jetstream held contracts with a number of state, county, and local government agencies, and they knew that if the allegations were substantiated, the company might be barred from further state contracts, a devastating blow. A former employee, Manuel Gomez, made a tape of a conversation with company owner John Field that offered evidence of kickbacks. The chief investigator of the Nevada Office of the Labor Commissioner, Gail Maxwell, was aware of the prevalence of Latinos as victims in such schemes. Her office collected millions of dollars for workers who were improperly paid or intentionally misclassified. "Over half are Hispanic employees," she observed. "They are the most exploited." Daniel O'Shea, who represented the Southern California–Nevada Council of Carpenters, seconded Maxwell's sentiment: "Not one white guy was ever asked to kick back money to the company."

The response to the story revealed how much ground Latinos have gained. *El Tiempo Libre*, the big Spanish-language free weekly, ran a cover story, "Pagan Para Trabajar" (pay to work); *City Life*, the alternative weekly, ran a story and an editorial; and both the major newspapers, the *Sun* and the anti-labor *Review-Journal*, prominently featured the situation. The story crossed from Spanish to English, highlighting not only the power of labor in a city under construction, but the increasing visibility of what had long been the shadow of Latinos throughout the local scene. Disparate interests also fused, creating new alliances. The Carpenters Union helped bring the story to the fore, and Jetstream failed to explain their actions to the Clark County School Board. The company was barred from school district work, a loss of millions in revenue.

These small victories may portend a pattern, but it is hard to look at Latino laborers without seeing construction work as a trap. It is the bottom of the city, generally apart from the upward mobility that service work offers. It seems reserved for newcomers, a price to pay to have even a claim at the kind of work that can sustain a family. Even in 2001, the protection of workers only became bilingual in certain circumstances.

Life for Latino immigrants is not easy anywhere and it can be especially hard in Las Vegas. Immigrants from rural Mexico and Central America know little about cities, much less ones devoted to crass capitalism. Few social and governmental institutions grace Las Vegas. The spread-out nature of the city makes it hard to get around even with the efficient Citizens' Area Transit system. Only networks of family, friends, and people hailing from the same village or region provide an entry point.

Latinos need three things when they arrive in town: a work card, required of anyone who works in gaming or where alcohol is served, a health card, and a car. These are the tickets to the middle class in Las Vegas, a way out of the low-wage construction trap. Two of them involve the mechanisms of government; the third involves the private sector. Attaining them does little to persuade people that they're valued by the society they've joined.

Despite the state's libertarian leanings, government-sponsored workplace regulation has a long history in southern Nevada. Since 1947, Nevada law has required licensing of workers where liquor is served and gaming is present. As is common in Nevada, counties establish the criteria for work laws. Generally workers must be twenty-one years of age; they must have the proper documents from the Immigration and Naturalization Service, a concern for many immigrant workers; they must not have an extensive criminal history or any outstanding warrants for their arrest. The sheriff's card, as it is colloquially called, is required of all casino workers. You can't get a sheriff's card until you have a job in a casino, but you can't keep the job without it. Without an employer's referral, the county won't issue the card, creating a symbiotic relationship between the state and industry. The techniques of alcohol management card is required for work in places that serve alcohol. Food servers and child care workers need a health card, for which they must pass a hepatitis A/tuberculosis skin test, attend a food handling preparation class, and view a movie about health and safety in the workplace. Child care workers face other requirements as well. These minimal standards are supposed to ensure that service in casinos and restaurants is free of criminals, illegal workers, and obvious health hazards.

The entire work card process has spawned an enormous bureaucracy that spends public dollars to facilitate private business. The county commission and the Las Vegas City Council invest much of their time reviewing card denials. The business of government can consist of one pleading after another for restoration of the cards on which an individual's livelihood depends. Work cards were even more widely required: as late as 2001, for example, astrologers were covered under the rules. A license to read tarot cards required a work card, as did many other occupations that have nothing to do with gaming or serving food or alcohol. Unions didn't oppose the rules, seeing in them another way to assert their usefulness. Las Vegas was a happy police state, where even advocates for workers accepted the needs of the industry above their own. Despite efforts to rewrite the rules, the work cards provided one more piece of evidence that Nevada's brand of libertarianism favored business over the individual. It also spent considerable state dollars fulfilling a human resources department function.

For Latinos, the maze of regulation was particularly daunting. Confusing and rightfully regarded as arbitrary, even discriminatory, the system seemed designed to frustrate people who needed to work and were ready to start. The bustling crowds of the Clark County Health Department reminded me of a Latin American bus station when I walked through the doors one morning. The new building, only weeks old at the time, already showed the wear of heavy use. Hundreds were in line at 8 A.M., all seeking the essential prerequisite of work in Las Vegas: the health card. All ages, male and female, the crowd spoke almost exclusively Spanish. They came in groups, sometimes entire families, and the one who spoke English translated for the rest. The small sign-up room was packed. The spacing between people was not American at all. Instead it reflected cultures of shared space, where people were accustomed to being physically close to one another. I gasped for air. The TB testing area had a medical feel to it, but the nurses who administered the tests were already cranky. They dealt daily with impatient humanity, people who felt that their needs had an urgency that the rest of the world did not share. One young man crashed through the line, shouting in broken English, "You check my test, I go work." The purplish ring above the vaccination mark on his arm guaranteed he wasn't going anywhere, but he wasn't listening. The nurse had to call for security to get the man to a doctor. The auditorium where applicants watched a film that completed the process was overflowing. People poured out as it ended, and all I could think of was herding. There wasn't a lot in the process to give you faith in your new society.

I sat down next to a ten-year-old boy who spoke a little English and was translating for an attractive girl of about seventeen, his sister, who'd just arrived from El Salvador. When she smiled, I saw that half her teeth were stainless steel, gleaming in the fluorescent light. He asked me what a vaccination was as he filled out a form. I explained it to him as best I could and he asked his sister if she'd had one. She didn't know, so he asked me what to do. I told him he'd better put down that she hadn't. Then came the tough question. The boy was reading in English and came to the word pregnant. He didn't know it, and when I told him in Spanish, he blushed bright red. It's hard to be the mediator between cultures when you're young. It is even harder when there's money at stake and the rules aren't clear.

Cars are crucial symbols of status as well as the easiest way to get around. Las Vegas is a spread-out car city, as is every other southwestern metropolis, and even for immigrants cars are proof of success. The bus system transports many, but almost everyone prefers a car for the freedom it offers. For young Latino men especially, an automobile demonstrates virility as it has in Anglo America for a very long time. There is no more American symbol than the automobile, and acquiring one fills all kinds of desires for a good-sized segment of the Latino population as well as everyone else.

The used-car dealerships on East Fremont Street and Boulder Highway ooze of predation. "Se hablo Espanol," the signs scream, but the vehicles—all nice-looking, but a little long in the tooth and a little worn for the upscale market—all smack of created desire. "¿Sin credito o mal credito?" No credit or bad credit? Let us finance you. GMF Motors, one of the sleaziest of the local used-car dealerships, trumpets its commitment to the Latino community—*20 años al servicio de la comunidad hispana.* Twenty years of service to the Hispanic community. GMF does not advertise its shady business practices, its interest rates that are higher than the Stratosphere tower and the unwitting buyers who find themselves with leases instead of purchase agreements for their vehicles. GMF has provided cars and financing to the Latino community for a long time, well before the explosion of the Latino population, before Ricky Martin hit the pop charts and Latino became hip. It's the old relationship between the ghetto merchant and the ghetto that Malcom X wrote about and that Louis Farrakhan points to as oppression. These days, the old ghetto market is worthy of any business's attention.

Such a vulnerable market brings out the sharks, predators of all stripes. Illegal aliens can find forged ID cards, a driver's license, social security card, and work card for about $200 on Bonanza Road. Their quality varies, and tales abound of people who thought their fake ID was good enough until *La Migra*, the Immigration and Naturalization Service, showed up. One guy, a native Angeleno whose family had been in the high-interest auto loan market for a long time, salivated at the prospects in Las Vegas. He didn't want to work too hard, he established, and Las Vegas gave him ample opportunities to charge 29 percent interest on cars and reap a fortune. I asked him why so high. "Risk," he said. "These folks don't have credit, and so no one else'll take them. I like the immigrants because they haven't yet figured out that bankruptcy is an American sport." Within a couple of years, he'd purchased an East Fremont used-car dealership, closing the circle of vertical integration and reaping profit not only from the loans, but from the vehicles themselves.

It is economically dangerous to be Latino, immigrant, and not to speak English in Las Vegas, but maybe no more so than it has ever been in the United States. Italian, Jewish, Irish, Greek, and Polish immigrants have always been fodder, people who gave up themselves in order to give their children a chance. But there is something different here, something more textured about the nature of exploitation. In early-twentieth-century America, the emphasis on transforming immigrants was about culture,

CASH A CHECK HERE

about raising them—in the terms of the time—to the level of Americans and continuing the self-proclaimed national mission of civilizing the world. In this era, culture has been replaced by consumerism. Belonging has become a function of goods instead of values. These immigrants aren't being welcomed into American society. They are told to be part of the market, to buy and pay interest, and to remain in their own world. While the health card center and East Fremont streets show class distinctions, they also show race as ingredients. From melting pot to stew, maybe we'd moved to à la carte without realizing it.

A population above 300,000 means that there is a distinct and prominent Latino culture in Las Vegas, even though Las Vegas lacks a historic Latino area—a south side of Tucson, a southwest Albuquerque, or an East L.A. Instead Latinos have spread all over the city, enabled in part by the ability to earn good wages in the service industry, but equally by the enormous geographic growth of the city. Some areas in North Las Vegas reported Latino population as high as 85 percent in the 2000 census, areas around downtown top 50 percent and are often predominantly Latino, the old neighborhoods on the east and west sides are increasingly Spanish-speaking; Latinos are truly everywhere in the metropolitan area. Even in most suburban elementary schools, the number of kids with Spanish surnames tops 25 percent. Only the private schools resist the trend.

The growing population has spawned a visible world that is Spanish-speaking and aimed at Latino taste. New businesses sprout regularly, restaurants and nightclubs prominent among them. You can find countless lunch trucks that attend to construction workers on their breaks and on any kind of job site. *Vaquero*—cowboy—one is called; others are offshoots of well-known Mexican restaurants. Even the *tacquerias* have arrived. Roberto's was first, followed by Tacos Mexico in 1994. Dozens of smaller mom-and-pop restaurants thrive, and nightclubs flourish. Three radio stations, two television stations, three weekly Spanish-language newspapers, and two telephone directories all cater to the Latino community. *El Mundo*, the oldest Spanish-language newspaper in Las Vegas, increased from forty-eight to seventy-two pages to accommodate new advertising from national chains. Donrey Corporation, the corporate owner of the *Review-Journal*, bought another, the weekly *El Tiempo Libre*. Mainstream business now coveted the Latino market. You could live a life in Spanish in Las Vegas and never be inconvenienced.

NIGHT CLUB

The Latino middle class has emerged in recent years, partly born in Los Angeles, but increasingly immigrant as well. Latinos from L.A. have settled in great numbers for the same reasons as everyone else: economic opportunity and low cost of living. Middle-class wages for service work provide opportunity to own a home or start a business. Unionized service workers like Lilia Guzman, who came to Las Vegas in 1994 after fifteen years in Los Angeles, most often experience the benefits. This Acapulco native and her family could never get ahead in California. Her job as a prep cook was a grind, with few benefits to augment low pay. Las Vegas gave her paid vacations, a living wage, health insurance, and the opportunity to move up, all as she chopped vegetables at the Mirage. In 1996, even with a now-disabled husband, she saved enough to buy a five-bedroom house in an up-and-coming neighborhood in North Las Vegas populated by other Mexican-Americans, many of whom had also come from Los Angeles. "Oh, it's a thousand times better," she told *Los Angeles Times* reporters Nancy Cleeland and Lee Romney. "There's nobody left in Los Angeles."

Opportunity comes in all shapes and forms in Las Vegas, and the only ingredient that binds it is hustle. Las Vegas remains an entrepreneurial town, a place where it's easy to start anything because even the most established operations are unable to cater to the entire community. Las Vegas has grown so rapidly that there are gaps in every service offered to anyone. It's an entrepreneur's dream, general and niche market alike begging for goods and services. For young Latinos, especially those born in the United States who are bilingual, Las Vegas puts stars in their eyes, but for an entirely different set of reasons than anyone would expect.

Manolo Sáenz and José Rodríguez impressed me when I met them. In their twenties, they both worked two full-time jobs. Muscular and heavyset, exuding drive, Manolo was a second-shift janitor. Born in El Paso, he'd moved to Las Vegas as a young boy and come up through its schools. He might have been in a gang. He'd never really say, but he did admit that he "wasn't doing no one no good" in those days. By his early twenties, Manolo married and found a purpose, work and family. During the days, he sells auto insurance to the Hispanic community for an Anglo broker on commission. Come five o'clock, he puts on a uniform and cleans the university. Later José, lean and thoughtful, with a sardonic air, join him. The custodial work gives them a salary and benefits, retirement and health care, a path to the future, although on a janitor's salary they couldn't quite fulfill their expectations. The commission work, their hustle jobs, gives them a chance to move up the ladder, to make some money to renovate their homes, and to gain the prestige and status that came from being self-made. Like immigrants of generations ago, they work second jobs, in their cases jobs with claims to being white-collar that their primary jobs don't possess. Despite the solid pay at the university and the benefits, I don't expect them to be there for long. Their eyes are looking higher, to suburbs and swimming pools, dance lessons, and private schools.

Manolo and José are Mexican Americans, typical of the second generation of any immigrant group in the United States. They seem straight from the pages of a Horatio Alger novel, the pull-yourself-up-by-your-bootstraps ethos of fiction. Their cultural tastes and aspirations are American, but they speak with the soft lilt that native Spanish speakers carry in English. They're strivers, pushing forward, embracing the moment in all its consumerist passion. Without real opportunities at education and maybe not even seeing the need for it, they intended all along to rise economically, socially, and in every other way they could. Striving was an integral part of their ethos, doing better for themselves and their families crucial to their self-definition. When the Anglo insurance broker they work for raised her share of their take and started charging them more for their cubicles, they sought a better deal. An insurance broker I knew was thrilled to hire them. He offered desks, a car, and a small expense account, and took a much smaller bite of their take. When I later asked if I owed him for helping my friends, he laughed and said, "Are you kidding? Those guys have the market of the future in the palm of their hands. You did *me* the favor."

But the strain of working two jobs all the time, of never seeing the wives and kids, of never swimming in the pool that their work paid for, strained relationships. The wives complained they never saw the men, but without the second job the families couldn't live in the style they'd come to enjoy. Both men preferred that their wives stayed home. A combination of culture and common sense dictated the choice, but any way you looked at it, the guys worked and their families enjoyed the fruits of their labors. They didn't grouse about it. They defined their status by their accomplishments, but they did know that they were missing their kids' lives. "The only time I ever see my son," José said to me one day, "he's asleep." He ended up leaving the insurance business for a third-shift job washing busses for the school district. It didn't pay as much or offer the same upward mobility, but it let him be home during the day. José's workday starts at 5 P.M. and ends at 7 A.M. the next morning. Here was the price of success, the hardest part of the climb to the middle class.

"We've moved to Summerlin," one of the toniest addresses in town, Ruben Maldonado, another of the young Latinos I'd come to know, told me. Ruben was an El Salvadoran who moved to New York as a small child and came to Las Vegas with his mother at about fourteen. He too had flirted with gangs, but left that life as soon as he could. He wanted more, and by the time I met him his desire and energy were paying off. "Me, my wife, the baby, and the new one on the way. We love it up there," he said as I teased him about living with the rich white people. "It's clean, it's quiet, and it's safe." The area they'd chosen, an apartment that cost almost $800 a month, abutted against a subdivision with a man-made lake in its center. A physician I knew lives in the upscale subdivision next door. Ruben and his wife take their one-year-old to the lake, feed the ducks, and breathe the heady air of aspiration.

Ruben then announced he'd quit his second job. "My wife's got a job now," he told me. "She's learning to do those laser eye surgeries." It was a real shift for Ruben. As long as I'd known him, he'd worked two jobs and his wife stayed home. Now in their nice suburban apartment, with a second kid on the way, they could become a split-shift family. She works days. He works evenings and stays with the kid during the day. At 4 P.M., he takes his son to the boy's grandmother's house, and his wife picks up the youngster when she gets off work an hour later. It isn't easy, but it is considerably better than where they came from.

This transformation in Ruben's family illustrated another of the perils of Las Vegas, one that is pronounced for Latino families. Latino women hold the community together, and they are prominent in families, in churches, and in the Culinary Union. "We are family," an organizer shouted at the 2000 Culinary Union Shop Steward's Convention, "and we all know where the power is: with the women." Union housekeepers make solid middle-class wages, with the toke as much as $35,000 a year, and receive benefits like pension programs and health care. Women's economic success sometimes supersedes that of Latino men, who more often face nonunion jobs with lower wages and fewer benefit options. In a largely Catholic culture that still maintains male dominance, the economic success of women can imperil social relations. Even though 10.5 million American women earned more than their men in 1998, most were upper-middle-class whites who'd made the transition to parity in relationships as only the privileged could. Even in educated families, this reversal of economic roles and redistribution of responsibilities could bruise egos. For immigrant families, well-paid women and poorly paid men presented a complicated devil's bargain in which status and power, never far from economic prowess, became inverted in a way the old country never permitted. Opportunities and beliefs can run hard against each other.

While Ruben and his wife made about the same money, the difference is more pronounced in occupations like construction. Much construction work is done on subcontracts, and a worker might take home $200 or $250 a week. For an immigrant alone, sending as much as possible home to Mexico or trying to bring a relative out of El Salvador, this was a significant sum. For a man with a wife and kids here, these are shit wages, the kind that keep your family poor. A woman bringing in as much is essential. One bringing in more is better, but a tacit threat. Money gives women independence, choices, and could challenge a traditional man from a patriarchal culture that promotes docile acceptance from women. Economics changed the power structure and in some cases the rules.

For Latina women, the United States could be liberating. Leonard Bernstein's "America," from *West Side Story*, nailed this idea. The women want to stay. "Okay by me in America," Rita Moreno sang, articulating the perspective of more than three generations of Latinas in the United States. America improves their lives, gives them options and opportunities, grants them freedom, and liberates them from being under the control of men. For many men, America is simply oppressive, grinding, relentless, and full of images beyond their reach. The women are free from the constraints of the village, their traditional home-bound role, and even the church. Like Rosie the Riveter of World War II, they don't want go back. If they have to, it's with a terrible sense of loss.

"I'm learning Spanish," the perky suburban housewife said with a laugh, "so that the next time a housekeeper steals from me, I can fire her myself!" Like many in Las Vegas's suburbs, she'd found it necessary and desirable to hire some household help. Her first housekeeper was a young Mexican girl who spoke no English, but seemed to work hard. The relationship worked well for a couple of weeks, and the woman, raised to be considerate and slightly uncomfortable about hiring help in the first place, did all she could to level the inherent differences in status that came from an off-the-clock employer-employee relationship. To offer the girl lunch, she made the time-honored hand gesture of spooning to her mouth; the young girl beamed. The woman even cleaned the house before the housekeeper arrived, she said to make sure the girl didn't waste time doing the basic stuff, but equally much to minimize any sense of degradation in the work. The girl earned $40 for three to five hours of work, not a bad wage for any- one without marketable skills other than a strong back and a willingness to work. The house looked clean, the woman averred, and since her husband had no political aspirations, she thought she'd keep the girl.

Then a few items began to disappear, first a twenty-dollar bill left in a pottery bowl, then a few other small items. The housewife set a trap, leav- ing another twenty-dollar bill in the same bowl, covered but not complete- ly obscured. She was relieved to find it where she left it after the girl finished. Maybe something else had happened, maybe the missing stuff dis- appeared some other way. One day, a few weeks after the woman decided that she must have misplaced the missing money, she searched for a pair of mother-of-pearl earrings, pretty but not monetarily valuable, an heirloom from her grandmother. They were nowhere to be found. This time she was certain: the girl had been stealing.

The language barrier added tension to an already stiff, even brittle relationship. The woman wanted her earrings back. They were a keep-sake, valueless except as a memory of a cherished grandmother. She was even willing to pay to get them back. But she couldn't bring the subject up. She had no evidence, nothing but a feeling that grew stronger every day. Communication was hard enough with the language barrier, and her message would be insulting. She stewed, and tension mounted. When the girl came to work, you could have cut the air in the house with a knife. After agonizing about the situation for almost a month, she decided to confront the cleaning girl. She brought in an Argentinian friend fluent in Spanish, who asked the girl if she'd seen the earrings. The woman would pay to get them back, she told the young girl. When the girl denied seeing them, the Argentinian pushed. She said that the homeowners thought the girl took them. The young girl became indignant: "If they think I took the earrings, then I don't want to work there anymore." The Argentinian explained that she was already fired. She couldn't quit. The girl showed no remorse and made no admission. Her feelings hurt, maybe rightly, maybe as a mask to cover her perfidy, she left. The ear-rings were gone. The woman decided then and there to learn Spanish. Next time, she'd handle her own dirty work. The woman chalked it up as a learning experience. In her house ever after, to pull an "Enadina," the girl's name, meant to be dishonest and deceitful.

The next household helper was different, a thirty-five-year-old Nicaraguan woman who had left a bad marriage to a doctor in Managua to clean houses in the United States. She made between $100 and $150 a day, usually doing two or three houses a day, five days a week. The money made her comfortable, allowed her to send for her kids, and let her live a relative-ly easy life. She spoke English well, proof of an upper-middle-class Central American upbringing, and did not feel that the work was beneath her. "It's better than having that creep beat me," she told the stunned housewife.

This relationship went smoothly. The Nicaraguan woman was trust-worthy. Within a month, she was given a key to lock up when she left. She came regularly and on time, did the work, and the two women chatted and became *simpático*. When the couple replaced the husband's lounge chair, they gave it to the housekeeper. When the housekeeper needed a new car, the husband, a veteran of the auto business, got her a better car loan than she could have without his help. When the woman took sick, the couple vis-ited her in the hospital. The relationship became seamless, effortless, congenial, as friendly as a once-a-week relationship based around payment could be. When the housekeeper's boyfriend arrived from Oregon, she called one morning, just before she was supposed to arrive. "Is it okay if I bring him to work with me?" She asked. The wife was a little unsure of leaving a stranger in the house alone, but she had learned to trust the Nicaraguan. "Sure," she said, maybe a little grudgingly. The couple came and worked in the house by themselves. When the housewife arrived home, she found a note: "Thanks for your trust," it closed, "love, Nena."

"I'm so worried about Marquesa," a well-off suburban mom intoned over coffee one morning. Marquesa was her Mexican live-in housekeeper and nanny, *sin papeles,* who had been with the family since their oldest, then twelve, was three. In her late twenties, Marquesa was a Mexican Indian from a small village in the central highlands. Her English had become passable over the years, but she was never terribly forthcoming about herself. When she first arrived, she knew one phrase in English. "She no home," Marquesa would shout into the phone when anyone would call. The family had taken her in and depended on her as if she were one of them. She was integral to everything the family did, going on trips with them, on vacation, skiing, and to family functions across the country. Nothing worked in the house when Marquesa wasn't there. Always in the background, almost always with one child or another in her care, Marquesa smoothly fit into a world that to her must have once seemed like another planet.

Marquesa was the real head of the household, a majordomo in the classic sense. She was responsible for the children, and as the family became more affluent, she was given a helper. The second housekeeper was essential in getting the work done, but far less a part of the family. Her job was largely confined to housework. It involved little of the interaction with the family that was characteristic of Marquesa, and the number-two housekeeper was not invited on family trips and vacations. Friends joked that they were the only family whose housekeeper had a housekeeper, but with three children, a dog, two busy adult schedules, and a gorgeous home to maintain, the arrangement made sense. A few, probably envious, observed that the children knew Marquesa better than they knew their parents, and a pretty good case could be made that she saw the kids more than the parents did. Such is life for the prominent, the perennially booked, the people who try to do it all and have it all at the same time.

Marquesa experienced a level of comfort in her life in this well-off

Parking Garage

Desert Passage

MGM
Miss it
and you miss
Las Vegas
David Cassidy
THE CITY OF
ENTERTAINMENT
MGM
GRAND

MGM Grand

RIVIERA

SLOT MACHINES

suburban family that she couldn't have dreamed of as a child. She had her own suite in their home, complete with cable TV, bathroom and shower, telephone, and every other amenity that any American teenager craved. The family bought her clothes, and she was often dressed in Polo shirts and designer jeans. Marquesa wasn't married, and if she had prospects, no one in her English-speaking circle was aware of them. Nor did she seem to miss having her own social life, often choosing to stay with the family on her own time. Sunday was her day off, and when she left, she spent the day with her brother's family across town. She treated the children, especially the youngest, the only girl, as if they were her own, and the children reciprocated her affection.

Marquesa reminded me of older nuns I once interviewed. They had grown up early in the twentieth century in rural Quebec, poor, in small towns, in a very macho culture, often with drunken fathers who came home and beat their wives and the kids. When faced with an adulthood that offered few options, grinding poverty and marriage to a man who drank too much and came home to wale on his own family or a move to an unfamiliar and perhaps dangerous urban area to seek a job that was likely to be equally grinding and pay poorly, a "marriage" to the church made considerable sense. It offered personal freedom, the security and stability of the powerful institution, and no beatings.

For Marquesa, the parallels were strong. Born poor in a small Mexican village, her role was proscribed from birth. With few options, crossing the border and giving herself over to a generous and powerful family that could provide her with freedom, comfort, and safety in return for her labor more than made sense. She benefitted from the family's professional and social advancements, moving up in status and amenities as the family became more affluent and more widely respected. The choice between the life her origins could offer her and the one she was living in an essential but subsidiary role in her American family was hardly a difficult one. For Marquesa, from the highlands of Mexico, from a family of countless siblings consigned to hopeless poverty, there was no choice at all. The polo shirts, the private VCR and TV, and her own phone! It was a no-brainer.

The pull of her natural family remained strong, and every two years Marquesa went home to Mexico for Christmas, crossing the border both ways. "She said she'd be back before New Year's," the woman continued, a tone of concern in her voice. *La Migra*, the border patrol, stepped up its patrols as New Year's Eve 2000 approached. Reports of arrests scared this suburban family. One of the crucial components of their busy family life could be caught in the larger swirl of politics and chaotic silliness that marked the change to the year 2000. Marquesa was a member of the family and they missed her. December was a tense month.

Marquesa returned safely, but she was visibly bruised. Her face had marks, a huge swollen area around one eye and discoloration on the other cheek. When I inquired about the bruises, she turned away. I heard that it had taken her twenty-four hours to get across the border, that she'd been chased by the border patrol, and that the two *coyotes*, the young Mexican men who spirit people across, had demanded an extra $500 from her. When she failed to produce it and refused to promise to do so, one struck her in the face. An older man traveling with the group objected and helped her escape. By the time she returned, a new caginess had appeared in her eyes. Life with the family insulated her, protected her from the outside, but only as long as she was inside its boundaries. When she ventured out to family and friends, the protection did not venture out with her. There was also fear in her eyes now, a sense that sooner or later she would have to choose between the life she'd made for herself and the world she came from.

The family was traumatized by Marquesa's experience. The wife was horrified. Like a lot of people in the upper-middle-class suburbs, she'd overestimated the power of their chosen insularity and the reach they had beyond it. One night, she held a symbol of that distance in her hand. It was a pastel-colored polo shirt she'd given Marquesa, ripped and muddy from the trip. The second housekeeper had brought it to her. She'd found it stuffed in the bottom of a pile of laundry. Marquesa was part of their family, they all felt, and they had an obligation to her. The husband decided to see if he could get her a green card. He is a man of influence, a sizable donor to political campaigns. But when he went after a green card, he landed in a morass. Conventional influence was not sufficient; *mordida*, the border word for bribery, was out of the question. The rules were the rules, and Marquesa remained *sin papeles*.

Lee Heldman had been a junior executive, wearing a coat and tie and grinding out his seventy-plus hours a week to make a living for his family when he got sick of it. A friend had built a landscape business, working outside in shorts alongside four Hispanic men, and was looking to sell. Lee jumped at the chance. With some of his own money and a lot of the bank's, he found himself in the landscape business, riding around in a truck with lawn mowers and "eating at the taco roach-trap truck" with the guys, he said with his ever-present laugh.

Lee was hardly an experienced businessman, but the first thing he noticed was the work ethic of his employees. "Those guys work," he observed in amazement one night, echoing every other employer of Latinos I talked with. "They really put out." Of the four, three were paid hourly wages; the fourth was a subcontractor. The subcontractor was the oldest, the best and most experienced worker, had been in the United States the longest, spoke English the best, and led the crew in every social way. I asked why he was not on salary. "I don't know," Lee answered, puzzled. "He's always done it this way."

I didn't want to ask too many damaging questions, so I left it alone and retreated to the realm of speculation. Clearly here was a man with a lot of experience in the United States, who'd been north of the border for twelve years, during two of the government's amnesty efforts, who had all the traits that Americans prize in their workers, and I knew that he was financially penalized by the subcontracting arrangement. Hourly landscape crews don't get retirement benefits, but they do pay into Social Security, and were eligible for unemployment, though that was a remote prospect in the booming valley economy, were probably covered by worker's compensation statutes, and maybe even received a health care package. Add to that the subcontractor's self-employment tax of almost 15 percent, and it was easy to see that the best worker might have more freedom, but he was clearly paying for it. I couldn't understand why someone as savvy as this man would have passed on amnesty, unless it was because he couldn't qualify for one or another reason. To the casual observer, that spelled felony—somewhere along the line, sometime in the long-forgotten past, maybe even south of the border. He was an outstanding worker, had not been in any kind of trouble during Lee's or his friend's ownership of the company, a period of more than five years. Something in the past was holding this man back, keeping him from enjoying the full benefit of his work and experience, or so my imagination told me.

Another scenario was possible too. If you're not a Mexican citizen or if you foreswear citizenship, any property you own in Mexico is subject to confiscation, as Americans with ninety-nine-year leases on oceanfront property in Punta Banda in Baja California learned the hard way late in 2000 when the Mexican government seized their homes. Maybe this man owned property and didn't to want to risk its seizure. At least this explanation made economic sense, but it sure seemed convoluted.

I spoke with Raquel Casas about him. Casas is herself an American success story, the daughter of migrant farm workers who picked fruit as a child, made her way first to Fresno State, then to Yale University, and finally to a job close to home at UNLV. She and her siblings, all college-educated, were the real winners in the pull up to the middle class, the children of the generation who came north ahead of the great onrush of immigrants who came in swelling numbers as economic, political, and social conditions worsened in Mexico and Central America. That earlier generation found stability—albeit marginal and sometimes quite poor—and they became integrated into their own communities in places like the Central Valley of California. America took advantage of them; but in the desire for labor at cheap rates, the nation looked past the origins of workers as long as the workers made no demands. When they did, tension followed and the innate contempt with which many in the Southwest regarded Mexicans and their descendants emerged. Raquel's parents had been part of the United Farm Workers of America, Cesar Chavez's movement to secure basic human rights and living wages. In testimony to the solidarity of workers in the 1960s, United Auto Workers president Walter Reuther stood on the picket lines with striking farm workers. Labor did not yet see immigration as a threat.

Casas pointed out that the man in question might also be expressing a cultural preference, and making a statement about identity. He might have refused amnesty, citizenship, and anything else the American government offered simply because he was in his heart a *Mexicano*, and the United States, with all its promise of freedom, equality, and opportunity, was simply not his country. He might have heard the Latino urban legend that becoming an American citizen required that you throw the Mexican flag on the ground and spit and stomp on it. He might have felt that the United States and its customs could never be his place. Her own father fit that pattern. Although he lived in California for most of his adult life, raised his children there, went to church there, and worked in the California soil, his heart remained in Zacatecas. After thirty-six years, he finally applied for American citizenship. The subcontractor might very well have the same powerful allegiance to his homeland, a similar reluctance to abandoning it in the embrace of another flag.

It was a cultural difference really, the strength of affinity in places where people see themselves rooted in layered generations. They are not just individuals, fulfilling their own destinies; they are amalgamations of their heritage, people who represent their families and cultures in the way that they live and in the decisions they make. To Americans, the idea that national identity is so valuable that it might cost money is foreign. Why did Jim Bowie, Davey Crockett, and others go to Texas to die at the Alamo in the 1830s? What brought them to Mexico to eventually foment revolution? They had to shed their American citizenship to get land in Mexican Texas, and with that land, profit. They had to become citizens of the Republic of Mexico and convert to Catholicism, which they did willingly and more than a little disingenuously. The malleability of identity has always been an American trait. The insistence on a past, any past, at the cost of wealth seems absurd to Americans. No wonder my imagination wove tales when the economics of the subcontractor's situation didn't make sense to me.

At about eleven in the morning, all over Las Vegas it seems, the army of gardeners, landscape workers, and yard men take their break. They park on the street or sometimes on walking or biking paths, put out the ubiquitous orange cones, and out of nowhere comes a soccer ball. Within minutes, they've divided up into teams and a match is under way. They pass the ball to one another, shouting with glee. Someone lofts a header toward the goalie standing between two orange cones. He leaps, seeking to deflect the ball. Either way, there are shouts, laughter, the sounds of people at play. The language is Spanish, and the scene could be anywhere in Mexico, Central America, or much of South America, or for that matter almost anywhere in the United States. I watched one group play in a small park just outside the gates of an upper-middle-class community. It struck me that in the spring sun, with the manicured park and the metal rails of the fence and the nearby guard booth, this could be upper-class Brazil, Paraguay, Mexico, or anywhere else with an enormous underclass and a few people with privilege. In the United States, privilege extends further down the socioeconomic ladder. In Las Vegas, it extends even further than in most places. There are $170,000 homes behind those gates. Yet to the young men playing soccer, even one such home must feel a million miles away, well out of the reach of his earnings from building, much less caring for the landscape around, similar homes. How might one conceive of owning one of these homes instead of tending the lawn and playing soccer in the park? How might one bridge the gap between transient or semipermanent labor and a job with benefits, with health care, with the resources to support a family?

It is hard to live in Las Vegas without recognizing that despite the enormous opportunity and the advantageous standard of living of the middle class, a good part of that prosperity is built on the backs of poorly paid construction workers. "Home Buyer Beware!" read the flyer handed to me by workers from Tejas Underground. The company was one of many subcontractors working in the valley, and its workers did the same work as union workers, but for half the wages. Tejas Underground subcontracted from Del Webb Corporation, which had many unionized subcontractors. The workers felt shorted. Same work, same pay, an old American refrain, here chorused by new Americans. Tejas Underground employees "want to be represented by a union and work under a union agreement so they can receive decent wages and benefits," the flyer read. "Ask Del Webb why they hire contractors to exploit their employees and infringe on their right to organize. Call Tejas Underground and tell them to show Tejas Underground employees the dignity and respect they deserve."

Nevada's right-to-work status ensures that manual construction work, like framing and sheetrocking, are low-wage jobs. While iron workers, union carpenters, electricians, and other tradesmen make solid wages and drive new pickups, further down the pecking order, the wages fall fast. At each construction site, a hierarchy emerges: you rarely see African American or Anglo guys framing houses. That work is done by men, newcomers, speaking Spanish. When the skilled craftsmen arrive in their glistening trucks that usually sport union bumper stickers, they are white—country, but definitely white. Privilege can be articulated even in trade work.

The success of democracy has a great deal to do with whether privilege can be translated more broadly in the future. Latinos have been invisible in the United States for a long time, overlooked as they work and even as they're playing soccer. The key to attaining the full benefits of American life is securing recognition of their contribution. If privilege, even blue-collar privilege like high-wage manual labor, remains a perquisite of nativity, if thirty years from now the skilled tradesmen are still mostly white, some of the air will have gone out of the balloon of democracy and the American dream will be something other than what it is now. The Southwest, Aztlán, the Chicano name for their lost homeland in this desolate region, is the most visible part of the great current of immigration, but it is also a harbinger of a future that you see everywhere, from New York to Aurora, Illinois. Spanish-speaking immigration is more than a reprise of past immigration. In scope and character, it is a transformative phenomenon that has the power to remake American society. As was earlier immigration, Latino immigration is made up of the poor and the fleeing, with a smattering of the well-off. But it is nourished by proximity, by a fecundity unrivaled since restrictive immigration legislation was imposed in 1924. Integration into the main corridors of society is coming, but the terms of that new status have yet to be determined. Latino life in Las Vegas shows the Spanish-speaking future in its many dimensions. Following the aspirations of the many forward in time will answer significant questions about the openness of American society to a historical bootstraps-driven prosperity. That future is already in play in Las Vegas.

PART III

Building a New City

CHAPTER 8

The Tortoise and the Air

Life in a Libertarian Desert

THE DAY AFTER A RAIN, LAS VEGAS IS ONE OF THE MOST BEAUTIFUL PLACES on earth. Moisture changes the look of the city, replacing the usual grime with a sheen of wetness. The colors of the desert, from the brilliant blue sky to the crumbly gray and golden richness of old mountains and the deep reds and purples of the rocks, come out with a vengeance. The clear air telescopes distances and brings the unreal topography up close. The dirt is tamped down, the air is clear, and you can see forever. Strip hotels look like abstract expressionist landscape painting; could Christo have been here overnight? They glint against the backdrop of the mountains, stone-cold and unreal with the snow-covered peak of nearly twelve-thousand-foot-high Mt. Charleston behind them. The angles are powerful and even sensual, the sense of time vast in the barren, rocky expanses. The landscape feels lunar, airless, timeless, ancient. The scrub, low to the ground, reflects light off the dark slopes. The clarity is exquisite, the color sharp and clear, and the scene overpowering, even epiphanic. It'll steal your breath, make you gasp in a way that Americans reserve for their first view of the Grand Canyon.

But it doesn't rain very often in the desert. Only about ninety miles from Death Valley, one of the hottest places on earth, Las Vegas is among the world's largest dry cities. It lies in the double rain shadow of the vast

Sierra Nevada and the smaller Spring Mountains to its immediate west, which completely wall the valley off from the moderating influence of the Pacific Ocean. Climatologists suggest that 120 inches of water could evaporate off the valley floors annually. With average rainfall of about four inches each year, Las Vegas is hyper-arid.

Most of the time, the dust is up, and a haze envelopes the lower parts of the valley. The air is thick and dusty, the fate of all developed desert environments. The sun is hot, sometimes too hot even for the most devoted desert rat. Heat chases you everywhere. An hour in the sun and your steering wheel is too hot to touch. The pavement radiates. Squiggly lines of viscous air showing the purple of traces of petroleum rise. This Las Vegas can take your breath away too, but from the exertion of even casual walking. Breathing is like inhaling in a blast furnace. It sears your lungs, fills you with flaming air, and if you're not careful to drink water constantly, drains your energy. Sunscreen and a hat are essential. People wear sunglasses all the time, indoors, at night, everywhere, not to be incognito or cool. It's just habit. Some say it's a dry heat, but over 110 degrees, who cares? In the summer, people live before 10 A.M. and after 8 P.M. If you don't have to, you don't go out during the heat of the day. It can be so hot it'll make you wish for winter.

Industrial societies learned to conquer the limits of the physical environment. Boston, New York, and Chicago became easier with oil heaters, gas furnaces, central heat, and mechanized snow removal. It isn't an accident that places like Spokane have office buildings connected by aboveground indoor passageways or that Minneapolis–St. Paul parking meters feature an electric plug for your engine block heater. In Las Vegas as elsewhere in the South and Southwest, the advent of air-conditioning was the catalyst for habitability, the moment when real growth became possible and a permanent connection to American society became viable. Without technology, only a polar bear or a desert tortoise could live beyond the edges of humid-climate culture. With it, Americans were free to do what they do best: put their faith in what the biologist Garrett Hardin called "technological solutions to all classes of problems" and impress the template of their society on any landscape they found.

In Las Vegas, that template demanded special mitigation. The way Americans live was honed in wooded, wet climates. American history and literature demonstrated a justified fear of the winter, and dismissed the desert as an afterthought, treating it as a threat to be avoided instead of addressed. Deserts were the wastelands of American society, where it tossed its detritus and hid its immense flaws. After confirming the destructive power of nuclear weapons, Americans exploded their nuclear devices with wild abandon almost entirely in the desert. An estimated 200 million curies of radiation remain in the subsurface of the Nevada Test Site, less than seventy-five miles from downtown Las Vegas.

When deserts became part of the mainstream, old attitudes and the problems they spawned, along with new ones that accompanied growth, came home to roost. The uniformity of the expansive desert hid scars that a new society had to grapple with. Sparsely populated but fragile, the desert had enjoyed the de facto protection of small population; as it filled with people, Las Vegas had to reach consensus to solve basic needs: water, clean air, sewage disposal, electricity, and the rest of the grid on which American society depended.

While that was an easy enough task in cities with a big river, enormous salt caverns, great open expanses, or other obvious places to dump its crap, in the desert the surface is the extent of what you have to work with. Dig down and you hit caliche, a hard clay that stymies earth-movers and keeps new swimming pools shallow. Leave your waste—whatever it is—on the surface and it spreads and leaches, slowly, inexorably, eventually reaching almost anywhere. Building an infrastructure and mitigating its challenges was more difficult in the desert.

The first thing anyone asks when considering the future of Las Vegas's growth is: Where will the water come from? The question is an obvious one, but asking it belies a fundamental misunderstanding of the way water works in American deserts. The Southwest is profligate in its water use, consuming more water per capita than any other region, and Las Vegas is the prime culprit. The city has endured water shortages since the 1940s, but rarely as a result of a lack of supply. Instead the absence of distribution capability, of pipelines and storage tanks, has led to the city's failure to keep up with spiking demand. Water delivery is a technological question.

Nowhere does the American desire to use technology to obviate natural limits scream as loudly as in Las Vegas. The need for that technology is more evident there as well. Faith in technology compels American society forward and translates into pure belief in the desert. Barring a revolution in the way American society does business, nowhere in the desert is there less chance of running out of water than in Las Vegas.

Water will always be the straw man, the question the rest of the world asks that pulls attention from the real issues Las Vegas and any booming desert metropolis face. In the American West, water is an institutional question. Availability is not the real question. Free-flowing water has become a question of fee per acre foot, of who will pay how much for the water and who elsewhere will give it up for cash. The only genuinely determining factor in acquiring water is cost. Water is a commodity, marketed in the same way as any other consumable. Maybe someday, in a postapocalyptic future, there will be illegal freshwater dealers like the people who once traded oil to apartheid-era South Africa and got diamonds in return. Even though water is the basis of life, as long as it is a commodity in a market, cash rules. This is the principle on which the American West was built. The late Marc Reisner astutely observed that in this arid region, water flows uphill to money. Money is no problem in Las Vegas.

The distribution of water use in the Las Vegas Valley is certainly surprising. In 2000 the orgy of waterfalls and man-made lakes accounted for 7 percent of the total usage. Residential use comprised fully two-thirds of Las Vegas's water use, the nebulous category of "irrigation" claimed 9 percent, and all other uses, schools and government, commercial, and industrial, used 20 percent. The profligate display is Las Vegas to the core, masking reality and on closer inspection confounding and deceiving those who look only at the surface and actually believe it.

Even more perplexing, the waterfalls, pools, showers, toilets, lawns, and golf courses of all of urban Nevada, even including the profligate water use of nearly 400 gallons per day per person in greater Las Vegas compared to about 310 gallons in Phoenix, use only 20 percent of the state's water. The rest, as in every other western state, goes to agriculture and ranching, anachronistic activities that in Nevada survive only when subsidized by the federal government. Eighty percent of the water results in a minuscule percentage of jobs, revenue, taxes, and other income for the state. Its gross handle of $1 billion per annum is less than one-fifteenth of the gaming win alone and looks even smaller when income from tourism and entertainment are figured in. Nevada would dearly miss the MGM if it couldn't get enough water, but if all of Nevada's agriculture and ranching dried up and blew away, urban Nevada might not notice for years.

Reallocation, the process that figuratively takes water from the cotton fields outside of Yuma, Arizona, to water parks like the Schlitterbahn in New Braunfels, Texas, makes plain sense in Nevada. It also inspires passionate outcry. I was pilloried in print and hung in effigy for making this argument in a syndicated column in 2000. Writers and editors from all over the West wanted my scalp for merely suggesting that there was better use for western water than irrigating subsidized crops that only the federal government will buy.

Las Vegas's water begins with the 1922 creation of the Colorado River Compact, the "Law of the River," the adjudication of the Colorado River that stemmed from California's imperial need for water. After cannibalizing southern California and draining the Owens Valley, Los Angeles needed even more. The Colorado River, the lifeblood of the West, became the logical source, and for a decade California grappled with entrenched interests in Upper Basin states like Colorado and Wyoming. They had little need in the 1920s for that water, but they could see that their chance at the brass ring of industrial prosperity depended on being able to reserve water for use in the future. In the process of reaching agreement, the Upper Basin and California colluded against Arizona and Nevada. Arizona resisted, never signing the Colorado Compact, and Congress changed the law to allow the compact to take effect in 1927 without Arizona's acquiescence. Little Nevada just took its lumps, garnering all of 300,000 acres feet per annum from the river, compared to California's 4.4 million. The relationship between California and its neighbors, the junior partners in western growth, was made clear. Like it or not, California would do its own thing. Nevada and Arizona could come along or resist if they chose. Their decision would not affect the outcome of water distribution.

So it remained until after 1945, when growth in the rest of the West accelerated as California blossomed into the sixth largest economy in the world. Until 1945, most states didn't use their entire allotment, but postwar growth quickly changed that. The Colorado Compact allocated more than 16 million acre feet per annum to the various states, but the Colorado River routinely generated only 12 to 13 million in an average year. Someday, somebody somewhere was going to be left dry. California wasn't going to be the loser, and as long as Colorado congressman Wayne Aspinall, the king of the Water Buffaloes, the western congressmen who brought home the bacon by tying their votes to the inclusion of projects in their districts, reigned as chairman of the House Appropriations Committee, the Upper Basin—Colorado, Utah, Wyoming, and most of New Mexico—certainly wasn't going to suffer. That left Mexico, which had its 1.5 million acre foot allowance delivered at the border and immediately diverted to the fields around Mexicali—this is why the Colorado River rarely reached the Gulf of California between the 1930s and the 1980s and even now only produces a trickle in the wettest of years—and the junior Lower Basin states. Arizona fought long and hard. The multibillion-dollar, thirty-years-in-the-making Central Arizona Project, a testament to former secretary of the interior Stewart Udall's power and prowess and the single biggest boondoggle in the long, pathetic history of federal water projects, became one of the strategies Arizona used to defend its share of the river. Nevada and the part of New Mexico included in the Lower Basin mostly stood by and watched, having long ago learned the lesson that when the big dogs tear into each other, the best survival strategy for the little dogs is to stay out of the way and hope nobody looks at you and licks their chops.

Growth in the interior West and the changing economy put incredible pressure on water adjudication, flawed to begin with and entirely a creature of political power. In the lower basin, Arizona grew first, adding retirement as an industry. As California set the tone for the nation, migrants flocked to the Golden State, spilling into neighboring states. When the Cold War ended and California's vaunted aerospace industry fell apart, Nevada grew and Las Vegas began to use first 60 percent, then 70 percent, and finally 75 percent of the 300,000 acre feet allotted to it from Lake Mead. The numbers were a little misleading. Las Vegas, like nearly every other city along the river, received credit for the treated sewage it deposited in the lake, meaning more than 227,000 acre feet came to Las Vegas in the average year. Still, reality aside, the die had been cast. Growth everywhere meant greater demand for water, and the Upper Basin showed no willingness to share. Even as the twenty-first century dawned, the old western adage "whiskey's for drinkin' and water's for fightin'" remained even truer than it had been a century before.

The fighting commenced. The question became whether agriculture and ranching could hold its century-old share of the water at the expense of western cities, where more than 90 percent of the region's population resided. In the Lower Basin the power base that rural interests held had long since evaporated. Rural Arizona was overwhelmed by the cities. By 1980 the Tucson-Phoenix-Flagstaff corridor, the nascent megalopolis, was home to more than 75 percent of the state's non-Indian population. California's Central Valley was a great consumer of water, but by the mid-1990s even rural interests in California recognized that reallocation was a certainty. Only in Nevada did rural and ranching interests hold on, resisting the inevitable and promising a fight to the death over land, a commodity entirely worthless without water. This was the romantic and sometimes bizarre world of the Sagebrush Rebels, held up as a symbol but as a group too parochial to recognize that they would soon be pushed aside even by their most passionate supporters. Even as they bellowed and brayed, the changes in the urban West doomed them to noisy irrelevance.

Everywhere anyone looked, western cities boomed. Phoenix, with 40,000 people in 1950, got huge and then surged again, from 1.6 million in 1980 to more than 3.3 million in 1999. New subdivisions spread out into the desert, freeways clogged, and Phoenix took on the look of a little Los Angeles. Albuquerque grew so fast that Corrales and Rio Rancho, formerly nearby small towns, became part of the city. Albuquerque even overran Petroglyph National Monument, created to preserve petroglyphs that had become surrounded by the rapid growth of West Mesa. Low wages and a docile but educated population made Utah desirable for high-tech industries, and Salt Lake City found itself buried in traffic, made worse by its run for the 2002 Winter Olympics. Los Angeles . . . well, never mind. Urban growth came at the expense of rural areas. A greater portion of the population shifted to cities and took western states further from their rural roots. Every bit of that growth demanded services, and above all, water.

The upsurge in population in Las Vegas forced a reassessment of the local water situation. For most of its history, Las Vegas had been fed by the underground springs that gave the valley its name; in Spanish, *Las Vegas* means "the meadows," and the artesian water that percolated to the surface there had been the attraction for human beings since time immemorial. The railroad harnessed it, creating a private water company that distributed water to most of the city through the 1930s; dug wells for their water. In 1940 water still seemed plentiful in the Las Vegas Valley, but continuous growth soon demanded new structures. Voters approved a municipal water district in 1948 to bring water from Lake Mead, and in 1955 Las Vegas received the first water in its new pipeline. Demand soon exceeded distribution capacity, and a new round of water infrastructure development ensued. In 1982 the Southern Nevada Water Project completed a pipeline that let Las Vegas take its full share of Lake Mead. By that time, the underground water that had long sustained the valley still pumped, but before it reached the surface it was diverted to pipes that wound their way throughout the city.

The catalyst for both the shortages and the huge steps in infrastructure was growth. Even before its remarkable boom, the city had grown at a rate that consistently outpaced even the prayer that infrastructure could keep pace. All of a sudden, Las Vegas had much greater growth to contend with and the same flimsy infrastructure and weak traditions of leadership that prevailed thirty years earlier.

Into that vacuum stepped Patricia Mulroy, a visionary governmental leader of a sort rarely seen in Nevada or elsewhere in the West. As general manager of the Las Vegas Valley Water District, Mulroy intuited the future a full decade ahead of the rest of the region. In the 1980s she recognized that the nation had stopped building new dams and pipelines. The era of dam building was over, gone the way of the Water Buffaloes and former Bureau of Reclamation commissioner Floyd Dominy, who'd made those projects happen. The environmental movement fought dams, and after 1974 the federal agencies and the political representatives who staked their careers on development lacked the combination of political power and financial wherewithal to build. More water would have to come from redistribution of existing supply. Mulroy recognized that the future of water meant reallocation, and that that in turn guaranteed that the people who turned the changes in the structure to their advantage would come home the big winners. But reallocation was a hard sell, an alteration of the status quo sure to enrage its beneficiaries. Circumventing them demanded a certain genius.

The transformation required a declaration of war, but as it turned out, only as a feint. In 1989 Mulroy and the Las Vegas Valley Water District she headed fired a salvo designed to do more than get the attention of rural Nevada. Her proposal was inflammatory. Mulroy claimed 805,000 acre feet of water in twenty-six valleys across the state, some of which were 250 miles from Las Vegas. She claimed the Virgin River, an annual stream, even though it's barely wet most summers, that starts near Zion National Park and winds its way to Lake Mead. Because it was not navigable by nineteenth-century standards, the Virgin River had never been included in the Colorado River Compact. To her opponents, Mulroy's claim was outright assault. Despite her contention that she didn't want to "wipe out" rural Nevada, the cow counties saw the water grab as social genocide. When the water district initiated the research for an environmental impact statement, rural Nevada had no choice but to take the effort seriously. It was fightin' time in the new West.

The prospect of a battle royale brought other, more powerful, more recalcitrant, and newly vulnerable beneficiaries of the Colorado River to the table. A western water fight served only those who didn't have enough water. Worse, it could shed light on the absurd and archaic arrangements that made fortunes for some and left others dry. The Colorado River Compact had become an outdated document that originated in a time when agriculture and ranching reigned supreme in the West and the cities were neither big enough nor sufficiently independent of the rural economy to resist. Even the vaunted Bureau of Reclamation, the great western dam-building agency that wielded power like a club, had fallen on hard times. The wicked joked that the Bureau of Reclamation's nickname, "BuRec," now stood for Bureau of Recreation. But the compact created a water oligarchy, and as long as no one looked too closely and small-town congressional representatives bartered their votes in state houses and Congress, the rural West would hold tight to its federally subsidized prize. A great big stink about water in Nevada would do more damage to the status quo than finding a way to give a little bit of water to cities to preserve the rural areas' prerogative of subsidized water for no apparent economic purpose.

Mulroy had something to offer them as well. Her solution to the entire Lower Basin mess only cost a few hundred thousand acre feet of water each year. First she consolidated her power by bringing her opponents over to her side. Instead of building a dam and piping water to Las Vegas, she told the state engineer at a hearing, all that Las Vegas wanted was to let the Virgin River flow. Rather than dam the river and create a huge fight not only with rural Nevada, but with environmentalists throughout the nation, Mulroy proposed letting the river go where it has since the Hoover Dam was built: into Lake Mead. From there, two pipelines would take it to the Las Vegas Valley. Environmentalists were thrilled because Mulroy did not want to build a dam. Communities along the Virgin River were equally excited. Not only did they get water from the deal, they also received seats on the newly reconfigured Southern Nevada Water Authority board, a powerful regional authority that encompassed the Las Vegas Valley Water District. Mulroy created a regional management entity, and the rural counties could negotiate from a position of relative strength on the authority's board. Pulling all of this off required "major rethinking" up and down the Colorado River, Mulroy reminded the public, but it was a start.

The grease for this wheel was cash, the real gold Las Vegas had to offer. Water has never been a paying proposition in the West. Only one of all the reclamation projects in the region, in Carlsbad, New Mexico, ever paid for itself, and that happened only because the federal government took over a failed private project in 1908. For a long time, the lack of economic logic simply didn't matter. Farmers and ranchers controlled the statehouses in the interior West, and along with their well-placed representatives in Washington, D.C., that power guaranteed that no one cut the federal appropriations that covered the economic shortfall from the water that fed agriculture and ranching. The Law of the River was really just oligarchic control by a well-placed and wealthy few defending privileges they'd never earned. That changed first when cities in the interior western states overwhelmed the rural areas, and again when the Microchip Revolution altered the social meaning of American crops and natural resources. Did we really need that cotton from Yuma, Arizona? Did we really need to subsidize competition with farmers in the East, Midwest, and South with federal projects that couldn't meet their bills in the West? The fiction became harder to sustain, and when Mulroy knocked, even people who probably hated her recognized that she brought a few more years of coverage by providing a solution that quieted the issue down. No less an opponent of Las Vegas's water grab than Bill Clinton's secretary of the interior, Bruce Babbitt of Arizona, turned around on the issue. "Las Vegas needs an expanded water supply from the Colorado River," he agreed in 1998.

Mulroy also fixed the other side of the equation. Once the extra water for Las Vegas was in Lake Mead, it still had to get to Las Vegas. The answer was an expansion of the water delivery system, a "second straw" as it became known, to accompany the pipe completed in 1982. The project cost almost $2 billion, about what a dam and pipes from rural Nevada would have cost, and it had the added advantage of being large enough to carry future allotments of water beyond Nevada's 300,000-acre-foot limit. As always the question became who would pay for the project. The most palatable way in Nevada was regressive taxation—the sales tax. That way, the refrain went, the 36 million visitors each year helped subsidize locals. Seductive, the measure passed in 1998 despite populist, environmentalist, and senior citizen opposition.

Mulroy's endeavors took care of Las Vegas's short-term needs. The long-term future has more to do with a larger trend in the West, the reallocation of water from rural to urban uses. In California, reallocation was well under way as 1999 ended. For southern Nevada, reallocation of the river itself, as Mulroy suggested, was crucial. Again, Las Vegas's cash greased the wheels of water commerce. Irrigation districts have rarely been able to pay their bills in the West, and a shot of outside money is almost always welcome. The cash came thanks to the creation of a water banking system that let both Nevada and California "store" excess irrigation water in underground aquifers in

Arizona. The irrigation districts were paid for putting their water underground, instead of spreading it aboveground to grow crops.

With computer models showing that even without an increase in the state's Colorado River allocation, southern Nevada could thrive with a system of water banking and leasing, Las Vegas had not only the rationale but the means to ensure water well into the twenty-first century. Arizona farmers could provide the additional water that Las Vegas needed to sustain its growth. The transfer of the water that irrigates the cotton in Yuma seemed poised to begin, but the Schlitterbahn, the water park outside New Braunfels, Texas, couldn't afford to pay for it. Las Vegas wrote the check with a smile.

Confirmation of the new order came in early January 2001 in the waning days of the Clinton administration, when Bruce Babbitt signed an accord that officially gave California the surplus water it had long taken from the Colorado River in return for a commitment from the Golden State to conserve water. The fifteen-year agreement, Babbitt announced, "reverses a century of trying to solve these water problems by going to war." Babbitt had long demonized California—he joked that the strategy made his political career—but changes in demography and water demand led him to a new stance. California ceded power too. In return for permission to take excess water, it promised to annually decrease the amount it took.

The real beneficiary was southern Nevada. Pat Mulroy announced after the signing that Las Vegas was "out of the crisis mode." Under the agreement, southern Nevada received the right to store up to 1.2 million acre feet in Arizona aquifers as well as an additional 500,000 acre feet beneath Nevada. Most important, the new compact gave Las Vegas a fifty-year cushion, ending the urgency spawned by the decade-old prediction that the city would run dry in 2007.

Full-scale interstate transfers of water have yet to occur, but they're not hard to see ten years down the road. They'll probably occur when a city like Phoenix has to curtail its growth because of an impending shortage of water. Then one of the water-rich Upper Basin states, Utah or Colorado, will sell some water downriver. Although it is easy to imagine that the rural states would rather sell water to any city but Las Vegas, most observers envision a system of water auctions. When money talks, Las Vegas will always be in the picture.

No American city has ever ceased to grow because of a lack of water, and it's unlikely that Las Vegas will be the first. Los Angeles, Phoenix, Tucson, and the rest all found sources for their expansion, and at least for now Las

Vegas has used its greatest asset, cash, to redirect enough of the water for long enough to fashion a permanent solution. As long as water is a commodity—and there is nothing happening in American society to change that—and Las Vegas has cash, the exchange will continue in some form. Once slow to realize its water needs and rights, Las Vegas has come on fast. Southern Nevada is confident about its future access to water, so confident that water doesn't really rate on the list of environmental problems Las Vegas faces.

"Air quality is always a function of a growing population and economy," observed Russell Roberts, a tall, husky, and imposing figure in blue jeans and a flannel shirt with twenty years' experience in western air-quality management who was assistant planning manager for air quality in Clark County in 2000. "You look at places that have air-quality problems, they're places with vibrant growing economies and growing populations. You look at places that don't have air-quality problems and they typically don't have much of an economy." From Roberts's perspective, the equation was simple. Polluted air results from success in other endeavors. Communities that have problems with the quality of their air are doing something else right. Very often they're growing rapidly, adding population and new suburbs, creating jobs, building amenities, moving upward. They're also building highways, and people are driving farther each year, tearing up farmland or desert for new subdivisions, convenience stores, and shopping centers, and deferring the environmental cost of all those growth-related activities. Bad air almost always remains what it has always been: a sign of prosperity and economic success. "In trying to deal with that success," Roberts pointed out, "we sometimes forget that there's a resource out there that needs to be looked at."

Americans have long paid a price for that slip of memory. Until the 1970s, smokestacks meant progress and prosperity. Early in the century, when their emissions destroyed nearby crops, factories built their towers higher to spread the impact over a greater area but with less intensity. This didn't stop pollution, but it diminished or ended the liability of the individual factories. Farmers' crops weren't damaged enough to compel them to litigate. This fix, almost technological in character, worked as long as the new, larger zones of factory emission didn't overlap too much, as long as pollution wasn't everywhere. After World War II, fouled air became more common and threatening, and "smog"—the word is an amalgam for smoke and fog, first used in early-twentieth-century London—became the signature of southern California. But smoke-filled air remained a by-product of a healthy economy, and throughout the 1950s few people railed about it. Air pollution was part of the deal the children of the Depression made with their employers to ensure prosperity and security in the workplace.

In the 1960s fouled air became a symbol of what was wrong with the nation. Pollution galvanized the new environmentalism, based in quality of life instead of the efficiency of turn-of-the-twentieth-century conservation. Air became the bellwether: How could people have it all if a white shirt turned gray from soot by noon? Nobody, not even the iconic reactionary figure of Archie Bunker, was *for* pollution, especially not air pollution.

The image of a gas mask permeated the rise of environmentalism in the United States and nowhere more so than in southern California. Its smog may not have been the worst in the nation, but it was certainly the best known and most symbolic of the fouling of the American dream. After 1970 the threat of killer smog abated. People didn't feel imperiled, but they did feel threatened. Bad air meant coughing, wheezing, hacking, the diminishment of quality of life for the infirm and especially the retired. If environmentalism became a personal quest to the beneficiaries of the industrial America, it became so out of affluence, privilege, and a sense of entitlement that articulated a powerful sentiment that people should have it all.

The passage of the Clean Air Act in 1970 set the nation on the path to reactive mitigation, a reality still true thirty years later. Americans won't stop progress to keep their air clean, but they will resort to after-the-fact strategies to diminish the impact of their activities. After passage of the Clean Air Act, smokestack scrubbers, the Corporate Average Fuel Economy standards for automobile manufacturers, and oxygenated fuel in the winter became typical remedies. They addressed consequences, not behavior, and were implemented only after air got dirty. Once again, technology proceeded at a pace faster than the ability and the will to manage it.

Las Vegas's story was typical of the way that air quality served as the canary in the coal mine that everyone ignored. As growth accelerated in the 1980s, air quality was first impaired and then degraded. Like Phoenix, Las Vegas found that for all the advantages of growth, its consequences became a threat not so much to general prosperity, but to the most attractive feature of the town, the quality of life it offered. The new people who so loved their life in the desert complained loudly when they had trouble breathing or found the vistas hazy. Even though the EPA regulated only Class I areas, wilderness and national parks, the public expected government to give them clear sight lines. Retirees worried about the impact of bad air on their health. Acting after the fact meant an eternal game of catch-up, one that would at best end in a draw. No matter what air-quality planners did, their tools were sufficient only to slow the decline in quality. Air wouldn't get fundamentally better, but it wouldn't grow much worse either, a chip that could be used to stave off greater federal intervention.

This was Las Vegas's fate in the 1990s. After another round of amendments to the Clean Air Act in 1990, the Environmental Protection Agency set National Ambient Air Quality Standards that established a ceiling for the concentration of six categories of pollutants in the air that either harmed public health or threatened the environment: carbon monoxide, nitrogen dioxide, ozone, lead, sulfur dioxide, and dust, or PM10, regulatory shorthand for particulate matter smaller than ten microns in diameter. PM10 was pernicious because it could be inhaled into the deepest part of the lung and could cause serious difficulty for people with respiratory problems. Throughout the 1990s Las Vegas was in a state of "nonattainment," EPA lingo for air quality that doesn't meet federal standards, in two of the six catagories: carbon monoxide and PM10. Early in 2001 the Air Pollution Control District announced that it expected to be unable to meet standards for ozone by the end of 2001. Nonattainment had consequences that were especially dire in a place growing as fast as Las Vegas, where the designation had the potential to lead to complicated and onerous results.

The two areas of nonattainment—carbon monoxide from vehicle exhausts and PM10, the ever-blowing dust from tearing up the desert to build homes, schools, roads, malls, and everything else that seventy-thousand new inhabitants a year need—were rooted in growth. Carbon monoxide had been the bane of American cities, Los Angeles preeminent among them, and the structure of urbanization worsened the problem. As housing costs rose, people moved farther away, driving more miles on crowded freeways each day. The bargain was Faustian: housing was cheaper farther away, but the cost of vehicle upkeep, gasoline, and time spent in travel offset that financial advantage in many places. At the same time, each mile driven produced carbon monoxide, diminishing air quality, an impact residents didn't count among their difficulties but that had the potential not only to physically harm them, but also to bring down sanctions on the region in which they lived. In spread-out western cities, mass transit was a joke. Buses catered to the local poor; intraregional buses for daily commuting were rare. Nearly everyone drove. As Las Vegas's subdivisions reached farther into the desert, people drove more miles in more cars, releasing more carbon monoxide into the air.

The blowing dirt was an issue unique to desert cities. Dirt in the air almost always resulted from tearing into the fragile crust of the desert. Just a single vehicle or motorbike passing across desert terrain can initiate the process. Repeated passes set up a cycle of erosion and wind-born removal. Two types of soil are especially vulnerable, so-called desert pavement, a thin layer of stones forming a tarmac that effectively limits dust generation unless it is torn, and the much rarer cryptogramic soils that consist of biologic and geologic materials combined into an exquisitely delicate surface layer that can be destroyed by a mere boot print.

Blowing dirt accompanied urban growth throughout the Southwest. In Phoenix it had been especially problematic. Early in the 1900s Arizona's dry air was recommended as a remedy for tuberculosis and other respiratory disease. The image persisted long after Phoenix's air got bad. The hordes of retirees who moved there developed respiratory problems, a result of both age and the dry desert air for people with breathing problems. In Las Vegas, dust from the never-ending process of clearing the desert became a feature of daily life. As graders and earthmovers came, they tore the cover off the desert, and when the wind blew, the dirt billowed into the air. Anti-dust ordinances require construction sites to prevent air pollution. Every morning and often twice a day, trucks spray water to keep down the dust.

The circumstances of growth inaugurated regulatory mechanisms. By the late 1980s, the Las Vegas Valley had achieved perennial moderate nonattainment, a situation federal agencies winked at, but also had to address. The Clean Air Act Amendments of 1990 upgraded standards and demanded response. Areas of moderate nonattainment had to implement emission control standards "as expeditiously as practicable," a phrase as ambiguous and undefined as the "all deliberate speed" clause in the 1954 *Brown v. Board of Education* decision. Such areas were also required to implement an oxygenated-gasoline program during the winter and an enhanced vehicle inspection program, and to produce forecasts of the dread VMT—vehicle miles traveled—to anticipate increases in travel to assist planning. These were to be included in a State Implementation Plan and delivered to the EPA by November 15, 1991. On that very day, the Clark County Commission approved an SIP plan that purported to show that the area could meet federal standards for carbon monoxide by December 1995. So far so good.

Except that growth continued and air quality worsened while the county scrambled to implement the plan. Almost seventy thousand people moved to Las Vegas in 1992 alone, precipitating more than twelve thousand housing starts, road construction, malls, schools, and other ancillary development. That was just an ordinary year in the middle of the extended boom, but it seemed like construction was everywhere and the air filled with dirt as a result. Average miles driven per vehicle rose, and even with better average gasoline mileage and cleaner fuels, the improvement in air quality did not meet EPA standards. Even the prohibition of wood-burning fireplaces in new homes did not solve the problem. On January 8, 1993, EPA reclassified much of southern California and the Las Vegas Valley to serious nonattainment status, introducing more rigorous reporting and mitigation. It leveled deadlines, requiring a plan for the Las Vegas Valley by 1997 that would show how acceptable air quality could be attained by 2001. There was a stick that accompanied this carrot, a drop-dead date of attainment for PM10 by December 2006. The Clark County Commission accepted this new mandate.

Improvement in the carbon monoxide category seemed within reach: the combination of improvements since the 1970s and the introduction of oxygenated fuel in 1996 nearly offset the increase in cars on Las Vegas roads. Studies determined that carbon monoxide pollution was a lot like crime: a relatively small number of offenders, 50,000 to 70,000 "high emitters" out of a total of more than 700,000 vehicles, accounted for more than 75 percent of carbon monoxide pollution. Better testing and compliance with smog controls considerably slowed carbon monoxide emission. "Carbon monoxide is going to be a historical problem," Roberts anticipated late in 2000. "We've got that licked and we've done that without having to turn this community upside down," he assured me. "That'll buy us twenty years and then we'll see what growth does to CO levels."

PM10 was an entirely different matter, far more complex and difficult to address. The Air Quality Division spent a great deal of its time on the problem, their efforts culminating in the *Particulate Matter (PM10) Attainment Demonstration Plan*, another of the series of documents filed with the EPA to keep the federal government from asserting its authority over the county's. The attainment demonstration plan had one small goal: to show that the strategies the county implemented would lead to attainment by the target date of 2001. The full implementation plan, what Roberts called a "huge task, a state-of-the-art cutting-edge PM10 plan," was in preparation as

2000 ended. Rules in place had already made the cost of digging up the desert much higher. The Clark County Health District implemented a permit system that tracked every activity with potential to disturb the surface and create dust. New APCD regulations seemed likely to break southern Nevada's traditional hands-off attitude toward landowners by requiring controls on "vacant disturbed land," widely recognized as a significant source of dust pollution. The combination of water trucks and chemical palliatives to keep the dust down, site-specific measures implemented on a case-by-case basis, more comprehensive site clean-up procedures, and a hotline to report blowing dust and violators all contributed to creating stasis.

But this wasn't truly a solution; it was more like a holding action. The reactive model made real gains over time impossible as long as growth continued. The mitigation measures cut the amount of dust from existing construction and even predicted the amount of growth, but new construction, even when it complied with the five rules for dust management adopted by the district board of health, meant that the dust in the air stayed constant in quantity.

Air-quality management remains a reactive process, in which communities grapple with consequences instead of launching proactive measures. "There are limits to technology in terms of emission reductions, there are limits to political acceptability of some of the options, in any scenario there is a finite number of control measures you can apply to reduce the impact," Roberts wearily observed. One of the end results, however unintended, of meeting the demands of the Clean Air Act, Roberts continued, is that "we've gotten by for thirty years by fixing it on the back end, sometimes successfully, sometimes not." The current system could buy you time, but it left you with two enormous problems: sooner or later, you'd have to rely on a new technological fix to solve the ongoing problem, and no matter what you did, you'd run up against the hard fact that as long as growth continued, all solutions were short-term. No matter what you accomplished, you'd lose your gains and the entire process would begin all over again.

Roberts advocated a new approach, the inclusion of air quality as an infrastructure cost, front-ended into the development process in the same manner as other fixed costs. "Treating air quality as infrastructure like we treat sewer, water, parks, and all the other things is the way to go," he insisted. "I hope we can convince people that you have to treat air quality as an infrastructure issue." If air quality was an infrastructure concern, reactive mitigation might not be necessary. The eternal cost of buy-down of impact on the air could be avoided. "It's not my idea," Roberts averred, "its just not an idea that's been implemented in this country as a whole."

Roberts's proposition reverses the historical pattern of pollution management. The history of mitigation had been reactive rather than proactive, and under most circumstances it simply hasn't worked very well. Los Angeles is the poster child for the immense shortcomings of reactive mitigation in air-quality management. The South Coast Air Basin there has the largest local air district in the world. Its annual budget tops $100 million, it has eight hundred employees and a dedicated board and staff, and it enjoys every other reactive advantage possible. For fifty years the region has been in nonattainment. Even during the last few years, when air has actually gotten better, reactive management remains a Band-Aid, illustrating an uncomfortable reality. Air-quality managers "deal with symptoms, not the disease," Roberts admitted.

The weakest spot in the reactive arsenal was its vulnerability to public inquiry. After the National Environmental Policy Act of 1970 and the Resource Conservation and Recovery Act (RCRA) in 1976, the public had greater oversight of environmental issues. The 1990 Clean Air Act amendments set absolute standards for offending air districts. If they didn't meet them, they were vulnerable to the third-party lawsuit, the tool of the environmental movement in the 1980s and 1990s. When air-quality goals were ignored or simply not attained, any environmental group might sue. Under the Clean Air Act, the EPA had to act even if it didn't want to, raising the stakes for air-quality management. "The old days of doing as good as you can even if it's not good enough, then we'll figure it out later are pretty much over," Roberts insisted. "Because you're gonna get sued, you're gonna lose, and EPA's gonna be forced to implement sanctions or take over your program."

Air quality had become part of local politics in a new and logical but counterintuitive way. It had become a handmaiden of the powerful, who manipulated it for their purposes. In 1999, as Sheldon Adelson, the perennially petulant owner of the Venetian, battled a proposed monorail and the expansion of the Las Vegas Convention Center, a small, ad-hoc local environmental group, the Nevada Environmental Coalition, retained Patton Boggs, one of the most aggressive law firms in Washington, D.C. The firm filed suit, charging that the plans for both the monorail and expansion violated federal PM10 standards and that the state's air-quality implementation program was inadequate. Although the Venetian and its parent company, Sands, Inc., refused to comment, they enjoyed a long relationship with Patton Boggs. The suit demanded that both projects be halted until they were in compliance with the Clean Air Act.

The Clean Air Act gave Adelson another way to bend the county to his will. Adelson vigorously opposed the planned monorail, one of the measures the county attempted to alleviate traffic in the resort corridor, mostly because he rejected early offers to have it include his property. The monorail bypassed the Venetian, and facilitated a plan for expansion of the Las Vegas Convention Center, the rival of Adelson's Sands Convention Center. "The litigation itself is more far-reaching," said Manny Cortez, president of the LVCVA. "If they say the county and the city haven't complied with clean air standards, that means all construction in the valley will cease." Not only the monorail and the expansion, but twenty thousand homes under construction in 1999, hundreds of thousands of square feet of commercial construction, flood retention basins, and desperately needed roads were all threatened. "This is anti-growth litigation!" an exasperated Cortez wailed.

Hardly. The measure was typical Adelson, a way to jam up everyone else to achieve his ends. By 1999 the thorny and self-righteous Adelson had developed a reputation for such tactics. Anti-growth wasn't his posture. He wanted to limit his rivals' ability to compete. The Clean Air Act became another tool for someone who could afford high-priced lawyers who knew all the tricks. Adelson knew little and cared less about clean air; what he sought was a business advantage, and the law gave him an opening he used as a club in his ongoing effort to bend the already weak institutions of Las Vegas and Clark County to his will.

Adelson's attempts to use the Clean Air Act to stop projects added credence to Russ Roberts's arguments for a new paradigm. Unless air quality is added to the list of infrastructure concerns factored into the development process, the Las Vegas Valley is likely to remain vulnerable not only to third-party lawsuits from the well-intentioned as well as the hard-nosed, but to the range of impacts of bad air as well. In December 2000 a sanctions clock began ticking as a result of Las Vegas's inability to formulate an acceptable plan. If the region could not produce an acceptable air-quality plan, in June 2002 new businesses might face the impact of EPA sanctions, and after December 2002 federal funding for nonessential highways, sewer lines, and sewage plants could be frozen. Ultimately air quality is much more than a set of standards implemented by the EPA and manipulated by officials, business leaders, and others. The air we breathe is a public health question of crucial importance in a region getting older and dustier at the same time. "Somebody's health is suffering," Roberts reminded me. "It's not just a [social] welfare thing where you can't see the mountains. There's a certain justice in it. We all breathe the same air, the developers' kids and you and me."

If air quality was the quintessential issue for an aging, quality of life—minded population, nothing clearly articulated the fat and happy stomach of the environmentalism of affluence like the Endangered Species Act. A product of the heady time when Americans truly thought they could permanently solve problems like poverty and disease and they possessed a pie big enough that pieces of it could be kept out of commercial use forever, the passage of the Endangered Species Act in 1973 came at a time when the conditions that spawned it—and nearly every other piece of environmental legislation that followed the Wilderness Act of 1964—were rapidly coming to an end. That environmentalism was a product of wealth, idealism, and optimism, once-abundant traits that became scarce after the mid-1970s. Bipartisan environmentalism came apart as the economic rules of post—World War II American society ceased to apply. The combination of Vietnam War—era inflation and the OPEC oil crisis brought a halt to American prosperity, inaugurating twenty-three consecutive years in which the real value of wages fell. As the nation lost industries like electronics and nearly gave up others like automobiles, holding back resources for social rather than economic purposes made sense to fewer politicians. The Endangered Species Act became one of the prime targets, attacked over the building of the Tellico Dam in Tennessee by the late 1970s and vigorously challenged at every subsequent reauthorization. Designed for an era of plenty, it became controversial in a leaner time.

The Endangered Species Act had been designed with the cuddly, easy-to-love species in mind, but like a lot of environmental regulation its application was far broader. Even though its framers likely hadn't thought of desert species when they passed the bill, the law applied equally to the weird little fish, fowl, and animals who inhabited the micro- niches of the Mojave Desert. Among these creatures was a slow-moving reptile, the desert tortoise, the Nevada state reptile, whose presence in the greater Las Vegas Valley illustrated the degree to which the ESA was truly the product of a full-stomach society.

In 1989 growth in Las Vegas reached an early apex, the first of many in the following decade. Since the mid-1980s, the town had added as many as four thousand people per month. More than five thousand housing starts were expected in 1989, and builders, developers, and the rest of the growth coalition—people whose economic interests depend on growth—were cautiously hopeful that the worst years were behind them. Las Vegas's image was changing, people were coming to town, and they intended to capitalize on the transformation of the desert.

At the same time, the desert tortoise, an indicator species of ecosystem health, declined in population throughout the Mojave Desert. Designated a sensitive species in 1980, the tortoise had faced the impact of development not only in the Las Vegas Valley, but throughout the eastern Mojave. From China Lake Basin, snuggled against the Sierra Nevada, to Nye County, Nevada, north of Las Vegas, tortoise populations plummeted. Even in protected areas, such as the Desert Tortoise Natural Area near Ridgecrest, California and the Chuckawalla Bench near Palm Springs, the numbers of tortoises declined by 50 to 70 percent. Between 1980 and 1988, BLM biologist Kristin Berry announced, desert tortoise populations in the western Mojave had declined by as much as two-thirds. Determined and provocative, Berry battled not only her own agency but developers and their allies to call attention to the plight of the desert tortoise.

The tortoises faced a dire situation throughout the eastern Mojave. Developers, ranchers, and off-road vehicle enthusiasts attributed the tortoise's demise to the shortfall of rain in the late 1980s, but a condition in the tortoises called URDS—upper respiratory distress syndrome—seemed the more likely culprit. URDS had been a common ailment among tortoises in captivity, but its spread to the wild suggested that something new threatened the tortoise's survival. URDS left the reptiles so weak that they could no longer feed themselves or even in some situations retract their head and forearms under their shell, an essential protection for an otherwise vulnerable species. The diminishment of habitat that resulted from growth in greater Las Vegas, Pahrump, a Nye County town that by 2000 had reached almost thirty thousand people, and Barstow and the area around it in eastern California, combined with a remarkable increase in predator species also contributed. Ravens, scavengers who craved tortoise eggs and multiplied by at least 600 percent as humans moved into the desert, and other predators found the tortoise easy prey, and the survival of the species came into question. Although named California's state reptile in 1972, that status offered the tortoise no protection. Nor did any of the other California or Nevada designations. Nevada's "species of concern" label, applied in the 1960s, and its rare and protected status, attained in 1978, protected only the animal, not its habitat. Developers could destroy as much land as they chose as long as they didn't hurt the tortoise itself.

Only ESA recognition could protect the tortoise, and Kristin Berry set out to attain it. In 1984 environmental groups proposed listing the tortoise as a threatened species. Throughout the remainder of the 1980s, the U.S. Fish and Wildlife Service deferred action. On May 31, 1989, after the spread of URDS and the observed population crash, the Defenders of Wildlife, the Environmental Defense Fund, and the Natural Resources Defense Council informed the Fish and Wildlife Service that they intended to sue for protection of the tortoise. On August 4, 1989, Secretary of the Interior Manuel Lujan Jr., a New Mexican and no environmentalist by any measure, determined that the situation warranted an emergency listing of the desert tortoise, immediately kicking in Endangered Species Act provisions. Full-stomach environmental regulation met libertarian private property, and a death struggle seemed likely to ensue. It didn't.

The filing sent shivers through Las Vegas developers. It occurred at the exact moment when the up-and-down growth of the previous five years was poised to finally shoot upward. Between 1985 and 1990, Las Vegas went through an almost classic boom-bust-boom-bust in growth. One year, the town set a new record for housing starts; the next, the construction companies that so benefitted the year before went under. But by 1989 big national players had seen what Las Vegas had to offer, including Summa Corporation's Summerlin, the enormous development on the city's western edge that became the largest master-planned community in the world. The company had invested more than $60 million in infrastructure, located almost entirely on prime desert tortoise habitat, and its project and everything else in the valley—flood control projects, new schools, roads, and homes—all came to a grinding halt. With the desert tortoise listed, all work in affected areas was halted, and developers could not discern any clear process for mitigation.

A combination of chaos and opportunism followed. Even though permits already issued by the county required full compliance, some developers simply bulldozed their land, turtles and all, ensuring that when inspection took place no turtles would be found. Efforts to avoid the law took place at night. In summer and fall 1989 the sound of bulldozers echoed in the Las Vegas Valley as much as twenty hours a day. Enforcement fell to the Fish and Wildlife Service, which had one agent for the entire valley. Illegal bulldozing continued even after the emergency listing.

The sixty-day notice that the environmental groups filed also put developers on alert. The very day that Lujan declared the tortoise endangered, the City of Las Vegas, the Nevada Development Authority, the Southern Nevada Homebuilders Association, Summa Corporation, and six other development companies asked the federal courts for a restraining order. This was business as usual. Environmental regulation, especially the applications of the ESA, almost always drew this response from affected parties. Developers and other opponents of such listings usually had deeper pockets than environmental groups. They relied on the courts and the expensive process of litigation. In the late 1970s state and local courts and in some cases even federal courts had ruled against the ESA. Business had to be allowed to proceed or a political bloodbath that involved everyone in the valley was sure to follow.

The one local government entity that hadn't entered the lawsuit, Clark County, moved toward a different solution. Seeing itself as a stakeholder and a facilitator, the county talked to the parties in the lawsuit, the five incorporated municipalities in the county, Las Vegas, Henderson, Boulder City, Mesquite, and North Las Vegas, the Nature Conservancy, environmental groups, recreation interests, and ranchers and miners. On August 28, 1989, officials formed the Clark County Desert Tortoise Habitat Conservation Plan Steering Committee to seek a way through the wreckage. Their goal was no less than a solution that simultaneously complied with the ESA and let the developers continue.

The motivation was money. With development forces heavily invested and a recession that was driving Californians east by the thousands, there was too much profit at stake to run the risk of stopping to fight. In a low-tax state like Nevada, growth paid whatever portion of the bills that tourists didn't cover. Impact fees, user fees, and the like were an essential part of the budget of every governmental entity, and the threat of the end of that revenue brought people to the table. The City of Las Vegas estimated that the tortoise listing would cost it $11 million in lost revenues during the first year alone. Developers recognized that the vast profits aching to be taken from the construction of new subdivisions were in peril. They'd experienced the ups and downs of the previous years and with the opening of the Mirage, the Excalibur, and all the other planned hotels, and the $60 million investment by Summa Corporation, anybody with the heart of a developer recognized that this was the moment. Litigation, even if successful, would take too long. They had to build now. The only way was to reach some kind of compromise. If enlightenment couldn't drive the process, enlightened self-interest could be found somewhere close by.

What made the strategy possible was a clause in the ESA that permitted "incidental taking" of individual members of a listed species if a plan to further the survival of the species as a whole was created. Elsewhere, the ESA had been used to create something called a Habitat Conservation Plan. A similar mechanism for Clark County might very well permit genuine compromise, save the tortoise, and not wreck the local economy. In a community that had been on the periphery for so long, the chance for growth and the legitimization that came from it was too valuable to be too expensive. Under the circumstances, if an HCP cost a lot, so be it. The developers knew they could make more, the city and county knew its revenue stream, dependent on growth, would continue, and tortoise advocates figured they could save the species.

Here was incontrovertible proof that the ESA was a full-stomach phenomenon. Developers said they would pay for the privilege of building, and the Clark County Short-Term Habitat Conservation Plan was cobbled together. Tortoise advocates received $2.3 million to protect the tortoise. Advocates wanted the money for research, land acquisition, and a conservation center south of U.S. 95 as it bent toward Boulder City, away from the main corridors of regional growth. In exchange, developers were allowed to build on seven thousand acres at a fee of $250 per acre. This provision extended to land that was already in the process of development by the listing date. In reality, that privilege was extended to anyone who paid the $250 per acre fee, and a lot of land that had barely been graded on August 4, 1989, became eligible for development.

Money truly talked, as it almost always does in Las Vegas. Developers paid for their oft-assumed privilege of developing anything in sight, and environmentalists received enough money to remove 841 tortoises to their new habitat. On July 24, 1991, less than two years after the initial listing, the short-term HCP came into being. It was not without problems. Addressing only the Las Vegas Valley, it inspired some Sagebrush Rebellion–style complaining from rural communities. But the short-term plan led to a long-term HCP that covered the county and raised the impact fee to $550 an acre, development continued, and the tortoises were protected. The battle between developers, the environmental community and the law in Clark County ended without protracted litigation. Not everyone got everything they wanted, but nearly everyone could live with the result.

The roots of the ESA in a time of affluence and optimism made it possible to mitigate with the application of dollars. The law had been written based on assumptions that made it viable in 1990s Las Vegas. Full-stomach environmentalism met full-stomach capitalism. Everyone, even developers, became environmentalists when enough money was involved, and in 1990 in Clark County, there was more than enough money to go around. Even more stunning, Las Vegas initiated a pattern that ten years later had been extended to seventy-nine species in the county and that Secretary of the Interior Bruce Babbitt acclaimed as a model for the nation in resolving ESA disputes. Babbitt hailed the 2000 multispecies plan as the example he intended to use to show people how ESA compromises could be accomplished. The law had been applied with so little rancor in Las Vegas that the experience heartened people on both sides of environmental disputes. Rarely had developers and the environmental community been able to find a solution that everyone could live with. Even Kristin Berry, the tortoises' champion agreed: "In Las Vegas, every effort was made to come up with something that would benefit tortoises *and* be workable for developers." The idiosyncratic town in the desert, the one that everyone pointed to as the worst example of excess, had something significant to offer American environmentalism.

Deserts are still dumps in the American imagination, places that are inhospitable to the descendants of the culture of wood that so shapes American attitudes even today. They are ugly by the standards of a society that regards mountaintops and tall trees as beautiful, barren to a culture that embraces open bodies of water or flowing rivers as a manifestation of its prosperity and quality of life. Even after a half-century of widespread air-conditioning, a phenomenon that makes a hot desert summer little different than a northern plains winter in its degree of discomfort, Americans still look down on the desert, still think they've compromised if they come to live in it. If they do, they re-create the land they came from, roll out the template of suburban Ohio and with water and fertilizer and the swimming pool in the backyard, try to hold on to a small vestige of the life of places where more than eighteen inches of rain, the minimum for agriculture without irrigation, falls each year. They make faux oases from the desert landscape, inaugurating a process of ecological transformation and mentally separating land that they define as sacred—because it is green—from the rest of profane desertscape that surrounds them.

Yet deserts hold a considerable piece of the future of the nation. Despite the environmental revolution and the plethora of legislation, little has genuinely changed about American attitudes toward nature since the early 1960s, when the eminent biologist Raymond Dasmann asked why we bring the water to where the people are instead of the other way around. We still do and we probably always will. That we mirror the oligarchic patterns of desert civilizations should come as no surprise to any observer of the American scene. Americans still believe in technological fixes, maybe not with the wholehearted enthusiasm of the 1950s and 1960s, but as a nation we prefer that solution to a change in behavior.

The growth of Las Vegas depended on that preference. First air-conditioning, then water infrastructure, and finally air-quality mitigation suggest a game of catch-up, of creating a habitable desert by transforming it, exchanging accommodation for amenity, supported by the institutions and technologies of a society sharpened in far wetter places. It's a mismatch, one visible daily from my window and always apparent from the air. If you come from the desert and fly over Indianapolis or Columbus, the trees and the amount of open green space jump out at you. The landscape you're accustomed to is brown and spare; in the Midwest, in the Northeast, in the South, the world is lush, green, and overgrown. After a decade in the desert, that cramped, crowded, overgrown look will make you claustrophobic, but the institutions built in the desert hail from that wetter, colder world.

American institutions are an awkward fit in American deserts, but that has never stopped us from trying to impress them on the land, nor is it likely to. Southern Nevada and greater Las Vegas are the point of that transition, pursuing the transformation of the desert with greater aggressiveness than peer cities like Phoenix and Tucson. With money to throw around to ease the tensions that come from the Endangered Species Act and the Clean Air Act, with unending and as yet unerring faith in the technological fix, Las Vegas is decidedly retrograde. The values of the people who settle the desert are consistent with the rest of their society except for the remarkable vigor they enjoy and the faith they place in their society's ability to transpose its imagery, goals, and structures between people and the physical world they inhabit. Much new development in Las Vegas, from Martinique Bay to The Lakes, alludes to the desert's most obvious lack.

Maybe Las Vegas is not so unusual in this respect. Maybe its people simply articulate with clarity and lack of pretense the same thing that the rest of the nation believes, that nature is a canvas for American society and there's no resource like human ingenuity.

Las Vegas is where Americans most use culture and technology to buffer themselves from the desert. Tinted school bus windows, fill-your-own soft drinks at fast-food restaurants, and the free purified drinking water in every Starbucks (which I was assured is a local adaptation) attest to the little things we do to make the desert habitable. Such a life is possible because of technology, air-conditioning most prominent, and only as long as we're a society that can sustain itself through an enormous figurative pipeline of things the desert doesn't provide. For as long as it exists, Las Vegas will be a testament to the ability of humans to transform a difficult natural setting into a comfortable one. This practice explains why so many intellectuals, artists, and cultural critics come to Las Vegas, look at it, and say it can't be sustained. They lack faith in industrial and postindustrial society, as well as the recognition that what Las Vegas does is unfamiliar only to people with northern and western European antecedents. To Spaniards from the arid Iberian plains and Incas from the highlands of South America, or even the sheepherders of the Bible, the strategies of a desert city make considerable sense.

Las Vegas's ability to manipulate its environment is equaled only by its ability to persuade American society of its virtues. This bizarre juxtaposition of similar traits holds the key to understanding how Americans live in the desert. There, they see what they want to see and ignore the rest, whether it is air pollution, endangered species, or water; when they can't ignore it anymore, they turn to technology to solve the problem. There's a purity to this faith that dismays the cynical and puts off the righteous, but after the initial rage at the naivete of such belief, some appreciation for the simple and unpretentious devotion to faith should follow. Many say that our time in Las Vegas is short, that it can't be sustained. In reality, Las Vegas is no more implausible than Boston or Minneapolis–St. Paul. The webs that sustain modern life are more evident in Las Vegas, but they're no more important in the desert than in the frozen north. Once again, Las Vegas illustrates the problem. More telling, it offers a solution that capitalists can embrace. Sometimes, even the enviros can go along too.

CHAPTER 9

Rolling to a Stop

The Weight of Traffic

I-15 and U.S. 93-95 loop around downtown Las Vegas, joining just to the north and the west of the old core of the city. Called the "Spaghetti Bowl" for its long, strandlike circles of road, the meeting point of these two highways was long the best of many examples of what was wrong with traffic in the fastest growing city in the nation. Conceived in the late 1950s and built in the 1970s with money from the Interstate Highway Act of 1956, I-15 fulfilled the axiomatic role of highways after World War II. "If you got it, a truck brought it," the saying went, and trucks traveled in droves on the new interstates. I-15 gave Las Vegas an easy connection to southern California and the mythic postwar paradise of the California Dream. Its intersection with U.S. 95 linked the existing road to Hoover Dam, making Las Vegas a new crossroads.

In the twenty years following its completion, the Spaghetti Bowl became a nightmare. The interchange built for a town of 300,000 people served a community of more than 1.4 million, and "clogged" didn't begin to describe its condition. The number of cars that navigated that interchange each day, who changed from one freeway to the other, grew so fast that traffic came to a complete halt. As Las Vegas expanded to the northwest, three lanes of stopped cars stretched back for miles to the west each morning; by 2 P.M. every afternoon, equally long lines waited impatiently facing north. Inbound drivers in the morning and outbound drivers in the afternoon had the sun in their eyes. Dante's Inferno couldn't have been worse: never-ending commutes in bumper-to-bumper traffic with the sun in your eyes in more than 100 degree heat surely constituted postmodern hell. Even though Las Vegans in 1999 spent an average of only thirty-four hours per year gridlocked in traffic, a far cry from Los Angeles's nation-leading eighty-two and about the same as cities like Norfolk, Virginia, and Minneapolis–St. Paul, Las Vegas's one freeway felt like it might rival Los Angeles's many.

Here was the problem of the industrial and postindustrial city: too many people wanted to be somewhere at the same time, and the delivery systems to get them there were not adequate. Roads weren't jammed during most of the day. They were useless only at specific times. But the chaos those hours created had a disproportionately negative impact on workers, housewives, casino executives, and even tourists. By the mid-1990s American cities ground to gridlock and people learned to accommodate. They staggered their travel times, learned how to breathe deeply and relax, listened to books on tape, or chatted endlessly on their cell phones. Sitting in your car was a fact of life. You went on autopilot and didn't think about it. Traffic was a consequence of being who and where you were.

Las Vegas's rapid growth exacerbated the dilemma, but it was only a small-scale version of the problems that vexed Atlanta, San Francisco, New York, Chicago, and every other major metropolitan area. Americans love cars for convenience and status—and conversely, for the insularity and anonymity they provide. Twentieth-century cities lacked the structure of their predecessors, and created during the automotive revolution, faced every manifestation of the problems it brought. Without mass transit, they were planned around automobile access, a model that by the 1990s guaranteed plenty of time stuck in traffic. There was no getting around the crux of the issue: in Las Vegas, as in every other major American city, it became harder and harder to simply get around.

Like beauty, traffic is in the eye of the beholder. The Spaghetti Bowl was only the most poignant example. In a community where 577,517 cars had been registered in 1990 and 890,298 were on the road as 1999 began, what else could happen? Las Vegas's roads had been built for another city, a small-town city, and they bore no relationship to the needs of the ever-expanding millennial metropolis. The way people reacted depended on where they came from. If you hailed from greater Los Angeles, you wondered what people complained about. If you called a smaller city or a rural area home, driving in Las Vegas seemed like punishment for the most venal of sins.

Nor did salvation appear imminent. With growth above 70,000 people each year throughout the 1990s and a net gain of more than 100,000 in 2000 alone, Las Vegas seemed well on the way to fulfilling culture critic Mike Davis's contention that it repeated the deadliest sins of Los Angeles's twentieth-century growth, energy and water consumption run amok, sprawl, pollution, and traffic, and diminished quality of life, as a consequence of the never-ending desire for greater convenience. The traditions of libertarian Nevada certainly encouraged private automobiles. So did the ethos of post–World War II America, where millions regarded their personal space as sacred and their vehicle as the article of their deliverance. The Spaghetti Bowl became the local symbol, but there were plenty of other examples of traffic gone haywire. The intersection of Rainbow and Sahara perennially reached the top ten nationally for annual accidents; the Strip, with its combination of pedestrians, cabs, and service vehicles, locals and tourists, became its own peculiar purgatory. At 2 P.M. on President's Day weekend 2001, I crept along in Strip traffic. A trip from Tropicana to Spring Mountain, one major and two minor interchanges and a total of less than two miles, took forty minutes.

The traffic was everywhere, on streets, avenues, and arterial roads, made worse by every dimension of Las Vegas. Truck traffic delivered goods to the city-states of the Strip; eternal construction, designed to facilitate more traffic, slowed movement. The enormous parking garages at every one of the hotels, emblazoned with their "free parking" signs, encouraged driving. In Las Vegas, it might take a while to get there, but you never had to hunt for a place to park. Acres of parking and even valet parking were free. Accommodating tourists hurt locals. Free parking served as another of the enticements of Las Vegas, another way to be better for visitors. Developing alternative forms of transportation is not an issue in Las Vegas as it is in other growing cities.

The response to increase in traffic was to build more roads, and each provided a measure of relief. A new road seemed open—wide open for a couple of weeks or even a month, the equivalent of an oasis in the desert. Then as if by magic, the road, street, arterial, or even highway suddenly filled, and breathing space was a fleeting memory. The roads seemed to birth new cars. They drew traffic to them like magnets and negated all the gains of recent construction.

In its traffic as much as in any other way, Las Vegas typified the dilemma of urban America. From the nightly traffic jams on the Strip, hour after hour of cars crawling along in a bizarre ritual of cruising, to the long lines at intersections, longer traffic lights, and the peripheral sense of being surrounded while behind the wheel, Las Vegas had achieved an undesired normative status. Most would have preferred not to be normal in this way, but everyone was equally culpable in the problem. Almost every one of the 700,000 newcomers of the 1990s of driving age had at least one car. It was easy to point fingers, but hard to find the real villains in the mass of cars sitting in stop-and-go traffic.

Highway development had been a crucial piece of Las Vegas's growth. When Highway 91 to Los Angeles was paved in the 1930s, it shifted the community's dependence from rails to pavement and pulled Las Vegas into Los Angeles's orbit. Highway 91 also spurred the city's expansion. Along this road, Thomas Hull built the El Rancho in 1941 at the corner of what is now Sahara and Las Vegas Boulevard, and soon Guy McAfee, the corrupt vice captain turned gambling entrepreneur was calling the road "the Strip" after his beloved Sunset Strip. The shift from rails to roads focused Las Vegas's dependence on a closer and more concrete source of power than either the railroad or the federal government.

When I-15 was completed in the early 1970s, its construction accelerated the process that had begun with Highway 91. A little desert town with limited claim on the American imagination and less on its resources needed an arterial to meet the growing demands of its primary industry. Trucks streamed to Las Vegas. The quantity of freight argued for close proximity between the highway and the hotels on the Strip that had become the real economic engine of the city; eventually Las Vegas became an important trucking depot, centered around Cheyenne Avenue and I-15 in North Las Vegas. Options for the location of the interstate, one to the west and two to the east, existed, but made little sense. "Where else would you put it?" one old-timer asked. "Two miles either way and you're in the desert."

I-15 and later U.S. 95 had other consequences that eventually reshaped local mobility. The big wide new highway provided an avenue for the spread of the city to the west. In the 1950s most Las Vegans lived east of the Strip, and the bulk of the city's residential growth remained south and east. Before 1960 only Charleston Avenue crossed the railroad tracks and continued all the way west to the Spring Mountains. In the 1970s the Oran K. Gragson

Freeway, U.S. 95, extended the city's reach along the old Tonopah highway, toward Red Rock Canyon and Mount Charleston, laying the basis for the eventual northwestern growth of metropolitan Las Vegas.

I-15 also completed what local planners later called "the Great Wall of Las Vegas." The railroad tracks had once defined the westernmost boundary of the town, and the old Los Angeles highway, which became the Strip, ran almost parallel to the tracks. The interstate followed the same line, creating three clear lines that isolated east from west. Alone, none disrupted traffic. Together, they formed a wall that divided the city into different quadrants, impeded travel, and created different development patterns. The Great Wall of Las Vegas made travel on the surface streets into a stress-filled daily struggle that portended road rage and every other ill of urban life.

There were many consequences of this daily scourge, but the greatest social result was the division of the city into separate halves. By the 1980s the goal of most Las Vegans was to avoid crossing the Strip on the way to and from work. It was simple to attain. All you had to do was work on the same side of the Strip as you lived. This solved the problem for individual drivers, but accentuated the evolution of separate regional identities within the already diffuse metropolitan area. The east and west sides had been in a status war since the 1950s, when developments competed for social preeminence. The completion of the Great Wall only accentuated the parallel evolution of remarkably similar communities on both sides of town.

By the late 1980s even staying on your own side of town meant inexorable waiting in traffic, but the real struggle began when you contemplated crossing the Great Wall. Psychically the three strands provided an enormous obstacle; the reality was sheer torture. You might spend forty-five minutes waiting to cross the Strip at Tropicana or Flamingo, and then get held up crossing above the interstate for every bit as long. "It became nigh on impossible to get across," one commuter remembered with angst. Even worse, the Strip had become gridlocked. On a Saturday night, it might take an hour and fifteen minutes to go from the Tropicana to a show at Caesars. The casino owners couldn't accept the traffic. "People should be eating, they should be gambling, they should be seeing a show," one remembered. "They shouldn't be sitting in traffic." The opening of the Mirage made the long-simmering problem more than real. Traffic became the city's newest crisis.

The transformation had been brief but significant. The Strip started life as a highway and became an urban street. When it consisted of low-slung casinos adjacent to the street, truck and car traffic easily turned into the properties and were swallowed in their enormous parking areas. There were fewer hotels, they were not close together, and the road functioned as a thoroughfare. As the Strip became a crowded street, the combination of slow-moving trucks, rubber-necking drivers, and traffic lights that allowed drivers to turn left into each property all slowed traffic to a crawl. Nor did busses have their own lane, further tangling motion on the streets. The addition of pedestrians exacerbated the crisis, bringing everything to a complete stop.

As was typical in Las Vegas, the political will to solve the problem was intrinsically tied to the horse in the one-horse town. The agony of gridlock brought only sympathy from elected officials. Any solutions stemmed directly from the casinos' problems, not those of the legions of commuters. As the traffic crisis loomed, the new era of self-contained resorts began. Hotels no longer discouraged patrons from visiting other properties. The Strip itself became an attraction, bringing its own constituency who walked, cabbed, or even drove its length simply to look. Unhappy customers, those who missed their dinner reservations or got crummy seats at a show because they were late, wouldn't come back.

Public transportation remained a Band-Aid on a much larger problem. Las Vegas invested in the Citizen's Area Transit, which in 1997 won the American Public Transportation Association's System of the Year award. In 1998, 247 buses carried 46.5 million passengers for an average of 188,512 per bus, far more than most cities. The system's heaviest use came from the lower economic sectors: maids and carless construction workers, minimum-wage labor headed to serve the affluent. Visitors to the Strip, who made up more than 25 percent of CAT ridership, skewed the totals. CAT buses are everywhere, serving all the major arteries, albeit some only once an hour. The mantra of local riders is "Don't miss the bus!" In 2000 the CAT system carried 4 million passengers per month on its three hundred buses and each bus featured a wheelchair lift to accommodate disabled passengers. Despite these remarkable strides, buses have yet to make a dent in local traffic.

As in most western cities, the problem in Las Vegas is cultural. Americans regard the lack of a personal vehicle as a failing of the individual, their perspective itself a manifestation of the cult of the individual in American society. Postwar Americans grew up seeing the automobile as the primary embodiment of freedom and regarding convenience as a moral imperative, and these ideas persist at all costs. New cities, those that grew up in the twentieth century, are not designed for pedestrians. Public transportation in the postwar West was usually an afterthought, an admission of failure and anathema to the forces of growth that aligned in favor of freeways and the subdivisions they spawned. In the end, the sprawl of western cities impeded mass transit and consigned it to a narrow slot in transportation. It existed, it seemed, for the sole purpose of affirming class distinctions by conveying carless workers to low-wage jobs in the suburbs.

County commissioner Bruce Woodbury, a Stanford-educated attorney who typified the old guard, had emerged as a leader on the county commission and he spearheaded the drive for a master transportation plan. Woodbury was often mistaken for a real community leader; he had earned a reputation for calmness on the fractious county commission. Before 1990 his major accomplishment had been a regional flood control district funded by a quater-percent sales tax increase. Flooding was a real if infrequent problem in the desert, and Las Vegas had paid a severe price. A 1975 flood floated all the cars in the Caesars Palace parking lot and drowned two men in North Las Vegas. Intermittent floods threatened the Strip. President Ronald Reagan declared Clark County a disaster area in 1984, and heavy summer rains in 1990 starkly confirmed that the days of letting the rare torrents find their own way from pavement into the dry landscape were over forever. Woodbury fashioned the $700 million Flood Control District, securing his position as the only commission member with a claim on leadership.

Woodbury's approach to solving the city's traffic problems avoided many of the niceties of modern planning. He bandied about the figure of $100 million in annual new revenue that he insisted was necessary to solve the traffic problem. When asked about the purpose of the money, Woodbury talked of a beltway around the valley. A new freeway had the ring of panacea about it, and without much study or analysis, the concept became policy. Las Vegans were as wedded to the combination of freedom and insularity that automobiles promised as were the residents of any city in the land, and Woodbury regarded his job as making it possible for them to exercise their desire. Once again, the way Las Vegas highlighted the core of American self-indulgence became crystal clear. The only solution to gridlock was more money spent on more and hopefully better roads.

Funding the project presented a major obstacle. Nevadans hated taxes, and politicians lacked the will and the standing to impose them even for the best projects. Nevada's anti-tax history was long and storied, and even to solve the valley's most pressing infrastructure problem taxes were anathema. People expected government to function without resources, and the Las Vegas *Review-Journal* actively encouraged the notion that the government that governs best, governs not at all. Even worse, newcomers took out more in services than they paid in taxes, guaranteeing that growth exacerbated rather than solved problems.

When government needed money, it usually looked to taxes on visitors. Special interests stymied every effort to tax locals, and by 1990 there were many of them in the valley. Every time the county suggested a new tax to fund improvements, some special-interest group would cry in pain that they were bearing the burden of growth alone. This was Nevada after all; couldn't visitors pay for the road improvements the metropolis needed? When the county retrenched, planned anew, and offered another option, another other interest group would scream even more loudly. "You let them off," the refrain went. "Why are you sticking it to us?" As weak as ever and devoid of political leadership, county government searched for a pie-in-the-sky solution that didn't cost anyone but solved all the region's transportation issues.

Nor did the county have a reservoir of experience on which to draw. Few people in southern Nevada had ever seen such intense and consistent growth. After 1985 the pace accelerated and the small-town responses of the past no longer sufficed. Although Las Vegas imported its new business leadership, the public sector lagged in its ability to recruit talented officials to what seemed, even in the 1980s, a peculiar backwater. Leadership for a regional transportation master plan had to come from unexpected places. At a luncheon meeting, Henry Chanin, a tall, sandy-haired forty-year-old former investment banker who had become deputy director of the airport authority, made a couple of suggestions. "I was yanked from the airport," he remembered, "and was working for the county manager in a newly created position called 'special projects manager.'" Chanin was told to assemble a transportation master plan and devise a funding program for it.

The planners crafted a proposal that they called the "fair share funding plan," spreading the burden among as many constituencies as possible. It included an increase in the sales tax, one of the bellwethers of Nevada's regressive system and a rarity in that it split the pain between visitors and locals. An increase in the room tax, paid by visitors, was offset by a higher motor vehicle privilege tax, paid by residents. An increase in the jet aviation fuel tax, also passed on to visitors in increased airfares, was included, and redirected from the state to the county. For the first time, developers paid a fee for residential and commercial construction to fund Woodbury's beltway. A gasoline tax increase was earmarked for the improvement of local streets. A quarter-percent sales tax increase went to mass transit. All of the sources of funding allowed the county to float bonds against them; construction could begin before collecting the revenues. The formula meant that as growth accelerated, the county received more money to fund the roadways that made the region habitable. Newcomers, the five thousand people who moved to town each month, began paying their share with each purchase they made while everyone reaped the benefits. As a fund-raising mechanism, the structure was an enormous success and it helped to alleviate the problem that new residents did not pay in taxes what it cost the county to serve them. In 2000 alone, the fair share funding plan raised $166.4 million.

The county lacked the power to authorize such a plan, but the need was so pressing that planners gave the legislature a push. Nevada remained top-heavy. Despite the reality that Clark County made up more than 60 percent of the state's population and outpaced growth in the rest of the state every year, the legislature ran as it always had: by the north, for the north, and with little concern for anything in the South. "Our notion was to go up to the legislature and make them an offer they couldn't refuse," Chanin told me. They hoped that a large majority of voters would provide a cudgel by approving the plan in a November 1990 referendum. The 68 percent margin startled almost everybody, including the planners. When the legislature received the proposal, even the most rabid northerners recognized that approval was a foregone conclusion. Clark County taxed itself for improvements and all the legislature needed to do was affirm the choice. In January 1991 the legislature approved, and Clark County was "on its way, off to fix the problem," Chanin smiled. "Except of course the problem didn't quite get fixed."

Even after the vote, the county recognized that the plan's support remained tenuous. The opposition even to taxation that spread the pain and served everyone's primary objective remained so great that county officials looked for ways to lay off the burden on available partners. McCarran Airport looked to be a likely candidate. McCarran was an older urban airport, backed up against the Strip on one side, suburban development on another, and commercial areas of the city everywhere else. An integral component, it required much from the environment around it, had resources, and could be persuaded to recognize that a traffic plan worked to its advantage. By the early 1990s the airport was in real trouble. Gridlock nearby had devastating implications, and the county master transportation plan offered a solution. Under existing statute, airports could build roads for airport traffic and McCarran Airport agreed to pay to connect the airport roadway system and I-15. The FAA acquiesced, and the airport built a section of road that alone cost more than $200 million. The roadway "was a gift," Chanin remonstrated. "The airport paid for it." Traffic did diminish, some vehicles and especially taxis accessed the city by the longer southern connector route, and I-215, called the Roadrunner Route, the planned fifty-three-mile beltway around the city, began, built with airport dollars.

The opening of the airport tunnel and the connection to I-15 on December 31, 1994, was a celebratory moment. The county threw an enormous roadside party for the opening. Almost five thousand runners ran in a combination road race and fun run called the Tun-o'-Fun Race and a large crowd rooted them on. Radio stations broadcast live, people ate hot dogs, and county commissioners patted each other on the back, and with good reason. The airport tunnel was a rarity, proof that government could work in Clark County. One of the few projects that served locals as well as visitors, the airport tunnel seemed to prove that the city could function even as it grew. The constellation of power in greater Las Vegas had finally been marshaled for the purpose of solving the problems of the fastest growing city in the nation.

Even before the airport funded local roadways, Clark County cast its lot with the idea of a beltway. It became the linchpin of the entire transportation plan, the single feature that the community believed it could not do without. Las Vegas invested its future in the beltway, and its construction became the single greatest transportation priority of the 1990s.

By the early 1990s, beltways were an old ruse that created myriad problems. Evolving out of 1930s efforts to build bypass highways, they initially guided traffic around congested downtowns. As trucks became a staple of American transportation, these byways became more heavily trafficked. After the Interstate Highway System began, the metropolitan beltway became the way to relieve downtowns of commercial traffic, through travelers, and even some commuters. Few envisioned that beltway interchanges would become the focal points of what Joel Garreau later labeled "edge cities," communities adjacent to major cities that are not truly part of them.

By the 1980s almost every American city of any size had at least one beltway and many had more. The Washington, D.C., beltway was the most famous, offering hope of easy transportation in the 1960s and spawning a metaphor that endures today. True to the "inside the beltway" slur, such roads often prompted false hope. When they opened, they promised to solve traffic problems, but in reality they simply deferred them, pushed them farther into the surrounding countryside. Such roads spawned a new urbanism, drawing not only cars, but houses, strip malls, and the like to them with remarkable speed.

The process of extending roads farther into surrounding hinterlands spoke to the peculiar confidence and incredible sense of abundance that lay at the heart of postwar American thinking. Long after evidence around them conclusively demonstrated a finite universe, Americans believed that their world was infinite. A network of roads deferred any talk of the scarcity of space; a new road meant new everything, and once American cities spread outward the momentum they created was unstoppable. Even the baby boomers, who came of age with 1960s environmentalism and its emphasis on limits, accelerated this pace, still acting as if they could always have it all. In their world, they were not to be denied anything, and freedom, space, leisure, and access figured prominently in their constellation of values. Roads and cars made it all possible, providing the basis of much of rock 'n' roll, the soundtrack of the post-1945 world. From cruising down the road in a Mercury '49 to Bruce Springsteen, the motion of cars defined American young. If roads couldn't be denied anywhere else in the United States, Las Vegas was the least likely place to hold back the highway.

Las Vegas came late to the federal highway dollars derby. By 1990 federal funding for highways had fallen dramatically on a per capita basis from the heyday of the interstate highway program in the 1960s, and there was nowhere near enough funding to build a beltway in Las Vegas. In the Rust Belt the interstate system was largely complete, and little national political impetus in favor of further highway funding existed. Congressional representatives from large industrial states controlled transportation funding, and Nevada lacked the political clout needed to secure special appropriations that constituted the real pork that Washington, D.C., could offer a small state. Rapidly growing and still politically weak, Nevada found itself without access to precious federal resources at a crucial moment in regional development.

The planners envisioned their own solutions to the problem of paying for a huge roadway development. The master planners reached an agreement with the Nevada Department of Transportation to earmark existing federal dollars to make I-15 exits into flyover ramps, breaching the Great

Wall of Las Vegas. The ramps were designed to move traffic on the interstate above and across the highway, eliminating two of the stoplights that made crossing the interstate excruciating. When they were completed in the late 1990s, it was hard to remember that it had ever been different as you departed I-15 and crossed directly to the Strip without encountering a traffic light.

The fair share funding plan also targeted a room tax increase to pay for two large superarterial streets that crossed the Strip, the interstate, and the railroad tracks without a single stoplight. Such streets solved one of the gaming industry's major problems: the terrific cross-traffic that stalled commuters and made visitors unable to get to their destinations. The first, called the Desert Inn Arterial, conveyed east-west traffic from Paradise Avenue east of the Strip to Valley View on the west side by design, providing no access to the interstate or the Strip. When it opened in mid-1996, the DI superarterial was a huge success. Presto! In an instant, people could cross the Strip and be on the other side of town. Las Vegas's Great Wall had been breached and the smiles gleamed on the faces of local drivers. The fate of commuters and visitors in vehicles had been separated, hopefully for eternity.

The second superarterial did not fare as well. Drawn in 1990 to bisect the golf course at the failing Dunes Hotel, the road transected a property that had been in serious financial trouble for a decade, one of the last outposts of mobbed-up operators in the new city. Morris Shenker remained the major shareholder at the Dunes through 1985, when a skimming scandal brought on by the Russian organized crime network in the United States, forced his ouster. A Japanese businessman, Masao Nangaku, bought the hotel, but soon unloaded the property; Caesars Palace officials, sure that Steve Wynn, who coveted the property, was buried in debt from the Mirage, tried to lowball Nangaku. Wynn circumvented them. In 1992 the Mirage Group spent $75 million for the troubled 164-acre property, a cost of about $450,000 per acre. The sale included the eighteen-hole golf course, through which the superarterial was to pass. Wynn was the most powerful individual in Nevada, and his influence counteracted the approval of the voters, legislators, and the desire of the public. In 2001, after the completion of the Bellagio on the Dunes property, the street had not been built and the estimated cost for a route that was acceptable had tripled to $120 million. Some of the money put aside for the superstreet had been diverted to landscaping the medians on the Strip. The resulting palm trees are lovely, but they do nothing to move the ever-growing volume of cars.

Without the second arterial, the beltway became even more important. Construction began in the early 1990s, focused almost exclusively on the southeast portion, between U.S. 95 and I-15. That section was crucial to the future of the entire valley. Traffic studies revealed that completing the road to U.S. 95 offered the fastest relief. The new route was expected to ease congestion on existing surface streets. The county focused its energies there, leaving the heavily trafficked northwest to use gridlocked U.S. 95 and the dreaded Spaghetti Bowl.

The decision was clearly tactical, a function of the limits on the degree of relief road construction could offer. "We very carefully explained that you can't build a beltway half a mile here and a half a mile there," Chanin remembered, "and expect it to have any impact on traffic." This formula required an ideal of cooperation, a foreign sentiment in individualistic southern Nevada. Even though such a perspective underpinned the entire county-wide transportation plan, commissioners in districts that did not immediately benefit warily watched and calculated the frustration of their constituents. Those in the far western part of the valley were most unnerved. Their voters sat in traffic for hours every day while the county turned its attention elsewhere. It remained to be seen if the soft cohesiveness of southern Nevada could withstand the frustration of a gridlocked public. Yet this self-funded project was widely considered proof of greater Las Vegas's planning viability and the answer to regional problems as late as 1995.

In 1996 county commissioner Paul Christensen, long a power on the commission, went down to defeat, and his loss sent a shudder through the political community. Christensen hailed from an old Las Vegas family, with roots that reached back to a time before Bugsy Siegel showed up in town. He never met a developer he didn't like, one observer of the city noted, but his district increased by more than 75 percent during his term and the newcomers didn't care how powerful his family was. Christensen's constituents decided he was too parochial. Like the rest of the community, Christensen was stunned by is loss. He decided he lost because he'd permitted the county to build the beltway in the southeast without getting anything for his northwestern district. Other commissioners recognized that Christensen's fate might be their own and responded with a political maneuver to ensure that they wouldn't suffer the wrath of voters. They rose up with one voice and insisted on a part of the beltway in their individual districts immediately. The loose confederation that underpinned the plan disappeared overnight. County staff rushed to provide each commissioner with what they demanded. "You know how it is," one participant sighed. "The politicians are the whores, and staff just changes the sheets." Instead of building real freeways with overpasses, the county extended what was essentially a frontage road, two lanes each direction and broken up by stoplights and stop signs. Within three years, nearly every commissioner had at least a piece of the "beltway" in their district and all breathed a little easier.

The self-interested political pressure upset the calculus of road-building and hindered the solution of the region's traffic problems. The frontage road through the valley's southwest accelerated development there, one of the few areas that had yet to encounter unbridled growth. The airport's takeoff and landing zone, called the Cooperative Management Area, prevented residential development in much of that area, but the roadway provided access beyond the area, ensuring that the lull in development was over.

The result was a hybrid, a combination of freeway and four-lane road that was referred to as a beltway, but was more reminiscent of the county frontage roads that parallel highways in places like rural Texas. In 2001, after a decade of building, the roadway stretched from just west of U.S. 95, the Las Vegas–Boulder City freeway, to Decatur Avenue on the near west side. From there, it became a road with posted speeds of forty-five miles per hour, but traffic sailed along at about seventy miles per hour. Traffic lights and four-way stops marked the interchanges. Speed limits changed rapidly, usually ignored by drivers whipping by at twenty or more miles per hour over the limit. The roughly $5 million it cost to build each overpass slowed the process, even though the fair share funding program raised more than $165 million each year. The result was tragic. Five deaths were reported in high-speed accidents on the faux beltway between November 1999 and March 2001, the saddest a two-year-old crushed to death when a driver ran a red light at one of the interchanges and broadsided the boy's parents' car.

Local funding built the beltway, such as it was, but early in 2001 the drawbacks were as apparent as the advantages. A section in the southeast, from Green Valley Parkway to Gibson Road, debuted during summer 2000 with only two lanes each direction. It was underbuilt from the day it opened and soon was as crowded and slow as any arterial street in the valley. To many who drove the road, the two lanes each direction seemed a terrific waste, a guarantor of huge difficulties when the county widened the road to the inevitable three lanes each way. Commissioner Bruce Woodbury proudly opened the road to traffic, announcing another step in the city's salvation from its dilemma, but people no longer believed him. The problem became more widely recognized, and as it did, commissioners from the northern districts where the faux beltway had not yet begun demurred on the chance to have frontage roads instead of freeways. They insisted on waiting until their districts could have the real thing, overpasses and interchanges included.

The county claimed that it lacked sufficient funds to build a third lane each direction between Green Valley Parkway and the eastern end of the freeway and would come back and add it later, but knowing observers recognized disingenuousness in the claim. The county took in so much money that it could not spend it fast enough, but the funds did not show up as surplus on the county's ledger. Instead, the money was committed to the various projects, often for the purchase of right-of-ways, and so appeared to have been spent. The community didn't quite reap the benefit. The eventual fifty-three-mile C-shaped road was projected to cost about $16 million per mile. As late as 2001, official county documents asserted that complete build-out of the beltway would take another twenty years, about the time it would have taken with federal highway funding.

Piecemeal and self-funded, Las Vegas's beltway was testimony to the problems of trying to fulfill every desire of the baby boom generation. Geoff Schumacher, one of Nevada's most astute journalists, called the beltway a "symbol of failure" of the community's ability to address unchecked growth, as well as a "triumph of engineering and a blot on the desert." As cars filled roads that begat more roads, a postwar definition of freedom as mobility came crashing down. Addicted to cars, Las Vegas could find only conventional solutions. "We have failed to learn from the mistakes of other cities," Schumacher mused, and "so we have the beltway." Inadequate in the long run, such roads offered an illusory hope, brief windows without gridlock that closed as quickly as they opened. Such opportunities tempted and tantalized and provided enormous political capital, but they could not satisfy. The grind of the daily commute wore on and on.

Moving people around the city is one issue, but it is a micro issue in a town where most people's livelihood depends on visitors. Much larger and more significant is the problem of getting people to Las Vegas in the first place. Despite an expenditure of almost $400 million in the 1990s, by 1997 the traffic on I-15, the artery from southern California, had outgrown the road. In 1998, 6.25 million people, almost 20 percent of the valley's visitors, drove in from southern California; in the first nine months of 1999 there were fifty-five fatalities on the road, most between Barstow and the Nevada border town of Primm. On any three-day weekend or holiday, the two lanes of traffic each direction between Barstow and Las Vegas—and at the worst moments, all the way to San Bernardino—were bumper to bumper, headed toward Las Vegas on Friday and back to California after New Year's Day, King Day, Presidents' Day, Memorial Day, the Fourth of July weekend, Labor Day, Thanksgiving, and Christmas. Some called the 275 miles "the world's largest parking lot." The four-hour trip could take as many as ten, a price in aggravation that drivers were generally willing to pay. Many started partying long before they hit Nevada, and the road opened to three lanes each direction only about ten miles from Las Vegas; a parade of deadly accidents along the highway consistently led the evening news. If the Spaghetti Bowl was Dante's local Inferno, here was a more devious torture, a road crammed with people doing exactly what you were doing, partying behind the wheel, with equal disregard for the rest of the species.

This particular traffic tie-up offered tacit encouragement of the expansion of Indian gaming in California. In 1998 Proposition 1A, which allowed Indian tribes to operate Las Vegas–style gaming in the Golden State, passed by an overwhelming margin. Although California Indian groups went on television and pleaded with the public to allow this chance at self-sufficiency, the traffic problem on I-15 contributed to its success. No Indian casino in California could expect to compete with Las Vegas's spectacle. Even Foxwoods, the Pequots' wildly lucrative Connecticut casino, offered at best B-grade entertainment, and in Las Vegas, where Paris Las Vegas opened in 1999 as a quaint little $760 million project, the ante was much higher. Las Vegas owned the cachet of being the pinnacle, and no Indian casino, even a well-financed one, could anticipate topping the five-mile edifice of the Las Vegas Strip.

But they could capture a share of the market. Proximate, small casinos easily siphoned off a constituency that drove by. People on vacation didn't want to spend it on I-15. Imagine if you'd been in traffic for six hours on the way to Las Vegas and you passed a sign on the side of the road that said, "If you just want to gamble, you're through with your trip" or some other version of the signs that dot American highways that say, "If you lived here, you'd be home by now." If you were sick enough of the traffic and the trip, Nevada gamers rightly feared, an Indian casino somewhere in the Mojave Desert might just do the trick.

The casino industry recognized this problem, investing more than $50 million toward the defeat of Proposition 1A, but it lost resoundingly. Californians wanted gaming closer to home, and Las Vegas accurately perceived a threat to one of its primary markets. It didn't hurt that California permitted eighteen-year-olds to gamble while Nevada held to a minimum age of twenty-one. California Indians enjoyed a captive market by age and location, and analysts predicted a 3- to 5 percent decrease in California visitation, enough to send a little shudder through Wall Street as the earnings reports for the first quarter of 1999 were readied for release.

Some observers found the gaming industry's opposition to the expansion of Indian gaming in California to be more than a little disingenuous. Since Atlantic City opened for gaming in the 1970s, Nevada companies had played a major role in casinos everywhere. Mississippi, Louisiana, Missouri, Illinois, and even Michigan, which sought gaming to relieve Detroit's Rust Belt woes, were all served by Las Vegas companies. Las Vegas operated Indian gaming for various tribes in dozens of locations, providing expertise, structure, and operational skill that no one else could offer. If Las Vegas gamers felt nauseated by the expansion of gaming, a look in the mirror yielded one of the primary catalysts of their indigestion.

Proposition 1A provided a wake-up call. It transformed the traffic on I-15 from the problem of individual drivers into a major issue for the gaming industry. State government understood the relationship with clarity. The Nevada Department of Transportation gave California a $10 million contribution to a road-widening project between Victorville and Barstow, and the Nevada and California congressional delegations cooperated to allow $24 million of Nevada's annual $190 million in federal road money to be spent in California as Las Vegans sat miserably in traffic. In early 2001 the gaming industry had only begun to confront the larger implications of the packed road that delivered so many of their patrons.

Even more pressing was the need to get people to Las Vegas by air. During the 1990s visitation to the city doubled, from approximately 18 million in 1989 to 36 million per annum in 2000. McCarran Airport was crucial, delivering 19,090,000 people on scheduled and charter flights in 1990 and topping 33,669,000 in 1999; 46 percent of all visitors to Las Vegas arrived through McCarran, an enormous percentage that reflected changing patterns in American travel. Vacation flights remained considerably less expensive than business travel, making Las Vegas a high-volume, low-margin market for the airlines. Until the mid-1990s, a combination of low cost, lack of time, and a general sense of financial well-being filled airline seats at record pace, prompting airline industry analysts to call the period a golden age for airlines. Americans became accustomed to air travel, and Las Vegas became one of the major beneficiaries.

Since the late 1970s, the airport had planned ahead. Its goal was never to be a bottleneck, never to be singled out as the cause of any decline in visitation. Most who watched the airport agreed that more than any other single entity, the airport had succeeded in accommodating the unbelievable pace of growth. The airport constructed a new terminal, the C gates, in the late 1980s, and then added another spectacular new terminal, the aesthetically sophisticated D gates, one of the first places that melded the casino, shopping mall, and airport seamlessly into one, in 1998. One new runway and the extension of another to accommodate jets added capacity, and new roads such as the airport tunnel accompanied the gates. In 2000 McCarran Airport remained a functional if sometimes crowded airport and decidedly not a funnel. It remained "local government's best response to transportation problems," averred Henry Chanin.

There were limits to the ability to make the visitor numbers grow with the existing airport. Even after the opening of the D gates, its new capacity of 50 million people per year meant that if the airport delivered 50 percent of the market and the number of visitors grew at the 2000 rate, by 2007 the airport would reach capacity. After that, increases in annual visitation would slow if not halt, and instead of an ever-growing market, which had driven the city throughout the 1990s, Las Vegas would cannibalize itself. More rooms and a fixed or much more slowly growing stream of visitors meant that the gains of one organization would come at the expense of another. Demand for Las Vegas as a travel destination remained heady, even intoxicating. In 1997 David Ehlers, chairman of Las Vegas Investment Advisors Inc., insisted that he had "long believed that the problem with Las Vegas visitor counts is not a lack of demand, it's the lack of capacity to bring the visitors here." His sentiment was widely shared in the business community. "It's not that there aren't more people who want to come to Las Vegas even now," echoed one developer early in 2001. "There just isn't an efficient, economical way to get them here." Nor did the gaming industry seem inclined to do anything about it.

The airport's problems were those of air travel in the late 1990s writ large. McCarran's urban location simultaneously charmed visitors, who were ten minutes by cab from Strip hotels, but threatened the airport's ability to serve its traffic. Unlike Denver International Airport, located on the prairie thirty miles east of Denver, McCarran was surrounded. Flying home one Sunday afternoon brought me so close to the city that from my seat I could distinguish the players in my regular pick-up basketball game. By 2001 the airport had done all it could. No land for new runways existed, so increasing the number of passengers per plane was the only option. But its airport gates weren't set up for larger planes, leaving the long-term growth of visitation in jeopardy.

Even more threatening, as the demand for airplane seats nationwide reached a near crisis in the late 1990s, Las Vegas found its allotment cut. Airlines did not make as much money per seat on Las Vegas flights. The combination of price-sensitive vacation travelers and the discount packages that defined the local market meant that on a per seat basis when demand almost exceeded supply, business travelers between Chicago and Los Angeles offered far higher profit per traveler. The major airlines cut their flights to Las Vegas to maximize profit from market conditions. Southwest Airlines and America West Airlines, which together accounted for 53 percent of flights to McCarran, both limited seating. In early 1998 McCarran Airport's overall arrival numbers fell 4.3 percent, about 35,000 people. The threat of a lack of seats prompted flamboyant former America West Airlines head Mike Conway to raise $50 million, including $30 million from Harrah's and the Rio, for a new Las Vegas–based carrier, National Airlines. National claimed it would fill a niche in the market, and for the first year of its existence, it succeeded wildly.

The success was short-lived. The casinos never saw National Airlines as their own. As the economy slowed after George W. Bush's election in 2000, seats to Las Vegas magically appeared and National's niche faced assault from the major carriers. The casinos could not afford to antagonize the major airlines. They depended on all the airlines to bring them passengers, and if one of the big four carriers perceived the casinos as competition, the airlines could confidently move their seats to more lucrative routes, knowing that the casinos aren't airlines, and even more, don't want to become airlines. Despite numerous amenities like more legroom, National wasn't that special. By early 2001 Delta Airlines had already imitated one of National's best innovations. They too offered check-in at hotels—Bally's, the Imperial Palace, Luxor, Mandalay Bay, and the Sahara among them—and the demand for the new service grew daily until September 11, 2001, ended off-site check-in of baggage.

Although a casino-backed airline wasn't the answer, the gaming industry fell short of providing solutions to its own problems. No issue was as important in the long run than access to the city. In the 1990s the city nearly doubled its room capacity. Clogged freeways and no airline seats meant a classic bottleneck. Visitors wanted to come to Las Vegas and there was plenty of room when they arrived. But they were jammed up in transit. "These guys spend $5 million on a fish tank," an analyst from Deutsche Bank observed, "but they won't cooperate on anything that would benefit them all."

One of the raps against Las Vegas is that it isn't really a city. There are no high-rises that aren't hotels, no urban spaces like Central Park in New York, nowhere to walk to or from, and there's no promenade, no place to see and be seen in a pedestrian framework. Las Vegas is a western city. Like its peers, it is built for the automobile, where neither the topography nor architecture welcome the pedestrian unless space is specifically designed for them. It is hot much of the year, too hot for most walkers except early in the morning. The streets are wide, and except on the Strip, little is compelling about the city's street-side architecture or landscape.

But in these drawbacks Las Vegas is not alone. Except for older cities like San Francisco, western cities aren't built for walking, as I learned trying to reach the Delta Center in Salt Lake City for a Utah Jazz game. The blocks stretched on endlessly, and walking was not a pleasure but a purpose, a way to reach a place for a specific event. You don't walk to the store for phyllo dough in Las Vegas. You're unlikely to stroll home from work, pick up a baguette, chat with the butcher, and whistle your way to your own front door. In Las Vegas, daily tasks are accomplished mostly by car.

Las Vegas does have a promenade, a de facto one created not by planners but by the feet of thousands. It's a typical western promenade, an enticing urban play space devoted to the pleasure of visitors. Every day, tens of thousands stroll the Strip and drink in the spectacle. There are so many pedestrians that drivers find it impossible to turn into a parking garage or the driveway of a restaurant. The constant slowing of traffic has as much to do with ubiquitous pedestrians, who think that because they're on vacation, so is the rest of the world, as with the volume of cars. Yet the promenaders persist, and as long as each new casino hotel embraces the passersby as components of the revenue stream, the aesthetics of the Strip will include space for walkers and gawkers in more complicated and sophisticated ways.

The sight of people walking in Las Vegas was a symbol of one of the transformations the town had undergone. People don't walk when they're headed to play at the tables. They do so when they're seeing the sights, bagging the visual trophies that stand in place of experience. By walking the Las Vegas Strip, the multitude of visitors did more than change the flow of traffic. They also helped reinvent the meaning of this city in American society. Instead of a place to play, Las Vegas became something to see. Whether it qualified as one of the wonders of the world, as people once perceived nearby Hoover Dam, was arguable, but Las Vegas had become an experience unto itself.

At first walking the Strip was dangerous. As recently as the early 1990s people crossed six- or eight-lane heavily trafficked arteries like Flamingo and Tropicana at street level. They'd line up like lemmings, pressed against the metal rails that kept them off the street, awaiting the "walk" sign. They'd swarm across, hoping to reach the other side before the light changed. It was a peculiar form of risk for a city devoted to letting you relax. Stragglers were always in genuine danger, as were the inebriated. Mobile Las Vegas had little experience with pedestrians.

The annual death toll for pedestrians on the Strip could be staggering, averaging upwards of forty people a year in the 1990s. Many of these fatalities were alcohol-related—hell, they were caused by alcohol—one of the consequences of being a designated sinning zone. People came to Las Vegas to play and they thought they were invincible. Some were lucky, too many were not, and the city had another problem to address. In the mid-1990s the new construction on the Strip posed a solution that led to the reinvention of local space.

It was a simple solution really, a response to the change in visitors' behavior. Clark County built pedestrian overpasses over the Strip, better to meld millions of walkers and hundreds of thousands of cars. They kept cars from hitting people and they made the traffic flow better, imperceptibly faster perhaps, but at least the illusion of motion persisted. There was another advantage. The moveable metal guard barricades that the county set up on the corners to discourage people from crossing the street at ground level added a little flair. They reminded some of the barriers London police use in Trafalgar Square and Piccadilly Circus. The corners of the Strip at Tropicana and at Flamingo took on a Jetsons quality. At ground level, behind the barricades, the corners were reminiscent of European cities; on the overhead crosswalks, they seemed like something out of Fritz Lang's *Metropolis*, futuristic and postmodern, the foot traffic of the future.

The Strip also had another device for moving people, this one straight out of Disneyland. Steve Wynn built a monorail between the Mirage and the adjacent Treasure Island, which opened in 1994; at the Bellagio in 1998 he built another one to the Monte Carlo. Wynn planned to link all of his properties with the monorail, but Caesars Palace, positioned between Mirage and Bellagio, would not permit Wynn's tram to cross its property. Wynn lost the game of transportation tic-tac-toe and found himself with two separate pieces of unconnected tram.

With the construction of the Luxor and Mandalay Bay, Circus Circus Enterprises created a monorail that served its three properties at the south end of the Strip. Boarding at Mandalay Bay, a passenger could ride to either the Luxor and Excalibur, obviating the need to walk between these neo-city-states in hot weather, occasional cold, and infrequent rain, and allowing an easy and free flow of people between three adjacent properties owned by the same company. The monorail reprised one of Las Vegas's oldest strategies: keep them in the hotel. After seeing the spectacle became part of the town's attraction, properties that could control the flow of their patrons benefitted, both from the presence of visitors and the eternal Las Vegas illusion of providing something for nothing.

Another monorail linked the MGM, at Tropicana Avenue, and Bally's, at Flamingo Road, a distance of a little more than one mile. Opening in June 1995, it allowed people to avoid a longer walk, but it was less scenic, for it traveled on the back side of the hotels, close to Koval Lane, the first street east of the Strip. In 1997 more than fifteen thousand people used it each day to reach a variety of destinations, serving almost like a subway for the Strip. Visitors used it, but so did hotel workers, shoppers, and people on their lunch break. Even locals out for a night on the town could use this monorail. They might park in the enormous parking garage at the MGM and hop the monorail to their ultimate destination, a restaurant or a comedy club closer to Flamingo Road. Las Vegas rarely resembles European or even older American urbanity, but the Bally's—MGM monorail offered a glimpse of that kind of public culture.

The pedestrian overpasses and the two monorails created more than transportation. If you linked them, you could negotiate the best parts of the Strip without using a private vehicle or a taxi. One July day, I took my wife and kids to the monorail depot at Mandalay Bay. We rode to Excalibur, walked through the casino and across the overpasses to MGM, where we boarded the monorail for Bally's. Departing there, we crossed above the Strip twice more and found ourselves on the people conveyor to Caesars

Palace and the Forum Shops. After browsing the shops and eating lunch, we walked next door to the Mirage, took the tram to Treasure Island, waited around for the first pirate show of the evening, and then reversed the process. Even on a crowded day, the trip took a little more than an hour, required less discomfort and exertion than walking in the summer heat, and was easier on the psyche than driving the same distance, parking, and walking in. The only drawback of the monorail-overpass combo was the radical change in temperature every time we left or entered a casino. Outside, the temperature topped 110 degrees; inside, it couldn't have been more than 70, a jarring contrast that didn't give the body the time to adjust and left me with the sniffles.

Here was an antidote to the attacks on Las Vegas's urbanity, I mused. This was an urban promenade, and thousands seemed to agree with me. The promenade made the most seductive parts of the Strip into a giant outdoor mall of competing franchises. Early in the morning, guests use the same walkways as part of their daily exercise routines. I saw joggers along the route, watching the sun come up as they ran. Reaching from Treasure Island to Mandalay Bay, it encompassed almost all of the new Strip, leaving out only Sheldon Adelson's Venetian across the street from Treasure Island. The promenade created urban pedestrian space in Las Vegas, and parallel developments such as Las Vegas's first elite high-rises, Turnberry Place, the $750,000 to $3,000,000 per unit luxury towers complete with high-end restaurants and spas, and Park Towers added to the urban impression as they initiated the first systematic attempts to build Las Vegas vertically rather than horizontally. But Turnberry expected that 70 percent of its 740 units would not be their owner's primary residence.

Turnberry, Park Towers, and other such urban developments, like the monorails, overpasses, and the promenade, created pedestrian and urban living space primarily for outsiders. Locals used the trams and the walkways, but they were designed for the comfort of visitors, convention-goers, and shoppers, people who just wanted to visually drink in the Strip. Las Vegas' growing urbanity seemed contradictory, like the fake tinytowns that the architect Jon Jerde designs. Community isn't a designable event; only the illusion of physical community is. Tourist towns cater to their visitors ahead of the locals. Most of the changes that Las Vegas's transformation in the past twenty years has yielded have not been geared to the needs of residents. Despite its novel and futuristic implications, Las Vegas's promenade was regressive, a sop to image instead of community, part of Las Vegas's company-town past, when locals didn't matter.

. . .

Infrastructure and livability are incredibly closely linked. The rate of growth has been so great in the past two decades that it would not really be possible to keep up, but good planning, implementation, and strategy can and should mitigate some of the impact. Nevada's unusual tax structure and its weak government limit the chances of dealing with growth, for greater Las Vegas and indeed the state depend on the dollars that development offers in order to maintain a key feature of Nevada's attractiveness to newcomers: the absence of anything resembling progressive taxation. Even more, Nevada is peculiarly oligarchic. So few hands hold statewide and local power that political columnist Jon Ralston, the state's most prescient political commentor, labeled the state legislature the "Gang of 63" for their slavishly obsequious capitulation to the powers that be. The bulk of public money spent in the past two decades has been spent catering to the industry that is still the most important one in Las Vegas and is the engine that drives Nevada besides. There are ancillary benefits for residents, but they're few and far between and they don't solve the problems growth creates.

The bottom line is that Las Vegas has become less livable in the past twenty years, and in twenty more it'll be even less so. "I remember someone telling me, we were growing at four thousand to five thousand people a month, look at the first ten cars and double it, and that's what its going to look like three years from now, double it again and that's two years from then," one city planner said. "Where are they going to go?"

The window for solutions opened and closed before anyone realized it. As long as the city perceives highways as the answer, Las Vegas's traffic problems will grow worse. The roads that promised salvation when they were new have become more crowded, and there is little hope of long-term improvement short of a catastrophe that destroys the reasons people move to Las Vegas. Planners have long understood that you can't build roads and make traffic disappear, but without the creativity and political will to invent and implement alternatives that appeal to the driving public, little can slow the gradual degradation of life for the people who live in greater Las Vegas. One planner projected that a twenty-minute commute in 2000 would require fifty minutes in 2020. The expansion of U.S. 95 west of the Spaghetti Bowl promises Nevada's first high occupancy vehicle lane, but no one truly expects people to car pool as a result. More and more, people will live and work in the edge cities, the suburban enclaves like Green Valley,

Summerlin, and even the currently remote but increasingly consumed Boulder City. Those places will, like Riverside and Antelope Valley in southern California, become worlds of their own, separate from the larger issues of the metropolitan area. As that continues, Las Vegas will more and more resemble greater Los Angeles, less and less linked together by shared experience and interests. The result will likely be another sprawling southwestern metropolis that serves the few and pounds the many into submission.

When the regional transportation plan public hearings debuted in the early 1990s, Henry Chanin and the others who advocated the plan sincerely believed that they would succeed. "I used to close by telling my audience, 'When you look back,'" Chanin remembered, "'you will remember this as the night that the Los Angelization of Las Vegas stopped cold.'" Well-intentioned, they faced a hydra, a many-tentacled beast that grew new limbs every time they hacked one off. The combination of baby boomers' expectations, weak governmental institutions in the state and county, and the fundamental irascibility of Americans when it came to their favorite personal transportation device doomed the response. Even in a perfect world, unbridled desire and limited space foreshadowed the eternal traffic jam. "They didn't empty the spaghetti bowl," observed one exhausted commuter after he spent half an hour gridlocked on the road about three miles west of the interchange. "They just passed it down the table." In Las Vegas, the illusion of hope and collective greed combined with facile government to make resolution a dream. I once told a national television audience that if Las Vegas reached 2 million people, I didn't want to be here. I probably will be here when that happens in about 2007. I have no illusions that when the two millionth person settles in, all of us will be sitting in traffic.

CHAPTER 10

The Instant Metropolis

Building a City without Basements or Closets

I PARKED IN FRONT OF THE SMALLISH AND ORDINARY HOME, WONDERING why I'd been told I had to see it. I rang the doorbell, and the door to this modest-looking house opened into a stunning interior. The unexceptional exterior hid an enormous pie slice-shaped home complete with an atrium with marble floors, exquisite statuary, an indoor swimming pool, and nearly six thousand square feet of living space that were all impossible to discern from the street. I felt like I'd entered a James Bond movie from the 1960s. The house once belonged to a 1960s-era casino owner, a mob boss turned legitimate by Nevada's idiosyncrasies. It reflected his roots, the inherent fear of calling attention to himself that was the hallmark of such operators. They felt their roots in the underworld; most believed that anything the outside world could see could be taken from them. While they feared attention, they had no aversion to luxurious living. Modest exteriors that did not encourage the curious hid fabulous palaces within. Elegant living happened behind closed doors in the old Las Vegas.

A few weeks later, I stood in the living room of a friend's new home. At more than $1 million, the property was equally exquisite, with its own porte cochere, twenty-foot-high doors, and marble steps. The enormous living room had forty-foot ceilings, beautiful soffits, and stunning art, including a Joan Miró, on the walls. The sunny west side of the house was floor-to-ceiling double-pane glass that offered a beautiful view of a championship golf course, rolling hills, and the outline of the Strip in the distance. A mechanical sun shade could be lowered to cut the heat and glare from the late-afternoon sun. A twenty-five-foot-long, twelve-foot-deep swimming pool lay beyond the beautiful glass wall, its most notable feature a waterfall that made the pool seem to go on forever. More than ten thousand square feet, the house was a palace, but designed by the homeowners, it reflected their personal warmth, love of entertaining, and desire to affirm their arrival on the scene. The new Las Vegas openly displayed its private wealth in ways that its predecessors could not.

The wealthy were not the only ones building in Las Vegas as the new century began. "There are two seasons in Las Vegas," the twenty-year veteran of the city's construction industry told me, "summer and construction. A big builder in Connecticut builds three houses or so a year. Here you build seventy-five and nobody would even notice." The landscape of the Las Vegas Valley bore him out. The edifice of the Strip in 2000, visible from almost anywhere in the community, offered miles of gleaming architecture and cost billions in construction. Very little of it existed in 1990. Every photograph of the Strip from that decade shows construction cranes, so ubiquitous that they could easily replace the mountain bluebird as the state bird. Two billion dollars was recorded in commercial and public construction in 1999 in Clark County, a year in which the Strip had very little new construction. Equally prominent, the concentric ring of new subdivisions stretched like a belt from the southeastern corner of the valley to the Northwest. In 1999 the valley recorded 21,216 new home sales, with a valuation of nearly $2 billion. Thousands of graded and lined home sites in every direction promised more of the same. "Every new hotel room meant a job, a paycheck, a house, and a mortgage," one developer noted as he added up the consequences. The fifty thousand new hotel rooms of the 1990s guaranteed even more home construction. Even more stunning, when Strip construction hit a lull in 2000, housing starts did not diminish, suggesting a new independence from gaming-related construction in the local housing market.

Along with tourism and gaming, real estate development drove Las Vegas, transformed its look, created its revenues, made its economy, and continued the growth that marked the 1980s and 1990s. Clark County and every municipality in it depended on development dollars to pay their way.

Each municipality raised its fees for everything from expediting the approval of planning documents to new sewer hookups to pay for the infrastructure to assess, record, and maybe even manage growth. The county commission granted variance after variance to developers because the impact fees they paid provided a good chunk of the county's budget. When asked if the valley was addicted to growth, Jim Gibson, the mayor of Henderson, by 2001 the second largest city in the state at 208,000 people and the fastest growing city in the nation for the most of the 1990s, hesitated. After a moment, he answered affirmatively. "The impact fees on development pay for everything else," he admitted.

Urban sprawl is a fact of life in a city that has nearly doubled in population and physical size in the last decade. New subdivisions emerge so fast that it is impossible to keep up. They spawn business districts of strip malls that seemingly weren't there yesterday. Even the police need maps. New streets and subdivisions open with such regularity that the most recent directory is out of date within weeks of issue. I sat behind a patrol car at a stop sign, watching him pull the map book off the dashboard to locate his destination. "They update our map books weekly," said Dave McKenna, a sergeant with the Henderson Police Department. "It's the only way we know where anything is."

Homeowners experience the same dilemma. In the early 1990s we bought a house on the outskirts of town, naively hoping to enjoy the desert for a long time to come. Within five years, we were surrounded, so we packed up and again moved to the edge of town. We won ourselves a brief respite. Three years later, we had neighbors all around us, a new middle school completed, a second elementary school under construction, and nearby, a resort hotel—casino and its variety of retail. I couldn't find any land within a dozen miles that wasn't already graded for new homes.

Greater Las Vegas appears to be running out of street names, but developers assign their own street names and the permutations appear infinite. Simple errors in spelling have extended the range of possibilities. Streets like Jane Austin, named for the eighteenth-century English writer Jane Austen, Manua Loa Street, named for the active Hawaiian volcano Mauna Loa, and Doc Holiday Avenue, for the nineteenth-century tubercular gunfighter Doc Holliday, are common. Even Bugsy Siegel's name was misspelled on one street, prompting an irate letter to the newspaper that mocked not only developers, but also the civil servants who had signed off on it. Even worse were streets like Icey Creek Drive or Pinacle Way, common words that anyone with an eighth-grade education should be able to spell.

While the misspellings are comical objects of ridicule, they're also indicative of the burden growth places on the region. People don't misspell street names because they're stupid. Such errors occur because there are so many streets being named so fast, so many permits issued, so many of everything else associated with development, that people can't keep up. There isn't time to check the spelling, and on a certain level, who cares? It really does just increase the options, albeit at the cost of minor embarrassment. When you name between sixty and a hundred streets a month, there's got to be room for a little creativity.

Weak government apparatus doesn't contribute much to solutions. Government in the Silver State has never been powerful. Nevada has long been the citizen's state, even though its freedoms really extend to business a great deal more than to the individual. Small-town thinking in local government is endemic and if not venal at least morally challenged. Before the community can truly change, opined John L. Smith, "it takes leadership for the long haul, people who want to do more than just make a score," and that time has not yet arrived. The Clark County Commission routinely grants any developer's request, and the stories of shopping bags of campaign cash are legion. "The hookers here say 'no' more than the county commission," Peggy Pierce of the Sierra Club quipped to a national television audience, nailing one of the dilemmas of Las Vegas's peculiar circumstances: everything was possible but each required a trade-off.

The Las Vegas Valley has become a Catch-22. Future growth pays for current growth; current growth pays for last year's, and services always lag. Every year, the quality of life declines. Costs rise a little bit, it becomes marginally harder to accomplish everyday tasks, and more things that Americans expect government to do go begging. The valley is engaged in a game of catch-up that it can't possibly win, the single greatest threat to Las Vegas's future. The region's most winning attribute has been the exceptional quality of life it offers at a remarkably reasonable cost. As costs rise and quality falls, Las Vegas faces the problems of most American urban areas. The city's move to the norm is so recent and its hold on respectability sufficiently tenuous that preserving quality of life is crucial. Nothing, not even highways, reflects the dangers and the promise of Las Vegas like construction.

The story of building Las Vegas begins with Del E. Webb and the corporation he founded. After a successful career in construction, Webb came to Las Vegas at the behest of the Valley National Bank of Phoenix, which held a $600,000 note from Billy Wilkerson, the impresario who started the Flamingo after World War II. As Wilkerson floundered, Webb stepped in to protect the bank's investment. The powerful construction magnate found himself in a different world, one in which Bugsy Siegel called the shots. Siegel was extravagant and bizarre; Webb was an opportunistic and efficient builder. Their relationship contained considerable tension. Every account includes Siegel's reassurance that mobsters "only kill each other" in response to Webb's alarm at the twelve notches on Siegel's figurative gunbelt. Webb was apparently not too intimidated. Las Vegas legend attributes much of the cost overrun at the Flamingo Hotel to Webb's men checking materials in at the front gate, billing them to Siegel, and then driving them out the back gate to other Webb jobs. From the Flamingo, Webb moved on to build hotels, high schools, civic buildings, and other structures throughout the 1950s, paving the way for even greater involvement in Las Vegas and its primary industry at the time, casino gambling. A 1961 exchange of stock let the Del Webb Company own the Sahara. The construction magnate was now a casino owner, and by 1965 the company had more than $60 million invested in Nevada.

Webb foreshadowed the future of Las Vegas. He was a legitimate businessman who could see the potential in gambling. He and his partner Dan Topping continued to own the Yankees, and sports betting was legal in 1960s Las Vegas. In 1960 the Webb corporation had gone public, requiring every shareholder to pass gaming board investigation, an impossible circumstance for any publicly traded company. Webb circumvented concerns by devising a system of operating companies that leased the casinos from the corporation. As far as Major League Baseball was concerned, Del Webb owned the Yankees but not the casino; the Nevada Gaming Commission affirmed this fiction. The Sahara became a profitable venture for the company, and Webb bought other casinos, including the Thunderbird, the Mint in downtown Las Vegas, and a new casino at Lake Tahoe. He also maintained a relationship with Howard Hughes. The two men had been friends before Hughes retreated into solitude, and even after, he would meet with Webb on occasion. Webb handled much of Hughes's business, by some accounts $1 billion worth. By 1978 Del Webb's seven thousand gaming employees were the largest number in the state.

In the 1980s a changing market upset the conventions of the Las Vegas Valley, and the Webb Corporation became the catalyst in a regional transformation. When suburbanization swept the nation after World War II, led by Levittown on Long Island, outside New York City, construction companies around the country built new homes by the thousands. Until the Sahara deal, Webb focused on commercial construction in Las Vegas and the residential retirement community of Sun City outside Phoenix. The combination of the Sun City model and Del Webb's willingness to treat gaming as any other industry inaugurated the wholesale suburbanization of Las Vegas.

In the early 1980s the housing market in greater Las Vegas took off. Home-building was driven by the volume of population growth. In each decade between 1950 and 1980, population doubled, and with more than 460,000 people in the valley in 1980 compared to only 50,000 in 1950, greater Las Vegas regularly needed more places for people to live. Somebody had to provide them, but there were significant obstacles. Local builders remained small, unable to secure enough capital to build on the scale the city's growth demanded. Until the late 1980s national builders weren't very interested in Sin City.

Prior to the 1980s, housing construction in Las Vegas suffered from the same maladies as every other industry in town. Las Vegas's stigma scared away some businesses; others chose southern California or Arizona instead of a new location that was perennially short of capital. Most construction was idiosyncratic and individualistic, and other than the government-sponsored development of Boulder City in the 1930s, planning was usually happenstance when it occurred at all. Builders were generally recent arrivals, people like Ernest Becker, who came to Las Vegas for the opportunity he sensed and pioneered the westward expansion of the city by building west of the railroad tracks and what became I-15.

Becker was a southern Californian, scion of a family two generations deep into real estate development when he arrived in Las Vegas after World War II. Before he built, the railroad tracks marked the western boundary of the town. Charleston Boulevard, one of the main east-west thoroughfares, was only paved as far west as Highland Avenue, today the first major intersection west of the interstate. In 1952 Becker debuted Charleston Heights, near the corner of Decatur Boulevard and Alta Drive, a mile west of the paved road. The tract was a harbinger. In the next decade Becker prepared lots for as many as sixty-three subdivisions. At his peak in the mid-1960s, Becker turned out three thousand developed lots a year. Construction seeded other endeavors for the family, including a slot route, an operation that owns and services slots machines located in bars, grocery stores, and convenience stores, in the 1970s. In 1988 the Beckers opened Arizona

Charlie's, an early neighborhood casino, which the financier Carl Icahn owned in 2000.

Las Vegas was a working-class town in those days, and the homes that Becker and his competitors built were small, California-style versions of bungalows and the tract homes that swept the nation after World War II. Most had carports instead of garages and they averaged between twelve hundred and fifteen hundred square feet. They were usually one story and low to the ground, with an occasional hint of a rounded Moorish arch. The city's neighborhoods from that era reveal eclectic if not always tasteful character, a wide array of styles, sizes, and shapes. In those days, individual builders constructed neighborhoods, often house by house. Other than leading with the garage, a less than welcoming overture, the houses bore little resemblance to one another. Often they were cinder-block tract homes; A-frames, modern-styled homes, and others were interspersed, and as in many smaller cities, surprisingly nice homes were separated from modest ones by only a block or two. "Ordinary" described the architecture of non-Strip Las Vegas in the 1950s and 1960s.

The most prestigious addresses in town were in the Scotch 80s, west of the railroad tracks and the interstate and between Sahara and Charleston on Rancho Drive. While the neighborhood was not quite stately, it offered spacious ranch-style homes on large lots. Some homes had tennis courts and guest houses, and the successful gravitated to the area. Nearly a half-century later, both neighborhoods housed remnants of the old Las Vegas elite. Proximity to hospitals made it home to a number of physicians. Las Vegas's Mayor Oscar Goodman and his wife Carolyn resided there in 2000; until the mid-1990s Steve and Elaine Wynn called the area home.

Tucked inside the Scotch 80s stood the most exclusive neighborhood in town, Rancho Circle, a block that had "guard gates before there were guard gates anywhere," one resident recalled. Mansions abutted one another on the ten-house street. Rancho Circle was reminiscent of other ultra-exclusive urban enclaves, Washington Square in Henry James's New York and Audubon Place in New Orleans's Garden District among them. In the 1960s and 1970s "that's where anybody who was anybody lived," remembered one neighbor. Here was luxury, the first suburban enclave in Las Vegas that separated its owners from the rest of the city by wealth and status.

East of the Strip, the primary exclusive neighborhood developed around the International Country Club, now the Las Vegas Country Club, which began in 1967. The country club started as a championship golf course with upper-range and high-end condominiums, perfect for the Las Vegas of its day. Throughout the 1970s the area enjoyed powerful cachet. Frank "Lefty" Rosenthal, the man at the center of the Stardust scandal, Allen Glick, its ostensible owner, and Dan Chandler, the wayward son of former Major League Baseball commissioner A. B. "Happy" Chandler and a top-level employee at Caesars Palace, all lived there. Home to developers, mobsters, and casino bosses, the country club was the not-too-subtle merging of Las Vegas's past with its future.

Other exclusive neighborhoods developed. Southeast of the Strip, east of Eastern Avenue and south of Tropicana Avenue, an attractive neighborhood of spacious homes came together. Celebrities who called Las Vegas home favored the area, for it was far enough from town to protect their privacy. Wayne Newton built an exquisite mansion, called Casa de Shenandoah, south of Sunset Road and stocked it with exotic animals. On Eastern Avenue, long before the street became a major north-south thoroughfare, comedian Redd Foxx had his "Casa Redd Foxx." Sammy Davis Jr. lived in the same area, along with many of the city's elite, and by 1980 a growing number of the leaders of the emerging professional class.

The first truly master-planned community in Las Vegas, Green Valley, took shape in the mid-1970s. Engineered by Hank Greenspun, the irascible publisher of the *Las Vegas Sun*, who had bought land in the 1950s and held it, Green Valley represented an innovation in regional community-building. Its model offered a truly master-planned, mixed-income community, replete with amenities. Nothing quite like it had ever been built in Las Vegas, and its beginnings were rocky. After two national companies could not meet their obligations, Greenspun formed the American Nevada Corporation, but barely avoided bankruptcy on more than one occasion. In 1975, when his then son-in-law Mark Fine, who had worked at Chemical Bank and at the investment bank of Loeb Rhoades, Inc., took over the project, its prospects were tenuous at best.

Fine's expertise played a crucial role in developing Green Valley, engineering land sales and recruiting the best builders in the valley. U.S. Homes, a national builder; Pardee Homes, a division of Weyerhaeuser Corporation; Al and Mart Collins of Collins Brothers Homes, twenty-five-year veterans of valley construction; and the Metropolitan Development Corporation, which started building in 1972, constructed subdivisions, all subject to the strict covenants American Nevada insisted upon. The company intended a community, not a collection of houses, and Greenspun knew better than anyone the weakness of the public mechanisms in Clark County. By the early 1980s the area around Green Valley Parkway and Sunset Boulevard held two hundred homes, schools, and a shopping center. The community's signature freestanding bronze sculptures soon followed, lending an air of permanence. The core area of a new town, privately planned with a development company acting as de facto municipal government, began.

Housing took off in Las Vegas as the nation recovered from the economic malaise of the late 1970s. The housing market benefitted from the decline in interest rates, and buyers, empowered by the close relationship between wages and housing prices, searched for new homes. U.S. Homes, Pardee, and Lewis Homes still dominated the local market. Pardee developed Spring Valley in the 1970s, starting with a one-square-mile tract and, in typical southern Nevada fashion, laying off the cost of infrastructure on the county. Smaller local builders such as Collins Brothers, or RA Homes, owned by Hal Ober, who came to Las Vegas in 1977 as U.S. Homes' initial representative in town and founded his own company in 1980, comprised the rest of the market. Proof of the new optimism came in 1983 when after a five-year slump building in Las Vegas returned to its 1978 level. As Wall Street invested in the Strip, large real estate developers eyed Las Vegas, recognizing the makings of an exceptional moment.

The late 1980s were a heady time for Las Vegas builders. In 1983 a 640-acre high-end development called Spanish Trails opened in the southwest, a forerunner of the amenity-laden master-planned communities that became a hallmark of upscale Las Vegas. Spanish Trail aimed at an elite market; its own country club and $9 million, eighteen-hole golf course offered the gracious living that Americans craved. Construction at The Lakes, a thirteen-hundred-acre project in the far west valley, began. A Collins Brothers development, The Lakes was scheduled for five thousand homes and included a thirty-acre lake in its center, one of the last man-made water features approved by the county commission. It included developments such as Coral Cay, with homes that cost as much as $221,000 for the 3,415-square-foot model, the Trinidad. Smaller and less well appointed homes were available for as much as $100,000 less than the Trinidad. As migration to Las Vegas increased, the prospects for developers became more enticing.

Cautious optimism became giddy excitement in a hurry. American Nevada insisted upon diversity of housing, and Green Valley's reasonable prices nicely positioned the community as the nation rebounded. Its success prompted parallel developments. Housing unit permits, which only rarely topped 10,000 prior to 1987, suddenly jumped in 1988 to 26,448, a result of Summerlin. The new standard has remained above 20,000 units per year ever since. After a few initial lean years, Summerlin became a desirable commodity. In 1994 it sold $70 million worth of property.

By 2000 Summerlin and Green Valley had become complete communities, still under construction, but with clear-cut identities of their own and public images that were widely understood. Summerlin attained an upscale, almost elitist image, a result of the early emphasis on construction for the upper end of the housing market. It eschewed apartments and multifamily condominiums, concentrating instead on first-time home buyers. The area also acquired a reputation for uniformity; one prospective buyer turned away, saying, "They all jog at the same time out there!" Green Valley faced similar complaints, especially from people who lived in the core of the city. Despite such contentions, people flocked to the new areas, creating communities that were not at all rooted in the past. Together Green Valley and Summerlin reinvented daily living in the Las Vegas Valley.

The growth of the suburbs created two entirely new cities, geographically dispersed and far different than the one city that came before them. These eerily similar pods, almost visual mirror images of one another, grew up independent of each other and of the rest of the city. Northwest and southeast, the same amenities existed, jogging trails and community parks, restaurants like Applebee's and Chili's. By 2000 they each had their own hospitals and retirement communities, and genial if sometimes heated competition rose up between them. "Enjoy the quiet in Summerlin," one advertisement touted, tacitly accenting rival Green Valley's proximity to the airport. Green Valley billboards targeted drivers on U.S. 95, the most horrid traffic in the entire valley, reminding them that the southeast had much easier access to the Strip, downtown, and commercial areas. Even residents got into the game, proponents of each charging that the other side of town was more (or less) elite, depending on the context, was less friendly to newcomers, had better schools, and was closer to the idyllic community of American myth. As the psychic distance between them grew, they became two entirely distinct communities, in parallel universes that shared little and competed eternally.

The pull apart happened gradually as the pace of growth accelerated in the 1990s and especially as the number of meeting places between the two

SUBURB

suburbs diminished. In the early 1990s greater Las Vegas was still one city, and travel across it did not inhibit ongoing relationships. Crosstown friendships were common, and it seemed that once a weekend, everyone piled in the van and headed to spend the day seeing friends on the other side of town. Community-wide organizations thrived, and the sense of being in one city, bound by many strands of connective fiber, was strong. A combination of growth and traffic interceded. What had once been worth the effort quickly became an inconvenience, then a burden, then an experience to dread. The strain increased, first making what had been day trips into overnight stays—I remember loading the car to go on a sleepover for the whole family at our friends' house in the far northwest—and finally into an ordeal. A crosstown trip occasioned a cost-benefit analysis; did you really like someone enough to make the trip?

Ancillary reasons to fight the traffic also diminished. As both suburbs grew, they offered a full complement of convenient amenities. New businesses located in the newest parts of town and some of the best restaurants in the world opened on the Strip, mid- to high-end chain restaurants opened in both Green Valley and Summerlin. You didn't have to leave your side of town except for specialty experiences, an old favorite restaurant or a little clothing boutique. Even those soon opened a second store near you. Doctor's offices that had only been centrally located now opened satellite facilities east and west. Even more, the suburbs drew off the core who could get out of the city. Soon crosstown friendships grew soft as the opportunities to renew acquaintance without the schlepp diminished. Friends became more casual, children who had once played together turned into total strangers, and the sense of small-town proximity disappeared.

In part, the diminishment of community-wide ties resulted from the nature of the planned communities. Green Valley and Summerlin were designed to be self-contained, as complete as the casino-hotels that dominated the local skyline. They offered their residents everything they could possibly need, affirming both the baby boomers' sense of being entitled to it all and the cocoonlike insularity of similar places elsewhere. Again, Las Vegas reflected crucial trends in the nature of American life with great clarity. Transparent in its actions and aspirations, it spoke to the core of the impermanence of postindustrial American culture.

The world of planned communities was not aesthetically sophisticated. Architecturally and to an increasing degree culturally, suburban Las Vegas took its lead from Los Angeles and especially Orange County. Its architecture was "basically vanilla," remembered Steve Bottfeld of Marketing Solutions, which researches the desires of home buyers and builders. As long as Las Vegas remained fundamentally a working-class town, it had all the visual charm of Peoria. Las Vegas was "a visually impoverished environment," UNLV architecture professor Keith Eggener, who soon fled to Columbia, Missouri, used to moan. The pseudo-Spanish-style houses with their red tile roofs, surrounded by cement block walls, created living that was intensely private. Blocked in and oriented toward the backyard instead of the front of the house, they gave anyone who wanted it their own private Los Angeles suburb.

The communities grew progressively more lavish during their brief histories. The differences in the styles, sizes, and amenities of homes built during Green Valley's two decades showed the evolution of expectations as well as the home builders' marketing to increasingly affluent buyers. The first areas, built in the late 1970s or early 1980s, were typically small, about a thousand or twelve hundred square feet, with one-car garages, and often looked like cut-down Swiss chalets. They sold for between $60,000 and $80,000, with a few more expensive properties interspersed. Most were two stories; many had private swimming pools. The neighborhoods were arranged around little parks in their center, creating the illusion of a small village around a commons or a courtyard. While all the parks had playgrounds, only a few had community swimming pools, essential in a place where a pool can be the center of social life for much of the year. These homes fit people of modest means who were fleeing the city to build an older sense of community, an assumption that home builders shared with everyone else in the late 1970s.

The next wave, built in the early to mid-1980s, placed greater emphasis on single-family amenities and less on the community. The subdivisions were bigger and more spread out, laid out in blocks instead of around squares. They included houses of as many as four different sizes. These were very reasonably priced homes for ordinary people. In the early 1990s the median home price stood at $113,000. In 1992 a 2,200-square-foot model, with four bedrooms, a family room, a dining room, and a kitchen alcove, could be had for $129,900. The different size of the houses were supposed to ensure demographically mixed neighborhoods, creating the elusive ideal of community by placing retired people and young families next to each other.

As Summerlin took shape across town from Green Valley, it mirrored the developments in the southeast. One subdivision, Capriana at Smoke Ranch, a 1,926-square foot home with three bedrooms, two and a half baths, and family room, began at $116,900. A 1,217-square-foot model with two bedrooms or a bedroom and a den began at $94,990. In 1991 at Desert Shores, a parallel development of The Lakes with its own faux lake adjacent to Summerlin, 1,710 square feet started at $142,900 and 2,782 square feet complete with a "bonus room" began at $173,900. Affordable by any measure of housing cost, such homes increased Las Vegas's appeal to newcomers.

Las Vegas real estate had pulled a neat trick, one of the many of the city's atypical formulas. The city's housing costs mirrored the Midwest, where homes remained considerably cheaper than on either coast. But Las Vegas offered the equivalent of a coastal experience in its entertainment if not always in the range and diversity of its cultural features. For a discriminating high-end art museum devotee, Las Vegas in 1991 was surely lacking. For an average American who worked for a living, the shows, music, and casinos offered better than much else in Nobrow American culture.

Exchanging a home on either of the expensive, high-tax coasts for one in Las Vegas promised the ordinary American a significant improvement not only in the house they lived in, but in their commuting time, their tax burden, the weather, recreational opportunities, and the other features that made up the amorphous idea of quality of life.

Until the 1990s, developments like Via Romantico, a moderately expensive subdivision with Italian-named streets and homes with faux pillars that seemed decadent to me when we first viewed homes, passed for upscale. It offered a mini–Caesars Palace theme, wildly Roman on a very small scale. The amenities spoke to Las Vegas's idea of class from a time before the suburban revolution, from a moment when Las Vegas could still provide eyewash, could cut corners, and simultaneously offer people the script that promised them they were special. In such homes, you had to search for the very few closets.

By the early 1990s amenities in the upscale market had changed the look of housing. The influx of national builders brought not only more sophisticated infrastructure, but also architectural design that was more pleasing than its predecessors. More than mere red tile roofs, California influence became a predominant feature; the stuccoed houses, usually sand, pink, or another vaguely desert tone, were most often shaped in the form of conventional American single-family dwellings. The contrast, the stucco in place of wood, the muted desert tones instead of the bright wood and paint of much of the rest of the nation, created an atmosphere that paralleled Santa Fe's faux adobe uniformity. Other southwestern influences also appeared, especially in custom homes, and a range of other influences became if not common at least visible. Even Midwestern styles could be seen.

The three-car garage became the ultimate symbol of status. Between the late 1980s and the early 1990s, a mini-revolution occurred in this simple functional device–turned–amenity. Without basements—as a result of the hard pan caliche clay just a few feet below the surface—homes lacked adequate storage space. A 2,500-square foot home might have only one significant closet, usually a wraparound under the staircase or a walk-in in the master bedroom. People had nowhere to put the stuff they accumulated and the homeowners associations refused to let them leave boats and RVs on the street. One result was the proliferation of rental storage sheds. The other was the three-car garage, built-in storage space.

By 1995 resale homes were doomed if they didn't have a third bay in the garage. Even though garages were rarely climate-controlled, which meant that anything left in them was subject to the brutal and insistent heat of the extended summer, the space was an easy place to dump the detritus of daily life, all the stuff you collect in a lifetime and never look at again. The third garage bay announced something else, too, a step up from the two-car model that articulated the ever-consuming local passion with ways to define "better" in material terms. Without it, you had used up goods; with it, you had a claim on the disappointed home buyer who couldn't wrangle their way into new construction. Reasonably priced homes, perfectly good in every way except that they had only two bays, sat for months as home buyers bought smaller homes on smaller lots for slightly more money because they had a third garage bay.

In the 1990s suburban Las Vegas became truly upscale. A significant number of well-off newcomers bought new homes in record numbers. Most were in the newest suburbs, each tonier than the last, and there the newcomers met locals who moved from the city. This environment was part of a niche for homes in the $250,000 to $500,000 range. As much as 40 percent of buyers were from out of town, and in some neighborhoods the ratio was higher. In one development of more than a hundred homes, only one couple had been raised in the valley. Such homes were not quite palaces, but they were very nice: $250,000 could buy as much as 3,500 square feet on a small suburban lot and put a family in the most desired school zone in the entire district, easily improving the lot of the average family. Especially for people who came from either coast, Las Vegas housing was elegant and gracious at an extremely reasonable price.

Throughout the 1990s Las Vegas housing costs remained almost constant. A shortage of sources of developable land and fierce competition among builders in the frenzied climate kept prices down. There were only three major sources of land in the valley: the two companies and the Bureau of Land Management. They offered land in three-hundred-acre parcels, and developers scrambled to buy and build as quickly as possible so they could be ready the next time land became available. This put a premium on fast construction and quick sales, and nothing sold faster than houses with a price advantage. The municipalities in the valley lacked sufficient inspectors, and with the pressure from developers and politicians who took their money, inspections often became pro forma. Building code violations were rampant, and no one had the resources to check to make sure the violations were fixed. A strange kind of derby followed, where municipalities charged higher fees for immediate assessment and presumably approval of developers' plans, so the process could continue at an even more dizzying pace.

An ongoing array of complaints and lawsuits against home builders became part of the din of growth. Some home owners charged that inspectors colluded with builders; others noted the absence of inspectors as their new homes rose. In one case, Richmond American settled with home owners who videotaped rainwater rushing out of their walls during a rare storm; in others, home builders stalled, made patchwork repairs, or ignored construction defects. Renegade builders left homes half-completed; some pool companies fleeced consumers, leaving gaping holes in minuscule backyards across the valley. One orchestrated bankruptcy by a pool company led to hearings at the state legislature. Even though by 2001 a number of home owners' associations had filed class-action suits against developers and both Summa Corporation and American Nevada Corporation, construction continued unabated. The enormous number of new houses diminished the desirability of the resale home market. New construction didn't cost significantly more than existing homes. As prices remained constant, more people found their way into new homes, spurring even more construction.

Although new home construction costs inched up at a rate far slower than in Nevada's neighboring states, as the 1990s drew to a close the market turned upward. Developers ran for the fringes where land was cheap, built fast, and sold; providing parks and schools in areas without master planning taxed smaller developers and usually ended with either substandard services or government footing the bill. Less attractive in a community that placed a premium on the new, resales dragged behind, tenuous at best. In 1998 developers claimed that cheap land was running out, forcing them to make lots even smaller or to raise costs. Master-planned acreage had risen in cost from $50,000 an acre to as much as $100,000. Squeezed to a 5 percent margin, developers claimed, they could not afford higher costs and looked to offset the increase with smaller lots and higher prices. The division of acres into smaller lots, six to an acre instead of five, resulted, as did other mechanisms to pass costs to consumers.

Developers routinely pointed to higher land costs as the source of any increase in housing prices, but the real impetus for rising home prices came from outside Nevada. Although locals who watched the market might balk, Californians in Las Vegas brought a different scale for housing costs. Even in the early 1990s, when a lot of newcomers were working-class people, Californians regarded Las Vegas housing as cheap. Newcomers looked at available housing stock, found it both familiar and affordable, and routinely were able to afford hundreds more square feet than in southern California and still have money left over. They contributed to a softening of ceilings in the market, and as the decade drew to a close, houses grew marginally but noticeably more expensive.

The range in housing cost in Las Vegas had always been small. The high-end custom home market had been very limited as long as casino workers comprised Las Vegas's primary population. There simply weren't all that many people who could afford high-end construction. As the new suburbs grew, their emphasis on diverse housing and tract home construction guaranteed that most houses fell within in the middle of the housing market. A few tracts of high-end homes were built, occasional subdivisions full of palaces like Tournament Players Club in Summerlin or Hillsborough in Green Valley, but the market primarily aimed at the middle class.

As Las Vegas became acceptable and even fashionable, more affluent people who made the town home sought more expensive, flashier houses. Specialty neighborhoods inside high-end tract homes provided another level of insulation from the outside world. Having a custom home, designed and built individually, became an important social marker. These developments proliferated, ranging between $500,000 and $1 million. Some leapfrogged to the middle of the desert, forcing the extension of infrastructure to exclusive subdivisions, usually at the expense of less-expensive subdivisions closer in. Swank subdivisions were often behind gates, some of which had guard booths as well. The entire subdivision might have a guard booth and gates, and the 5,000-square-foot, $450,000 semicustom tract homes within the outside gate often encircled a golf course and an inner sanctum of larger and significantly more expensive homes, which could be reached only by entering a code at a separate gate. Gates seemed to promise both privacy and exclusivity in Las Vegas.

The gates were soon everywhere, a function of status rather than of security. Most gates were hardly a deterrent to criminals. They remained open to accommodate construction traffic, you gave the code to the pizza place so they wouldn't have to call from the gate when they arrived, the exterminator had it, and so did the carpet layer and every other tradesman. The landscaping companies, with trucks full of Latino workers who mowed lawns and trimmed trees, also had the code, as did your kids' friends, the ice cream guy, and even the door-to-door salesmen. One suburban mom who carpooled had the entry code for six different subdivisions on a notecard attached to her visor. She needed it to drop the kids off, she said. Most high-end gated communities were located in areas that experienced the lowest levels of property and personal crime, far from urban blight, homeless people, and the day labor markets. Yet gates provided a measure of specialness, something home owners craved as they differentiated their tract home and neighborhood from all the others. Subdivisions with homes that cost as little as $175,000 advertised gates, although usually without the guard in the booth.

Gated communities are symptomatic of a society in which the connections of proximity have frayed, but in Las Vegas in particular they seem a reflection of the community's preoccupation with the self. Nobody who thought about it could truly believe that living behind gates would keep them safer, but many enjoyed the status that they assumed accompanied the pronouncement that you needed a code to reach their house. To some, gates announced their prosperity; to others, they promised that you would be left alone. To even more, they served as a calling card, a pronouncement that the owner had made it. In every case, they were part of the upscaling of local amenities.

As the 1990s ended, a new trend was apparent. Along the golf courses in Summerlin, in places like Dragon Ridge above Green Valley, and at Lake Las Vegas, the houses that crews labored on were much more than starter castles. At Lake Las Vegas, the last man-made lake permitted by the county commission, some lots by the golf course or the lake cost as much as $1 million. The promise of exclusivity and remote solitude made the houses as much statements about their owner as places to live. Instead of simply opulent, they became truly ostentatious, sometimes magnificent, palatial, enormous, and amenity-laden, with marble floors, soffits, designer architecture, $200,000 swimming pools, and an array of artistic touches that drove prices through the roof. Such homes had never before been built in southern Nevada; they resembled the palaces of nineteenth-century mining barons. "A $5 million, a $10 million, a $15 million house, is not unusual," Henry Chanin observed. "It certainly was. The wealthiest people in the casino industry, nobody lived in that kind of housing. It just wasn't here. The Californians brought that."

"Californian" in this formulation is code for the class of wealthy people who are independent of place, a version of author Christopher Lasch's transnational class of moneyed individuals who eschew national obligations. "I probably won't live there at all," said Mel Durao, a fifty-seven-year-old resident of Tiburon, California, who owned two homes in Pebble Beach, one in Tiburon, and was buying a $3 million condo in Las Vegas's

Park Towers. "I thought [Las Vegas] would be a good place to go on occasion"—to see a show, dine in elegant restaurants, or play a little golf. More than 70 percent of such buyers came from outside Las Vegas, and their arrival in significant numbers transformed high-end development.

Lake Las Vegas became the prototype of a new, far-more-than-upscale market. An actor, hotel owner, and area developer who controlled substantial holdings around Lake Mead, J. Carlton Adair dreamed of developing a high-end resort. In the late 1960s he acquired land in an exchange with the Park Service and envisioned a community like those under construction at Aspen, Colorado, or in Hawaii. Adair's resort included a man-made lake and other amenities. He anticipated the future by twenty years, but Las Vegas, its constituency, and its housing market were not yet ready. The market Adair envisioned did not yet exist, and his development went bankrupt. Only after Transcontinental Properties bought the development in 1990 did the project transform into a high-end resort community, complete with a Hyatt Hotel, exquisite restaurants, and a championship golf course.

While only a very few can afford to live in places like Lake Las Vegas, such construction altered the housing market. Las Vegas's affordability depends on the relationship between the cost of living and the wage scale. It is different from every other destination resort in the country because the average worker can afford to live there. Aspen's workers commute from downvalley, from as far as sixty miles away. Steamboat Springs, Colorado, mandated affordable housing and paid for it with municipal dollars, but even such a dramatic step didn't make the town any more affordable. In Santa Fe, New Mexico, in 1998 the average wage was $12,000 a year and the average home cost upwards of $200,000. There was simply no way that someone making the average wage—or even a couple both making the average wage—could afford the average home. In Las Vegas the median family income reached $40,514 in 1997 and the median price of a home in 1999 was $143,000. The opportunity to grasp the prize of home ownership for the perfectly average family existed. They could often afford the mortgage on a home. It might not be their dream, but it got them far closer to the middle class than it would have in any comparable city.

High-end construction pulled the housing market upward. In 2000 the median housing price climbed by a remarkable 10.9 percent to almost $160,000. Throughout the enormous housing boom, Las Vegas's prices had stayed below the rate of increase in every surrounding state. In 2001

Coldwell-Banker determined that the cost of 2,200-square-foot home in
Las Vegas was on par with Cheyenne, Wyoming. New home price increases
rarely outpaced the value of existing homes, and on the rare occasions that
they did, the difference wasn't significant. Although attributing the spike in
2000 to the cost of a handful of palaces completed that year was easy, it was
a portent of much more. The draw of big dollars was powerful. High-end
homes encouraged builders to inch up the price of other homes, reflected
in the more than 10 percent increase. Finally, the community's overall success and the prosperity that accompanied it began to implode. The consequence of such a move could be dire.

When Mike Davis assailed Las Vegas's shortcomings, he pointed to the community's lack of parkland on a per capita basis as a central flaw. No American
city had less park space per person, Davis thundered, proof of the fundamental venality of the company town. At the instant he spoke, he was technically correct. Greater Las Vegas did have less parkland per capita than any
city in the nation, 1.9 acres of developed parkland per 1,000 people compared to a national average of more than 4 acres. Plenty of explanations to
explain this deficiency existed—a 50 percent increase in the population in a
seven-year period, the regressive tax structure of the state, and the presence
of growing numbers of senior citizens who voted against anything—but
Davis's assertion was still true. What he couldn't see was the opening of a
window that changed the entire trajectory of the Las Vegas Valley. It came
from an unlikely place, the city of Henderson, long known as "Hooterville"
after the town in the 1960s situation comedy *Green Acres*.

Henderson started as an industrial city, and in the 1980s it was still one
of the least desirable places in the valley. The town was perceived as lower
class and industrial, dirty, lacking amenities, and thoroughly backward, a
sentiment reinforced by the 1988 explosion at the Pepcon chemical plant
in the city's downtown. The blast blew out windows four miles away. In May
1991 a leak in a storage tank sent a cloud of chlorine gas into the air in one
of the worst such accidents in American history. Thousands were evacuat-
ed and more than three hundred were hospitalized. One of the town's high
schools was called Basic High School, after Basic Magnesium Inc., the
World War II—era industrial enterprise that started the town. *Basic* had other
meanings, as J. Bruce Alversen, who became a partner in a prominent Las
Vegas law firm, discovered when he interviewed with a major university he
hoped to attend. "They actually asked me why I graduated from a basic high

school," he heartily laughed a generation later. "The guy said, 'Couldn't you at least have graduated from advanced?'" The stigma was pervasive. Thinking that "Henderson" sounded less stigmatized than "Las Vegas" and not as pretentious as "Green Valley," my wife told a former Las Vegan that that's where we were moving. Her response was "why do you want to live *there*?"

The people in Green Valley didn't think of themselves as residents of Henderson, and the cabal that ran the city was happy to indulge that self-deception. City leaders took the dollars that suburban development poured into local coffers and added to the city's minuscule infrastructure. Henderson's roughly 25,000 people in 1980 had one library, a small downtown, and a few baseball fields. Green Valley and its environs grew so rapidly in a fifteen-year period that in 1999 the city surpassed Reno as the second largest in Nevada. In effect, an entirely new city grew up, larger than the one that preceded it, that took the same name but shared few of the characteristics of industrial Henderson.

The tension that resulted was pervasive and enormous. The people who grew up in the industrial town were proud of their city, and resented the newcomers and the transformation they brought. Henderson had its own iconography, a small downtown, and a number of venerated local institutions. Its people regarded themselves as a separate community with an important history, closely tied to World War II and apart from Las Vegas. The newcomers referred to their hometown as "Green Valley." Locals fumed; they regarded referring to Green Valley as independent community as a slight on their hometown and believed that Green Valley looked down on Henderson. "There's no such town as Green Valley," a friend from Henderson insisted, wagging his finger in my face. "It's all Henderson." Technically, he was correct. Actually two separate communities, leaning in different directions, inhabited the loose rubric.

Old Henderson also took considerable umbrage at what its people regarded as the pretensions of Green Valley. "All you Green Valley people are snobs," the principal of a Henderson middle school railed at a suburban mother who sought a zone variance for her child to attend school closer to home. The mother insisted that wasn't the case; dropping the child in Henderson required an extra twenty-minute drive each morning, she protested. Both she and her husband worked on the Strip, west of their home, and traveling seven miles to the east and then those seven plus twelve more to the west seemed too much of a disruption to the family's already chaotic daily life. The principal refused to relent, coveting the upper-middle-class children of Green Valley to help raise the standardized test scores of his largely blue-collar school. The tension took social forms as well. Green Valley sprouted youth baseball leagues for teenagers; Henderson's main baseball field, Morrell Park, suffered from the reputation of being dangerous. The idea that their kids could get hurt while playing baseball propelled parents to start their own leagues. All such steps, well-intended or spiteful, accented differences and drove a wedge between the two communities that shared the same name.

A physical distance existed between the two communities, a visual demilitarized zone of undeveloped land that clearly illustrated the psychic division between the two. In 2000, at Gibson Avenue at the base of Black Mountain, undeveloped land stretched for a full mile to the west and at least six hundred yards to the east. One direction looked toward Las Vegas for jobs and amenities; the other included the self-contained community that preceded rapid growth. The mile of space inbetween could seem equal to that between the Allied and German trench lines in World War I. Breaching the barrier and creating a community out of the two distinct parts required more than simple construction. Deft manipulation of signs and symbols was crucial.

With an increasingly upscale profile but resisting being a bedroom community for Las Vegas, Henderson campaigned to change the city's image. In 1982 the city opened an award-winning convention center. Although the industrial plants paid the city's bills, after the 1991 chlorine release they became controversial. In 1992 a long-delayed $9 million beautification project on Boulder Highway was completed, and a $1.8 million downtown beautification began. National retail chains looked favorably on Henderson, and residents were finally able to shop at the big stores without driving to Las Vegas. At the same time, suburban growth raised the average household income of the eighty-thousand-person town to $52,425, well above any other municipality in the state.

Despite its newfound status as an affluent community, Henderson still struggled with questions of identity. "Like a butterfly, the city is gradually shedding its cocoon," the *Sun* trumpeted in 1993, but the community had not decided what it wanted to be. Most of old Henderson was sure it didn't want to be a bedroom community or the old industrial town it had been, but its ability to be independent was circumscribed at best. As population soared, the city's ability to redefine itself was limited. If Henderson didn't have much to offer its thousands of new residents, it had little claim on their talents in any other way.

The most powerful institutions the city could muster to support its reinvention were libraries and public parks. Parks and libraries offered shared space and commonality of values, civic interaction and socialization. They combined education, relaxation, and social cohesiveness, all desirable traits in a growing community. Their very nature minimized differences and magnified similarities. They were crucial building blocks, pieces of the puzzle of quality of life that served the community and enhanced its reputation. They were also cornerstones of any model of changing outside perceptions of the city.

Parks connoted the change in status most clearly. When Henderson was a blue-collar industrial town, it could little afford such extravagances. In 1960 the city contained just two parks totaling eighteen acres, and as growth continued, the limited services the community provided contributed to its negative reputation. By 1990 the lack of parks had become a crisis. Henderson was home to 140,000 people, but its 707 acres of developed and undeveloped parkland in 1994 would have sufficed only for a smaller city. A mix of public involvement and the participation of private developers in a grand scheme helped the city's developed and underdeveloped parklands increase by 150 percent to 1,895 acres in 1998. The professional park community recognized Henderson's achievement. Faced with soaring population increase, hampered by new residents' limited identification with Henderson, and experiencing enormous development, the city fashioned a dramatic and meaningful response. When Henderson bested Springfield, Missouri, Columbia, Maryland, and Scottsdale, Arizona, for the National Recreation and Park Association's 1999 National Gold Medal for Excellence in Park and Recreation Administration, Henderson had attained a kind of respect never accorded any other Nevada community.

Park development in Henderson outpaced that of the rest of the Las Vegas Valley, but by 2000 other governmental entities were attempting to bring the per-person average acreage up to more acceptable levels. In 1999 the City of Las Vegas opened two large public swimming pools and five new parks ranging in size from one to thirty-nine acres. Other municipalities followed, and the canard that greater Las Vegas lacked park space was being addressed at breakneck speed.

Henderson garnered other accolades as the city fashioned a comprehensive response to growth. It maintained an enviable quality of life without raising the very low local property taxes. *Money* magazine rated

Henderson among the fifty safest American cities in 1997. The city had the highest per capita income in the state, in some zip codes in new developments topping $70,000. It offered the most extensive trail system in Nevada besides its new parks and recreation facilities. With the state's most stringent development standards, the city pushed the cost of much of its infrastructure onto developers, receiving land for parks, fire stations, and police stations as well as roads, water, and sewer infrastructure through local improvement districts charged to developers. All of the city's seven golf courses used raw or reclaimed water. In 2000 Henderson truly seemed to have not only met but mastered the challenge of rapid growth. Communities all around the country looked to the town that had once been known as Hooterville as a model.

Mastering growth did not solve identity issues for Henderson. The city claimed the virtues of a bedroom community, something Henderson did not want to be. Even more problematic, the solutions came from the new areas, in the impact fees from developers of the city's twenty-five master-planned communities, and was returned to them as amenities for those communities. Some developers produced turnkey public parks as part of their agreement with the city, but often they were so judiciously located that if you did not know the park existed you'd never even think to look for it. As a result, the benefits of growth were distributed unevenly, exacerbating the already existing tension between Green Valley and its environs and old Henderson. The city was still searching for an identity that could bind the old and new towns together.

The problem increasingly stemmed from intellectual orientation. Green Valley looked toward Las Vegas, and as Henderson annexed more land to its west in order to secure the revenue that came from impact fees, the community shifted even further away from the old downtown. A major downtown redevelopment project stalled, leaving old Henderson begging for a piece of the larger city's new action. Coupled with the shivers that the idea of being a bedroom community sent down the old city's figurative spine, Henderson needed a boost for its downtown.

As such an impetus often does, it arrived bundled with its own baggage. Richard L. Moore had been president of the Community College of Southern Nevada since 1994 and was acclaimed as a visionary educator—as long as no one looked closely at his record. A snappy Claremont-educated economist who previously headed Santa Monica College in California, Moore brought tremendous energy and a casual disregard for rules and regulations to his post. He had not quite been run out of California, but the state legislature did pass rules governing spending in public education that were widely referred to as "Richard Moore laws." A fast-talking outsider who promised the moon could always find a place in Las Vegas, and Moore was likely the last of the big-city used-car salesmen to carve a niche in small-town Las Vegas.

By 1999 Moore found his aspirations thwarted. The house of cards he built started to collapse, but the Teflon-coated Moore concocted an exit strategy. He threw his support behind Kenny Guinn in the 1998 gubernatorial race and parlayed Henderson's aspirations into a $500,000 planning grant for the establishment of a new four-year college, Nevada State College, to be located in Henderson. To Moore, the planning grant, which paid his salary and that of a crony, Orlando Sandoval, was the same as establishment of the college.

Moore made his career in southern Nevada by telling people what they wanted to hear and there was nothing that Henderson wanted to hear more than that it had a role in serving higher education in the state. A college town provided an ideal solution to the dilemma of the industrial town turned bedroom community. "If there was ever a community suited for a state college," Mayor Jim Gibson told an approving audience at his 1999 state of the city address, "Henderson is it." Visions of Bloomington, Indiana, danced in the heads of city leaders; images of pennants and racoon coats, goldfish-swallowing contests, and hordes of students turning old Henderson's downtown, Water Street, into UCLA's Westwood tantalized the business community. Moore fed on those dreams, immediately abandoning the logical idea of a state college to produce teachers to meet the annual demand for two thousands new teachers in favor of a Claremont-style residential college. "Oxford on the Colorado," Moore had the audacity to say, and Henderson lapped up the fantasy. "I think Richard Moore's wonderful," gushed city councilwoman Amanda Cyphers at a 1999 City of Henderson strategic planning retreat.

The project offered the city another benefit. Planned for a tract of three hundred acres north and west of the intersection of Lake Mead Boulevard and Boulder Highway, land donated by LandWell Company, the real estate arm of BMI, the proposed site would offer a tie-in to stalled downtown redevelopment. The location made town leaders salivate; it would transform industrial land into suburban land, further removing the stigma that dogged Henderson, and bolstered downtown commerce. The site had a stigma; rumors of toxic substances below the surface persisted. Despite this, the college was to become the cornerstone of Landwell's upscale 2,400-acre Provenance development. The city promised that construction would not begin until assurances of the site's safety were received, and an accepting public supported the college.

The entire project resulted from a community's desire for a different self-image. Nevada State College presented itself as a residential college, one of Moore's objectives that clearly tied into those of Henderson. Residential students were hard to come by in southern Nevada. Las Vegas was the only population center in the state, and its students preferred the commuter lifestyle in which school became just one of a menu of options in their daily life. Even the more established UNLV, with more than 25,000 people comprising more than 14,000 full-time-equivalents in 2000, had only 1,800 students in residence. American university education had been moving toward urban commuters for a more than generation. Few other states established new residential institutions, especially at the state college level. Despite the weight of evidence to the contrary, Henderson remained committed to the invention of itself as a college town.

By 2001 Moore's luster had tarnished. He'd been implicated in a number of scandals at the community college and there had been talk of indictment. But this was, after all, southern Nevada, and being indiscreet, shady, and even ethically challenged never kept anyone from public power. With the support of powerful politicians, Nevada State College was funded by the legislature. Despite fervent promises that the new college would not reallocate the existing capital improvement budget for the university and community college system, the money for the college came directly from the budgets of UNLV and the down-in-the-mouth University of Nevada-Reno, barely able to hold its own in a state that had left it behind. Even before budget approval, Moore's cart-before-the-horse style inspired the nonexistent college's website to offer a campus design competition. Moore had accomplished a characteristic sleight-of-hand; he'd seamlessly joined a city's aspirations to his own, selling a panacea that only an economically flush community with real doubts about its identity would buy.

Henderson may have conquered most of the problems associated with growth, but in 2001 it had not been able to resolve its own fears about its status. The college remained a chimera, a dream of respectability that the second-largest and most affluent city in Nevada did not really need, but one that its leaders strongly believed affirmed its new status. Henderson could have could have hinged its future elsewhere, but its history condemned it to a gamble to assuage its insecurities. It risked its remarkably high quality of life to change its image. Its marriage to a manipulative educator may turn out to have been a bold move. It may also become an expensive failure that curtails Henderson's ability to serve its rapidly growing population.

Nor were Henderson's problems unique. The City of Las Vegas faced its own dilemma. Downtown Las Vegas and its northwestern suburbs reprised the battles in Henderson on their own terms, pitting retirees and their overwhelming desire for stasis against Las Vegas mayor Oscar Goodman's passionate drive to redevelop downtown. In a world of finite resources and with a city government that relied on Goodman's charisma for its clout, the struggles between downtown and the older neighborhoods around it and the new and more upscale northwest were titanic battles between old and new factions. Anywhere you looked in the Las Vegas Valley, growth produced winners and losers, and constituencies fought to ensure they would be among the winners. The Hobbesian war of all against all could not have been any more divisive.

"Smart Growth," the headline in *CityLife* announced in 1999. "So far we've got the *growth* part down." Reporter Steve Sebelius pointed to two possible strategies for Las Vegas: trying to direct and focus the growth through higher fees for water and sewer lines, or conceding that growth was inevitable and trying to ensure that government services kept up. The former was a pipe dream, something hard to engineer even in places that tolerated much greater government intervention, and certainly unlikely in a place that prided itself on an absence of constraints on individual decisions. The latter was business as usual, a license for developers to demand that government ease their burden by allowing them to do as they pleased. The haphazard building style had begun long before growth took off, and like many dimensions of Nevada's political and cultural structure, it had become an anachronism in a rapidly growing place. The lack of regulation was convenient for the powers in the community, who secured their position by contributing to political campaigns with abandon. A look at the growth demonstrated that new power shaped the town—and that power was in development.

Developers have become a new kind of growth coalition for greater Las Vegas, further evidence of the normalization of the region. Like growth coalitions anywhere, these entrepreneurs influence issues with cash and clout, wearing down public regulatory entities with a barrage of paperwork and ongoing appearances before the county commission. Planners seek solutions, but they are hamstrung by the disparity in power between the developers and staff professionals. In one well-known instance, the county set aside a wetlands park, a combination of lower elevation flood plain and the area's sewage district retention zone that would purify the treated wastewater it returned to Lake Mead. The park, complete with erosion control structures, a cattail marsh to purify waste water, a research center, and recreational trails, seemed a valve for pent-up urbanism. As it was being fashioned, developers came to the commission, seeking variances for the land surrounding the nature reserve, and were granted their requests. Even though the wetlands park became a local cause célèbre, a favorite project for corporate civic service, by its groundbreaking in February 2000 the project had been compromised by the typical configuration of developer self-interest and tepid response from weak government. In spring 2001, while the hundred-acre core of the park was under construction, a nearby tract once slated for inclusion had bulldozers for a new subdivision tearing at the ground. "Sometimes I think the master plan for Las Vegas is written in pencil," observed Deanna White of the Sierra Club.

The new power formed along the same lines as the old, bleeding together the forces that built the Strip with capital that couldn't have been found in Las Vegas before the 1970s. The same names of a generation before, Del Webb and Summa Corporation, were prominent, their cachet improved by the passage of time and by the crossover from casino and hotel construction and ownership to the growing housing market. Such companies grew from specialized entities to multifaceted conglomerates, not only building, but vertically integrating development from purchase of the land to sales to the consumer. The strategy created considerable political power to accompany the wealth generated by growth. The expansion of Las Vegas played right into the hands of the powers of a generation ago, allowing them to change shape and to take center stage in the fastest growing city in the nation.

The people who opposed growth or merely wanted to influence its direction found themselves with neither the tools nor the resources to oppose the new oligarchy. State senator Dina Titus introduced in 1998 the idea of a growth ring similar to that of Portland, Oregon, but it made little headway. The models for slowing growth were largely noxious. The faux elitism of authors like the new urbanist James Howard Kunstler, who argued for front-porch culture without considering the implications of de facto class-based segregation, or the elitist strategies of communities like Boulder, Colorado, where government bought open space that turned into a club against the middle class that the affluent college town hired to serve its insular needs, neither solved problems nor were politically palatable in southern Nevada.

The region seemed caught in a conundrum: its traditions and its needs were pitted against one another. Nevada's traditions exalted the primacy of the individual, the right to be free as the individual defined it and especially to use property as its owner saw fit. This worked fine in a state of 150,000 people, but when one metropolitan area topped 1.4 million, the ability of all to act in their self-interest without creating chaos brought daily living to a halt. As developers gained power, they shifted the cost of growth to their customers, the new home owners who'd come in search of an affordable paradise. Besides the possibility of prosperity, it was the idea of freedom that made Nevada attractive, but as the new century took shape, freedom increasingly meant the developers' right to pass on to consumers the basic costs of development. The mechanisms to temper such power simply weren't there, and weak government offered little recourse.

People still came by the thousands, with expectations that exceeded the region's ability to respond and even local and state government's vision of its responsibilities. I drove west out of the valley on U.S. 95, the old Tonopah Highway, on one sunny spring morning in 2001 and found that, much to my surprise, the city now reached almost to the boundary of the Paiute Reservation. This was a full five miles farther than my last trip the year before. A new high school was near the highway; the Centennial Parkway extended past businesses and endless homes. It looked as if an entirely new city, one that truly hadn't been there five years before, was firmly in place. The newcomers there found what their predecessors during the previous fifteen years had found: a city overwhelmed by the arrival of so many people, a place that not only grew with weedlike speed, but that simultaneously overwhelmed every existing institution. The greatest consequence of growth turned out to be not environmental problems, but social ones. People had to fashion community from the chaos of a community that had doubled in size in a decade. The mechanisms they found for the task were truly novel.

CHAPTER 11

Community from Nothingness
Neighborhoods of Affinity

"When we first moved here, people pulled their cars into their garages and put the garage door down before they opened their car door," Fran Sutherland, an attractive, fortyish Atlanta native reminisced about her first year in her new suburban Las Vegas neighborhood. "I couldn't believe it! We'd moved here from New Orleans, where kids played in the street, but here there was no one, no one at all." Her husband, Gary, a powerful-looking man of about forty-five with broad shoulders and Irish good looks who was a sales manager for a glass distributor, nodded in agreement. "We put two rocking chairs on our front porch, the only ones in the neighborhood." Gary had been a college hockey player, and within weeks, he'd rounded up the neighborhood kids and taught them how to play. They began on roller blades, with sticks flying and Gary coaxing something resembling team hockey from the chaos. By the time we met, five years later, their street was full of kids playing, and Gary coached not only high school hockey, but a junior high club hockey and a team in the city youth hockey league. "We've still got our rocking chairs, and we're still the only adults out front," Fran laughed. "But the kids are all out here."

The Sutherlands had crossed Las Vegas's great divide, the line between transience and community, almost without trying. They looked around, found nothing intriguing, and turned their adopted neighborhood into a template for their desires. The clay wasn't what they expected, but they modeled community from the raw material around them. Undeterred by architecture that kept people apart, by the daunting heat, and by social assumptions that seemed designed to put them off, they struck at the group that is always in search of people to do things with: kids. That adults hung back while the kids shouted joyously as they chased after hockey pucks in the street should come as no surprise.

"It took me a while to get used to it here," Fran continued. "My kids had grown up outside, in south Florida and in the bayous, fishing and hunting, and it didn't seem to me that even with a pool we could do the same things here." Las Vegas was hot, searingly so, most of the year, and people responded the way they do to the winter in northern states: they did everything they could to stay inside, out of the sun. Between ten in the morning and eight at night, the sun bakes. It saps moisture from the body and broils the skin. People cover their windshields with portable shades and drape towels over their steering wheels, but opening a car door in the summer always emits a rush of hot, unpleasant air. People go into work at five in the morning to find a parking place that will stay in the shade all day. The only safe place is a pool, and there is one in almost every walled-in backyard and at every apartment complex.

For people who expected the outdoors to provide conventional amenities, Las Vegas required adjustment. The Sutherlands made theirs. The impetus of street hockey and the filling of the neighborhood—they were in the first tract of homes that opened, and successive waves brought more families with more children—meant that all of a sudden, opportunities for almost anything existed—if you could see a dry, stark, concrete world as a possibility. The washes, the concreted drainage ditches used to prevent fearsome desert flash floods, provided a place for children to play when it was dry. They were also incredibly dangerous when it rained, and for the benefit of longtime residents as well as newcomers, every rainy season, public service advertisements constantly urged people to stay out of the washes. Eighty-seven percent of Nevada was federal land, some of it only twenty minutes' drive from the Sutherlands' home, and it offered opportunities for family outings, overnight camping, and the outdoor activities the couple wanted to enjoy with their children. "They still play flashlight tag, hide-and-seek, all the kids' games we played," Fran pointed out. "They just do it without the trees."

The Sutherlands are typical of Las Vegas's newest additions, the graft-ed upper middle class. Like many others, they are drawn to the town because of the opportunity it offers, and when they arrived were shocked by how different it was from other places they'd lived. The signposts of cul-tural familiarity, both visual and cultural, were absent. Las Vegas was truly a backyard culture, a place where everyone had a pool not only to keep cool but as a way to choose their friends. Life in Las Vegas was driven not by geography or proximity, but instead by affinity. Your neighbors were not the people who lived next door to you, but the ones you shared activities with, the parents who chatted as they watched their children during karate or gymnastics class or Little League games and practices, or who shared an interest in dancing and belonged to your church, synagogue, or more recently, mosque.

The key to the difference was Las Vegas's transience. Like most Las Vegas newcomers, the Sutherlands expected to find a town with formed institutions. Even children noticed the difference. "My kid says, 'You're only the new kid in school for three weeks here,'" one amused parent noted. Las Vegas had to build continuity even at the most basic level, the schoolyard. Hierarchies changed rapidly. Anyone who had gone to school with the same people from first through twelfth grade found the fluidity disconcerting. If there had ever been a core in Las Vegas life, it had long been overwhelmed by the tidal wave of newcomers. Nowhere was that con-stant tide of new people more evident than in the suburbs that appeared almost like magic on the edges of the city.

The new suburbs have distinctive traits in the postmodern United States. They lack the dynamic core of the mid-twentieth century, the lay-ered and textured structure of space that characterized the United States into the 1970s, but instead spread out and contain row after row, mile after mile of the same restaurants, chain stores, ball fields, churches, and every-thing else that forms the basis of postmodern community. The most decentralized urban areas since industrialization, they revolve around a series of indistinguishable centers, all providing the same commercial enti-ties. These fixtures mirror one of the problems of the future, the way in which private commercial space stands in for public space. Without such private space—stores, coffeeshops, and restaurants—most suburbs would have no social space at all.

Most suburbs, from Metairie, Louisiana, and Overland Park, Kansas, near Kansas City, to Orange County, California, also have older cities nearby, with long traditions of community and identity, ways of defining local reality that graft the new communities onto a limb of the existing regional tree. Such suburban areas are extensions of changes in the cities on whose edge they perch, creations of the perception that demographic change is decline. They hinge on the older cities and their psychic importance, extending older dominion in a new and different way. They exclude, commentators such as Ray Suarez say, on the basis of race, but if he's right, the new suburbs do an outstanding job of using class differences to mask race.

Las Vegas was different. The older city to build off of was there, but it hadn't been around long enough to stabilize the constellation of ideas, attitudes, and practices that define a city. In 1975 Las Vegas lacked the base of older cities, the generations of neighborhoods around factories, the deep traditions of place that shaped American memory. It was a blue-collar company town, beholden to gambling. Its parks and pools were subpar, its main attraction for locals exactly what brought its visitors, the Strip. As a result, Las Vegas's pattern is unlike that of other American cities. Although the old downtown, Fremont Street, is in an eternal slump, the new downtown, the Strip, was built for tourists. More typically, the growth belt rings the older Las Vegas, precipitating its decline. Anchored by Sun City, brimming with well-off retirees, Las Vegas has grafted on its own upper middle class of professionals and managers that 1970s Las Vegas didn't have and, in its own mind, didn't need.

The growth of the suburbs has slaughtered urban neighborhoods in Las Vegas as it has everywhere else. "I call it the 'Bic lighter syndrome,'" one local investor said with disdain. "We use them and throw them away." The blight shows in even the best older neighborhoods. Young families flee to the suburbs to join middle-class newcomers who uniformly land in the endless new housing tracts. It is, as Suarez contends, a reflection of race, especially as the city becomes increasing Latino, but it is simultaneously a function of class. The suburbs draw people of all colors whose values are classed white.

In 2000 the demography of the valley bore out the change. The 2000 census showed that Clark County's population had increased by 85.6 percent since 1990, in no small part attributable to the growth of non-white groups in the valley. Latinos increased 264 percent in the decade, to 302,143, more than 20 percent of the population. African Americans increased 9.1 percent, to 124,885 people. Statistically, African Americans and Asians were distributed throughout the valley. The newness of the city mitigated against historic patterns of discrimination, and a significant portion of African American migrants were retired middle-class workers. Even African American youth were integrated into the city at large. Suburban African American and Asian families were common, integral parts of the new city.

Las Vegas's economy makes suburban living possible for many. The straight equation that money begats class had little meaning in a city based on prosperity for the unskilled. Observers like David Guterson attacked the town for its gated communities, but inside the gates was a different story. In Las Vegas, money and class had little direct relationship. Anyone, valet parking attendant, professional gambler, or even two-income service-industry workers, could have enough money to participate in middle- and even upper-middle-class life. Under duress, a skycap at McCarran Airport copped to making $80,000 a year; fearing I was with the IRS, he likely underreported. Las Vegas has been economic paradise for the blue-collar tradesperson with a brain for more than two decades, and the Mercedes-driving parade of the high-school-educated never ends. Dealers at the Bellagio routinely top $75,000 a year, allowing them to live next door to aspiring corporate managers.

Easy accessibility confused the meaning of status, complicating the exclusivity of neighborhoods. Even high-end houses were not all that expensive: $500,000 in Las Vegas in 2000 still bought a palace; $350,000 an upscale suburban tract home of 3,500 or more square feet with a pool. Nice homes could house dirtballs, people you wouldn't want your kids around. "Just because they have money," insisted one suburban mom, "doesn't mean they've got class." The gates could restrict access but they couldn't keep out the outside world, especially one where two unskilled incomes easily topped $100,000 a year. Money got you inside the gates, a disconcerting scenario for those who sought gated communities to wall off the problems of the outside world. They attained status, not safety, then realized that part of the price of living in Las Vegas was that anyone could attain the elite position they craved.

The suburbs became a meeting ground of newcomers to town and the winners in old Las Vegas. The growth belt drew anyone from the city with aspirations. Those who made enough money left declining neighborhoods in the city for the suburbs. Older areas, built during earlier growth, turned rental. Older people who couldn't or wouldn't move remained and found themselves living next door to bikers and other threatening types. Immigrant families, usually Spanish-speaking, became common in these

neighborhoods, and barred windows and fences with locked gates suggested growing fear. So did the gates around apartment complexes, where safety was clearly the goal if not always the reality. Often immigrant families as
well as older people felt threatened by the less stable elements.

The losses of these neighborhoods became the gains of the suburbs,
where well-off service-industry locals with social aspirations lived alongside
the grafted upper middle class. This proximity was novel, something rarely
found in the 1990s in the United States, and it sometimes disrupted both
groups. Neither was entirely comfortable with the other; not only were
there class and occupational differences, but point of origin was also a
problem. Californians, most numerous among newcomers, were no more
popular in the Silver State than they are in any other place where
California's influence reached. In the early 1990s an average of six thousand people each month traded in driver's licenses at the Nevada
Department of Motor Vehicles office on Sahara Avenue. As many as two-
thirds came from California. "Californicators," some called this multitude
with derision; long-time southern Nevadans observed that if someone did
something stupid while driving, they always had California license plates.
On the rare occasions that such vehicles sported Nevada plates, their
license-plate holder identified the car as having been purchased in
California. The Californian newcomers were different from long-time
Nevadans, and even different from people from the Midwest, the East
Coast, and elsewhere.

Californians are only the point people for change and the animosity
that transformation inspires. Despite the way they are held up as objects of
ridicule, they are pivotal. They bring the values that cause and create
change, the demands for institutions that the old company town never
asked for, as well as a sense of entitlement. They are catalysts for the rapid
transformation that has made Las Vegas a true twenty-first-century frontier town. Las Vegas lacked the formed institutions of industrial America,
and people who arrive expecting such a structure are disappointed. The
people who succeeded saw a need and determined to fill it themselves.
When faced with transience, they made community, literally and figuratively, into a solution.

There are front-yard cultures in Las Vegas, where people know and
embrace their neighbors, have block parties, and exhibit the glue that
bound communities in an older American memory. That world was all

white; these new front-yard cultures are multiracial and multiethnic, bound by more than proximity. These are minicommunities where people share fears and aspirations: fear of decay in the cities they left behind, fear of the streets, of crime, of gangs, of losing their children as a cost of the time it takes to eke out their hard-won middle-class existence. They aspire to safe streets and schools, time with their families, and real human interaction with neighbors who become friends. These the multiracial "white" 'burbs, where people who want what we've unfairly come to think of as "white" suburban living come, no matter what their color, race, or ethnicity.

In my old neighborhood, the combination of aspirations and fears actually worked. Our block had streetside life, people trimming trees and tending flowers, talking to each other, and they knew about each other's lives. Owners occupied most homes, and one couple, Mike and Sandy, with a span of children reaching from teenagers to a toddler, had an ever-open garage door, through which Mike watched the action. "Bailey," he'd shout after their youngest at dinnertime or sunset, "it's time to come in." It seemed like the American neighborhood of myth, with the never-ending football game among the shared backyards and kids called by parents who put a damper on the fun.

One of the primary catalysts in the conviviality of this little enclave was an African American couple from Chicago, Clark and Anne Pero. They and their two children arrived about 1993, fresh from the snow of the Midwest, and rented one of the 2,200-square-foot houses. Although most assume that the smaller houses would be the first to "go rental," a phrase that describes how neighborhoods fall quickly out of fashion, the opposite was true. Retirees often owned the smaller homes; families who might move on, either when they had another child and outgrew the home or when they made enough money to climb the housing ladder, owned the larger ones. The rentals were regarded as a threat to property values, neighborhood culture, and stability, but there was never a better addition to a neighborhood than the Peros. They were typical of newcomers, especially minority ones, ecstatic at the chance at life in the Last Detroit.

Clark worked in the change room at a casino and was a gearhead to boot. He drove a souped-up early-1980s Mustang II and spent a good portion of his free time under the hood. In their garage was the body and chassis of a classic Camaro, waiting for an opportunity to be restored. Every day, Clark left for work, often using his torqued-out engine to zip by me with a wave; in the evening, the garage door was open and he had his tool set out, fixing something on somebody's ride. Anne sat on the porch, and their two children, Clark Jr. and Brittany, played out front. On the weekends, they were out early in the morning and stayed out all day. Always with a smile, always with a wave and a "how you doing," talkative and pleasant, the Peros were the ones who knew everything that went on—who in the neighborhood was thinking about changing jobs or buying a new car or putting in a swimming pool, whose kid went out for football or wrestling or was in dance class or karate, and whose in-laws were coming to visit. It was impossible not to stand and chat, sometimes for an hour or more. More than friendly, they were central. Seamlessly they made neighbors of us all. I started to refer to my block as "the nicest street in the world."

These were people trying to better their situation, all enthused to be in a neighborhood where adults were out front, the kids were well-behaved, and there was a feeling of shared space. All had high school educations or perhaps some college and they'd clawed their way up in the tumultuous society around them. They shared more than anything that divided them. Clark once told me of his neighborhood in Chicago: "It had gone to hell," he said. "Taken over by gangs and punks." He and Anne wanted more for their kids, and ensuring that the streets were supervised, that public space belonged to the neighborhood and not to any faction that might stake a claim to it, was part of that. The sentiment was instinctive rather than spoken, for Clark preferred hanging around home and tossing back an occasional beer with his neighbors to going out to dinner or even to a baseball game. Mike and Sandy were similar. Blue-collar to the core, they'd fled an older Las Vegas that was disintegrating, and in this neighborhood they'd made their stand. Their aspirations and fears coincided with the Peros', and together the two families created a mythic American neighborhood, the kind we're all certain used to be common and are now long gone.

Such a vision of community was simultaneously a reflection of experience and a creation of television. Intimacy, goodwill, and interaction in community, called by some "social capital," may once have been commonplace in the United States. The tales of Nathaniel Hawthorne illustrated its power and even oppression. Sinclair Lewis showed its limits. Sherwood Anderson, Thornton Wilder, and the rest of a generation of writers exalted it. In the 1960s urbanist Jane Jacobs still found its ingredients even in the modern metropolis. The memory of this connectedness shaped American perceptions of what a neighborhood should be.

World War II precipitated the demise of small-town America and changed the fundamental basis of the relationship between people in neighborhoods. Suburbanization played a crucial role, for new communities replaced the glue of internal ties with the lubrication of external linkage. When the southern California suburbs came together after World War II, they were populated by two groups of people: those who left tightly woven and often ethnic urban neighborhoods, and those the war and its aftermath propelled from the equally tightly knit small towns of rural America. The adults who inhabited these new suburbs had grown up in a world of kinship, ethnic loyalty, and neighborhood fraternity. They made these new places as they remembered home. This time the difference was that instead of sharing religion, family, or ethnicity, they shared stage of life, aspiration, and even occupation. The aerospace suburbs of southern California were populated by engineers and their families, people from all over; the nearby slightly less well-off ones were filled with firemen, policemen, and clerks. They made community from the memory of closer ties, foisting upon their children the barbecues and touch football games, block parties, and drive-in movies. "We were blithe conquerors, my tribe," David Beers remembered in *Blue Sky Dream*, his memoir. "When we chose a new homeland, invaded a place, settled it, and made it over in our image, we did so with a smiling sense of our own inevitability."

But those neighborhoods could be oppressive, too, constraining, stultifying, trampling. For the ones who set the standards, who hosted the barbecues, who starred in the pick-up games, who enjoyed the social games—the drunkenness, the flirting and its consequences the increasing rate of divorce and the shattered lives of children—it was a joyous world. For those uncomfortable with closeness bred by proximity, who'd just as soon be left alone, or the children subjected to the taunts of bullies or whose home lives were wrecked by the affairs among parents, proximity seemed too close, a threat to their lives. The experience left an imprint. As adults, they felt reticence about their neighbors, wanting to know them enough to discern who belonged and who didn't, but not so well that you'd leave them a key in case of emergency or that they'd feel like they could stroll over and chat at any time. It was a fine line between unfriendliness and the creation of structure in a community, designed to defend, but not to insist on participation. After all, they were only neighbors and you didn't choose your neighbors like you choose your friends.

This trend would be no more pronounced in Las Vegas than it is in any other place, if not for the transience of the city's inhabitants. When people move into subdivisions en masse—when it appears that they roll out a carpet with the homes on it and say "that one over there, sir, the third on the left, that's yours"—absence of mechanisms to promote even the rudiments of community is accentuated. There's no welcome wagon, no one to greet you, no one to come by and say, "Welcome to what passes for a neighborhood." For some, this lack of such basic institutions was hard to fathom. "It didn't make sense," one housewife said. "Every place else I'd moved into a new subdivision, we'd all become friends. At least we had the builder to bitch about." In Las Vegas, that didn't routinely happen. Few invested in their geographic neighbors. Instead, they created neighborhoods of affinity, communities based on interest, not proximity.

Neighborhoods of affinity are a tricky business. They involve relationships that used to be second-tier—the parents of the other kids on your son's Little League team—but that subsequently achieve primacy. In transient situations, they become the foundation of community. They take on a front-line importance, making up for the dearth of relationships that date back to eighth grade. Such relationships embody communities of interest, not of space, and are accentuated by the reality that parents who let their preteen and young teenagers move about unsupervised court disaster. Because of the "Soccer mom" phenomenon, the prevalence of carpools and chaperoned children's activities, communities of affinity have taken on new roles in neighborhoods across the nation.

For Las Vegas's grafted upper middle class, the skyline itself is a daily reminder of the perils of postmodern life. The town's dominant industry is a threat to parents' aspirations for their children, a morass that can draw their kids in if the parents aren't vigilant. The city sells excess and self-indulgence, both very dangerous for youth. Las Vegas is visibly casual about sexuality. "I don't know how to explain bare butts to my five-year-old," one mother complained about the "no ifs, ands, or butts" billboard picturing five thong-clad backsides that advertised the Riviera's Crazy Girls neoburlesque show. Gambling can be a problem for anyone, but especially the young. With high-interest credit cards to cushion any short-term losses and the self-perception of invincibility of so many, deep debt is a mathematical certainty. Unlike parents in the 1970s, who looked around suburbs and mistakenly perceived little danger for their children, parents today who insist that their children succeed spend much time making sure distractions don't get in the way. In Las Vegas, the distractions are bigger and closer than in most places and more socially acceptable, too, but they're different only in degree, not in kind. In Las Vegas the institutions to which parents elsewhere might turn their kids over—organizations, activities, sports—aren't in place. Parents themselves have to take action to ensure that their kids are safe and occupied. Las Vegas is not Bloomington, Indiana, or Spokane, Washington, and everyone who lives there knows it. The question becomes: What will they do about it?

If you're a couple like Andy and Sandy Fry, you create structure in your child's life. The Frys came to Las Vegas in 1975 when Andy, a former basketball player at a small college, was hired to teach history at UNLV. From Virginia, they drove across the country, crossed the Hoover Dam, passed the old casino at Railroad Pass, came over the hill, and looked down at the Las Vegas Valley. The old Boulder Highway bar district, full of low-rent biker bars, strip joints, junkyards, and liquor stores, gave Sandy her first view of her new home. She burst into tears, a common response for educated middle-class women. The view wasn't their image of what they wanted, but it was their new life. Their son, Bryan, was an infant when they arrived, and the Frys settled in to watch and shape the transformation of their adopted home. Sandy stayed home until Bryan was ready for school. Once he reached first grade, she returned to teaching and became the most popular first-grade teacher in the city. Everyone wanted their children to be in Mrs. Fry's class.

The years Sandy stayed home with Bryan were critical. The Frys sacrificed; even successful university professors are only on the margins of the upper middle class, and one income did not stretch terribly far. But the key was attention to a kid's needs in the shadow of the Strip, growing taller, wider, longer throughout the 1980s and 1990s. Bryan showed a talent for music, so Sandy took him to music lessons in their one car, and Andy bicycled to the university. By the time Bryan reached high school, he was an outstanding student as well as a standout musician, a member of the school band and ultimately valedictorian of his high school class. All three Frys were casual about Bryan's success, but all who knew them knew that besides good fortune and good genetics, parental involvement and vigilance played a pivotal role.

That vigilance is important in transient communities and especially in neighborhoods of affinity. Through the 1970s, kids controlled their interactions; they rode their bikes, walked to parks, and visited their friends on their own. Nowadays, until a teenager receives a driver's license, parents play a significant role: they drive often and everywhere, and in doing so they manage, shape, and sometimes even control their kids' relationships.

But there's still the absence of institutions, the lack of formal structure, to overcome. Without community structure, neighborhoods of affinity are simply random meetings, chaotic events that happen independently. One newcomer said to me, "People here always want to know how long you've been here. They're new too, so they can't know any more people than we do." I opined, "They check you out by how long you've been. If you've only been here a short while, you might not be in deep enough to stay. So they don't invest. Once you've been here awhile, they'll feel more comfortable. They're as afraid of loss as you are." Building community from nothingness is always tenuous.

Everybody hates home owners associations. Mike Davis calls them "microscopically parochial interests" in his renowned story of Los Angeles, *City of Quartz*. In *Privatopia: Homeowner Associations and the Rise of Private Residential Government*, political scientist Evan Mackenzie describes the associations as tools of developers wielded against the very home owners they're supposed to serve, and even my students groaned at their mention. In an individualist society, home owners' associations—or more correctly common interest developments—are oppressive, parochial, tyrannical, and downright mean. Everyone, or at least anyone who was ever late with an association dues check, has their horror story. They built a back porch that wasn't even visible from the street and spent a year wrangling with the self-important people on the architectural committee, a missed payment racked up thousands of dollars in fines and fees, or the management firm lost their check and it took two years to straighten out the mess. Nobody except developers and the tight-lipped creeps who run for board seats and want to snoop in your backyard likes them. Nobody, not even members of the boards themselves, trust them.

But home owners associations play a significant role, one that makes them palatable to the busiest among us, who are willing to put their civic rights in blind trust and to accept property values as the pinnacle of American civilization. Especially in transient places without firm institutions, or where larger, community-wide institutions are in decline—which is to say everywhere—home owners associations stand in lieu of the social fabric of the mythic America. With confidence in state and national government at an all-time low and local government regarded as the province of special interests, the HOA becomes simultaneously a hedge against the decline of the centralized state, the closest thing to the grassroots democracy Tocqueville envisioned and a way to ensure the conformity of image that is at the heart of stability in a liberal consumerist society. In an age when people operate under the premise that government works for someone else, when they work twelve-hour days and only nod to their neighbors, home owners associations provide the vast majority with a security blanket. They yield smaller lots and yards and have lots of restrictions, but they keep purple houses and old cars off the block. Done properly, they seem to function in place of community relationships, in place of the shame of being the worst house or yard on the block, in place of sharing life with your neighbors.

Romantic critics like James Howard Kunstler will squawk at this. The political will charge racism or more astutely classism, and libertarians will decry the loss of individual freedoms, but home owners associations are part of a pattern. Americans are more willing to cede some of their freedoms for guarantees of safety and stability, especially if they can send a check and not be bothered with the details.

But HOAs are not voluntary organizations, not something people choose to belong to, like a church or the Girl Scouts. In the new suburbs, HOAs are not a choice, and they come with the baggage of other forced obligations. Most who buy homes in associations do so without understanding that they have responsibilities beyond their check for dues. On the surface, an HOA does not require much. A home owner has to pay on time, abide by the codes, covenants, and restrictions, and attend a meeting once a year, but most have no sense of belonging to the association. Many associations can't get a quorum on the first try. People routinely send proxies back that give the board their vote, giving up rights of considerable social and even economic value without a second thought. No one attends HOA meetings, *Los Angeles Times* reporter Tom Gorman observed, reading their absence as a lack of civic feeling and an indicator that people don't feel they belong. The only time they do, managers say, is when there's a major issue, a 100 percent increase in dues or someone has painted their house in polka-dots.

Despite their cheery newsletters that exhort people to better neighborliness, HOAs don't function like membership-driven trade organizations, nor are they like a subscription to a magazine. "It's a fiduciary relationship," explained Deborah Jones of Terrawest, which started in 1980 and by 1999 specialized in upscale suburban HOAs. "That's why it seems bureaucratic and cold." HOAs seem ominous, closer to a cross between the Guardian Angels, a pseudo—citizen patrol, and a hired security force to police social interaction. Like baseball umpires, the tasks HOA boards perform are mundane and invisible until a crucial moment with enormous implications. Mostly, you pay a fee and they maintain regularity in the neighborhood. Only when there's trouble does the HOA step forward in its overlapping and confusing roles to defend the integrity of the community. This is when the trouble starts.

"Governance works at any level because of participation," said Barbara Holland of H&L Realty, which manages more home owners associations than any agency in Las Vegas. "People don't vote in national elections; why should voting for a board of directors be any different?" But there's a disconnect. People who live in a neighborhood don't see running it as governance. Until the 1970s social rules governed such functions and most of the correction that followed happened informally. With the breakdown of conventional community, HOAs became more prominent precisely to fill the gap between social and official. It is deeply twisted terrain.

By default, HOAs assume an undefined role that can't help but inspire resentment. People who juggle two worklives, dance classes, Little League, Sunday school, and half a dozen other activities happily assign the responsibility for the world around them to hired guns. They can't do everything even though they try, and in neighborhoods of affinity, where proximity and sociability are often unrelated and most life goes on in walled-in backyards, the temptation to hire a semiprivate pseudo—police force to protect the value of your single largest investment is vast. In more than one strictly middle-class subdivision in Las Vegas, the HOA fee paid for maintenance of front yards. Close enough to feel insecure about the potential of their streets to fall from "desirable" to the dreaded "transitional," neighborhoods embraced an ethic of enforced order. They paid, and every lawn was eternally and uniformly green and manicured.

At the same time, "when it comes to people's homes, their emotions are so involved," observed Vicki Parris of Terrawest. "People who run multimillion-dollar corporations get on the board of directors and have heart failure over something like painting the curb red." Even telling them that by agreeing not to do whatever it is they want, they're helping prevent someone else from doing the same thing where they don't want it doesn't help. "You don't even want to go there with them," laughed Deborah Jones.

The consequences of pretending that people will maintain their property without coercion lets many look past the oppressive traits of HOAs. The look of neighborhoods without associations is usually less consistent, more erratic, and more worn. "Nice house, nice house, nice house, trashed yard, ten cars in front, broken windows, nice house, nice house," observed Barbara Holland. Buyers seek placidity, and if property values are all you care about, then an HOA is fine. One bad house on a block ruins not only its own value, but that of all the homes around it. No wonder that even people who aren't crazy about such organizations accept them. Home owners associations "maintain community," said one well-educated Las Vegan, fully aware of the inherent contradiction. "You can complain about your neighbor's dog without confronting your neighbor. Where I grew up [in Chicago], the alderman used to do that, but here they don't do anything."

In a strange way, the exchange smacked of an earlier America, one in which Paul Revere might be comfortable. Revere and his eighteenth-century contemporaries understood individual freedom as something located within the community's standards. They were free to do as they pleased, they thought, within the parameters that the community established for behavior. The reach to the home owners association as a tacit reflection of community standards, albeit, a cynic might say, of one lazy and dissolute community, was not terribly hard to make. The community stood in for the individual and the individual agreed to abide by the rules—as long as they were primarily applied to other people.

But everyone still hates their HOA and the rules it makes. They want to restrict others and not themselves, one more piece of evidence of a self-indulgent, self-centered world where people have abandoned any conception of mutually agreed-upon coercion. They might endure the restrictions, but they sure don't like them and they take out their frustration in many ways. Board members are specific and identifiable targets, for they must make "painful decisions," as Jones said. They can be sued and generally carry board insurance. "Who wants to be attacked personally?" Barbara Holland wondered, recounting tales of slashed tires and late-night phone calls. Board members are "living with their constituency right next door," she continued, "and they see them on the street every day." Their kids play with the kids of people they have to sanction. No wonder it's hard to find people willing to serve on boards.

Yet HOAs have coalesced in Las Vegas, and the institution is maturing. "We're taking baby steps," Jones said, "but we're taking them fast." The explosion of construction since the 1980s, the gargantuan size of projects, and the absence of other community institutions have made the HOA a springboard for local and even state politics. Like many other time-dependent activities, this formula favors Las Vegas's enormous retiree population at the expense of the rest of the community, but if people can lead in the fractious world of HOA boards, maybe they are good candidates for higher office.

The issue is larger than Las Vegas, but it has manifested itself in the new suburbs there. For all its flaws, the HOA has become the official representative of community, and neither Las Vegans nor Americans in general are entirely comfortable with the fact. Community can not be legislated any more than it can be designed, but the structure of new neighborhoods and the patterns of life mitigate against social resolution of conflict. As a result, almost every new home in Las Vegas's future will be part of an HOA. Henderson mandated that developers create HOAs as a condition of construction in 1998. The result has often been bland but oppressive authority at the grassroots, board members who inflict their personal biases and objectives on their neighbors, who are understandably resentful. Tocqueville's democracy? Closer to the world of Neal Stephenson's *Diamond Age*, in which miscreants are punished by authorities who monitor their every behavior and tattoo "poor impulse control" on the foreheads of those who can't control themselves. Postmodern community based on proximity has its own pitfalls.

The week before the NFL season starts, the *Las Vegas Review-Journal* prints a supplement that no other city in the nation offers. This special section lists NFL teams and the bars that cater to them. The newspaper sets criteria: the bar must show every single one of a team's games and must offer food and drink specials and giveaways of team merchandise during the games. Most years, each team, from the high and mighty Green Bay Packers, the regional Denver Broncos, Arizona Cardinals, Oakland Raiders, and San Francisco '49ers, and even the lowly Cincinnati Bengals, has a bar where it is the home team. The bar purchases the NFL satellite television package and picks its team, using the affinity people have for teams in other places to fill the house on Sunday mornings. It's a good deal for everyone; the bar offers free food and cheap drinks to go with the game. Its slot machines and video poker machines hum with activity instead of the strange quiet of off-season Sunday mornings. If the bar does really well, the fans come back at other times with different friends, and out of such strange loyalties—a Cincinnati Bengals bar in Las Vegas?—sometimes a clientele can grow and a business prosper.

These bars serve as community centers of a sort, gathering points for lost transients, people who identify strongly with where they come from, and just plain fans. In Las Vegas, you can root for the Carolina Panthers and find people who share your peculiar affliction and maybe even your hometown in the Carolinas or Tennessee. Not only stragglers and lost souls, newcomers and recent transfers feel this pull. So do all kinds of people. It's another of the ways to build community, to find not only common interests but sometimes common roots among people searching to belong in a new and still strange place. But a bar as a setting for community has its problems. Clientele varies, the atmosphere doesn't quite work, and sometimes places that are rough on Saturday night can't plane off those edges by kickoff time on Sunday morning.

From the farm town of Frankfurt, Kansas, Randy Beeman cut a big swath when he arrived in Las Vegas. Over six feet tall and more than 240 pounds, with a wad of chaw in his cheek and a big, big personality, Randy was a Kansas boy of a particular kind. He was rowdy and fun, loud and obnoxious, but in a good way, and was always at the center of some mischief or entertainment. We called him Big Country, after Bryant Reeves, the seven-foot crewcut basketball center, and they were two peas from the same pod. The nickname was both an acknowledgment of who Randy was and a tacit put-down, a reminder that this was a town where country boys with big heads could easily lose them. Randy didn't suffer fools gladly, although he sometimes resembled them. He bragged that he'd been shot in the leg during a fracas in a Topeka, barroom. His friends chided that if he'd been a little lighter on his feet and a little sharper, he might have gotten out of the way before he got hit.

Like nearly everybody from the southern plains, Randy was a Kansas City Chiefs fan, and in 1995, when Joe Montana still quarterbacked them and Marcus Allen had just showed up to run the ball, a Super Bowl looked possible. The Chiefs were a powerhouse, and everyone picked them as a winner. In Las Vegas, they had no bigger fan than Randy, so when the paper came out with the list of bars, I passed it on, knowing that a taste of home and the feelings of kinship that a group of Chiefs fans might inspire would help his adjustment to the postindustrial capital.

Las Vegas loves a winner, and in 1995 the Chiefs fit the bill. There are more fair-weather fans per square inch in the desert city than anywhere in the world, and when the Chiefs were winning, they had a flock of new fans. The first Sunday of the football season, Randy plopped his two boys, Augie, who was four, and Everett, three, into the car and went off to watch the Chiefs at the bar listed in the paper. Wearing his bright red Chiefs sweatshirt, he was looking for home away from home. Even the boys were decked out in official NFL gear. "I wanted the boys to feel their roots," he said afterward. "I wanted them to be around Chiefs fans, our kind of people." When they arrived at the bar, Randy was a little put off. It was a nondescript rag-tag place on a concrete parking lot among the sagebrush out by the interstate, decrepit and run-down and just a little dangerous. Appearances could be deceiving, though, so in went the Beemans to cheer on their club.

Randy ordered a Bloody Mary for himself, cokes for the boys, and settled in. He looked around; the clientele looked rough, but he'd seen worse. After all, he'd been shot in a bar fight. The game began, with the Chiefs running the kickoff back past the thirty yard line. Everyone cheered loudly, and Randy smiled and slapped hands with couple of fans. He smiled his Big Country grin, as high-wattage as the neon lights themselves. Here was community, here was commonality, and the Chiefs looked like a winner. Las Vegas could be like home. It was nice to find the culture of the plains, where everyone knew everyone else and they all cared about the same things, especially in this city so different.

By the second quarter, almost 10 A.M. local time, the mood was changing. Folks were getting a little loopy; the beer was flowing, the cigarette smoke thickening, and the place seemed downright rowdy. The Chiefs turned the ball over not once but twice, and fell behind by a touchdown, then two. Two fellows by the bar were upset; they cursed louder and louder, using words that even worldly Randy had never put together. Randy wanted out. He didn't want his boys to see this, to hear this. It wasn't right. These weren't real Chiefs fans! They couldn't be. They didn't seem to respect the team, or worse, the game.

Turns out Randy was right. It was the Chiefs bar, but the primary attraction was the point spread. Most of the people were bettors, not fans. When the Chiefs fell behind, they made bettors nervous. The Chiefs were giving ten points, and an eleven-point deficit meant that the team needed three touchdowns to get the bettors off the hook with a push—Las Vegas—speak for a tie—but only two to win the game. The result was the loud cursing and the despondent looks even as the Chiefs rallied. When they finally won the game, only Randy and the boys were jumping up and down and waving their arms. The Chiefs hadn't covered the spread, and glum despondence settled over the bar. Some were out peanuts, others hundreds. As Randy hooped and hollered, the rougher looking guys turned a jaundiced eye toward him; what was he so happy about? The goddamn Chiefs hadn't covered—again. Big and strapping, Randy always loved a fight and it looked like one was brewing between him and a couple of drunks over cheering a win for his team in its own bar. Hacked off, Randy was ready to start swinging until he remembered his boys were there. This wasn't what he wanted to teach them. They hit the road, never to return. Afterwards, he watched the Chiefs at home. So much for team loyalty in a transient town. So much for community forged in other places and translated to the postindustrial city.

On Nevada Day, October 31, 1994, a state holiday, five couples and one member of a sixth met for breakfast at the Country Inn on Sunset Road in Green Valley. Brought there by Mark Goldstein, a prominent attorney, and his wife, Gail Alcalay, they discussed founding a synagogue of their own in the southeastern valley. The group included a developer, the owner of an airplane sales company, an assistant superintendent of the Clark County School District, and of course, me. Most of the women were stay-at-home moms, volunteers in local causes. All belonged to another older synagogue at the time; for various reasons, each was dissatisfied. Led by Goldstein, they envisioned something new.

Despite popular mythology and the movie *Casino*, postwar Las Vegas was really a Jewish mob town. Meyer Lansky led the parade, and it was his organization that held sway. Bugsy Siegel, Gus Greenbaum, Davie Berman, Belden Katleman, Morris Rosen, and others took the opportunity Nevada offered to ply their lives' work and to go straight in the process. It appealed to them in a way it seems not to have to other ethnic groups; it was as if at heart even the worst of them, the vicious Siegel, the drug-addicted Greenbaum, wanted to be good Jewish boys, successful and respectable, but gambling and its sidelines made money and was really all they knew how to do. No one seized this opportunity more than Morris B. "Moe" Dalitz, the one-time Cleveland bootlegger who became widely known as Mr. Las Vegas, a leading philanthropist, an emblem of the city, and its de facto goodwill ambassador. Dalitz, Sally Denton and Roger Morris suggest, intuited the symbiotic relationship between the aboveground economy and its subterranean counterpart and made it pay not only in dollars, but in a long and happy life.

This reach for normal status led to the creation of synagogues, for American Jews have always practiced their ethnicity through their faith. The first and largest was Temple Beth Sholom, a Conservative synagogue with a campus in east Las Vegas that was completed in 1958, near where the wealthy and the middle classes lived until the great suburban explosion. Even after a group split off to found Ner Tamid, a Reform congregation, in the early 1970s, TBS claimed nine hundred family memberships, huge for a community of Las Vegas's size. TBS was the primary Jewish institution in Las Vegas from its founding into the 1980s.

Temple Beth Sholom always had a few idiosyncracies. Its early presidents were often from the gaming industry and a few were if not notorious at least infamous. One president, Jack Entratter, the six-foot, six-inch former headwaiter who became the front man at the Sands, built the spacious social hall. Mel Exber, a cocky kid from Brooklyn who became co-owner of the Las Vegas Club, also became president of the congregation. Other donors were even more suspect.

Of all these men, Dalitz especially embraced the chance to leave his nefarious roots behind. In the mid-1950s, he coordinated the United Jewish Appeal efforts in Las Vegas, succeeding Jake Kozloff, Ed Levinson, Gus Greenbaum, and Sam Tucker, all of whom were tied to illegal gaming. Dalitz served as mayor of Paradise, the municipality that existed to prevent the city of Las Vegas from annexing the Strip. Dalitz's imprint was on every important philanthropic event in the city. By the end of his life in 1980s, Dalitz had become one of the most beloved people in town. The school building on the Ner Tamid campus was built with his donation and is named for him.

The grease for the wheels of this system was cash, usually from the casinos. Until the early 1980s, casino cash was loosely regulated, and executives' pockets bulged with dollars. They were the biggest givers in the city and could be counted on for donations to all kinds of causes. "When I was in charge of the Western High School homecoming [in about 1975], I needed cash," Emil Stein, now a Las Vegas opthomologist, remembered. "I went to see Benny Binion and he reached into his desk and gave me a wad of cash." This generosity also helped the synagogues. Like most religious institutions in the United States, the congregations ran annual deficits. Until the corporate era, the "angels"—the well-heeled people who made sure the synagogue was solvent at the end of the year—came from the casinos. At Temple Beth Sholom, a culture of reliance on this sort of gift resulted from the peculiar structure of the community.

The Jews who came to Las Vegas after World War II were largely blue-collar and closely tied to gaming. There were a few exceptions, such as Dr. Reuben Zucker, a physician, and Louis Weiner, Bugsy Siegel's lawyer, but most migrants were largely uneducated, from the streets, and excited about to be legal doing what they enjoyed most. Al "Gig" Levin, a bellman at the Sands, was typical. He and his wife came from Chicago in the late 1940s because he liked to gamble and recognized an opportunity. Las Vegas had Jewish cab drivers, waiters, and twenty-one dealers as well.

They mixed with an ordinary western small-town Jewish community that preceded the explosion of gaming, tailors, storekeepers, and the like. Since the railroad land auction in 1905, Jews had lived in Las Vegas, but only in 1932 did the community grow large enough to formally organize as the Sons and Daughters of Israel. For the next fifteen years, the group met at the Elks' Lodge and the Odd Fellows Hall, again characteristic of small Jewish communities with powerful ties to faith and culture but no real economic position. After the war, the Jewish mobsters brought their cronies, many who felt at least a nominal need to affiliate—if only when their mothers came to visit. In 1946 they dedicated a Jewish Community Center at Thirteenth Street and Carson, showing signs of permanence. This community struggled, as did many smaller western communities, but when the newcomers came and waved their money around, it was easy to see a future. By the time they built a synagogue, being Jewish was an asset in Las Vegas. It seemed that everyone of importance was Jewish. The mobsters made it easy to belong; they were wealthy and a little dangerous, but not stuck-up. The dues for the synagogue were not high, and the presidents could produce cash at will for classrooms and projects. The annual revenue shortfalls for the synagogue never caused much concern; one wave of the hand from Jack Entratter or Mel Exber and the shortfalls were gone.

But this bred a version of Jewish culture specific to Las Vegas. Here too the Jews were city-builders, but there was a twist, a deviance built into it. "I call it a Jewish con man culture," one long-time resident said. "Where I grew up, at the end of the year the three angels looked at each, decided whose turn it was, and that guy ponied up his check for the balance." As long as the cash came from the casinos, no reason existed to push the members of the congregation—by the mid-1970s that included doctors, lawyers, developers, and the array of professionals that have become the Jewish community in the popular mind—to support their synagogue in more than a nominal way. When controls came in on casino money, when corporations rather than individuals owned the casinos, the river of cash that made life easy dried up.

For the younger grafted-on professionals who came after 1980, this was an unacceptable situation. Not only was the old culture just a little shady, but the synagogue was aging and its members seemed uninterested in the problems of raising young children. Added to the growing cultural rift was a geographic problem: the synagogue was located far from the city's suburban enclaves, where many local Jews had settled. Even more, city-wide institutions seemed irrelevant. After a period of negotiation, the eleven who met on Halloween decided to start their own synagogue. They named it Midbar Kodesh—"Holy Desert."

They began slowly, holding Friday night services first once a month, then twice a month, in a nearby middle school. As many as a hundred people came, surprising the founders. They anticipated demand, but this many people meant new responsibilities. Within a few months, the founders pledged some money and rented a storefront on Eastern Avenue, just across from the runways at McCarran Airport and down the street from a saloon called Finnegan's. They joked among themselves that after services they could walk over for a beer. They converted the space into a synagogue; like small congregations of all faiths, everyone from the more than thirty-five families that now comprised the group pitched in, painting the walls, building a few partitions to make classrooms, and cleaning the place so that it felt like a religious building instead of the office and warehouse it really was. Every synagogue has an eternal light; the one this new congregation found happened to be red. The smart alecks in the congregation thought this was more than appropriate, given their location. Services began that spring, and in 1995 a Hebrew School and a preschool opened at the makeshift temple.

From there, the growth took off. The number of members grew, first to fifty family units, then a hundred, then nearly two hundred, in the space of three years. By the fall of 1998 High Holiday services drew almost six hundred people, filling the Henderson Convention Center. The founders looked at each other in amazement. "I had to pinch myself to believe it was real," said Goldstein. New members showed up weekly, in search of prayer, fellowship, and education for their children.

The congregation drew from distinctly different constituencies, much as suburban neighborhoods did. Some were locals who migrated to the suburbs. Others were newcomers for whom the synagogue was the only Jewish institution in Las Vegas they'd ever heard of. The cantor, Robert Fisher, recognized how important it was to erase the line between longtime local and newest arrival. Fisher often intoned that "the future leaders of this congregation don't even know they'll live in Las Vegas yet." It was a telling remark that described how community could be made, by blending the assumptions of different groups with shared goals. By early 1999 the remarkable had happened: the eleven people who had started a synagogue just four years before and the many who had joined the congregation had raised enough money to break ground on the first Jewish building ever constructed in Henderson.

The microphone crackled on a sunny January day in 1999, and the chief executive officer of American Nevada, Brad Nelson, stepped to the podium at the Midbar Kodesh Temple groundbreaking. Nelson knew a lot about what makes community. "It's the people," he said in what could have been interpreted as corporate public relations. "It's the people who make neighborhoods, not the builders, not the houses or the streets." Nelson captured the spirit of the best side of the postmodern city. When people wanted something and were willing to put in the effort, there appeared to be no barriers to stop them anywhere in the Las Vegas Valley. What this transient community needed was more people like the ones who found synagogues and hockey leagues, more people who think of more than their own personal needs, who practice activities of enlightened self-interest, who see hope in a new city rather than fear, and who push their collective weight upon it. Opportunity drew people to the new Las Vegas. When they succeeded, their efforts made it more than row after row of houses separated by concrete-block walls and unconnected by human endeavor.

When I got over the shock of the shooting at Columbine High School, the first question that came to mind was why Littleton, Colorado, and not Las Vegas? Las Vegas, not suburban Colorado, was everyone's idea of anomie, of alienation, transience, and lack of community—precisely the traits that most said caused the tragic and senseless rampage. Busy parents and weak institutions, both Las Vegas traits, took their share of the blame too, as did popular culture run amok, again something that popular perception attributes to Las Vegas. So even though Littleton was an aberration, by conventional measure, Las Vegas seemed ripe for such a tragedy, a backdrop to paint this horrible psychosis upon. The only group of people I knew who could explain why it didn't happened were recent graduates of Las Vegas high schools, the people who make up my classes at UNLV. I rounded up a group of them and started listening.

In those sad days in the aftermath of the shooting, when a national cry of pain and finger-pointing were inextricably intertwined, high school cliquishness and the power relationships it spawned came to the fore as a causative factor. Youth are cruel to each other; they create canyons of distance out of slivers of difference. But we all knew that. Isn't that why so many of us hated high school and even if given our youth back would never go through it again? Las Vegas high school graduates noted the same problems everyone felt, but with a twist that I at first thought small. The power of cliques in their schools, they assured me, was muted by the sheer transience of their institutions. Turnover was remarkable. One teacher told me that 30 percent of her kids at the start of the year aren't there at the end; in the inner city, Steve Boston of Roy Martin Middle School averred, the turnover rate can top 70 percent. So for Las Vegas kids, the firm fixed position that made high school a torture didn't hold. In or out, it was hard to tell, and whatever you were, with five new students a day, it didn't last for long. Despite the mythic structure of high schools that has existed since the 1970s—jocks or socials, kickers or cowboys, freaks and their variants, from hippies to Goths, and always, those who simply don't count—no group had the upper hand long enough to inflict consistent misery. The oppressiveness that sent the Colorado kids over the edge certainly existed, but in comparatively small ways. No one group had enough control to terrorize others, at least the way these winners—after all, my students were in college—remembered it.

It was funny to hear the transience so often called the cause of social dislocation regarded as a mitigating factor in preventing violence, but once they explained that hard-edged social boundaries were soft because of it, I understood. Fluidity characterizes everything about Las Vegas, especially its schools. That fluidity does a lot of dislocating things, landing Nevada among the worst in high school drop-outs, teenage pregnancy, and other pathologies, but it also tamps down friction. It gives people an out, an escape, a way to invest elsewhere in a heartbeat. When new people show up every day who are immune to the past, when school is only one dimension of even a teenager's life, when teenagers don't socialize in the narrow networks of a Littleton, but instead live in a larger social setting, the slights of the teenage day, the reach for power, the hierarchical pecking means far less. It's less central, less definitive, and consequently less defining and less likely, at least for now, to engender a violent response.

A sense of hope pervades especially blue-collar and immigrant Las

Vegas, the students noted, further mitigating the impact of transience. All of the people who come to the desert, from casino-industry workers to maids who clean private homes, expect to do better than they did wherever they came from, and many of them do. Possibility infects their cultural doings with a subtle optimism, a sense of success impossible elsewhere with their skills. Many new Las Vegans were rescued from the scrapheap of economic demise, and their lives, while not necessarily everything they'd anticipated, were noticeably better than before. This optimism was transmitted, even in the worst situations, to their kids, who sensed possibilities that extended beyond the moment. "Kids elsewhere would love to have the opportunities that I do," Dineen Barkhuff mused in the clearest explanation of Las Vegas's promise to today's young, "and they just don't." Kids in Las Vegas weren't as immersed in the insularity of high school.

But a lot of this was rationalization, pondering at a time when everyone was asking questions of themselves and their world, counting themselves fortunate for not being in the wrong place at the wrong time. Maybe Las Vegas had just been lucky; maybe the transience that led to opening two new high schools a year was a precursor rather than an inoculation from the random psychotic violence of Columbine and its peers. There was no shortage of arrests for weapons possession in Las Vegas high schools and middle schools, nor were high-school-age kids in Las Vegas any different from anywhere else. Maybe it was simple urbanity that protected Las Vegas in 1999; realistically, Littleton shared more with Pearl City, Mississippi, or Jonesboro, Arkansas, than it did with Las Vegas. Maybe Las Vegas simply hadn't reached the point of Littleton. Maybe as the fluidity solidified, as Las Vegas's growth tapered off, as it would sooner or later, as the relationships ceased to shift like desert sands, the hard firm culture of American high schools would take hold. Maybe what had protected Las Vegas in 1999 depended on the chaos of the moment. When that chaos was resolved, the chances of a similar incident might grow.

With the synagogue nearing completion, I felt an absence. I needed that start-up feeling, the impossible endeavor, that charge against all odds, a push for something of value to more than my family. At a school meeting, a guy handed me a flyer. "Forming: New Little League," it read. The idea piqued my interest and I went to the meeting. Little League of America wanted to form a new league in my neighborhood. The nearest one had more than fourteen hundred kids and nowhere near enough fields. I listened, and before I knew it I was on the sponsorship committee. I sat out in the parking lot with one of the guys until 11:30 P.M., drinking a few beers, and when I got home I announced to my half-asleep wife that I'd found my tribe.

Within a year Paseo Verde Little League was being hailed as a model. The group of twenty or so at the core had started an organization, made it pay its own way, come up with a loose set of rules, enrolled more than five hundred kids, and kept conflicts to a minimum. It exhausted the group, but when we cleaned up after the Opening Day ceremonies as the second season started in 2001, the pride was palpable. Neighborhood organizations built on a commonality of interest could work; even in the twenty-first century, people could band together for civic purposes and produce something of value that not only worked but might endure. Watching kids play games and parents chat as I carried bag after bag of ice to coolers that held soft drinks, I could not help but think that the basis of a better-managed world was within reach.

Las Vegas is one start-up after another, a city being built from the ground up at the same time as its boundaries of style, scale, and space are being reinvented. The people who work on start-ups, no matter what they initiate, are somehow of a piece. They share traits and ideas, a way of looking at the world. They're the ones who are most at home in the new Las Vegas, for the vacuum it long has been is perfect for their needs. They understand that they won't always succeed, that the odds of overcoming transience are enormous, and that every institution they build is fragile. But there's a enthusiasm, a sincere if maybe misguided belief that the work we do today will matter tomorrow. After one Little League meeting, I said to one of the guys, "You know, four years from now, we'll start something else up and it'll be the same bunch of us." He nodded assent. I continued, "And you know what'll be different?" He shook his head no. "We'll all be four years older!" We hopped in our vehicles and drove away with smiles born of a kinship that transcended education, religion, place of origin, or any other marker. We were builders, people who started institutions that would last for our children—and if we're lucky, for our grandchildren. It really does come down to people.

Epilogue

THE WEEK PARIS LAS VEGAS OPENED IN FALL 1999, MY WIFE AND I ventured into the Eiffel Tower restaurant. On the eleventh floor, the restaurant was elegant and even exclusive, entered only with a reservation. A bouncer at the elevator doors on the first floor checked against the reservations list. The elevator lifted us, its doors opened, and a stylish bar lay in front of us, the introduction to a well-appointed room.

We sat as the sun went down and the lights of the Strip came up. From our vantage in the only-days-old Paris, the newest Las Vegas, the epitome of postindustrial chic, unfolded. The Bellagio was directly across the street, its choreographed fountains shooting jets of water into the sky to the sounds of opera amid colored lights reflecting the water as if it were a dance. At Caesars to the north, the new tower reflected the lights of the Strip, solidifying the leading casino brand. To the south stood the Monte Carlo, a $300 million spillover casino-hotel, and New York, New York, middle-class iconography painted on the most American of canvases. In the distance, the golden glow thrown by the thirty-eight-story tower of Mandalay Bay completed the futurescape of postmodern entertainment and service.

Eerie and exhilarating, the view from the Eiffel Tower didn't exist a

decade before. I couldn't see anything that had been on the Strip in 1990. None of the past was there; no Sands nor Dunes, two mainstays of the old Strip; no low-cut motel or beach-club casinos on the Strip of the 1950s or 1960s; and especially no wise guys. Instead the walkways were crammed with tourists, mom and pop from everywhere with kids who sought to make the new Las Vegas their own. Here was the new atop the old, Las Vegas's peculiar trick, maintaining illusion with each new facade. This Las Vegas was worth billions. It had all the right signs, symbols, and brands and could endlessly titillate. The script was perfect if you like that sort of thing. My view was also late Roman, the self-adorned. In a decade, Las Vegas distilled what the public wanted, even begged for, as always, as long as the public was willing to pay.

When McCarran Airport expanded in 1963 to offer the city a market beyond California drivers, not everyone embraced the idea. Some of the Strip hotels feared that the new Paradise Road exit, which carried traffic about one mile east of their properties, might encourage visitors to forego the Strip for downtown Las Vegas, where the trains still brought visitors to spill out into the night. Bypassing the Strip, they were certain, would kill it, leave it "dark" and forlorn, a relic of an idea in the desert, becoming more desiccated by the moment. Even after the Rat Pack made the Strip home, after Frank and Sammy brought attention none of the legion of skilled publicity men and women who labored for Las Vegas could buy, the owners were afraid that the attractions they'd worked so hard to build were simply not enough, too flimsy to withstand the diversion of traffic to a nearby street. They didn't realize what they'd accomplished, how permanent even their first attempts to create pleasure space were, how successful their translation of vice into recreation had already become.

The new Las Vegas has no such fear. Glen Schaeffer, Steve Wynn, Kirk Kerkorian, Sheldon Adelson, Paul Pusateri, the late Arthur Goldberg, and the others who built the new face of Las Vegas willingly sink billions into the Strip even though casino gambling is legal in thirty-seven states, even after California passed Proposition 1A in 1998, which permitted Native Americans to operate Las Vegas–style casinos in the state, even though forty-eight states offer a lottery. They take for granted something their predecessors could not bring themselves to believe. They've made Las Vegas into entertainment, brought it to a place where it stands on its own, where the sum of the city's parts is, if possible, greater than the whole. In 1963 Las Vegas was a town run by gamblers and hoods. In 2000 it had become a town

devoted to entertaining and funded by Wall Street, providing everyone with any experience they want.

If it sounds like Disneyland, it is. To call Las Vegas "Disneyland for adults," is trite; to regard it as someplace that provides adults with the feelings we expect children to have at Disneyland makes more sense. Las Vegas encourages you to become selfish and petulant. You can stomp your figurative feet to get attention, and if you pay, you get what you want all day and all night. Here is Las Vegas's genius: in a self-indulgent, self-centered society. what could be better than attention for a fee—that didn't feel like you were paying for it.

Las Vegas has become the rhythm of America. The day after Martin Luther King Jr. Day in 2001, I sat with photographer Virgil Hancock in the bar at Red Square in Mandalay Bay. "Las Vegas looks like its going through a little downturn," he observed as he looked around the half-empty bar. His timing was off; he hit the one day of shoulder season, a Tuesday, after New Year's, the Consumer Electronics Show, the King Day three-day weekend, and before the madness of the Super Bowl. With 36 million visitors annually, the shoulder season is short. Las Vegas mirrors the pace of American life, combining holidays, rituals, and ceremonials. King Day, Super Bowl, Chinese New Year, Presidents' Day weekend, the NCAA Tournament and especially the Final Four, Memorial Day, the NBA Finals, Fourth of July, Labor Day, the NFL season, the World Series, Halloween, Thanksgiving, Christmas, and New Year's Eve: anybody's holiday or event will do. Every night can be New Year's Eve if you want it to be and instead of seeing it as decadence as Americans once perceived such behavior, the never-ending party is what American culture espouses in the age of the self.

Entertainment and the self have become two of the important pillars of the age of Nobrow world culture. In a time when nearly everyone wants to be a consumer, when entertainment is culture and the cult of the self dominates, Las Vegas has preeminence. The Desert City has been providing this experience for better than half a century, first to a society that disdained it and thought it at best a deviant release, then to a descendant culture that embraced the willing deception. From Eminem to Donald Trump, American life is all about the self, and even after the terrorist atrocities, that doesn't seem to be changing. As our attention spans become shorter and our desires become more parochial and maybe even perverse, what will stop Las Vegas from continuing? Not water, maybe air quality, but short of a revolution on the scale of George Orwell's *1984*, Neal Stephenson's *Snow*

Crash, or Margaret Atwood's *The Handmaid's Tale*, Las Vegas is likely to remain at the pinnacle of a peculiar realm, one that people crave but that they simultaneously have to see as dissolute to guard themselves from the very weaknesses Las Vegas exploits.

In postmodern America there are only two truly egalitarian things left: the casino and the traffic jam. The traffic jam is egalitarian because helicopters have yet to become the daily toy of choice of the superrich; your Mercedes and my Ford get stuck the same, and all the CD players, cell phones, and leather upholstery in the world don't change that fact. In the casino, who you are makes little difference. Everybody's happy when you win—white, black, brown, yellow, red, pink, green, or blue, they stand at rapt attention when the bells go off and the coins clank in the metal trays with their unmistakable ring. Everyone smiles, pats you on the back, gets close to share in the glow. They think they're next. You've done what they're going to do.

This faux conviviality is indicative of the transformation of American society and the ways that historical ties have unraveled. In theory, we were

AIRPORT

once more involved with each other and less enamored of devices. Television and the technological revolution of the last twenty years, especially personal computers, the Internet, and cell phones, have redefined communication. In the process, we've cut out many of the older patterns of interaction. Shopping on the Internet may save time but it has little of the familiarity of going downtown and none of the social dimensions. Private space that seems public, where we think we're secure, helps assuage the transition, and shared activities that are intensely personal and fundamentally competitive like pulling slot-machine levers cross a series of boundaries that transcend old and new forms of interaction. If your machine hits, you're the only winner; when it hits, you're instantly part of a community of aspirants. In this respect, Las Vegas once again finds itself measuring the pulse of the nation.

The doomsayers and the morose all predict the demise of Las Vegas, arguing that the appetite for what it offers will diminish or that so many places will offer Las Vegas–style amenities that the city will lose its luster. Maybe they're right, but I doubt it. It's easy to predict the end of anything. As local columnist John L. Smith says, "If you predict the end of the world long enough, sooner or later you're going to be right." But if Las Vegas's history is any guide, the city's ability to respond to changes in culture can not be underestimated. Since the legalization of gambling in 1931, Las Vegas has provided Americans with what they weren't supposed to have at home and made whatever it was permissible if not flat-out okay. This sleight of hand was accomplished by the city's fundamental malleability, its lack of commitment to any version of its past or present.

There are dangers to the stability of prosperity, to be sure. Gaming greases the wheels. Las Vegas works for locals because the cost of living and the wage scale bear close relationship to one another. Wages alone don't do the trick. The combination of the toke and the low cost of housing make life easy. Anything that disrupts the parity is a threat, and in 1999 and 2000 the spate of high-end housing construction aimed at newcomers drove the cost of homes up for the first time in a decade. There was no parallel increase in wages, and a tug at the fabric of prosperity resulted. At the same time, WalMart sought to open enormous superstores with nonunion labor in the grocery section, long a unionized activity in Las Vegas's chains and another of the places where high-wage, low-skill work created middle-class families. The United Food and Commercial Workers Union challenged this move, and even though the county commission passed an anti-superstore ordinance in 1999, WalMart built, presenting another challenge to working-class prosperity. Idiosyncratic entrepreneurs also pose a potential threat. As construction neared completion at the Venetian, Sheldon Adelson claimed he had been overcharged, sued his general contractor, and refused to pay the subcontractors. The decision confirmed his reputation for venality, even if most in town knew full well he had a point. Rumor had it that considerable material delivered to the site and billed to Adelson was diverted for other purposes, but he nearly tipped the local construction trades into a minirecession. The attacks of September 11 poked a hole in visitation, driving down revenuew and inspiring layoffs, but Las Vegas's prosperity isn't in peril, nor is it inherently perilous. It does stand on a number of pillars, and each has to support its weight for the mix to work.

Rather than a string of carcasses in the desert, Las Vegas in 2050 will likely be the center of its own universe. Surely by then it will be a megalopolis that stretches to the California border and beyond, encompassing Boulder City and even Hoover Dam to the southeast. It will reach far north and west. The mountains around town will be covered with homes, hospitals and health care facilities will be more prevalent, and the roads will be so crowded that reminisceces of today's traffic will elicit fond memories of a simpler time. Las Vegas will host its own major league sports teams and maybe the NCAA championship football game. By then it will truly be creating entertainment as well as consuming it.

There are obstacles to this rosy picture. Global warming could make the desert entirely unhabitable—it's close as it is—the U.S. Department of Energy could site all the nuclear waste from every nuclear power plant in the country about a hundred miles away at Yucca Mountain, and Americans and the people of the world could embrace a culture of self-denial, could react with puritanical fervor against entertainment, pleasure, and self-indulgence. Any or all of these could make Las Vegas an anachronism, a version of the mining ghost towns scattered throughout Nevada and the rest of the interior West.

These externalities are real threats, but they don't define the trajectory of Las Vegas. Capitalism is a warrior culture, a hierarchical mode, and Las Vegas is its epitome. "Every single casino host in Las Vegas would rush to the airport to pick up Saddam Hussein and offer him a stay in their hotel," said one casino insider, and he nailed the essential feature of capitalism in all its forms: greed. In Las Vegas, ordinary people feel special;

people who feel that they are special can be catered to in a manner that suits their self-indulgence. Las Vegas anticipated the transformation of American culture not out of innate savvy but as a result of a lack of other options in the city. The reinvention of American culture as purely the self catapulted Las Vegas to prominence. The city took sin and made it choice, a sometimes ambiguous choice that many in American society from the privileged to the ordinary couldn't handle, but a choice nonetheless. Combined with a visionary approach to experience that melded Hollywood and Americans' taste for comfort and self-deception, Las Vegas grew into the last American frontier city, as foreign at times as Prague but as quin- tessential as Peoria. In Las Vegas, you can choose your fantasy; in the rest of America, you don't always get to pick.

Selected Bibliography

Abbott, Carl. *The Metropolitan Frontier: Cities in the Modern American West.* Tucson: University of Arizona Press, 1993.

Baker, George P., and George David Smith. *The New Financial Capitalists: Kohlberg Kravis Roberts and the Creation of Corporate Value.* Cambridge: Cambridge University Press, 1999.

Barber, Phyllis. *How I Got Cultured: A Nevada Memoir.* Reno: University of Nevada Press, 1994.

Barlett, Donald L., and James B. Steele. *Empire: The Life, Legend, and Madness of Howard Hughes.* New York: W. W. Norton, 1979.

Beers, David. *Blue Sky Dream: A Memoir of America's Fall from Grace.* New York: Doubleday, 1996.

Berman, Susan. *Easy Street.* New York: Dial Press, 1980.

——, *Lady Las Vegas: The Inside Story behind America's Neon Oasis.* Los Angeles: A&E Books, 1996.

Brill, Steven. *The Teamsters.* New York: Simon and Schuster, 1978.

Burbank, Jeff. *License to Steal: Nevada's Gaming Control System in the Megaresort Age.* Reno: University of Nevada Press, 2000.

Darlington, David. *The Mojave: A Portrait of the Definitive American Desert.* New York: Henry Holt, 1996.

Denton, Sally, and Roger Morris. *The Money and the Power: The Making of Las Vegas and Its Hold on America, 1947–2000.* New York: Alfred A. Knopf, 2001.

Drosnin, Michael. *Citizen Hughes: In His Own Words: How Howard Hughes Tried to Buy America.* New York: Holt, Rinehart, and Winston, 1985.

Dunne, John Gregory. *Vegas: A Memoir of a Dark Season.* New York: Random House, 1974.

Earley, Pete. *SuperCasino: Inside the "New" Las Vegas.* New York: Bantam Books, 2000.

Endlich, Lisa. *Goldman Sachs: The Culture of Success.* New York: Alfred A. Knopf, 1999.

Findlay, John M. *Magic Lands: Western Cityscapes and American Culture after 1940.* Berkeley: University of California Press, 1992.

Finnegan, William. *Cold New World: Growing up in a Harder Country.* New York: Random House, 1998.

Fleming, Ian. *Ian Fleming's Thrilling Cities.* New York: New American Library, 1964.

Gitlin, Todd. *The Twilight of Common Dreams: Why America Is Wracked by Culture Wars.* New York: Metropolitan Books, 1995.

Gottdeiner, M., Claudia C. Collins, and David R. Dickens. *Las Vegas: The Social Production of an All-American City.* Malden, MA: Blackwell Publishers, 1989.

Greenspun, Hank, with Alex Pelle. *Where I Stand: The Record of a Reckless Man.* New York: David McKay Publishing, 1966.

Halberstam, David. *Playing for Keeps: Michael Jordan and the World He Made.* New York: Random House, 1999.

Hannigan, John. *Fantasy City: Pleasure and Profit in the Postmodern Metropolis.* New York: Routledge, 1998.

Hess, Alan. *Viva Las Vegas: After-Hours Architecture.* San Francisco: Chronicle Books, 1973.

Kaplan, Robert D. *Empire Wilderness: Travels into America's Future.* New York: Random House, 1998.

Lacey, Robert. *Little Man: Meyer Lansky and the Gangster Life.* Boston: Little, Brown and Company, 1991.

Land, Barbara, and Myrick Land. *A Short History of Las Vegas.* Reno: University of Nevada Press, 1999.

Leach, William. *Country of Exiles: The Destruction of Place in American Life.* New York: Pantheon, 1999.

Lewis, Oscar. *Sagebrush Casinos: The Story of Legal Gambling in Nevada.* New York: Doubleday, 1953.

Lilliard, Richard G. *Desert Challenge: An Interpretation of Nevada*. New York: Alfred A. Knopf, 1948.

Lind, Michael. *The Next American Nation: The New Nationalism and the Fourth American Revolution*. New York: The Free Press, 1995.

Littlejohn, David, ed. *The Real Las Vegas: Life beyond the Strip*. New York: Oxford University Press, 1999.

Martinez, Andrés. *24/7: Living It up and Doubling Down in the New Las Vegas*. New York: Villard, 1999.

McCracken, Robert D. *Las Vegas: The Great American Playground*. Reno: University of Nevada Press, 1996.

Messick, Hank. *Lansky*. New York: G. P. Putnam's Sons, 1971.

Moehring, Eugene P. *Resort City in the Sunbelt: Las Vegas, 1930–1970*, 2nd ed. Reno: University of Nevada Press, 2000.

Nye, David E. *American Technological Sublime*. Cambridge: MIT Press, 1994.

Odessky, Dick. *Fly on the Wall: Recollections of Las Vegas's Good Old, Bad Old Days*. Las Vegas: Huntington Press, 1999.

Ostrander, Gilman M. *Nevada: The Great Rotten Borough, 1959–1964*. New York: Alfred A. Knopf, 1966.

Pearl, Ralph. *Vegas Is My Beat*. Secaucus, NJ: Lyle Stuart Publishing, 1973.

Pileggi, Nicholas. *Casino: Love and Honor in Las Vegas*. New York: Simon and Schuster, 1995.

Pine, B. Joseph, II, and James H. Gilmore. *The Experience Economy: Work Is Theatre and Every Business a Stage*. Cambridge, MA: Harvard Business School Press, 1999.

Putnam, Robert D. *Bowling Alone: The Collapse and Revival of American Community*. New York: Simon and Schuster, 2000.

Ralston, Jon. *The Anointed One: An Inside Look at Nevada Politics*. Las Vegas: Huntington Press, 2000.

Reich, Robert. *The Work of Nations: Preparing Ourselves for Twenty-first Century Capitalism*. New York: Alfred A. Knopf, 1991.

Reid, Ed. *Las Vegas: City without Clocks*. Englewood Cliffs, NJ: Prentice-Hall, 1961.

Reid, Ed and Ovid Demaris. *The Green Felt Jungle*. New York: Trident Press, 1963.

Reiff, David. *Los Angeles: Capital of the Third World*. New York: Simon and Schuster, 1991.

Richardson, Jack. *Memoir of a Gambler*. New York: Simon and Schuster, 1979.

Rome, Adam. *The Bulldozer in the Countryside: Suburban Sprawl and the Rise of American Environmentalism*. New York: Cambridge University Press, 2001.

Rothman, Hal K. *Devil's Bargains: Tourism in the Twentieth-Century American West.* Lawrence: University Press of Kansas, 1998.

Seabrook, John. *Nobrow: The Culture of Marketing, the Marketing of Culture.* New York: Alfred A. Knopf, 2000.

Sheehan, Jack, ed. *The Players: The Men Who Made Las Vegas.* Reno: University of Nevada Press, 1997.

Siegel, Fred. *The Future Once Happened Here: New York, D.C., L.A., and the Fate of America's Big Cities.* New York: The Free Press, 1997.

Skolnick, Jerome H. *House of Cards: Legalization and Control of Casino Gambling.* Boston: Little, Brown, and Company, 1978.

Smith, John L. *Running Scared: The Life and Treacherous Times of Las Vegas Casino King Steve Wynn.* New York: Barricade Books, 1995.

Spanier, David. *Welcome to the Pleasuredome: Inside Las Vegas.* Reno: University of Nevada Press, 1992.

Suarez, Ray. *The Old Neighborhood: What We Lost in the Great Suburban Migration, 1966–1999.* New York: The Free Press, 1999.

Thomson, David. *In Nevada: The Land, the People, God, and Chance* New York: Alfred A. Knopf, 2000.

Turner, Wallace. *Gambler's Money: The New Force in American Life.* Cambridge, MA: The Riverside Press, 1965.

Valenti, John, with Ron Naclerio. *Swee'pea and Other Playground Legends.* New York: Michael Kesend Publishing, 1990.

Venturi, Robert, Denise Scott Brown, and Steven Izenour. *Learning from Las Vegas.* Cambridge: MIT Press, 1972.

Yaeger, Don, with the cooperation of Jerry Tarkanian. *Shark Attack: Jerry Tarkanian and His Battle with the NCAA and UNLV.* New York: HarperCollins, 1992.

Index